Publications of the Institute of Business and Economic Research

Recent publications in this series:

Economic Development of Communist China
by Choh-Ming Li (1959)

Introduction to the Theory of Interest
by Joseph W. Conard (1959)

Antitrust in the Motion Picture Industry
by Michael Conant (1960)

Economic Doctrines of Knut Wicksell
by Carl G. Uhr (1960)

A Theory of Accounting to Investors
by George J. Staubus (1961)

Organization, Automation, and Society
by Robert A. Brady (1961)

HOUSING POLICY—THE SEARCH FOR SOLUTIONS

HOUSING POLICY—THE SEARCH FOR SOLUTIONS

A Comparison of the United Kingdom, Sweden, West Germany, and the United States since World War II

BY
PAUL F. WENDT

Publications of the Institute of Business and Economic Research, University of California

UNIVERSITY OF CALIFORNIA PRESS
BERKELEY AND LOS ANGELES, 1963

UNIVERSITY OF CALIFORNIA PRESS
BERKELEY AND LOS ANGELES, CALIFORNIA

CAMBRIDGE UNIVERSITY PRESS
LONDON, ENGLAND

SECOND PRINTING, 1963

LIBRARY OF CONGRESS CATALOG CARD NUMBER: 62-11497

The opinions expressed in this study are those of the author. The functions of the Institute of Business and Economic Research are confined to facilitating the prosecution of independent scholarly research by members of the faculty.

Preface

This study reviews and evaluates national housing programs and policies in four countries, the United Kingdom, Sweden, West Germany, and the United States since World War II.

The basic research was carried on in western Europe in 1958 during the author's sabbatical leave from the University of California. Financial assistance from the Institute of International Studies, University of California, Berkeley, made it possible for the author to extend his visit to West Germany and Sweden through the summer of 1958. The Real Estate Research Program, Institute of Business and Economic Research, University of California, Berkeley, provided research, editorial, and typing assistance in 1959 and 1960.

The number of persons who assisted in the gathering of information for this study is too large for complete enumeration. Dr. Reimer and other members of the secretariat of the United Nations Economic Commission for Europe made available a substantial number of published and unpublished reports bearing upon European housing. Dr. W. Fey and Dr. Klemt, of the Federal Ministry of Housing of West Germany, were helpful in providing statistical data, arranging for personal visits to German housing projects, and reviewing the chapter on West Germany.

Professor Alf Johannson, director of the Swedish Royal Housing Board, and members of his staff provided statistical and other data and reviewed many aspects of Sweden's postwar housing policies with the author. Stina Thornell and Dr. Per Holm provided guidance and assistance in the gathering and interpretation of data. Folke Dreber, of the Royal Building Board, arranged interviews with the International Siporex Company, the A. B. Ytonghus Company, and other private building and financing companies in Sweden, and assisted in many other ways during my visit. Owe Lundevall, of the Tenant's

Savings and Building Society (HSB), and A. Carlsson, of the Royal Housing Board, furnished statistical information and reviewed early drafts of the chapter on Sweden. The entire manuscript was reviewed by Roland Artle, a visiting professor at the University of California in 1960; his comments and suggestions on the chapter on Sweden were particularly helpful.

Professor Guy Arvidsson, formerly of the Swedish Riksbank and now at the University of Lund, and members of the staff of the Skandinaviska Banken and Svenska Handelsbanken in Stockholm assisted in assembling data on Sweden's postwar monetary and mortgage market developments. Professor Harald Dickson, of the Göteborg School of Economics, and Carl Edler offered gracious and hospitable assistance in arranging for visits to housing projects in southern Sweden.

Strategic assistance in providing statistical information, arranging for interviews with leaders in the British building industry, and reviewing drafts of the chapter on the United Kingdom was furnished by Peter Trench, director, and C. Gordon Rowlands, secretary, of the National Federation of Building Trades Employers. Mr. Trench's kindness in providing the use of his car and chauffeur in London for a day was a most pleasant highlight in the author's otherwise arduous research travels.

Garrett Holden, of the Building Societies; E. R. Young, chief estates manager of the National Coal Board; Frank Hellings, attorney; P. D. H. Stock, estates officer, Imperial Chemical Industries; Norman Waitte, of Waittes, Ltd.; Sir William Holford; Sir Alexander Killic; and William Calverly, builder, assisted the author in reviewing various aspects of the post-World War II housing situation in England.

Special thanks are due to Dr. Nathaniel Lichfield, of the Ministry of Housing and Local Government, who as a colleague at the University of California in 1959–60 was a constant source of help in securing and interpreting British housing data and in reviewing chapter iii.

Victor Mortenson and Eugene Brady served as research assistants in 1958–59 and 1959–60, and aided in the assembly of historical data for chapters ii, vi, and vii, and in the preparation of the first drafts of the chapter on West Germany.

I am especially indebted to my colleagues, Sherman Maisel, Albert H. Schaaf, and Wallace F. Smith, who reviewed and provided many helpful criticisms of the chapter on the United States and the concluding chapter. Miss Marybeth Branaman, of the Real Estate Research Program, reviewed the entire manuscript; her many comments and suggestions were of great assistance.

Finally, the author acknowledges the painstaking efforts of Mrs. Flora Ellen Palmer in checking footnote references and typing the manuscript.

The views expressed do not reflect those of any persons named above or those of the University of California or the Real Estate Research Program, Institute of Business and Economic Research. The author assumes the sole responsibility for errors, omissions, conclusions, and evaluations.

No critical analyst of national economic policies can achieve complete objectivity. It is the author's hope that his personal prejudices have not intruded too greatly upon this attempt to describe and evaluate postwar national housing policies factually and dispassionately.

PAUL F. WENDT

Berkeley, California

Contents

I INTRODUCTION 1

II THE NEED FOR STATE ACTION AND POSTWAR HOUSING PRODUCTION 4

III THE UNITED KINGDOM 13

Housing Policy as Influenced by World War I—*14;* Housing Policies, 1922 to 1939—*18;* Post-World War II Situation—*21;* Housing Policies of the Labour Government, 1945 to 1952—*24;* Housing Policies of Conservatives, 1952—*31;* Housing Finance—*36;* Building Societies—*42;* Life Insurance Companies—*43;* Local Authorities—*43;* The Housebuilding Industry—*45;* Review and Evaluation—*49*

IV SWEDEN 62

Housing Policy During World War II—*66;* Post-World War II Housing Policies—*68;* Rent Control—*70;* Housing Finance—*77;* Family Income and Other Subsidies—*85;* Post-World War II Housing Production—*85;* Postwar Changes in Property Ownership—*88;* Dominance of Multi-Family Dwellings—*92;* Costs of Postwar Government Housing Programs—*94;* Review and Evaluation—*97;* Eliminating the Postwar Housing Shortage—*100;* Achieving Stability in Housing—*103*

V WEST GERMANY 111

World War I and Its Aftermath—*113;* Housing Under the Nazi Government—*116;* Housing Policy During World War II—*119;* Post-World War II Housing Situation—*121;* Currency Reform and Governmental Reorganization—*122;* Housing Policy and the First Housing Act of 1950—*123;* Housing Finance—*127;* Low-

Income "Social Housing"—*131;* Tax Incentives for Housing—*134;* Postwar Housing Production—*138;* Review and Evaluation—*142*

VI THE UNITED STATES 145

Housing Policy During World War I—*146;* Housing Policy During the 1920's—*146;* Groping for a Long-Range Federal Housing Policy—*147;* Federal Housing Programs in the Great Depression—*148;* Housing Policies and Programs in World War II—*152;* Trends in U.S. Housing Production and Characteristics—*157;* The Housing Situation Following World War II—*163;* Mortgage Finance—*171;* Evaluation of Federal Mortgage Credit Programs—*187;* Public Housing—*190;* Causes of Slums and Blight—*197;* Federal Aid for Slum Clearance and Redevelopment—*198;* Urban Renewal and Rental Housing—*200;* Costs of Federal Housing Programs—*202;* Evaluation—*204*

VII EVALUATION OF POST-WORLD WAR II HOUSING POLICIES 230

Housing Objectives and Policies—*230;* Comparative Changes in Housing Standards—*247;* Effect of Policies upon the Residential Construction Industry—*253;* Effect of Housing Policies upon Postwar Economies—*256;* Conclusions—*267*

INDEX 275

I | Introduction

Following World War II most western European nations faced critical housing shortages as a result of war destruction, obsolescence, cessation of building during the war years, high marriage rates, and the rapid expansion of urban population and incomes. Improvement in housing standards became a major social objective of most European governments after the war, and relatively high levels of residential construction were achieved in the subsequent decade. Studies indicate that as much as 75 per cent of the new residential construction in western Europe since 1945 has benefited from some form of government subsidy.[1]

The increasing financial burden of government housing programs, the wide variations in the types of subsidies employed, and the relative success of national housing policies have led to a critical reëxamination of housing policies in the United States and in many European countries in recent years. The comparative success of national housing programs is of immediate consequence to the many countries that are seeking to formulate policies for improving housing standards for their rapidly expanding urban populations.

The purpose of this study is to review the origin and development of post-World War II housing policies in the United Kingdom, Sweden, West Germany, and the United States. A comparison will be made between postwar national housing policies, production, and the relative improvement in housing standards in order to evaluate the effectiveness of alternative policies.

The post-World War II housing situation in selected western European nations and in the United States will be reviewed in chapter ii. In succeeding chapters for each of the four countries to be studied,

---

[1] United Nations Economic Commission for Europe, *European Housing Progress and Policies in 1953*, E/ECE/189 (Geneva, August, 1954), pp. 29–33.

the evolution of national housing policies, the record of housing production, and the impact of housing policies upon housing standards will be examined. A final chapter will provide a review and analysis of postwar housing objectives, policies, and programs, and their effect upon housing costs and standards and upon the economies of the individual countries studied.

The task is admittedly ambitious, since it involves difficult problems of data collection and interpretation, and, more importantly, complex economic, political, and social evaluations. The statistical task has been greatly simplified by a series of background reports on European housing progress and policies prepared by the United Nations secretariat of the Economic Commission for Europe, upon which the author has relied extensively.

Several factors make the evaluation of national housing policies difficult. First, national housing policies must be viewed against the background of historical precedent, general economic policies, and the comparative urgencies of the housing needs arising out of World War II. Second, the evaluation of such features of national housing policy as rent controls, tax exemptions, loan subsidies, or public housing involves basic questions of economic and political philosophy which are compounded by differences in attitudes and customs among countries.

As a framework for evaluating national housing policies in the final chapter, the author considers the following:

The relationship between housing needs and national housing objectives

The degree of consistency over time between housing objectives and housing policies

The record of national housing production in altering housing standards, controlling building costs and maintaining stability in housing production

The relationship between the national housing programs and policies and the general economic growth and development.

The relationship between national housing policies and general economic policies presents problems of particular difficulty. If national housing policies appear to have been relatively unsuccessful in terms of the third criterion above, is it the fault of these policies or because general economic policies were inconsistent with them? Should it be assumed, in other words, that the provision of housing has top priority and that all other national economic programs should be subject to the key importance of maintaining housing production and raising housing standards? It is the author's view, with which some others are in agreement, that national housing programs can and should be employed to encourage a somewhat greater allocation of resources to the improvement of national housing standards. By the same token, however, housing programs must be subject to the overriding importance of maintaining general economic growth and stability.[2]

It is concluded that national housing policies should be designed to operate within the constraints of national economic policy. Therefore, national housing policy will be subject to criticism when it appears inconsistent with general economic policy. It will still be arguable, of course, in making evaluations on these terms, whether a given housing policy might have worked quite well, given different general national economic policies.

The conclusions drawn from the evaluative framework outlined above involve a mixture of subjective evaluations and objective observations. An economist in a country which has relied extensively upon private investment in a competitive market economy for the provision of housing can be expected to view somewhat critically direct government intervention in housing. Unfortunately, this innate bias may seem all too evident to readers with a different social and economic philosophy.

The conclusion seems inescapable, from the data analyzed, that several alternative combinations of housing policies and programs can prove effective in raising national housing standards. The selection of that particular combination of housing policies to be followed in any country, must, in the last analysis, be a political decision. That decision will be based upon historical tradition and accident, the relative strength of public demand for housing, the degree to which housing is viewed as an appropriate sphere for governmental action, and the degree to which past experience dictates reliance upon public or private enterprise to fill these demands.

[2] See, for example, Leo Grebler, "Criteria for Appraising Governmental Housing Programs," *American Economic Review,* L, No. 2 (May, 1960), 321–332.

II The Need for State Action and Postwar Housing Production

World War II had devastating effects upon the housing stock of many of the European countries. The effects of war destruction in France, Germany, Poland, Greece, and Italy are reflected in the over-all decline in the number of dwellings in those countries from 1937 to 1952, shown in Table II–1. England and Belgium also suffered much damage as a result of the war, but were in a position to begin postwar reconstruction earlier and on a larger scale than were the before-mentioned countries. Switzerland and the Scandinavian countries, in contrast, are illustrative of nations which suffered relatively little damage during the war years. These and the following data and observations are designed to provide an overview and perspective of the postwar housing problem in Europe at the end of World War II. They will provide an introduction to a more detailed consideration of the postwar housing problems and policies in the United Kingdom, Sweden, West Germany, and the United States.

The imbalance between the supply and demand for housing created by the depletion of the housing stock was further amplified by the surge of population growth that took place in some countries in the fifteen-year period following the outbreak of World War II. While there were wide differences in population growth in various European countries,[1] the population of Europe as a whole increased 8.4 per cent during that period. The broad changes in population and in the housing stock of European nations from mid-1937 to mid-1952 are shown in Table II–1.

A better indication of the extent of the postwar housing shortage can be gained from the data in Table II–2, which shows the number of dwellings and rooms per thousand of population and married women

[1] Owing to such factors as war losses, systematic elimination of whole population groups by Germany, postwar migration, traditional differences in birth rates, etc.

in selected western and central European countries in 1953. This was the first year for which such comparative data were available. It can be noted that the ratios of dwellings per 1,000 inhabitants were rela-

TABLE II-1

CHANGES IN POPULATION, AND HOUSEBUILDING LESS WAR LOSSES, 1937 TO 1952

Country	Total population			Number of dwellings		
	Mid-1937 (000's)	Mid-1952 (000's)	Percentage changes, mid-1937–mid-1952	Estimated stock, mid-1937 (000's)	Change, mid-1937 to mid-1952[a] (000's)	(Percentage)
Albania	1,030	1,246	21.0	....	....	....
Austria	6,755	6,949	2.9	2,000	87	4.4
Belgium	8,346	8,725	4.5	2,458	556	22.6
Bulgaria	6,500*	7,390	13.7	....	....	....
Czechoslovakia	14,432	12,600*	−12.7	3,500	409	11.7
Denmark	3,749	4,334	15.6	1,088	249	22.9
Finland	3,150	4,091	29.9	708	277	39.1
France	41,200	42,600	3.4	13,140	−305	−2.3
Germany:						
East	15,000*	17,599	17.3	....	....	....
West	38,500*	48,478	25.9	10,331	124	1.2
Berlin	4,300*	3,344	−22.2	....	....	....
Greece	7,113	7,776	9.3	1,816	−170	−9.4
Hungary	9,100	9,460	4.0	2,342	140	6.0
Ireland	2,948	2,948	0.0	622	78	12.5
Italy	42,372	46,865	10.6	10,522	0	0.0
Netherlands	8,598	10,377	20.7	2,036	284	13.9
Norway	2,919	3,327	14.0	681	214	31.4
Poland	31,200	26,000*	−16.7	6,860	−967	−14.1
Portugal	7,416	8,549	15.3	....	....	....
Romania	15,512	16,300	5.1	....	....	....
Spain	25,043	28,306	13.0	....	....	....
Sweden	6,276	7,126	13.5	1,785	635	35.6
Switzerland	4,180	4,815	15.2	1,083	235	21.7
Turkey	16,725	21,983	31.0	....	....	....
United Kingdom	47,289	50,429	6.6	12,500	1,600	12.8
Yugoslavia	15,600*	16,729	7.2	....	....	....
Total	385,253	418,346	8.4	....	....	....
U.S.S.R.	190,000*	206,000*	8.4	....	....	....

Source: United Nations Economic Commission for Europe, *European Housing Progress and Policies in 1953*, E/ECE/189 (Geneva, August, 1954), p. 4.

Note: Data for 1937 relate to present territories. The change in the number of dwellings is estimated on the basis of new construction less war losses, no account being taken of other losses.

[a] Construction less war losses, except for West Germany, where the housing stock at the end of 1952 has been taken as a basis for calculations.

* Secretariat estimate.

TABLE II–2

HOUSING DENSITIES IN SELECTED WESTERN AND CENTRAL EUROPEAN COUNTRIES, 1953–54

Country	Population		Dwellings (000's)	Rooms (000's)	Dwellings per 1,000		Rooms per	
	Period (Dec. 31)	000's			Married women	Inhabitants	1,000 inhabitants	Dwelling
Austria	1953	6,964	2,100	7,350	1,310[c]	320	1,055	3.5
Belgium	1953	8,798[a]	3,050	11,271[c]	1,355[c]	347	1,324[c]	3.9[c]
Denmark	1953	4,392[a]	1,360	5,200[cb]	1,308	312	1,134	4.0
Finland	1953	4,163	1,084	2,700	1,248	260	649	2.5
France	May, 1954	42,775	12,300	44,900	1,287[c]	288	1,050	3.6
West Germany	1955	49,278	10,966	44,271	854[c]	223	898	4.0
Ireland	July, 1953	2,942	700	2,729	1,468[c]	238	924[c]	4.2[c]
Netherlands	1953	10,551	2,400	11,600	1,061	230	1,099	4.8
Norway	1953	3,375[a]	941	4,000	1,239	279	1,207	4.3
Sweden	1953	7,205	2,464	7,700	1,468	342	1,069	3.1
Switzerland	1953	4,904	1,384	6,677	1,316	282	1,362	4.8
United Kingdom	1953	50,954[a]	14,386	66,000	1,085	282	1,295	4.6
Total	–	196,200	55,052	215,500	–	270	1,098	4.1

Source: United Nations Economic Commission for Europe, *The European Housing Situation*, E/ECE/221 (Geneva, January, 1956), p. 46.

Notes: As far as possible, figures have been adjusted to make the statistical basis uniform, but nevertheless the results are comparable only to a limited extent. In principle, emergency accommodation is not included, but practices vary considerably. Vacant dwellings are in principle included. As far as possible, figures are adjusted to comply with the League of Nations definition of a room and of a dwelling; exceptions are given in footnotes. Population figures are generally of *de facto* population. Relative figures are based on the total population, i.e., not only the number of persons or married couples living in the dwellings registered, but also those living in emergency quarters, institutional households, etc.

[a] *De jure* population.

[b] The number of rooms in rural districts has been estimated by the Secretariat.

[c] Last census figure (the date of which would generally be earlier than that indicated in the first column).

tively high in Austria, Belgium, Denmark, and Sweden, about average in the United Kingdom, France, Switzerland, Finland, and Norway, and low in West Germany, Ireland, and the Netherlands. In Austria, Sweden, and Finland, however, the small size of the dwellings results in below-average ratios of rooms per 1,000 inhabitants and per dwelling for these countries. The United Kingdom, the Netherlands, and Switzerland, on the other hand, are characterized by their relatively large ratios of rooms per dwelling. Another and in certain respects more descriptive measure of the housing situation in a given country is shown by the ratio of dwellings per 1,000 married women, as shown in Table II–2. Measures of dwelling availability by this criterion emphasize the severity of the housing shortage in West Germany, the Netherlands, and the United Kingdom. West Germany is by all criteria below average, and her position was clearly the worst of all the countries considered.

Taken as a whole, Belgium, Denmark, Austria, and Sweden were seemingly in the best-balanced position as to housing. The United Kingdom and Switzerland were probably, by the same criteria, at or above average, while West Germany, having experienced relatively greater war damage, was critically below the average for western and central Europe.

Index numbers of the value of dwelling construction in selected western European countries and the United States, adjusted for changes in the price level, are given in Table II–3. They provide a measure of the relative rates of expansion in residential building among these countries since 1949. It can be noted that, relative to the 1950 level of construction, the level of residential construction during the three years from 1956 to 1958 has been greatest in West Germany, the Netherlands, Sweden, Austria, and Greece, while the United Kingdom, Switzerland, Norway, and Belgium have expanded dwelling construction at a somewhat lower date during the period. The expansion in the value of dwelling construction in the United States in 1954 constant prices was below that in many western European countries. Denmark and Ireland show stagnation or absolute decline, which is a reflection of the less severe housing problem and a relatively suppressed economic growth in these countries. The level of production in 1950 is, of course, of key importance in the interpretation of the data in Table II–3. Countries which had already achieved high levels of residential construction by 1950, such as the United States, Greece, Norway, and Sweden, necessarily showed a smaller percentage increase in using 1950 as a base period.

TABLE II-3

INDEX NUMBERS OF THE VALUE OF DWELLING CONSTRUCTION BY COUNTRIES, 1950 TO 1959 (EXPRESSED IN 1954 CONSTANT PRICES, 1950 = 100)

Country	1950	1951	1952	1953	1954	1955	1956	1957	1958	1959
Austria	100	100	103	110	130	140	147	143	147	n.a.
Belgium	100	83	77	89	106	99	103	123	116	n.a.
Denmark[a]	100	89	93	110	122	101	97	115	108	138
West Germany	100	99	105	129	140	160	172	174	178	196
Greece	100	75	81	110	121	131	148	146	180	n.a.
Ireland	100	100	95	82	77	78	77	51	41	n.a.
Netherlands	100	92	96	119	122	114	138	156	149	153
Norway	100	107	122	130	127	125	109	122	111	109
Sweden	100	87	88	106	121	122	128	136	142	148
Switzerland	100	122	100	122	156	167	167	144	122	n.a.
United Kingdom	100	98	117	152	158	142	138	132	124	140
United States	100	85	85	89	98	115	104	100	106	138

Source: Index numbers calculated by author from value data in Organization for European Economic Cooperation, *General Statistics* (Paris, January, 1960), and, for the United States: U.S. Department of Labor and U.S. Department of Commerce, *Construction Volume and Costs, 1915–1956, A Statistical Supplement to Construction Review,* pp. 2, 6, 40, 42, and *Construction Review,* VI, No. 9 (September, 1960), 55–59.

The estimated number of dwellings completed annually in European countries during the post-World War II period shown in Table II–4 provides a further basis for comparisons.[2] The relative growth in dwelling construction shown in Table II–3 is influenced, as can be seen from Table II–4, by the selection of the year 1950 as the base year. Table II–4 shows that the lower rates of growth for some countries from 1950 to 1958 were primarily a reflection of the high level of production in the year 1950 (e.g., the United States, Austria, and Belgium). Conversely, the rate growth from 1950 to 1958 was apparently made to seem relatively greater in Sweden and the United Kingdom by the selection of 1950 as a base year.

Although comparable housing production figures are not available for many countries for the year 1938, it is of interest to note the very substantial gains in annual postwar housing production relative to prewar levels. The gains, of course, are most notable in countries which experienced extensive war damage and high rates of population growth, such as the Netherlands and West Germany. The influence of aggressive postwar national housing programs is also evident in countries such as Spain, Italy, and Greece, which have had chronic housing shortages for many years. By contrast, comparisons with prewar levels

[2] For comparison, the last "normal" prewar year (1938) is included in this table.

TABLE II–4

Dwellings Completed in Selected Countries, 1938 and 1948–59
(In thousands of units)

Country	1938	1948	1949	1950	1951	1952	1953	1954	1955	1956	1957	1958	1959
Austria	....	26.1	29.0	46.2	13.0[e]	57.3[f]	38.2	40.5	41.6	42.0*	34.6	36.2	35.5
Belgium	19.6	24.4	36.2	44.7	35.5	33.3	39.2	44.9	44.6	43.8	49.9	46.8	46.4
Czechoslovakia	22.0[c,d]	21.7	29.1	38.2	30.9	39.3	39.0	38.2	50.6	63.7	64.3	53.4	68.3
Denmark	14.6	19.6	24.6	20.4	21.5	19.0	21.3	23.3	24.0	19.8	26.5	21.0	26.2
East Germany	115.0[b]	....	....	....	....	....	32.3	34.7	32.8	32.8	41.0	48.0	....
Finland	7.7[a]	23.0	29.0	26.0	28.5	31.2	29.6	32.2	33.2	30.5	32.7	30.0	30.0
France	....	40.2	60.6	70.6	76.7	83.9	115.5	162.0	210.1	236.3	273.7	291.7	320.4
Greece	....	18.8	21.7	48.7	43.9	59.9	51.1	44.5	56.1	62.2	51.2	54.4	....
Hungary	....	....	....	24.7	17.7	16.7	16.8	27.2	31.5	25.5	51.3	41.8	46.6
Ireland	11.3	2.4	7.0	12.8	13.1	14.5	13.1	11.7	10.3	11.6*	9.2*	6.1*	7.2*
Italy	49.8	37.0	46.1	74.1	93.5	117.2	150.4	177.4	215.9	231.6	273.5	276.0	295.0
Netherlands	38.4[a]	38.8	48.7	54.8	64.8	57.4	62.6	70.5	61.9	69.2	89.3	90.0	84.3
Norway	5.1[a]	16.6	18.3	22.4	20.9	32.7	35.1	35.4	32.1	27.3	26.5	26.4	26.5
Poland	....	....	....	68.0	66.0	65.0	79.0	79.0	94.0	94.5	122.4	129.0	137.6
Portugal	....	....	(14.9)	17.6	17.8	15.2	22.0	22.1	24.4	28.2	29.9*	34.2	33.8
Romania	....	....	....	....	49.4	45.0	45.6	54.9	55.9	78.5	78.4	84.2	....
Spain	....	62.1	55.1	53.4	56.5	63.3	67.2	87.2	112.2	121.8	98.0	101.5	114.0
Sweden	53.5	48.0	41.6	43.9	39.8	44.7	51.9	58.2	57.0	56.9	65.8	63.0	70.0*
Switzerland	8.2[a]	(23.0)	(17.9)	25.0	30.0	27.5	29.4	36.1	39.3	39.3*	38.7*	26.1	35.7
Turkey	....	....	....	....	....	....	....	(54.2)	(58.5)	(53.4)	(52.6)	(53.4)	(51.1)
U.S.S.R.	225.0[c]	....	....	....	....	....	1,245.0	1,351.0	1,512.0	1,636.0	2,197.0	2,602.0	3,042.0
United Kingdom	360.2	232.4	205.5	214.7	209.4	254.5	330.4	356.7	328.6	310.0	310.0	281.4	284.4
United States	406.0	931.6	1,025.1	1,396.0	1,091.3	1,127.0	1,103.8	1,220.4	1,328.9	1,118.1	1,041.9	1,209.4	1,378.0
West Germany	170.0[b]	....	215.0	360.0	430.0	452.0	514.6	542.8	538.1	560.5	527.8	488.4	554.9
Yugoslavia	....	....	....	....	26.6	34.9	38.2	34.2	29.8	37.0	44.7	61.7	60.4

Sources: 1938: United Nations Statistical Committee, *Statistical Yearbook, 1957* (New York, 1957), Table 122 (Exceptions, see footnotes [b] and [c], below); 1948–49: United Nations Economic Commission for Europe, *Quarterly Bulletin of Housing and Building Statistics for Europe*, V, No. 1 (Geneva, 1957); 1950–58: *Ibid.*, VII, No. 2 (1959); 1959: *Ibid.*, VIII, No. 2 (1960); United States, 1938–57: U.S. Housing and Home Finance Agency, *Housing Statistics, Historical Supplement* (December, 1958), p. 1; United States, 1958: *Ibid.*, September, 1958, p. 1; Sweden, 1948–56: Socialstyrelsen, *Sociala Meddelanden 1957* (Stockholm, 1957), Tables 4, 7, 8, 10; Sweden, 1957–58: United Nations Economic Commission for Europe, *Quarterly Bulletin of Housing and Building Statistics for Europe*, VII, No. 2 (1959).

Note: Data refer in the main to new and reconstructed units and those units made available by extension and conversion, located in residential and nonresidential buildings. Figures placed between parentheses are based on an incomplete coverage.

* Estimated.

[a] Not comparable with postwar data.

[b] Source: Länderrat des Amerikanischen Besatzungsgebiets, *Statistisches Handbuch von Deutschland 1928–1944* (Munich, 1949), p. 340. (West Berlin estimated by author.)

[c] Source: United States Works Progress Administration for the City of New York, *Housing—What's It Worth?* (New York, 1939).

[d] Year 1937. [e] January 1, 1951, to May 31, 1951. [f] June 1, 1951, to December 31, 1951.

of housing production are less impressive in the United Kingdom and Sweden, which had relatively high rates of housing production in 1938.

The very large recent gains in housing production in Hungary, Poland, Romania, Yugoslavia, and the U.S.S.R. reflect greater attention to the provision of housing in the economic programs of these countries since 1956.

TABLE II–5

PATTERNS OF INVESTMENT IN WESTERN EUROPEAN COUNTRIES, 1950 TO 1955

Country	Net national product per capita in U.S. dollars—Average, 1952–54	Gross fixed investment as per cent of gross national product, 1950–54	Dwelling construction as per cent of		Number of dwellings completed per 1,000 inhabitants, 1955
			Gross fixed investment, 1950–54	Gross national product, 1950–54	
Austria	370	21	21	4.41	6.0
Belgium	800	14	23	3.22	4.7
Denmark	750	18	17	3.06	5.4
Finland	670	25	27[a]	6.75	7.9
France	740	17	23[b]	3.91	4.9
Greece	220	13	32	4.16	n.a.
Italy	310	19	20	3.80	4.6
Netherlands	500	21	17	3.57	5.8
Norway	740	29	18	5.22	9.5
Sweden	950	19	23	4.37	7.8
Switzerland	1,010	...	...	...	7.7
United Kingdom	780	13	22	2.86	6.5
United States	1,870	16[c]	24[c]	4.32	8.1[c]
West Germany	510	20	25	5.00	10.3

Sources: Net national product: United Nations Statistical Office, *Per Capita National Product of Fifty-Five Countries*, ST/STAT/SER. E/4 (New York, 1957); Investment: United Nations Economic Commission for Europe, *Economic Survey of Europe in 1955*, E/ECE/235 (Geneva, February, 1956), pp. 57–63.

[a] Years 1951–54.

[b] Years 1952–54.

[c] U.S. Department of Commerce, Office of Business Economics, *U.S. Income and Output, Supplement to the Survey of Current Business* (Washington, November, 1958). Percentages calculated by the author.

High levels of postwar economic activity combined with an extensive commitment of resources to housing production to produce record European dwelling construction in the post-World War II years. Differences in the record of housing production reflect the relative severity of the postwar housing shortages in various countries as well as national housing and general economic policies.

Table II–5 shows the dollar equivalent of the per capita net national product in selected European countries from 1952 to 1954, and the relationship of housing investment to the gross national product and to gross fixed investment. The level of the per capita net national product in the United States relative to European countries is of primary significance. Even though the percentages of the national product devoted to gross fixed investment are smaller for the United States, the dollar investment devoted to fixed investment and dwelling construction is substantially higher than for European countries.

Table II–5 shows that Finland, Norway, and West Germany allocated higher proportions of total resources to residential construction in the period from 1950 to 1954, and that this was reflected in high per capita housing construction. Percentages of gross national product devoted to fixed investment and dwelling construction were lower for the United Kingdom during this period than for countries with comparable per capita incomes, and this was reflected in relatively low per capita dwelling completions.

Particular attention can be given to the relative patterns of housing investment in Sweden, the United Kingdom, West Germany, and the United States. West Germany, the country with the lowest per capita net national product from 1952 to 1954, devoted the highest percentage of gross national product to dwelling construction and completed the largest number of dwellings per 1,000 inhabitants in 1955. Sweden, with higher per capita incomes than the United Kingdom, devoted a larger proportion of resources to dwelling construction and recorded a somewhat higher rate of completions in 1955 per 1,000 inhabitants. The relatively high rate of completions in the United States appears to be primarily a reflection of the very high per capita net national product in the United States relative to other countries.

In comparing the number of dwellings completed per 1,000 inhabitants in Table II–5, it is important to observe that the number of dwellings per capita in no way reflects differences in the size and quality of dwellings constructed in the various countries. As will be noted in greater detail subsequently, postwar dwellings constructed during the period from 1950 to 1954 were of smaller average size in West Germany and Sweden than in the United States and the United Kingdom. It will also be seen that standards of convenience in dwellings vary widely among the four countries.

The four countries selected for study illustrate the wide diversity in housing policies employed during the post-World War II years. Sweden and the United Kingdom relied extensively upon housing subsidies, rent controls, and large-scale public housebuilding. In the period since 1953, housing policies in the United Kingdom were shifted toward relaxation of rent controls, greater reliance upon free markets, and the provision of owner-occupied housing by private housebuilders. West Germany employed direct government low-interest rate loans and tax incentives to encourage private investment in housebuilding; special tax subsidies were developed to encourage private ownership of housing, and rent restrictions were gradually removed. Following the removal of wartime rent controls and emergency war housing programs, federal housing programs in the United States were confined almost exclusively to measures designed to encourage the flow of mortgage funds for production of owner-occupied and privately owned rental housing. Publicly owned low-rent housing and urban renewal activities have thus far had relatively limited impact upon the national housing market in the United States.

It seems evident that the critical nature of the postwar housing shortages in western Europe resulted in more extensive government participation in housing markets. In view of the wide differences in national housing policies, it is of considerable significance to describe and measure the results of these programs. Chapters iii to vi will consider in more detail the background of national housing policies, the extent of the post-World War II housing problem in each of these four countries, the record of housing production, the evaluation of national housing policies, and the manner and effectiveness with which diverse housing policies operated in an attempted solution to the problems posed. Chapter vii will include a summary and evaluation of the post-World War II housing policies examined.

III | The United Kingdom

As a basis for a review of the post-World War II housing problem and policies in the United Kingdom, it is proposed to review briefly the background of British housing policies and programs. National concern with housing policy in the United Kingdom, as in the United States and many other countries, had its roots in the problems of public health and the eradication of slums.

While the housing problem in England received much public attention in the nineteenth century, the problem goes back far earlier. It was present in London and other large cities during the Elizabethan period. Queen Elizabeth I noted in 1593 that "Great mischiefs daily grow and increase by reason of pestering the houses with divers families, harbouring of inmates, and converting great houses into several tenements and the erection of new buildings in London and Westminster." [1]

With the passing of agriculture as England's premier industry between 1800 and 1840, and the movement of population from the field to the factory, housebuilding increased rapidly in British cities. It was in the latter half of the century, however, when the industrial revolution had come of age in England, that the housing problem became most acute and commanded public attention.

The first Act of Parliament in the field of housing, the Shaftesbury Act of 1851, had as its aim the provision of working-class homes by the local authorities. The next important step was the Torrens Act of 1868, which was concerned with the improvement and demolition of unfit houses. The third housing act, the Cross Act, passed in 1875,

---

[1] P. L. Leigh-Breese, "A Housing Review," in Institute of Housing, *Report of the Proceedings at the Twenty-Fifth Annual Conference* (Scarborough, September, 1956), p. 89.

charged the local authorities with the provision of new housing as well as the maintenance or elimination of old housing. Public concern over housing conditions led to the appointment, in 1884, of a Royal Commission on Housing, which in the following year recommended amendments to previous legislation. These were finally enacted in the Housing of the Working Classes Act of 1890. Among other features, this act facilitated the giving of land by local authorities for working-class dwellings in cities.[2]

Housing policy of that period emphasized the role of private philanthropic bodies or the "five percent philanthropists," as they have been called.[3] Government housing legislation initiated between 1850 and 1880 made it legally possible for the local sanitary authorities to deal with slums, but without financial help from the central government. Provision of houses by local authorities under the Housing of the Working Classes Act of 1890 was considered only as a last resort in the elimination of slums. Although further powers were given local authorities in the Housing Acts of 1894, 1900, and 1903, and by the Housing and Town Planning Act of 1909, the government assumed little direct initiative in the provision or subsidy of housing prior to World War I. World War I transformed the previously negative government role in housing to a major political issue of national importance as the government assumed enlarged responsibility for the provision of housing with the slogan "Homes Fit for Heroes." [4]

Housing Policy as Influenced by World War I

The fundamental factors which led to the abrupt transition in government policy were the rapid growth in family formation during and immediately following World War I and the practical cessation of residential building from 1911 to 1918. It was estimated that the housing "shortage" in England and Wales exceeded 600,000 units at the beginning of 1919 as a result of an increase of 848,000 families from 1911 to 1918, offset by an increase of only 238,000 dwellings during the same period.[5] When it is considered that these estimates made no allowances for replacement of substandard housing or for the continuing rapid

[2] Harry Barnes, *Housing: The Facts and the Futures* (London: Ernest Benn, Ltd., 1923), chap. vi.

[3] Marian Bowley, *Housing and the State, 1919–1944* (London: Allen and Unwin, 1947), p. 3. The author has drawn heavily from Miss Bowley's work in this section.

[4] *Ibid.*, p. 4.

[5] *Ibid.*, p. 12. See also John Roland Jarmain, *Housing Subsidies and Rents* (London: Stevens & Sons, Ltd., 1948), p. 31.

increase in the number of families after 1919, the political concern over national housing policies is readily understandable.

Basic conflicts in British housing policy which have continued to this day were evident in 1919. The Conservative view was that the housing problem was a temporary result of the war and that private enterprise would be able to assume the major task of removing the deficiency in housing accommodations. The opposite point of view was reflected in the 1917 report of the Royal Commission on the Housing of the Industrial Population of Scotland Urban and Rural:

> We are driven to the conclusion that the sources and forces that were available for the provision of working-class houses had—and this is quite apart from the difficulties brought about by the war—failed to provide anything like a sufficiency of houses, and that in particular they had failed to provide houses of a reasonable standard of accommodation and habitability . . . Private enterprise was practically the only agency that undertook the building of houses, and most of the troubles we have been investigating are due to the failure of private enterprise to provide and maintain the necessary houses sufficient in quantity and quality.[6]

In part, this report reflected the wide differences in housing standards in Scotland as compared with England and Wales. Only 26.5 per cent of the houses in Scotland in 1911 had more than three rooms, while 73.8 per cent of the houses in England and Wales had four rooms or more. Overcrowding was widespread and acute, and a large proportion of Scottish housing lacked any modern conveniences and was in disrepair. The differences in the severity of the housing problem in Scotland as compared with England and Wales have resulted in widely differing housing policies over the past several decades. These differences are reflected in rent policies, subsidies, and the relative responsibilities of public and private enterprise in Scottish housing. For these reasons, many of the statistical comparisons will show England and Wales separately from Scotland.

The immediate result of the critical housing shortages following World War I was the passage of the Housing and Town Planning Act of 1919 and the extension of the life of the Rent and Mortgage Interest Restriction Act. The former Act required that local authorities survey the housing needs in their districts and take steps to provide the houses needed for the "working classes." Housing policy was no longer geared to slum clearance or to the encouragement of private philanthropic

---

[6] *Report of the Royal Commission on the Housing of the Industrial Population of Scotland Urban and Rural* (1917), p. 292, as quoted in Bowley, *op. cit.*, Appendix I, p. 262.

rental housing, but rather to the outright assumption by the local government of responsibility for the provision of working-class housing. Local authorities were guaranteed against any serious losses on housing schemes, for the national government accepted financial responsibility for any subsidies needed beyond certain minimum costs to be borne by the local government. Rents for local authority housing built under this legislation were fixed independently of costs, and the prewar level of controlled rents in working-class housing was used as a general guide. Local authorities had no inducement to maintain rents at economic levels, and the result was that politically desirable low rents were generally fixed, with the national government footing most of the bill for the difference between costs and rents.[7]

The original 1915 Rent Control Act was replaced in 1920 by a new act which prolonged rent controls until 1923 and extended controls to houses of higher ratable values. The Act permitted increases in rents of 15 per cent by July, 1921, and permitted further increases if the landlord was responsible for all repairs and to offset increases in the rates payable since 1915.[8]

The subsidy policy under the Housing Act of 1919 was at first limited by establishing maximum quotas in July, 1921, and finally abandoned altogether by the Act of 1923. The primary reason for the abandonment of the subsidy scheme under the 1919 Act was the concern over the cost to the Treasury, which rose from £20,500 in 1919/20 to a maximum of £7,951,600 in 1924/25. It was estimated that the average annual cost to the Treasury from the time the subsidy came to an end in 1924/25 until 1938/39 was £6,796,100—equivalent to about £40 per house per year.[9] Rapidly increasing building wages and material costs from 1919 to 1921 were also attributed in part to the lack of incentives for the local authorities to economize, since the Treasury bore most of the cost, and to the lack of controls by the Ministry of Health.

Table III–1 shows that approximately 170,000 dwellings were built under the Act of 1919 by local authorities and an additional 43,700 by private enterprise. In addition, 53,800 houses were built with no subsidy by private enterprise from 1920 to 1923. The Act was amended and finally repealed, not because it had been ineffective in stimulating housing construction, but because it encouraged local communities to initiate large-scale housing projects bearing low rents and requiring

---

[7] Jarmain, *op. cit.*, p. 43.

[8] Bowley, *op. cit.*, p. 22.

[9] *Ibid.*, p. 26, n. 2. This compares with typical house rents of £25 to £40 per year.

TABLE III–1

Numbers of Houses Built in England and Wales Between January 1, 1919, and March 31, 1939
(In thousands of units)

In year ending March 31	By Local Authorities[c]: 1st experiment: Housing etc., Act, 1919	2d experiment: Housing Acts: 1923	2d experiment: Housing Acts: 1924	2d experiment: Housing Acts: Total	3d experiment: Housing Acts: 1930, 1936, and 1938, slum clearance	3d experiment: Housing Acts: 1935, 1936, and 1938, decrowding	3d experiment: Housing Acts: 1925, 1936, and 1938, general	3d experiment: Housing Acts: Total	Total, local authorities	By Private Enterprise[e]: Subsidized: 1st experiment: Housing etc. and Addit. Powers Acts, 1919[d]	Subsidized: 2d experiment: Housing Acts: 1923	Subsidized: 2d experiment: Housing Acts: 1924	Subsidized: 2d experiment: Housing Acts: Total	Subsidized: 3d experiment: Housing Acts, 1930 to 1938	Subsidized: Total	Unsubsidized	Total, private enterprise	Grand total, local authorities and private enterprise
1920[a]	0.6	...	...	...	...	...	...	...	0.6	0.1	...	...	...	...	0.1			
1921	15.6	...	...	...	...	...	...	...	15.6	13.0	...	...	...	...	13.0			
1922	80.0	...	...	...	...	...	...	...	80.8	20.3	...	...	...	...	20.3	53.8[f]	97.5[f]	252.0[f]
1923	57.5	...	...	...	...	...	...	...	57.5	10.3	...	...	...	...	10.3			
1924	10.5	3.8	...	3.8	...	...	...	...	14.3	...	4.3	...	4.3	...	4.3	67.5	71.8	86.1
1925	2.9	15.3	2.5	17.8	...	...	...	...	20.7	...	47.0	...	47.0	...	47.0	69.2	116.2	136.9
1926	1.1	16.2	26.9	43.1	...	...	...	...	44.2	...	62.4	0.4	62.8	...	62.8	66.4	129.2	173.4
1927	0.9	14.1	59.1	73.2	...	...	...	...	74.1	...	78.4	1.2	79.6	...	79.6	63.9	143.5	217.6
1928	0.2	13.8	90.1	103.9	...	...	...	...	104.1	...	73.1	1.5	74.6	...	74.6	60.3	134.9	239.0
1929	...	5.1	50.6	55.7	...	...	...	...	55.7	...	48.4	0.7	49.1	...	49.1	64.7	113.8	169.5
1930	...	5.6	54.6	60.2	...	...	1.6	1.6	61.8	...	49.1	1.1	50.2	...	50.2	90.1	140.3	202.1
1931	...	...	52.5	52.5	...	...	3.4	3.4	55.9	...	...	2.6	2.6	...	2.6	125.4	128.0	183.9
1932	...	...	65.2	65.2	2.4	...	2.5	4.9	70.1	...	...	2.3	2.3	...	2.3	128.4	130.7	200.8
1933	...	1.4[b]	47.1	48.5	6.0	...	1.4	7.4	55.9	...	...	2.4	2.4	0.1	2.5	142.0	144.5	200.4
1934	...	...	44.8	44.8	9.0	...	2.2	11.2	56.0	...	...	2.8	2.8	...	2.8	207.9	210.7	266.7
1935	...	...	11.1	11.1	23.4	...	5.7	29.1	40.2	...	...	0.8	0.8	0.3	1.1	286.4	287.5	327.7
1936	...	...	...	...	39.1	...	14.4	53.5	53.5	...	...	...	...	0.2	0.2	271.7	271.9	325.4
1937	...	...	...	...	54.7	2.0	15.1	71.8	71.8	...	...	...	...	0.8	0.8	274.4	275.2	347.0
1938	...	...	...	...	56.8	7.3	13.9	78.0	78.0	...	...	...	...	2.6	2.6	257.1	259.7	337.7
1939	...	...	...	...	74.1	14.3	12.5	100.9	100.9	...	...	...	...	4.2	4.2	226.4	230.6	331.5
Total Armistice to March 31 1939	170.1	75.3	504.5	579.8	265.5	23.6	72.7	361.8	1111.7	43.7[d]	362.7	15.8	378.5	8.2	430.4	2455.6[g]	2886.0	3997.7

Source: This table, the sources of which are the *Ministry of Health Annual Reports* and the six-monthly report *Housing*, is adapted from Marian Bowley, *Housing and the State, 1919–1944* (London: Allen & Unwin, 1947), p. 271.

[a] Including three months January to March, 1919.

[b] Houses transferred from the Housing Act, 1924.

[c] Excluding 15,365 houses built to house persons displaced under reconstruction and improvement schemes under the 1890 and 1925 Acts.

[d] All except 4,500 of the houses included in this column were built under the Additional Powers Act.

[e] Excluding houses with rateable values exceeding £78 (£105 in the Metropolitan Police Area).

[f] Including houses built by unsubsidized private enterprise up to October, 1922, estimated by the Ministry of Health as 30 thousand.

[g] Including 21,500 houses built by private enterprise with Local Authority guaranties under the Housing (Financial Provisions) Act, 1933, not shown separately for individual years.

large national financial subsidies which were not shared in to any important degree by the local governments.

Housing Policies, 1922 to 1939

The Conservative government, which came into power in 1922, enacted the Housing Act in July, 1923 (the Chamberlain Act), which limited subsidies to be paid by the Treasury to a maximum of £6 a house annually for twenty years and provided for participation by private enterprise or by local authorities.[10] No subsidy from local rates (taxes) was required, and houses could be sold or rented, provided only that they met defined minimum standards and were built by October 1, 1925. Local authorities were given powers to advance money to persons wishing to buy new houses or to guarantee payments to building societies. Landlords were also eligible for local government advances to finance improvements in rental dwellings. Although local authorities were still permitted to build housing, the Act placed the burden of proof on the local authorities to establish to the satisfaction of the Minister of Health that they could perform the task better than if it were left to private enterprise. The Act has been characterized as one "to encourage private enterprise to build small houses either for sale or for letting."[11]

The Rent and Mortgage Interest Restriction Act of 1923, although it extended rent controls until 1925, provided that housing becoming vacant would be freed from further rent restrictions. Although the Act envisaged the gradual freeing of the house market from government controls, rent restrictions were extended first to 1927 and then annually until a general revision of rent controls was made in 1933.

When the Labour party took office in 1924, the local authorities were once more granted the power to provide working-class housing without first having to establish that it could not be provided by private enterprise. The local authorities were thus established in the housing field, and, as will be seen, their powers and obligations were further broadened in the housing field during the post-World War II years. The Labour government's Housing Act of 1924 increased the amount of annual subsidies available to local authorities and so-called public utility societies to £9 per house annually for forty years in urban parishes, and to £12 10*s*. per house annually for forty years for houses in rural parishes. The Act provided that average rents for the houses built with the new subsidy were to be fixed in relation to the prevailing

[10] *Ibid.*, p. 36.
[11] *Ibid.*, p. 39.

controlled rents of houses built before World War I, but provided that higher rents could be charged if housing authorities incurred a loss in excess of £4 10*s*. per house annually on houses built under the Act. In effect, the total subsidy was thus shared by the national and local governments, but the share of the local government could be limited to a maximum of £4 10*s*. per annum per house for forty years. In the fixing of rents, although the local authorities were free to fix rents of individual houses as they pleased, few introduced differential rent schemes. (These were schemes to vary rents paid with financial abilities of the occupants.)

With the advent of the depression of 1930, the national government urged local authorities to take advantage of the fall in building costs to charge lower rents. It was argued that, since it was possible in 1931 to build houses without subsidy to rent at levels comparable with subsidized houses built in 1927, there was no reason for continuing the subsidy, and it was abandoned as of the end of 1932. Marian Bowley has estimated that the so-called Chamberlain subsidies, under the Act of 1923, cost the Treasury £2,600,000 per year after 1929, or just under £7 per house per year. The Treasury contributions under the higher Labour government subsidies from 1924 to 1934 cost £4,300,000 annually after 1934, and averaged approximately £8 5*s*. per year per house.[12]

The relative effects of the Conservative government's Act of 1923 and of the Labour government's Act of 1924 can be clearly noted in Table III–1. Private enterprise accounted for a high level of subsidized and unsubsidized house production from 1925 to 1929, when the Chamberlain Housing Act was in effect. During this period, building by the local authorities was at a very low level. As the Labour government's Act of 1924 gradually took effect in 1927 and following years, local authorities again increased their housing production to levels exceeding those of 1922 and 1923. Subsidized private housing dwindled off to little or nothing, but unsubsidized private enterprise housing continued at rising levels, particularly following the reversal in national government policy referred to above, beginning in 1930/31.

In the aggregate, there were 2,207,000 houses built by private and public enterprise from 1923 to 1933/34. Of this total, approximately 1.5 million were built by private enterprise, of which two thirds were unsubsidized. Private enterprise housing constructed during this period was primarily for owner occupancy rather than rental. Local authori-

---

[12] *Ibid.*, p. 47. Miss Bowley estimated that the cost to the ratepayers of the two subsidies was only £1 9*s*. in 1935–36—equivalent to 0.9 per cent of the total rate expenditure.

ties accounted for approximately 600,000 units, most of which were built under the Labour government's Act of 1924.

The notable revival of private enterprise housing from 1924 to 1934 not only modified the severity of Britain's housing shortage, but resulted in the adoption of a national housing policy from 1934 to 1939 which relied primarily upon private enterprise to provide new housing and generally restricted the scope of local government activities to slum clearance. The estimated housing shortage was reduced from 822,000 dwelling units in 1923 to 127,000 by September, 1934.[13] The Housing Act of 1933 embodied the recommendations of a Report of the Departmental Committee on Housing of 1933, which set forth the government's policy in these terms:

> . . . to concentrate public effort and money on the clearance and improvement of slum conditions, and to rely in the main on competitive private enterprise to provide a new supply of accommodation for the working classes—the provision by private enterprise to be supplemented where necessary by means of unsubsidized building by the Local Authorities.[14]

> . . . it is anticipated that, with the re-establishment of more normal conditions, economic forces, operating in a free field, will secure a large volume and variety of production at competitive rents, and private builders, housing companies, public utility companies, finance societies, and private investors will, it is hoped, all take a share in the ownership of working-class houses.[15]

In order to stimulate private investment in working-class housing, the local authorities were authorized to guarantee the additional interest and capital involved if building societies advanced 90 per cent of the value of a new house instead of the customary 70 per cent, and the period for repayment of loans was raised from twenty to thirty years. National subsidies were paid (1) to offset the cost to local authorities of acquiring sites for slum clearance, (2) if the burden imposed on the rates as a result of slum clearance schemes would be unreasonable, and then only up to £5 per house per year, and (3) from £2 to £8 per house per year over forty years to decrease overcrowding in rural areas. The subsidies were later consolidated by the Housing Act

[13] *Ibid.*, p. 49.

[14] *Ibid.*, p. 138, quoting from *Report of the Departmental Committee on Housing*, Cmd. 4397 (London: H.M.S.O., 1933), p. 4. It had been previously recommended by the 1932 *Report on Local Expenditure* that housing subsidies should be given only to those who were unable to buy or rent houses built by private enterprise.

[15] *Ministry of Health Circular to Housing Authorities*, No. 1334 (May, 1933), as quoted in Bowley, *op. cit.*, p. 139.

of 1938 to provide a uniform subsidy of £5 10*s*. per annum per house for forty years for local authority slum clearance and decrowding schemes. The local authority was required to pay £2 15*s*. of this total subsidy. Subsidies on high-cost sites and for rehousing agricultural workers were at the same time increased.[16]

The Housing Act of 1936 provided that local authorities should pool their housing accounts for all housing built under the Housing Act of 1919 and subsequent legislation. In effect, the costs, revenues, and subsidies under various Acts were to be pooled and the rents of individual houses adjusted at will. It was thus made possible for the local authorities to move toward the equalization of rents for houses of similar standards bearing different subsidies.

Although the program of slum clearance did not gain any momentum until 1934, a total of 272,836 houses were closed or demolished from 1930 to 1939 and an equal number built for replacement by local authorities.[17] Meanwhile, as can be seen from Table III–1, a private building boom of record proportions was experienced in England and Wales. This resulted in an average annual production of approximately 250,000 units from 1934 to 1939. Miss Bowley points out that 40 per cent of the total produced by private enterprise were typical working-class houses (i.e., rated at less than £13), and that, since half of these were for sale only, working-class families without the necessary down payments were required to rely on the filtering or the "trickle-down" process to improve their housing standards. By 1937, however, the Inter-Departmental Committee on the Rent Restriction Acts concluded that the shortage of houses of any class had ceased to exist as a national problem.[18]

Post-World War II Situation

The deterioration of existing housing because of the lack of maintenance during World War II, the virtual cessation of housebuilding during hostilities, and the war destruction combined with high rates of family formation to create a severe postwar housing shortage in the United Kingdom by 1945. The estimated housing stock at the end of the war totaled approximately 11,000,000 dwellings, as shown in Table III–2.

The Minister of Health had estimated in December, 1943, that

[16] Bowley, *op. cit.*, pp. 141–142.
[17] *Ibid.*, p. 153.
[18] Jarmain, *op. cit.*, p. 17.

TABLE III–2

HOUSING STOCK, 1931 TO 1945, UNITED KINGDOM

	Units
Housing census, 1931	9,399,000
Dwellings built, 1931–39	2,506,000
Dwellings built, 1939–45	162,000
Total	12,067,000
Less:	
Dwellings demolished (15 per cent of 1931–39 building rate)	382,000
Slum clearance to March, 1939 (Ministry of Health Report, 1938–39)	242,000
War-destroyed houses (Cmd. 6609, 1945)	200,000
Severely war-damaged (uninhabitable) houses	250,000
Total	1,074,000
Total remaining, 1945	10,993,000

Source: Political and Economic Planning Committee, "Housing Report" (unpublished report, Political and Economic Planning Committee, 16 Queen Anne's Gate, London SW 1, December 3, 1951). The committee of citizens responsible for this preliminary report was unable to reach agreement upon a final, published document. Hereafter cited as Political and Economic Planning, "Housing Report."

1,500,000 new houses would be required in order to provide each family with a separate dwelling and eliminate overcrowding.[19] A total of over two million wartime marriages and continued high marriage and birth rates added to the prospects for magnifying the housing shortage in the immediate postwar period. Further, over half of Britain's housing stock was more than fifty-five years old, so that a high replacement demand was forecast for the future.[20]

The great public concern with the immediate and prospective post-World War II housing shortage in England is reflected in the Parliamentary Debate on the white paper on housing presented by the

[19] *House of Commons Debates,* 5th series, 409 (1945–46), 1057–1058. Estimates of housing needs in England and Wales varied widely. The Economics Committee of the Royal Commission on Population estimated that a shortage of only 25,000 units existed in October, 1950, assuming one house for all married women, for all widows below the age of sixty-five years, and for 20 per cent of single women between the ages of twenty and forty-five years.

At the other extreme, Alexander Bloch estimated that a housing shortage of 2,908,000 units existed a few years before, assuming that 47 houses were needed for each one hundred adults (*Estimating Housing Needs* [1947]). Bloch's work is cited in the Political and Economic Planning Committee's "Housing Report" (on this unpublished report, see the source note to Table III–2); hereafter cited as Political and Economic Planning, "Housing Report."

[20] Heinz Umrath, "Activities of the European Labor Movement in the Housing Field" (unpublished report, Amsterdam, December, 1952), p. 69. On this report, see source note to Table V–3.

Minister of Reconstruction in March, 1945.[21] It was estimated by the government that 750,000 houses were required for people with no separate dwelling and that an additional 500,000 houses were required for slum clearance and to eliminate overcrowding. The government set forth its objective in March, 1945, as the production of 220,000 units in the first year after the war and annual production at the rate of 300,000 units of permanent housing by the second year. This was to be supplemented by the delivery of 30,000 temporary houses from the United States government, on lend-lease, starting in 1945. The Minister of Health in the Churchill cabinet stated in the House of Commons on March 22, 1945:

> The people need houses, they need them as soon as possible, and it is up to the government to leave no stone unturned to supply the maximum number of houses in the minimum period of time. This is just what we intend to do. But this period ahead of us is, it must be, and it must continue to be, a time of the greatest difficulty we have ever confronted in housing. . . . I submit—that in these inescapable circumstances, the government programme is, in fact, a tremendous commitment if we are to fulfill it—a programme of 220,000 houses, completed in the first two years after the defeat of Germany plus temporary houses plus repair of war damage. . . . The Government will provide subsidies for local authorities *and for private enterprise,* the government must control the volume of contracts let in a way that was not done after the last war, the government must control the private work—building and repair and decorative work done on private account, the government must control the prices of materials. . . . I believe the great majority of permanent houses during this period will be built by local housing authorities, most of them under contract with builders, large or small. The Government do not for one moment fail to appreciate the widespread desire for house ownership or its social advantages. Private enterprise was responsible for nearly three-quarters of the houses built between the wars, and will soon, I hope, be making a great contribution again. It is almost universally acknowledged to be essential that a start with private enterprise building should be made.[22]

Opposition members viewed the government's program as much too conservative and estimated that "we must have a long-term housing program of building 7,000,000 new houses over the next 15 years.[23] The Labour party's officially announced program, in the 1943 pamphlet *Housing and Planning After the War,* had called for the erection of at

---

[21] *Housing, Government's Policy and Organization for Carrying It into Effect,* Cmd. 6609, presented by the Minister of Reconstruction (London: H.M.S.O., 1945).

[22] *House of Commons Debates,* 5th series, 409 (1945–46) 1019 ff.

[23] *Ibid.,* p. 1060.

least 4,000,000 houses during the decade following the end of the war. Local authorities were to assume the primary responsibility for the provision of postwar housing, while the activities of the building societies and the speculative builder were to be subject to rigid governmental control. It was proposed that the central government advance capital to the local authorities for housing construction at "substantially lower rates than normal." The Labour party's statement was critical of the fact that "the wrong families frequently got the benefit of the [housing] subsidy," and recommended that wages be increased and that land and building costs be reduced to the lowest possible level in order to remove the need for housing subsidies. To control land costs, it was recommended that there should be a periodic levy of 75 per cent of the increases in annual site values of land in urban or built-up areas.

The Labour Minister of Health, Mr. Bevan, expanded on the government's housing policy in the House of Commons on October 17, 1945:

> Before the war the housing problems of the middle classes were, roughly, solved. The higher income groups had their houses, the lower income groups had not. Speculative builders, supported enthusiastically, and even voraciously, by money lending organizations, solved the problem of the higher income groups in the matter of housing. We propose to start at the other end. We propose to start to solve, first, the housing difficulties of the lower income groups. In other words, we propose to lay the main emphasis of our programme upon building houses to let. That means that we shall ask Local Authorities to be the main instruments for the housing program.[24]

Housing Policies of the Labour Government, 1945 to 1952

The housing policies of the Labour government were in effect from August, 1945, until the passage of the Housing Act of 1952, following the Conservative victory in October, 1951. The primary features of the Labour government's housing policy were:

Reliance upon publicly owned rental housing with executive responsibility for local housing programs vested in the local housing authorities

Review and approval of local authority housing proposals by the Minister of Health

Licensing of all private building by the Ministry of Works, with a complicated materials control priority system

Low-interest-rate loans to local authorities through the Public Works Loan Board

Annual Exchequer subsidies, for periods of sixty years, supplemented

[24] *Ibid.*, 414 (1945–46), 1222.

by compulsory local rate fund contributions varying in amounts according to the type and location of newly constructed or improved housing

Control of rents and sales prices of houses

Interaction of the "development charge" and other provisions of the Town and Country Planning Act of 1947 with controls over residential building.[25]

Rent control was a key element in the housing policy of the Labour government. An Inter-Departmental Committee on Rent Control reported in 1945 the following extraordinary variety of rent levels for similar types of dwellings depending on when they were first let.[26]

About 4 million houses of a ratable value not above £35 in London and Scotland, and £20 in the provinces, which had been built before 1919 and continuously controlled on the basis of 1914 rents plus a 40 per cent permitted increase on the net rent. The average net rent of these was about 6*s.* a week (9*s.* in London).

About 4.5 million similar houses which had been decontrolled. The average net rent of these was about 30 per cent more than before decontrol (50 per cent in London), although rents varied widely.

A further 1.5 million local authority houses (mostly post-1918), not controlled, whose average net rents were 7*s.* a week (10*s.* 6*d.* in London).

Finally, 3 million post-1919 private enterprise houses, mostly owner-occupied. Those to let had average net rents "appreciably higher" than prewar houses. These rents were not controlled until 1939.

The committee recommended that rent control should be continued for at least ten years, that existing limits of ratable value within which houses were controlled should remain unchanged, but that houses built after the war and local authority houses should not be controlled. The committee recommended further that local authorities maintain a register of all rents in each area and that a system of "rent tribunals" be established to effect adjustments in rent levels.[27]

The Rent Act of 1946, as amended by the Act of 1949, provided for the establishment of rent tribunals, for the maintenance of registers of rents by the local authorities, and for security of tenure by tenants in rental properties in rental disputes.

That rents were generally low in England and Scotland in 1947 is

[25] The development charge was a special fee levied at the time of development upon the developer or builder. For a discussion of this and its effect upon housebuilding see Paul F. Wendt, "Administrative Problems under the British Town and Country Planning Act of 1947," *Land Economics,* XXV, No. 4 (November, 1949), 427–432.

[26] *Report of the Inter-Departmental Committee on Rent Control,* Cmd. 6621 (London: H.M.S.O., 1945).

[27] *Ibid.*

TABLE III–3

PERCENTAGE DISTRIBUTION OF GROSS RENTS BETWEEN COUNCIL AND PRIVATELY OWNED RENTED DWELLINGS, UNITED KINGDOM, 1947

Weekly rent	Total	Council	Privately owned and other
Up to and including 10*s*.	38	26	41
10*s*. to 15*s*.	32	46	29
15*s*. to 20*s*.	14	22	13
Over 20*s*.	16	6	17
Total	100	100	100

Source: *The British Household, Social Survey, 1947,* as cited in Political and Economic Planning, "Housing Report."
Note: Gross rents include allowances for local rates.

shown by Table III–3, indicating that 70 per cent of all rented dwellings had rents of 15*s*. per week, or less. Somewhat higher proportions of privately owned houses were found to be included in the lowest and in the highest rental ranges, while Council houses were typically rented in the range of 10 to 15*s*. per week.[28]

Considerable variation existed in the proportion of income spent for housing in the United Kingdom before and after World War II. Families living in prewar houses in 1950 were generally paying 1939 rents plus rate increases, while those who had moved into new houses or converted flats were paying considerably more. It was estimated that the average working-class family before the war spent 12 per cent of its income on rent and that this proportion had declined to eight or nine per cent by 1950.[29] The Department of Health for Scotland reported the following increases in rents and earnings in Scotland from 1938 to 1955, using 1938 as base:

	1938	1949	1955
Average local authority rent	100	118	140
Average weekly earnings	100	207	323

It was estimated that the average weekly rent in Scotland in 1938 amounted to 10.5 per cent of average weekly earnings, and that it was 6 per cent in 1949 and 4.5 per cent in 1955.[30]

[28] *The British Household, Social Survey, 1947,* as cited in Political and Economic Planning, "Housing Report."

[29] Ministry of Labour, *Weekly Expenditure of Working-Class Households in the U.K., 1937–38,* as cited in Political and Economic Planning, "Housing Report."

[30] Department of Health for Scotland, *D.H.S. Circular,* No. 23/1956 (Edinburgh: H.M.S.O., June 30, 1956). The rent return published in 1939 (Cmd. 5913)

During the period from 1946 to 1951 the following additions were made to the supply of rental housing in the United Kingdom:

About 650,000 local authority houses (not controlled) with net rents ranging from 5*s.* to 30*s.*

About 150,000 private enterprise houses, of which about one ninth were for letting. These were subject to some measure of rent and price regulation as a condition of the license to build, and came under formal control as they were referred to the rent tribunals.

Some 90,000 dwellings made available by conversion or adaptation, an unknown number of which were offered for letting for the first time and were subject to control by the rent tribunals.

In England, as in other countries, there was considerable public dissatisfaction with rent controls following World War II on three major counts: first, prevailing rents provided no inducement for private owners to build houses to let; second, glaring disparities existed in rent between similar houses; and, third, current rents did not provide enough income for the landlords to keep property in good condition. This dissatisfaction provided the basis for the modifications in rent controls by the Conservative government, beginning in 1952, which are discussed below.

Extensive controls over housing were exercised under the Labour government by several government departments with considerable overlapping and conflict in jurisdiction. Up to 1951 the Ministry of Town and Country Planning was responsible for the approval of local plans, compulsory acquisition of land, the planning and development of the new towns, and, through the Central Land Board, for the assessment of "development charges" assessed against land developers. The Ministry of Health was responsible for the development of national housing policies and oversight of local authority housebuilding. The Ministry of Works was responsible for the licensing of all building as well as the control over sale and rental prices of new dwellings (under the Building Materials and Housing Act of 1945). The Ministry of Labour and National Service was concerned with the supply of labor to the building industry, while the Ministry of Agriculture was responsible for advice on the use of agricultural land for housing purposes. The above agencies with responsibility in England and Wales were paral-

showed that at May 16, 1938, the average rent charged by the local authorities for their houses was £18 17*s.* 7*d.* The return for 1949 showed that in November, 1949, it was £22 5*s.* 9*d.* (Cmd. 8046). In November, 1955, it was £26 6*s.* 10*d.* In the same period the rise in average incomes has been relatively much greater; as an indication of this, the average weekly earnings of male manual workers in main industries may be quoted. In October, 1938, the figure was £3 9*s*; in October, 1949, it was £7 2*s.* 8*d.*; and in October, 1955, it was £11 2*s.* 11*d.*

leled by similar or sometimes different agencies in Scotland. All in all, the administration of housing policy under the Labour government was enmeshed in a complex system of bureaucratic controls. It was somewhat simplified when, under the Conservative government, the Ministry of Housing and Local Government in 1951 took over the town planning, housing, and local government functions formerly vested in the Ministry of Town and Country Planning and the Ministry of Health in England and Wales, and regional offices with broad authority were established to provide liaison with local authorities on housing matters.[31]

The housing policies of the Labour government were under fire within two months of the Labour party victory in August, 1945, primarily on the grounds that government restrictions, rising costs, and the elimination of private enterprise housing were throttling the housing industry. Actual production of housing in the United Kingdom rose gradually from 55,400 units in 1946 and 139,690 in 1947 to 227,616 in 1948 and 197,627 in 1949. It can be noted that private enterprise building actually exceeded local authority construction in 1946. This reflected the greater speed in initiating private construction as well as the more favorable private investment climate. In mid-1949 the Minister of Health stated in the House of Commons that the objective of the housing program had been cut to an annual output of 200,000 houses, as compared with the earlier production objective of 400,000 per annum.[32] Following his statement, the new dollar crisis led to the devaluation of the pound and further cuts in the program were suggested by the government. Housing production remained slightly under 200,000 units annually in 1950 and 1951, and rose to 239,922 in 1952.[33]

One of the more serious developments under the Labour government's administration was that the relatively low levels of house production were accompanied by rapid increases in building costs. The report of a committee of inquiry appointed by the Minister of Health to look into the cost of housebuilding reported in 1948 that a typical local authority house which had been built at a cost of £400 in 1939 cost £1,200 in 1947.[34] Although a large share of the rise in costs was

---

[31] Central Office of Information, Reference Division, *Housing in Britain* (London: H.M.S.O., August, 1954), p. 7.

[32] *House of Commons Debates,* 5th series, 466 (1948–49), 1833.

[33] Central Office of Information, *Housing in Britain,* p. 5.

[34] Richard A. Sabatino, *Housing in Great Britain, 1945–49* (Dallas: Southern Methodist University Press, 1956). See also *The Cost of House-Building,* First Report of the Committee of Inquiry appointed by the Minister of Health (London: H.M.S.O., 1948), as cited in Sabatino, *op. cit.,* p. 9.

attributed to the general inflation in the economy, important factors influencing the rapid cost increases following the war were declines in worker productivity, lack of personal incentives, shortages, dislocations in labor and material supplies, organizational inefficiency, technical backwardness, and monopolistic practices. A British productivity team which came to the United States in 1949 to observe American methods of building found that, although the American building worker did not work any harder than his British counterpart, "average production per man-hour in America was 50 per cent more than in Britain." [35]

Richard A. Sabatino has attributed the reduced productivity of the British housebuilding industry under the Labour government to the fact that the program failed to limit the total demand for labor and materials and, thus, failed to maintain a smooth flow of labor and materials to housebuilding sites. He attributes major importance to the sudden cuts made in capital investment in December, 1947, which resulted from the necessity to reduce imports and reallocate scarce labor and materials to the export industries which could earn dollars. Cuts in the housing program were made at that time because of the heavy drain on the limited dollar supply caused by imports of lumber and by the need to transfer labor and materials to work in the export industries.

Comparison of the actual accomplishments of the Labour government's housing program with the pledgc to produce 400,000 units annually in the decade following the war leads to the inevitable conclusion that the promised program was utopian from the start and had not been thought out in terms of the total requirements of the economy. Sabatino and others have viewed the failure of the housing program as the result of loose and makeshift central planning, rather than as a failure of planning as such.[36] Others have assumed that the failure of the Labour government's housing program was the result of too much planning and too great interference in housing by the national government. As will be noted in chapter vii, many of the problems in administering national programs during the immediate postwar years can be attributed in important measure to the continued severity of the foreign exchange shortage in the United Kingdom, which necessitated cutbacks in national economic programs.

---

[35] Sabatino, *op. cit.*, p. 43.

[36] *Ibid.*, p. 36.

TABLE III–4

Rates of Annual Contributions Payable Under Housing Subsidies in England and Wales: Postwar Legislation

Type of subsidy	Housing (Financial and Miscellaneous Provisions) Act, 1946		Housing Act, 1952		1946 Act as amended by Housing (Review of Contributions) Order, 1954	
	Exchequer contribution	Rate fund contribution	Exchequer contribution	Rate fund contribution	Exchequer contribution	Rate fund contribution
	£ s.	£ s.	£ s.	£ s.	£ s.	£ s.
General standard subsidy for ordinary house	16 10	5 10	26 14	8 18	22 1	7 7
Special standard subsidy at Minister's discretion for houses for the agricultural population, or for areas of low rents and substantial housing responsibilities	25 10	1 10[a]	35 14	2 10[a]	31 1	2 10[a]
Extra subsidy at Minister's discretion in heavily burdened areas	Not exceeding 2 15	5 10, less amount in previous column	Not exceeding 4 9	8 18, less amount in previous column	Not exceeding 3 13 6d.	7 7, less amount in previous column
For houses on expensive sites, where the developed site costs more than £3,000 per acre: extra subsidy for each £1,000 or part thereof in excess, disregarding excess over £10,000	1 4[b]	8[b]	2 5	15	2 5	15
Subsidy for flats on expensive sites:						
Escalator provision according to cost per acre of developed site:						
Ordinary subsidy on sites costing—						
More than £1,500 but not more than £4,000	28 10	9 10	52 16	17 12	45 18	15 6
rising to—						
More than £10,000 but not more than £12,000[c]	35 5	11 15	60 18	20 6	53 5	17 15
Special subsidy for flats in blocks of 4 storeys or more with lifts, on sites costing—						
More than £1,500 but not more than £4,000	35 10	13 0	63 6	22 17	56 8	20 11
rising to—						
More than £10,000 but not more than £12,000[c]	42 5	15 5	71 8	25 11	63 15	23 0
Extra subsidies in areas subject to mining subsidence	Up to £2	Up to £1	Up to £2	Up to £1	Up to £2	Up to £1
Extra subsidies for preservation of character of surroundings	Up to £5[b]	Up to £2 10s[b]	Up to £5	Up to £2 10s.	Up to £5	Up to £2 10s.
Grants to persons other than local authorities for the building of new houses for the agricultural population	Up to £15	...	Up to £15	...	Up to £15	...
Grants to local authorities for hostels	£5 per bedroom[b]	...	£5 per bedroom	...	£5 per bedroom	...
Grants to local authorities for reconditioning	Three quarters of estimated loss[b]	One quarter of estimated loss[b]	Three quarters of estimated loss	One quarter of estimated loss	Three quarters of estimated loss	One quarter of estimated loss
Grants for building experiments	At discretion[b]	...	At discretion	...	At discretion	...

Source: *Report of the Ministry of Housing and Local Government for the Year 1955*, Cmd. 9876 (London: H.M.S.O., October, 1956). Appendix I, Table C.

[a] In this category the county council also makes a contribution, equivalent to that from the rate fund.

[b] The rates of contribution shown here were authorised by the Housing Act, 1949.

[c] Over £12,000 the subsidy (both ordinary and special) is increased, for each additional £2,000 or part of £2,000 in the cost per acre of the site as developed, by £1 10*s*. (Exchequer) and 10*s*. (rate fund) under the 1946 Act, by £1 19*s*. (Exchequer) and 13*s*. (rate fund) under the 1952 Act, and by £1 16*s*. (Exchequer) and 12*s*. (rate fund) under the 1946 Act as amended.

Housing Policies of Conservatives, 1952

The Conservative government, on assuming office in October, 1951, established a production goal of 300,000 new houses a year. During the subsequent five-year period the Conservative government gradually effected a major reorientation in housing policy in the direction of greater reliance upon free markets, private enterprise, and the building of houses for owner occupancy. As an initial step in stimulating house production, the Housing Act of 1952 increased the standard or "general needs" housing subsidies, as shown in Table III–4. As will be seen presently, these subsidies were subsequently lowered by the Housing Act of 1954 and the Housing Subsidies Act of 1956, and eventually abolished entirely. The development charge, a payment assessed against any developer of land, was removed by the Town and Country Planning Act of 1953. The government expressed its intention to "promote, by all possible means, building of houses for owner occupancy." [37] To this end the local authorities, who had in 1950 and 1951 issued licenses on behalf of the Minister of Works in the ratio of one privately owned house to each four houses built by the local authority, were given the discretion to license private housebuilding up to the same number of houses as they were building themselves after January 1, 1952. After January 1, 1953, the authorities were asked to license without question the building of private houses with a maximum of 1,000 square feet in blocks of up to 12 units, and to consider on their merits applications for houses between 1,000 and 1,500 square feet and in blocks of more than 12. After January, 1954, the licensing of privately built houses up to 1,500 square feet and in blocks of up to 50 units became automatic, while proposals for larger houses or blocks of over 50 were to be referred to the Regional Office of the Ministry for approval. After November 10, 1954, private enterprise housebuilding became free of licensing. Further, the fixing of maximum resale prices and rents for dwellings built or converted under license, which had been required by the Building Materials and Housing Act, 1945 (as amended by the Housing Act, 1949), was permitted to lapse in December, 1953, and was not renewed.[38]

As a result of these changes, the share of private enterprise in total housing production rose from 12.5 per cent in 1951 to 21.7 per cent in 1953, 28.5 per cent in 1954, and to 47 per cent by 1958.[39]

---

[37] Ministry of Housing and Local Government, *Houses, The Next Step,* Cmd. 8996 (London: H.M.S.O., November, 1953), p. 1.

[38] *Report of the Ministry of Housing and Local Government for the Period 1950/51 to 1954,* Cmd. 9559 (London: H.M.S.O., August, 1955), p. 12.

[39] It is estimated that private enterprise accounted for in excess of 50 per cent of housing production in 1959.

A Report of the Interdepartmental Committee on Rent Control had recommended in 1945 that rent controls be continued for at least ten years, but that postwar newly built or converted houses should not be controlled, and that rents should be adjusted upward to allow for increased cost of repairs and for increased ability to pay in local areas.[40] It was noted earlier that the policy of the Labour government was to control rents and selling prices for existing as well as newly built houses. The Minister of Housing and Local Government called attention in 1953 to the fact that "There is at present in England and Wales a hopelessly illogical system of rents."[41] He pointed to the wide variation in rents for similar quarters and to the fact that rents were too low to enable landlords to maintain the inventory of 7.25 million privately rented houses, of which more than 4.75 million were past sixty-five years of age. He recommended substantial increases in rents based on the fact that repair costs had increased three times over since 1939, the base year for many rental properties.

In a speech in the House of Commons on October 27, 1954, the Min-

---

[40] *Report of the Inter-Departmental Committee on Rent Control,* Cmd. 6621 (London: H.M.S.O., 1945).

[41] Ministry of Housing and Local Government, *Houses, The Next Step,* Cmd. 8996 (London: H.M.S.O., November, 1953).

The following newspaper report from the *Sunday Express Reporter* (London), August 3, 1958, illustrates the minister's contention:

MINER'S WIFE MUST SWOP WITH TENANT

TWO-HOUSE WOMAN LOSES COUNCIL HOME

A £15-a-week miner has got to swop his council home for the house his wife owns—because she put 7s. 6d. a week on the rent.

Miner William Fox, 45, pays 21s. 5d. rent for the council house in Ingshead-avenue, Rawmarsh, South Yorkshire.

His wife's tenant, 51-year-old Mr. Sydney Goulty, a father of eight, pays 19s. 9d. for a three-bedroomed house in Broad-street.

Mr. Goulty earns £8. His rent was raised from 12s. 3d. last December.

And, the Socialist-controlled Rawmarsh Council was told, Mrs. Fox said, it would go up again this week.

Mr. Goulty lives with his wife Minnie and three of their children.

Said Mr. Goulty yesterday: "I protested to the council that my landlady lived in a council house. It seems wrong that I should be subsidising her house through my rates and yet she should put up my rent.

LONGING

"My wife and I have been longing for a council house for years. This place has no bathroom or hot-water system."

Said Mr. Fox: "I have lived here 12 years and spent more than £200 on improvements.

"It is unfair that I should be turned out because of what my wife owns. I am appealing to the council against the decision."

And his wife: "I put up the rent because of the high cost of repairs."

ister of Housing and Local Government drew attention to the integral relationship between rent controls and housing subsidies and to the impact of housing subsidies on the national budget:

Local authorities own about 1-¼ million houses built before the war, and a further 1-½ million built since the war. The Exchequer subsidies which they are receiving on these existing houses amount in all to nearly £47 million a year. There is no doubt that, in general, council house rents are today being subsidised to a greater extent than the financial circumstances of the individual tenants require. This shows that the amount of the subsidy which the Exchequer is now paying out in respect of existing houses is unnecessarily large, and provides a margin which could properly be used for financing some part of the future housebuilding programme.

For a number of years there will continue to be a large demand for more houses and in many areas the shortage is still serious. But most, if not all, the authorities which have long waiting lists possess a big pool of existing houses upon which they are receiving large amounts of subsidy. These usually include many prewar houses, built at much lower cost. Provided, therefore, that they subsidise only those tenants who require subsidising, and only to the extent of their need, local authorities should be well able to continue building the new houses they require with appreciably less Exchequer assistance than hitherto.

We are not proposing that the rates of subsidy on houses already built or building should be altered; but we have come to the conclusion that the subsidy on future houses, built for general needs, should be abolished altogether. In order not to make the transition too abrupt, we propose, for a year or so, to pay a much reduced annual subsidy of £10 per house.

What I have said about the position of local authorities as a whole does not apply to the corporations of the New Towns. They do not possess any pool of low-cost prewar houses, and consequently, their rents are substantially above the general average. A special problem arises also in the case of authorities of small towns or districts which are being expanded to accommodate overspill population from congested cities. We propose, therefore, in these special circumstances, to provide a basic Exchequer subsidy of £24, an increase of £2 over the existing rate.

Unless local authorities will exercise more discrimination in giving rent relief to their tenants, there is bound to be a continued misuse of public money. At present, councils are discouraged from introducing differential rent schemes by reason of the fact that, no matter how much they increase their revenue from rents, they still have a statutory obligation to pay into the Housing Revenue Account a fixed contribution from the rates. We therefore propose to abolish this obligation. This will allow local authorities, if they so desire, to use any savings they may make to reduce the rate burden, and will give them for the first time an incentive to adopt realistic rent policies. . . .

The proposed changes in the subsidy rates will have the effect of slowing down the annual growth of Exchequer expenditure on housing.

But, since they will not affect the subsidies payable on houses already built, they cannot, of course, reduce the present total of the subsidy bill. Nevertheless, I believe that it will be generally recognized that the policy which I have announced represents an important step in the direction of restoring some measure of reality to housing finance.[42]

In line with the above proposals, the Housing Act of 1956 provided for a reduction in the general needs housing subsidy to £10 per annum and for its eventual abolition. Beginning in November, 1956, the subsidy on houses for general needs was abolished, except for one-bedroom dwellings, which were in particular demand for old people and small families. Subsidies for dwellings in "New Towns" and to meet urgent industrial needs were continued at £24 per annum, while a slightly smaller subsidy of £22 1*s.* per annum was continued for slum clearance or redevelopment projects, as shown in Table III–5. The Act of 1956 also provided that local authorities were no longer required to make a contribution from the rates to the Housing Revenue Account for every house on which they received an Exchequer subsidy. The object was to provide greater flexibility in the granting of local government housing subsidies. The Act gave the Minister the power by order to abolish or reduce all or any of the Exchequer subsidies payable under the Act or to reduce the period for which the subsidies were payable. Before making such an order, the Minister was required to consult with the associations of local authorities.

Under the Rent Control Act of 1949, rent tribunals were unable to increase the standard rents. This restriction was removed by the Housing Repairs and Rents Act of 1954, with the result that the proportion of applications for rent increases which received favorable action by rent tribunals in England and Wales rose substantially in 1954, 1955, and 1956.[43]

Initial steps toward the abolition of rent controls in England and Wales were taken by the enactment of the Rent Act, 1957. This law removed more than 4.5 million owner-occupied houses, and any other houses which subsequently are vacated, from rent controls. In addition, the limits of ratable (assessed) value below which rents were controlled were lowered, resulting in the release of an additional 800,000 dwellings from rent controls.[44] The Minister of Housing and Local

---

[42] As quoted in *Report of the Ministry of Housing and Local Government for the Year 1955*, Cmd. 9876 (London: H.M.S.O., October, 1956), pp. 4–5.

[43] *Report of the Ministry of Housing and Local Government for the Year 1956*, Cmnd. 193 (London: H.M.S.O., June, 1957), Appendix II.

[44] Robert Steel, *The Rent Act, 1957* (London: Royal Institution of Chartered Surveyors, July, 1957), p. 14. Section 11 (1) of the Act of 1957 provided that the

TABLE III-5

RATES OF ANNUAL CONTRIBUTIONS PAYABLE UNDER HOUSING SUBSIDIES ACT, 1956

Purpose	Subsidy			
	Houses, and flats, in less than 4 storeys	Flats in 4 storeys	Flats in 5 storeys	Flats in 6 storeys or more
1. Provided for general needs, i.e. any purposes other than those specified in 2–7 of this table (Section 3(2)).[a]	£10 per annum	£20 per annum	£26 per annum	£38[b] per annum
2. Provided by a local authority for the purposes of slum clearance or redevelopment as defined in Section 11(1). 3. Provided by a local authority for the purpose of rehousing persons coming from camps or other unsatisfactory temporary housing accommodation designated as such by the Minister.	£22 1*s.* per annum	£32 per annum	£38 per annum	£50[b] per annum
4. Provided by a receiving authority under a town development scheme. 5. Provided by a local authority for persons coming into their area to meet the urgent needs of industry in accordance with arrangements approved by the Minister. 6. Provided by the local authority of a congested or overpopulated area in some other area as part of a scheme of development of "new town" character. 7. Provided by a development corporation of a new town.	£24 per annum	£32 per annum	£38 per annum	£50[b] per annum

Source: Ministry of Housing and Local Government, Circular No. 33/56, July 17, 1956 (London: H M.S.O., 1956), p. 5.

[a] Abolished by order, November 2, 1956, except for one-bedroom dwellings, a nominal subsidy of 1*s.*, and upon application by an authority to meet unusual problems.

[b] The subsidy is increased by £1 15*s.* for each storey in excess of six.

Government (in Scotland, the Secretary of State) was further authorized by the Act to reduce the ratable value limits further by statutory order, subject to approval by each House of Parliament. The Act of 1957 substituted a uniform new rent limit based on the 1956 gross value

Rent Acts should cease to apply to any dwelling house with a ratable value exceeding £40 in the City of London, £30 elsewhere in England and Wales, £40 in Scotland. Ratable value means the value on November 7, 1956.

of dwellings for the intricate and multiple bases previously applicable. The Act provided for increases in rents owing to increases in services, rates, or improvements, and for gradual permissive rent increases upon the expiration of contractual tenancies.[45]

Housing Finance

Local authorities had been authorized by the Public Works Loans Act of 1875 to borrow for capital expenditures including housing from the Public Works Loan Board, and this was the only source from which local authorities could normally borrow under the Labour government from 1945 to 1951. After 1952 local authorities were permitted to borrow from other sources; as a result, advances from the Public Works Loan Board gradually declined from 85 per cent of borrowing by local authorities to 22 per cent in 1956–57.[46] The rates of interest charged by the Public Works Loan Board are fixed by the Treasury and in general are based upon open market rates, which in turn are affected by the bank rate. The rise in interest rates beginning in late 1951 was reflected in a gradual rise in interest costs for long-term loans to the local authorities for housing and other purposes from 3 per cent in 1948 to a high of 6.75 per cent in September, 1957, as shown by Chart III–1. The Conservative government took steps to defer local authority borrowing from the Public Works Loan Board during the period of monetary stringency from 1954 to 1957. This restraint was offset, however, by direct borrowing by local authorities in the open market, and, as a result, the volume of public housing investment was maintained at relatively high levels despite the monetary stringency.

The influence of rising interest costs was supplemented by direct measures by the Ministry of Housing and Local Government to restrict public expenditures on new housing in 1957, when it was announced that as a part of the government's anti-inflation policy the Ministry would endeavor to reduce new public housebuilding by approximately

---

[45] *Ibid.*, pp. 59–60.

[46] *Report of the Ministry of Housing and Local Government for the Period 1950/51 to 1954*, Cmd. 9559 (London: H.M.S.O., August, 1955); *ibid., for the Year 1955*, Cmd. 9876 (October, 1956); *ibid., 1956*, Cmnd. 193 (June, 1957); *ibid., 1957*, Cmnd. 419 (May, 1958); *ibid., 1958*, Cmnd. 737 (May, 1959). The amount of loans sanctioned by the Minister of Housing and Local Government to local authorities for new housing was as follows (in millions): 1945–46, £36.1; 1946–47, £222.2; 1947–48, £167.7; 1948–49, £185.1; 1949–50, £226.5; 1950–51, £227.4; 1951–52, £252.5; 1952–53, £351.7; 1953–54, £325.8; 1954–55, £280.0; 1955–56, £236.5; 1956–57, £221.9; 1957–58, £235.5 (All figures obtained from appendixes on local government finance in the foregoing reports.)

CHART III-1

BUILDING SOCIETIES' RATES, BANK RATE, AND YIELD ON 2.5 PER CENT CONSOLS, 1951-1959

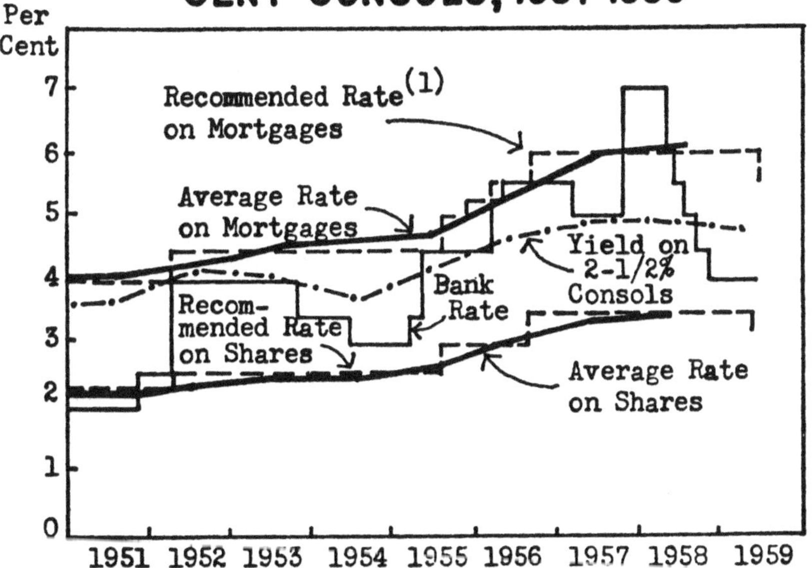

[1] Rate Recommended by the Building Societies Association.

SOURCE: *Committee on the Working of the Monetary System Report,* Cmnd. 827 (London: H.M.S.O., August, 1959), p. 101.

20 per cent by the financial year 1959–60. The rationale for this decision was stated as follows:

> As regards housing, some curtailment of expenditure on the building of new houses cannot be avoided. Since 1951 housing has been given a specially high priority, and expenditure on new housebuilding has absorbed a substantial proportion—between a quarter and a fifth—of all capital investment. As a result more than five million people have been rehoused in this period, and the housing situation in the country at large has been greatly improved. A decline in the building of houses by local authorities was therefore to be expected in any case, and has in fact already shown itself. Many local authorities have now built enough houses to meet the really urgent demands for more accommodation in their areas, and on that account have for some time been letting their building programmes run down. Many other authorities are approaching that position. Some urban authorities, furthermore, are starting to cut back their rate of building because of shortage of

available sites. Against this background, the Government must envisage some reduction in the current rate of housebuilding by local authorities. In its anti-inflation policy the Government will proceed on the basis that total expenditure of the building on new houses by authorities will progressively slow down in such a manner that in the financial year 1959–60 it will not exceed 80 per cent of the current level of expenditure.[47]

Table III–6 summarizes the total expenditures of local authorities on revenue and capital account for housing purposes. Expenditures on revenue account for housing rose from 12 per cent of total revenue expenditures in 1950–51 to approximately 16 per cent in 1955–56. Housing expenditures during this period were the second largest classification of local government expenditures, exceeded only by expenditures for education. Local government debt for housing purposes totaled £2,684 million as of March 31, 1955, and represented 71 per cent of the total.

Central government housing subsidies to local authorities are also shown in Table III–6. It can be seen that the technique of making annual grants for sixty-year periods resulted in a cumulative rise in the total expenditures to approximately £55 million in 1956–57. The annual rate of increase in central government subsidies was substantially reduced in recent years, however, as the Conservative government acted to reduce housing subsidies. The receipts on capital loans represent total borrowings for housing purposes through the Public Works Loan Board and in the open market during this period. The combined effect of rising interest costs and control by the Ministry of Housing and Local Government is reflected in the decline in both capital loan receipts and expenditures for housing after 1953–54.

Local authorities were also empowered to make thirty-year loans at fixed interest rates up to 80 per cent of value to private individuals for building or buying houses by the Small Dwellings Acquisition Act of 1899. Although originally limited to houses with a value not exceeding £400, the limit was raised to £800 in 1939 and was raised following World War II to £5,000. Meanwhile the percentage of loan to value was raised to 90 per cent. Local authorities were also empowered by the Housing Act of 1949 to advance 90-per-cent loans to any person for the purpose of buying or building houses or acquiring buildings for alteration or conversion into houses. Local authorities were also authorized by the Housing Acts of 1936 and 1949 to guarantee building societies against loss on loans made at higher proportions of purchase

[47] Ministry of Housing and Local Government, *Circular No. 54/57*, November 11, 1957 (London: H.M.S.O., 1957).

TABLE III–6

LOCAL GOVERNMENT EXPENDITURES FOR HOUSING, ENGLAND AND WALES, 1946 TO 1958
(In thousands of pounds)

Year	Revenue account						Capital account		
	Expenditure			Specific income		Balance of expenditures not met out of income			
	General	Loan charges	Total	Fees, rents	Govt. grants		Receipts on loans	Capital expenditures	Debt
1946–47	17,697	34,069	51,766	29,163	15,597	7,006	106,662	106,828	669,924
1947–48	37,336	38,203	75,539	40,145	26,573	8,821	192,154	210,612	849,357
1948–49	40,600	45,399	85,999	48,792	28,034	9,173	217,989	245,437	1,053,481
1949–50	42,960	53,200	96,160	56,932	29,132	10,096	217,155	222,794	1,253,912
1950–51	44,838	60,515	105,353	64,777	30,318	10,258	222,196	230,503	1,457,224
1951–52	47,958	69,080	117,038	73,853	32,021	11,164	249,536	254,697	1,687,224
1952–53	52,966	80,706	133,672	83,188	36,683	13,801	311,186	316,298	1,975,420
1953–54	57,496	95,892	153,388	95,798	42,316	15,274	332,481	338,621	2,282,235
1954–55	60,987	110,029	171,016	106,863	48,093	16,060	301,611	302,637	2,555,433
1955–56	66,781	124,074	190,855	118,039	54,048	18,768	268,454	269,074	2,791,838
1956–57	70,914	140,969	211,883	137,740	55,818	18,325	243,195	261,286	3,005,366
1957–58	74,279	158,053	232,332	155,494	57,825	19,013	235,693	244,756	3,201,176

Sources: 1946–47 to 1949–50: Ministry of Housing and Local Government, special tabulation prepared for the author. 1950–51 to 1957–58: *Report of the Ministry of Housing and Local Government for the Period 1950/51 to 1954*, Cmd. 9559 (London: H.M.S.O., August, 1955); *ibid., for the Year 1955*, Cmd. 9876 (October, 1956); *ibid., 1956*, Cmnd. 193 (June, 1957); *ibid., 1957*, Cmnd. 419 (May, 1958); *ibid., 1958*, Cmnd. 737 (May, 1959).

TABLE III-7

Advances and Guaranties by Local Authorities under the Small Dwellings Acquisition Acts and the Housing Acts, England and Wales, 1945 to 1959

Purpose	April, 1945, to March, 1951		April, 1951, to March, 1952		April, 1952, to March, 1953		April, 1953, to March, 1954		April, 1954, to March, 1955		April, 1955, to March, 1956		April, 1956, to March, 1957		April, 1957, to March, 1958		April, 1958, to March, 1959	
	Number of dwellings	Amount (£000)	Number of dwellings	Amount (£000)	Number of dwellings	Amount (£000)	Number of dwellings	Amount (£000)	Number of dwellings	Amount (£000)	Number of dwellings	Amount (£000)	Number of dwellings	Amount (£000)	Number of dwellings	Amount (£000)	Number of dwellings	Amoun (£000)
Advances made under the Small Dwellings Acquisition Acts:																		
1. For acquisition	32,215	25,040.0	12,335	12,725.4	8,670	8,632.7	10,337	10,270.3	15,431	17,111.4	17,587	19,158.4	13,161	13,263.6	9,632	8,800.1	7,252	6,755.7
2. For construction	8,590	8,803.8	4,025	5,162.0	4,758	7,137.5	6,352	10,020.8	8,017	12,802.3	7,559	13,323.4	4,616	8,366.4	2,475	4,248.0	1,567	2,677.5
Advances made under Housing Act, 1936, Sections 90 and 91 (1) (a):[a]																		
1. For improvements	34	9.1	—	—	—	—	—	—	—	—	—	—	—	—	—	—	—	—
2. For acquisition or construction	2,209	2,103.5	—	—	—	—	—	—	—	—	—	—	—	—	—	—	—	—
Advances to Housing Associations under Housing Act, 1957 (Section 119)	n.a.	n.a.	1,938	1,750.6	1,539	2,026.0	2,813	3,018.8	2,043	3,857.2	1,540	2,740.2	1,355	2,103.1	600	1,859.0	549	879.8
Advances under Housing Acts:																		
1. For acquisition	2,306	2,403.6	3,614	3,868.0	3,337	3,382.3	4,685	4,740.0	10,854	12,579.4	20,187	23,964.8	25,605	29,343.7	26,270	26,648.3	27,678	31,920.8
2. For construction	823	962.3	1,235	1,625.4	1,562	2,296.5	2,531	3,825.1	4,257	6,594.8	7,849	12,724.1	7,670	13,420.3	6,156	10,902.4	5,428	9,581.0
3. For conversion	15	10.8	43	21.1	29	22.6	45	41.6	85	82.9	194	124.1	213	183.8	215	202.4	149	98.0
4. For alteration, etc.	175	41.8	422	92.5	475	102.5	579	142.7	1,089	239.8	2,507	629.1	2,911	797.2	2,815	802.8	2,547	710.0
Dwellings for which guaranties have been given:																		
1. Housing Associations under Housing Act, 1957 (Section 119)	n.a.	—	59	—	61	—	26	—	74	—	119	—	7	—	—	—	—	—
2. Building Societies, etc., under Housing (Financial Provisions) Act, 1958 (Section 45)	99	—	20	—	1	—	2	—	10,698	—	16,041	—	10,509	1,283.8	10,118	—	7,952	—

Sources: *Report of the Ministry of Housing and Local Government for the Period 1950/51 to 1954*, Cmd. 9559 (London: H.M.S.O., August, 1955); *ibid., for the Year 1955*, Cmd. 9876 (October, 1956); *ibid., 1956*, Cmnd. 193 (June, 1957); *ibid., 1957*, Cmnd. 419 (May, 1958); *ibid., 1958*, Cmnd. 737 (May, 1959). All figures were obtained from Appendix I of the foregoing reports.

[a] Sections 90 and 91 of the Housing Act, 1936, were repealed as from July 30, 1949, by the Housing Act, 1949.

CHART III-2

GROWTH OF BUILDING SOCIETIES IN THE UNITED KINGDOM, 1913 – 1959

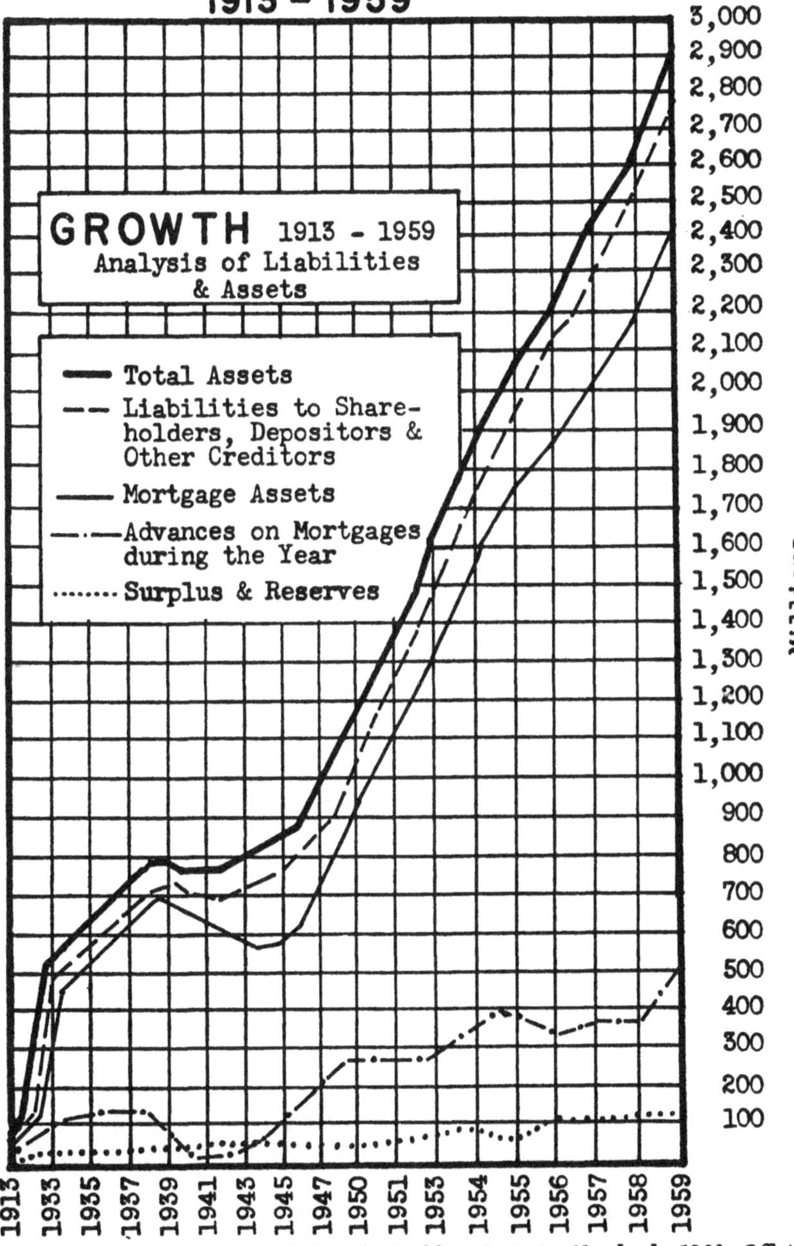

SOURCE: Franey & Co., Ltd. (eds.), *Building Societies Yearbook, 1960: Official Handbook of The Building Societies Association* (London: Franey & Co., Ltd., 1960), p. 50.

price on a basis that any losses would be shared by the Ministry.[48]

Table III–7 summarizes the advances and guaranties made by local authorities under the Small Dwellings Acquisition Acts and the Housing Acts during the period from 1945 to 1958. It can be noted that the magnitude of local authority advances for acquisition and construction was limited to an over-all total of approximately 45,000 dwellings for the six-year period ending in March, 1951. The annual number and monetary value of advances increased substantially from 1952 to 1955 under stimulus by the Minister of Housing for local authorities to make full use of their powers under these Acts to further private ownership of housing.

Appeals to local authorities in mid-1955 to limit capital expenditures, accompanied by a sharp rise in the interest rates shown in Chart III–1, resulted in substantial reductions in advances and guaranties under these Acts from 1956 to 1959.

Building Societies

The building societies, which have existed in England since 1781 or earlier, are the most important source of financing for private housebuilding. Chart III–2 shows the long-term growth in assets and mortgage loans for the member institutions of the Building Societies Association, which account for about three quarters of the total assets of all building societies in the United Kingdom. From approximately 3,000 around 1890, the total number of societies had declined to 755 in 1957, reflecting the continuous trend toward merger and consolidations over the years. The most rapid growth in assets occurred during the private building boom of the 1930's. The marked rise in mortgage loan advances following the Conservative government's shift in housing policy is noticeable after 1952.

The most usual type of mortgage loan available through the building societies is a 75-per-cent twenty-year loan repayable by annuity payments. The recent trend in rates of interest charged, shown in Chart III–1, reflects changes in prevailing money market conditions. Building societies usually reserve the right to vary the interest rate on existing mortgages by giving three or six months' notice to borrowers. Newly built houses certified by the National Housebuilders Registration Council as of good construction are eligible for twenty-three-year loans. The

[48] Loans to local authorities under the Small Dwellings Acquisition Acts were reported separately as follows (in millions): 1950–51, £16.1; 1951–52, £27.1; 1952–53, £21.9; 1953–54, £29.2; 1954–55, £56.1; 1955–56, £82.5; 1956–57, £4.0; 1957–58, £6.0.

National House-Builders Registration Council, an autonomous body formed in 1937 and representative of all housing interests, operates a voluntary scheme for the independent inspection of houses built privately and the certification of those which comply with agreed standards of construction. Further, if the borrower can give additional security, loans are made up to 90 per cent of value for periods up to thirty years. The typical form of additional security before the war was a local authority guarantee of the extra 15 per cent advanced. During the private housing boom of the late 1930's builders, through what was known as a "continuing arrangement," could deposit 10 per cent of the value of the houses to be built with a building society, which would then advance to purchasers up to 95 per cent of the value of the house on a thirty-year basis. Combined insurance schemes are also available, through which mortgage payments are linked with life insurance premiums to guarantee the unpaid balance on the mortgage if the mortgagor dies. For those in eligible age groups, combination mortgage loans and insurance policies are sometimes available up to thirty-five-year terms.

Life Insurance Companies

British life insurance companies lend considerable sums to their policyholders and to others secured by house mortgages. Total loans on house purchase in the United Kingdom by members of the British Insurance Association at the end of 1957 amounted to £410 million. Mortgage holdings accounted for 12.3 per cent of the assets of British Insurance Association companies at the end of 1956, which compares with 9.2 per cent in 1951 and 11.4 per cent in 1937. According to the recent report of the Committee on the Working of the Monetary System, the British insurance companies prefer to finance large blocks of office buildings, shops, and flats. However, they greatly extended their mortgages on house property to meet the demand, largely from their policyholders, during the credit squeeze in 1955–57. According to a recent study, life insurance companies expect the volume of house mortgage lending to decline. They follow a policy of accepting lending opportunities when rates are favorable, but do not seek out the business.[49]

Local Authorities

Although the local authorities have been authorized to make thirty-year loans up to 90 per cent of the value of the house at a rate of interest

[49] *Committee on the Working of the Monetary System Report,* Cmnd. 827 (London: H.M.S.O., August, 1959).

one fourth of one per cent above the rate at which the local authority was able to borrow from the Public Works Loan Board, few local authorities offer credit on these terms. In general, they tend to limit the terms of loans to twenty years, and to establish conservative valuations for purposes of determining loan values.

The mortgage credit terms available in early 1951 for purchase of a house costing £1,500 were summarized as follows in a confidential memorandum issued at that date:

	Deposit		Interest rate (per cent)	Number of years for repayment	Weekly payment (not including local rates)
	Per cent	Amount			
Building society:					
Plan 1........	25	£375	4.0	23 (Certified)	29*s.* 1*d.*
				20 (Uncertified)	
Plan 2........	10	£150	4.0	30 (Local authority guarantee)	29*s.* 10*d.*
				23 (Certified)	35*s.* 6*d.*
				20 (Uncertified)	38*s.*
Plan 3........	5	£75	4.0	23 (Certified)	36*s.* 8*d.*
				20 (Uncertified)	40*s.* 1*d.*
Local authority:					
Plan 4........	10	£150	3.75	30 (By annuity)	27*s.* 6*d.*
				20 (By fixed interest decreasing to 20*s.* 8*d.* at end of 20 years)	42*s.* 8*d.*

It can be seen that the weekly payments, which of course include amortization, far exceeded the median rents of 10 to 15 shillings per week including local rates referred to in Table III–3.

On May 4, 1954, the Minister of Housing and Local Government announced a special scheme to enable purchasers of smaller properties to obtain mortgages through building societies with partial guarantee by the local authorities with an initial deposit of, in some cases, only five per cent of the value. This scheme was modified in September, 1955, to provide that, for houses costing less than £2,500, building societies could advance up to 95 per cent of value on a post-1918 house and up to 90 per cent on a pre-1918 house. Although this and other measures by the Conservative government to stimulate privately owned housing resulted in a record volume of mortgage advances by the building societies in 1955, the extreme credit stringency starting in 1955, which culminated in the raising of the bank rate to 7 per cent in September, 1957, resulted in a sustained rise in mortgage interest rates charged by the building societies for new advances from the level of 4.5 per cent prevailing in March, 1952, to 5 per cent in July, 1955, 5.5 per cent in November, 1955, and 6 per cent in April, 1956. The reduction of the bank rate to 6 per cent in March, 1958, removed for a time the upward pressure on interest rates charged by the building societies.

The government published a white paper entitled "House Purchase; Proposed Government Scheme" in October, 1958, outlining arrangements for loans by the Exchequer to approved building societies in order to finance 95-per-cent twenty-year loans for the purchase of older houses and improvements to houses. Loans are to be made at the rate recommended by the Building Societies Association. The scheme also made provision for loans by local authorities up to 100 per cent of value instead of 90 per cent as previously loaned.[50]

The Housebuilding Industry

As in the United States, the housebuilding industry in England has been traditionally made up of small local enterprises. During the postwar period, the building industry in the United Kingdom was the subject of a great deal of criticism, and a number of studies were made of various aspects of the housebuilding industry.[51] The size structure of firms in the building industry during the postwar years is shown in Table III–8.

Sabatino and others have concluded that the post-World War II private housebuilding industry in England was a "backward industry of low productivity and high costs split into a large number of small, inefficient units engaged in a competitive scramble for work [and] producing a product to individual measurements by wasteful handicraft methods." [52] The old incentives of unemployment and fear of poverty, which had been instrumental in achieving relatively high labor productivity before the war, were substantially weakened by the postwar Labour government's full employment policy, and new incentives had not replaced them. Letters to the author from representatives of the British housebuilding industry suggest that Sabatino may have

[50] *Report of the Ministry of Housing and Local Government, 1958,* Cmnd. 737 (London: H.M.S.O., May, 1959), pp. 53–54.

[51] British Productivity Council, *A Review of Productivity in the Building Industry* (London, n.d.), p. 10.

[52] Sabatino, *op. cit.,* pp. 66–67. See also Ministry of Works, *Methods of Building in the U.S.A.,* The Report of a Mission Appointed by the Minister of Works (London: H.M.S.O., 1944).

TABLE III-8

SIZE OF BUILDING FIRMS IN THE UNITED KINGDOM, 1945 TO 1953

Size of firms, by number of employees	May, 1945		February, 1948		May, 1953	
	Firms	Employees	Firms	Employees	Firms	Employees
One-man firms	28,111	...	52,319	...	37,793	...
1 to 5........	26,441	60,861	45,014	105,948	42,046	98,756
6 to 19........	9,862	102,110	17,965	181,789	16,816	171,330
20 to 99.......	4,314	167,760	7,552	294,137	7,102	277,134
100 to 499.....	608	111,746	1,099	205,951	1,099	206,613
500 and over..	55	60,343	127	159,227	146	215,550
Totals....	69,391	504,820	124,076	947,052	105,002	969,383

Source: The British Productivity Council, *A Review of Productivity in the Building Industry* (London, n.d.), Table 1, p. 6.

Note: The figures for 1948 and 1953 exclude late returns not classified by size of firm. To arrive at the total number of operatives, 30,948 should be added for 1948 and 20,617 for 1953.

provided a somewhat distorted view of the industry. One of these letters points out: "It would have been unwise, and indeed impossible, for any private firm to have embarked on private housebuilding on a large scale at a time when application had to be made to the local authority for permission to build each individual house and the total number of private houses allowed in the whole country could be changed from month to month by ministerial edict. In addition, housebuilders had to face the various retarding influences, e.g., shortages of land and money and the bureaucratic control of land use."

The Girdwood Committee, which completed an investigation of the cost of housebuilding in 1948, found that a typical local authority house, which had cost less than £400 to build in 1939, cost £1,200 in 1947.[53] The committee concluded that the increase in building costs from 1939 to 1947 reflected changes in size, construction, and equipment of the houses built, direct increases in materials, wages, and other components of cost, and a decline in productivity. Direct increases in labor and materials were found to have kept pace with the general inflationary trend in the economy during and since the war. The committee called attention, however, to an apparent decline of 31 per cent in labor productivity in 1947 as compared with 1939, which was attributed to shortages, dislocations, and the lack of productivity incentives.[54]

---

[53] British Productivity Council, *op. cit.*, p. 10.

[54] *Ibid.*

A second report by this committee, in 1949, indicated that the introduction of incentive schemes had been effective in improving productivity on some 50 per cent of the houses currently under construction, but that productivity was still 20 per cent lower than before the war. A third report, in 1952, found no increase in output per worker between 1949 and 1951.[55] A special report by the Treasury noted a steady rise in productivity in housebuilding between 1951 and 1953.[56] Improved flow of materials, greater use of incentive schemes, careful preplanning, and larger-scale building operations were found to be the principal factors contributing to increased productivity.

The Report of the Private Enterprise Sub-Committee of the Central Housing Advisory Committee, in 1944, drew attention to the following factors which contributed to the relatively high efficiency and low costs of the private housebuilding industry in England during the interwar years from 1924 to 1939:

Ability to organize a continuous belt of production
Opportunity to acquire and plan sites in advance
Standardization of housing layout
Cheap money
Plentiful supply of labor and materials
Building costs in close correspondence with cost of living and stability of values
No competition between private enterprise and local authorities in the same field

For a number of reasons, many of which have been alluded to earlier, few of these conditions were present during the post-World War II years. As a result of the licensing regulations in effect under the Labour government, production was limited almost exclusively to publicly owned rental housing up to 1952. The delays in securing planning permission, the reluctance of landowners to sell land, and the reluctance of housebuilders to pay the development charges assessed under the Town and Country Planning Act of 1947 were contributing factors in discouraging private housebuilding. The elimination of the development charges by the Town and Country Planning Act of 1953 removed one factor deterring private development.[57] Further, shortages of labor and materials resulted in long delays in completing houses and in rising building costs during much of the post-World War

[55] *Ibid.*, p. 11.
[56] *Ibid.*
[57] Paul F. Wendt, "Administrative Problems Under the British Town and Country Planning Act of 1947," *Land Economics*, XXV (November, 1949), 427–432, and "A Reply from England on the Effects of the British Town and Country Planning Act, 1947," *ibid.*, XXVI (November, 1950), 397–400.

II period.[58] The influence of the credit stringency from 1954 to 1957 affected both public and private housebuilding, as noted earlier. In discussing "Problems in Building Modern Houses for Sale" the managing director of one of England's leading housebuilding firms stated that in consequence of the high bank rate prevailing in 1958 the building societies were temporarily unable to secure and to hold a sufficient volume of funds to finance a really large program of private housebuilding.[59] The most important element contributing to the failure of private enterprise housing to assume a more important position following World War II, however, was the assumption by local authorities of broad responsibility for provision of housing. This was explicit in the housing policy of the Labour government and remained a basic policy feature of the Conservative government. Commenting upon this factor, in the review referred to above, Mr. D. G. Howard said:

> As regards the standards of design construction and internal equipment of new housing, it would be true to say that public authorities have greatly improved their standards compared with pre-war, and the private developer has got to maintain a very high standard in order to equal the standards set by public authorities. . . .
>
> On the other hand, it must be pointed out that up to quite recently all houses built by public authorities have attracted a substantial state subsidy, which in every case is payable for 60 years, and this factor has tended to inflate the demand for this form of housing. Another factor which has tended to depress the demand for privately built housing has been the continued operation of the Rents Acts.[60]

It can be argued that the combination of these factors resulted in an atrophy of the private housebuilding industry in England as it was known before World War II. Meanwhile, the activity in the public housing sector immediately after the war attracted many of the larger housebuilding firms to the production of publicly owned rental housing. This is reflected to some degree in the expansion of the firms with 500 or more employees from 1945 to 1953 shown in Table III–8. Since 1952 many of these firms have reëntered private housebuilding on a substantial scale. Personal observation by the author confirmed the view that post-World War II housing and economic policies discouraged the revival of the private housebuilding industry to its prewar

[58] Sabatino, *op. cit.*, pp. 73–74. See also "Materials and Labour in Adequate Supply," in the *Financial Times Survey of the Building Industry, 1958* (London, July 14, 1958), p. 20.

[59] D. G. Howard, "Problems in Building Modern Houses for Sale," *Financial Times Survey of the Building Industry, 1958*, p. 42. Life insurance companies increased their lending during this period, but not sufficiently to offset the general mortgage credit stringency

[60] *Ibid.*

status, while encouraging improved design and construction standards in publicly owned housing and diverting the efforts of the most progressive firms in the housebuilding industry to the production under competitive bidding of local authority rental housing.

During visits to private housing developments and to local authority housing developments in mid-1958 the author gained the impression that publicly owned and developed housing had superior site planning and was on the whole better designed and constructed than typical private housing. The impact of competition from publicly subsidized housing, coupled with the shortages of land and adequate financing for private housebuilding, places a severe handicap upon the private housebuilder in the British market.[61] Despite the increase in publicly owned housing, however, the average Englishman still has a preference for living in his own house and recognizes that house purchase is a sound investment, particularly in times of inflation.

The relatively small number of large construction firms which participate in the bulk of local authority housing construction appear to have operated profitably in this sector of the housing market. It is, however, generally regarded as highly competitive and as one of the least profitable sections of a building firm's work. Nevertheless, public housing has been such an important segment in total postwar housing construction in England that it is looked to by many as a potentially stabilizing factor in housebuilding.

Review and Evaluation

Housing production in the United Kingdom, as shown in Table III–9, was maintained at high levels from 1953 on. Public construction dominated as a percentage of the total under the Labour government, but its percentage importance declined from 89 per cent in 1951 to 58 per cent in 1957 and to 53 per cent in 1958. Approximately 970,000 new dwellings were added to the housing supply during the six years from 1946 to 1951 when the Labour government was in power. Housing production during the following seven-year period, 1952 to 1958, under the Conservative government, totaled approximately 2,000,000 units, or double the former production figure.

It was pointed out earlier that shortages of labor and materials and difficulties in initiating large-scale public housing programs were important contributing factors to the failure of housing production to rise more rapidly under the Labour government. Easing of materials and manpower shortages and the encouragement of privately owned

[61] *Ibid.*

TABLE III–9

New Permanent Dwellings Completed in England, Wales, and Scotland, 1945 to 1959

Agency	Apr.–Dec., 1945	Jan.–Dec., 1946	1947	1948	1949	1950	1951	1952	1953
Public authorities:									
Local authorities	1,794	22,266	94,166	188,244	165,175	163,450	162,551	193,260	238,883
Housing associations	—	96[a]	880	1,831	1,408	1,631	1,797	2,153	7,924
Government departments	—	72[a]	490	2,666	4,483	5,512	7,899	10,189	9,051
Total public	1,794	22,434	95,536	192,741	171,066	170,593	172,247	205,602	255,858
Private builders	1,039	27,277	31,511	20,382	20,313	24,850	21,201	34,320	62,921
Grand total	2,833	49,711	127,047	213,123	191,379	195,443	193,448	239,922	318,779
Per cent, public	63.3	44.7	74.3	90.4	89.4	87.3	89.0	85.7	80.3
Rebuilding, conversions, and improvements:									
England and Wales	[No figures available (1945–1948)]				[3,178 (1949–1953)]				
Scotland	[6,136 (1945–1951)]							507	431

TABLE III-9 (*Continued*)

Agency	1954	1955	1956	1957	1958	1959	1945–51		1952–59	
							Total	Per cent	Total	Per cent
Public authorities:										
Local authorities	234,973	191,803	166,267	165,910	135,768	122,165	797,646	82.0	1,449,029	61.0
Housing associations	14,876	4,575	2,666	2,018	5,977	1,465	7,643	.8	41,654	1.7
Government departments	7,320	7,560	7,531	6,707	3,802	2,336	21,122	2.1	54,496	2.3
Total public	257,169	203,938	176,464	174,635	145,547	125,966	826,411	84.9	1,545,179	65.0
Private builders	90,636	113,457	124,161	126,455	128,148	150,708	146,573	15.1	830,806	35.0
Grand total	347,805	317,395	300,625	301,090	273,695	276,674	972,984	100.0	2,375,985	100.0
Per cent, public	73.9	64.3	58.7	58.0	53.2	45.5	—	—	—	—
Rebuilding, conversions, and improvements	14,056	36,668	36,997	38,413	36,635	83,153	—	—	245,922[b]	—

Sources: Ministry of Housing and Local Government, *Housing Return for England and Wales, 31st Dec., 1960*, Cmnd. 1271 (London, H.M.S.O., December, 1960); Department of Health for Scotland, *Housing Return for Scotland, 31st Dec., 1960*, Cmnd. 1269 (Edinburgh, H.M.S.O., February, 1961); Ministry of Housing and Local Government, *Houses, the Next Step*, Cmnd. 8996 (London, H.M.S.O., November, 1953); Secretary of State for Scotland, *Housing Policy, Scotland*, Cmd. 8997 (Edinburgh, H.M.S.O., November, 1953).

[a] Scotland included with private builders.

[b] Total figure for period 1954–59.

housing under the Conservative government resulted in a sustained rise in private housing production after 1951. Meanwhile, public housing construction continued and total housing production was maintained at relatively high levels even during the period of extreme credit stringency from 1955 to 1957.

Although substantial additions were made to the housing stock during post-World War II years, the volume of production never exceeded the record levels of the prewar years. The review of developments following World War II revealed that the maintenance of rents below the level of current costs and the centralization of responsibility for initiating housing programs in the local authorities resulted in a substantial drag upon the revival of the private housebuilding industry.

The subsequent elimination of the general needs subsidy by the Conservative government in 1956 found a wide gap between the costs of unsubsidized housing and typical rents for comparable space in local authority housing, making it difficult for private enterprise to build rental housing. It was of further importance that the reduced level of operations in the private housebuilding industry from 1939 to 1956 resulted in substantial organizational and technical obsolescence in this segment of the industry.

The gradually widening gap between housing costs and rents is illustrated by a tabulation published in the *Journal of the National Housing and Town Planning Council,* shown below. This shows that the local authorities, following the elimination of the Exchequer subsidy after November, 1956, found it necessary to make up, out of rates or from the rent pool, more than half the annual costs for new houses constructed. It will be observed that increased costs for building, maintenance, management, and repairs have not been allowed for in the estimates in Table III–10, so that the actual rent fund deficiency was probably greater than that shown.

These data permit some measurement of the extent of the housing subsidy required under typical rent and cost relationships from 1952 to 1956. Generally speaking, the occupants of both publicly and privately owned housing must make up the rent fund deficiency of local authorities through local rates assessed against housing occupants. According to the estimates in Table III–10, the total amounts of housing subsidies and rate fund deficiencies on new dwellings to be made up in this way have approximately equaled or exceeded typical rents paid in recent years. Further, loan charges on local authority housing debt, which amounted to £141 million in 1956–57, accounted for approximately two thirds of local government current housing expenditures. Local government loan charges exceeded rental income and

TABLE III–10

EFFECT OF INTEREST RATE AND SUBSIDY VARIATIONS ON THE RENT FUND DEFICIENCY OF LOCAL AUTHORITIES, 1952 TO 1956

	1952	Before November, 1955	Before November, 1956	After November, 1956
Assumed total cost of house	£1,525	£1,525	£1,525	£1,525
Rate of interest (per cent)	4.5	3.75	5.5	5.5
Annual loan charges	£70 5*s.*	£64 1*s.*	£87 5*s.*	£87 5*s.*
Maintenance, management, and repairs	£12	£12	£12	£12
Total	£82 5*s.*	£76 1*s.*	£99 5*s.*	£99 5*s.*
Notional rent (18*s.* per week)	£46 13*s.*	£46 13*s.*	£46 13*s.*	£46 13*s.*
Exchequer subsidy	£26 14*s.*	£22 1*s.*	£10	—
Rate subsidy	£8 18*s.*	£7 7*s.*	£7 7*s.*	£7 7*s.*
Rent fund deficiency	—	—	£35 5*s.*	£45 5*s.*

Source: County Council of Middlesex, County Planning Department, *Notes on the 1956 Housing Subsidies Act*, Office Circular No. 13/56 (London, November 16, 1956), p. 3, as cited in the *Journal of the National Housing and Town Planning Council*, May–June, 1956.

government housing grants by approximately £20 million in 1956–57. This represented an annual cost of approximately £6 for approximately 3.5 million publicly owned houses. Central government contributions to local housing programs amounting to £56 million during 1956–57 represent an additional cost of £16 per annum per publicly owned house which must be paid for by taxes. In order to ascertain the total costs of the housing program, it would be necessary to add the administrative costs of the Ministry and other public agencies participating in government housing programs. It seems evident that the apparent low housing costs under British rent controls and subsidies have represented a mirage, which disappears with the arrival of next year's tax bill.

The data in Tables III–10 and III–11 clearly portray the problems of the private housebuilding industry in the United Kingdom today. Lacking the Exchequer general needs subsidy or the local rate subsidy, the prospective private homeowner must be prepared to pay over twice as much in housing costs, including loan amortization, as are paid by the typical renter in council housing even after allowing for the income tax advantages of homeownership. (Loan amortization costs alone on a twenty-year loan of £1,500 at 4.5 per cent interest equal approximately £115 per annum.) At the same time, the quality

TABLE III-11

HOUSE BUILDING COSTS, ENGLAND AND WALES: SUMMARY OF INFORMATION RELATING TO TRADITIONAL THREE-BEDROOM HOUSES FOR WHICH TENDERS OR ESTIMATES WERE APPROVED BY THE MINISTRY OF HOUSING AND LOCAL GOVERNMENT, 1951–57

Period	Average floor area per house (including out-buildings)	Average tender price		
		Per house	Per sq. ft.	
Quarter	sq. ft.	£	*s.*	*d.*
1951: First	1,050	1,304	24	10
Second	1,037	1,359	26	2½
Third	1,031	1,403	27	2½
Fourth	1,011	1,396	27	7½
1952: First	984	1,380	28	0½
Second	952	1,391	29	2½
Third	932	1,391	29	10
Fourth	921	1,380	29	11½
1953: First	923	1,385	30	0
Second	913	1,387	30	4½
Third	914	1,382	30	3
Fourth	917	1,383	30	2
1954: First	909	1,378	30	4
Second	911	1,382	30	4
Third	919	1,381	30	1
Fourth	916	1,390	30	4
1955: First	912	1,402	30	9
Second	916	1,396	30	6
Third	914	1,432	31	4
Fourth	909	1,442	31	8½
1956: First	918	1,448	31	6½
Second	909	1,464	32	2½
*Third	910	1,487	32	8
Fourth	909	1,488	32	9
1957: First	915	1,494	32	8
Second	916	1,482	32	4½
Third	902	1,489	33	0

Source: *Report of the Ministry of Housing and Local Government, 1957*, Cmnd. 419 (London: H.M.S.O., May, 1958), Appendix I, Table H.

* The figures from the third quarter of 1956 onwards include new tradition houses, as the records do not now distinguish between traditional and new tradition houses.

of much of the postwar council housing is as good as or better than private housing available at the higher costs.

Large-scale public housing production in the United Kingdom during the postwar years resulted in a major shift in the characteristics of British housing and its tenure. It was estimated that approximately 11 million dwelling units remained in the United Kingdom as of the end of 1945. The total number of dwellings had increased to approximately 15 million by the middle of July 1957, as shown in Table III–12.[62]

TABLE III-12

ESTIMATED NUMBER OF DWELLINGS IN THE UNITED KINGDOM, 1951

		Millions of dwellings
Publicly owned		3.5
Privately owned:		
Owner-Occupied	4.65	
Rented—not subject to control by Rent Act of 1957	.82	
Rented—subject to control	4.89	
	10.4*	10.4*
Other rented houses not controlled		1.1*
Total estimated dwellings, July, 1957		15.0

Source: Robert Steel, *The Rent, October, 1957* (London: The Royal Institution of Chartered Surveyors, July, 1957), p. 12.
* Approximate—rounded to the nearest tenth.

The addition of approximately 2,300,000 publicly owned dwellings during the period from 1945 to 1959 and of only approximately 850,000 privately owned dwellings altered substantially the ownership of the housing stock in the United Kingdom. While housing was predominantly privately owned before World War II, almost one quarter was publicly owned by 1959. Further, the emphasis upon production of rental housing in the postwar period increased the importance of tenant-occupied dwellings as a percentage of the total housing supply.

Since census data are not available, it is more difficult to appraise the effects of England's postwar housing program upon the quality of housing. It was noted above that the average size of local authority houses was reduced by approximately 10 per cent during the period from 1950 to 1956. The space standards effective during most of the postwar period varied between 700 and 900 square feet for houses designed for four and five persons.[63] Privately owned houses constructed after 1954 were generally somewhat larger. It is more difficult to assess the influence of rent controls upon the condition of older

[62] Steel, *op. cit.*, p. 12.
[63] Ministry of Housing and Local Government, *Houses, 1952*, second supplement to *Housing Manual, 1949* (London: H.M.S.O., 1952).

housing in the United Kingdom since World War II. It is generally considered that the quality of rental housing has deteriorated during this period.

Increasing proportions of dwellings constructed by local authorities in recent years were in flats, as shown by Table III–13. The table also

TABLE III–13

ANALYSIS OF DWELLINGS BUILT BY LOCAL AUTHORITIES, ENGLAND AND WALES

	Percentage of all dwellings completed			
Number of bedrooms	April, 1945, to December, 1955	1956	1957	1958
One	7.0	10.6	13.3	17.8
Two	27.3	34.7	35.9	36.1
Three	63.1	52.8	48.7	43.9
Four or more	2.6	1.9	2.1	2.2
Flats (including the above)	17.7	26.7	30.8	35.5

Source: *Report of the Ministry of Housing and Local Government, 1958,* Cmnd. 737 (London: H.M.S.O., May, 1959), Appendix X, Table B.

shows the increasing trend toward production of smaller dwellings. The proportion of multistoried flats (more than four stories) increased to 11 per cent of all local authority dwelling construction and to 26 per cent of the total number of flats by 1958. As noted earlier, these trends resulted in part from the types of subsidies granted. It can be noted from Table III–4 that subsidies were higher for flats than for ordinary houses and that special subsidies were granted to facilitate construction of multistory flats on more expensive sites.

The data in Tables III–11 and III–13 suggest that the size of British housing units has declined during the postwar period. An increasing demand in the United Kingdom in recent years for one- and two-bedroom houses from the large numbers of childless and aged couples seeking a local authority house and the need to reduce costs were factors accounting for the government's encouragement of small dwelling construction. It is undoubtedly true, however, that postwar houses have had higher standards of convenience offsetting the trend toward smaller size. For example, it is now within the discretion of each local authority to decide whether or not to provide a second water closet for houses with three bedrooms, and separate inside bathrooms are provided in recommended house plans.[64] Postwar house

[64] *Ibid.*, p. 14.

construction, therefore, has most certainly had the effect of raising the convenience standards of the housing stock even though houses are smaller in size.

It is more difficult to appraise the influence of the postwar housing program on the condition of existing dwellings. In a review of government studies bearing on the condition of the dwelling stock as of 1949, it was concluded that the total number of houses in the United Kingdom requiring clearance approximated 2,000,000. This estimate was based upon assumptions that 11.6 per cent of the total of working-class dwellings in rural towns, 30 per cent of those in industrial towns, and 15 per cent of those in other urban areas were "unfit for human habitation and beyond repair at a reasonable expense.[65] In 1954 local authorities estimated that of approximately 13 million houses in England and Wales 850,000 (6.5 per cent) were unfit for human habitation.[66]

Progress in slum clearance was limited during the period from 1945 to 1951; it was estimated that during that period 44,721 houses were demolished or closed in England and Wales. As indicated in Table III–14, during the succeeding three years 40,552 houses were demolished or closed.

The Housing Act of 1949 provided for Exchequer assistance for owners prepared to improve or convert their property. Grants were made up to half the cost involved per dwelling, provided that the cost of the work exceeded £100, but not £600. (These limits were increased to £150 and £800 by amendment to regulations in 1952.) To be eligible, improvement plans must have the approval of the local authority and of the Minister, the houses must have an expected life of fifty years and must reach minimum standards established by the Minister. Exchequer contributions under this program, which were contributed mainly to private owners, rose to £215,000 in 1955–56 and to £546,000 in 1956–57. The number of conversions and improvements to dwellings in England and Wales under this program exceeded 100,000 during the three-year period from 1955 to 1957.[67] In combination with action on slum clearance and on elimination of unfit houses, this program made a notable contribution to the improvement in housing standards. New provisions in the 1959 Housing Act provide for government grants for the financing of basic necessities such as bath and water closet.

The Housing Repairs and Rents Act, 1954, required that local au-

[65] Political and Economic Planning, "Housing Report," chap. iv, p. 5.

[66] *Report of the Ministry of Housing and Local Government for the Year 1955*, p. 6.

[67] *Ibid., 1957*, pp. 138–139.

TABLE III–14

ACTION TAKEN ON UNFIT HOUSES: ENGLAND, WALES, AND SCOTLAND, 1945 TO 1958

England and Wales	April, 1945, to March, 1951	April, 1951, to March, 1952	April to December, 1952 (9 mos.)	1953	1954	1955	1956	1957	1958
1. Houses in clearance areas (Housing Act, 1957):									
Unfit houses demolished	34,450	10,522	6,823	4,063	5,424	8,066	13,777	21,099	28,376
Other houses demolished				156	461	495	593	933	1,521
2. Unfit houses elsewhere:									
Houses demolished				7,590	8,395	9,587	11,136	13,012	16,302
Houses closed	10,271	2,934	3,104	3,868	5,685	7,081	9,346	9,430	9,074
Total houses demolished or closed	44,721	13,456	9,927	15,677	19,965	25,229	34,852	44,474	55,273
Persons moved as result of:									
Demolitions	101,157	34,629	21,898	36,904	44,166	58,260	88,195	125,573	138,836
Closures	25,718	6,962	7,473	12,453	17,377	17,658	20,189	22,682	21,087
3. Unfit houses retained at end of year for temporary occupation under Housing Act, 1957:									
Sections 17 (2), 46, and 48	...	...	...	...	...	...	23,328	26,037	28,108
Sections 34 and 53	...	...	...	...	...	770	804	1,322	1,112
4. Houses which were made fit or in which defects were remedied as result of:									
Formal procedure under Public Health or Housing Acts:									

By owners	84,799[a] (By owners and by local authorities)	12,167[a] (By owners and by local authorities)	106,734	125,341	118,974	125,829	122,555	95,647	96,644
By local authorities (in default of owners)			5,880	9,748	6,663	8,994	10,516	8,737	8,125
Informal action by local authorities	425,502[a]	68,591[a]	219,253	268,697	255,882	230,809	215,500	178,713	176,447
Total	510,301[a]	80,758[a]	331,867	403,786	381,519	365,632	348,571	283,097	281,216
5. Houses reconstructed, enlarged or improved (Section 24 of Housing Act, 1957)	...	...	...	...	...	2,102	390	330	251
Scotland									
1. Unfit houses closed under Housing Acts	...	...	...	...	...	4,295	5,811	6,186	6,389
Not yet demolished at end of period[b]	...	...	...	...	...	4,295	9,189	12,851	15,739
Unfit houses demolished in clearance area	...	...	...	...	...	479	147	429	429
Unfit houses demolished not in clearance area	...	...	...	...	...	2,495	3,105	4,366	5,058
2. Unfit houses demolished under Town and Country Planning Acts:									
In comprehensive development area	...	...	...	...	...	507	569	309	670
Not in comprehensive development area	...	...	...	...	...	52	44	125	326

Sources: *Report of the Ministry of Housing and Local Government for the Period 1950/51 to 1954*, Cmd. 9559 (London: H.M.S.O., August, 1955); *ibid., for the Year 1955*, Cmd. 9876 (October, 1956); *ibid., 1956*, Cmnd. 193 (June, 1957); *ibid., 1957*, Cmnd. 419 (May, 1958); *ibid., 1958*, Cmnd. 737 (May, 1959). All figures obtained from Appendix I of the foregoing reports. Department of Health for Scotland, *Housing Return for Scotland, 30th June 1958*, Cmnd. 490 (Edinburgh: H.M.S.O., July, 1958), Table 13, p. 8; *ibid., March 31, 1959*, Cmnd. 728 (April, 1959), Table 13, p. 18.

[a] These figures relate to houses made fit as a result of formal procedure (or informal action prior to formal procedure) under the Housing Act, 1936 only. Corresponding figures for the Public Health Acts are not available prior to April 1952.

[b] Excludes houses closed or since demolished, and houses closed and reopened.

thorities submit to the Ministry proposals for dealing with slum houses in their areas and to start work. The following additional factors aided the rapid increase in the number of houses demolished in England and Wales from 1954 to 1957: (1) continuation of housing subsidies for purposes of slum clearance in the Housing Act of 1956, (2) the strengthening of demolition and closing powers by the Housing Act of 1957, and (3) the encouragement by the Conservative government of slum clearance despite the abandonment of the general needs subsidy and restrictions upon capital investment in 1956 and 1957. Table III–14 shows that substantially fewer houses were closed or demolished in Scotland during the postwar years.

Viewing the record, it can be observed that positive and effective steps were taken to improve the quality of the housing inventory in the United Kingdom, particularly in the years since 1954. Offsetting this, however, it must be recognized that the long-term debilitating effects of rent controls magnified the problem of slum housing and render its solution more difficult. Based on the author's personal observation, the standards of maintenance in the private housing sector in the United Kingdom are low compared with Germany, Sweden, or the United States, and this is owing in great measure to rent controls. It is reported, however, that a considerable improvement in maintenance standards resulted from the recent decontrol of substantial numbers of rental dwellings.

The success of programs of slum clearance in the United Kingdom can be attributed to the broad powers of clearance and redevelopment granted to the local authorities. The Housing and Repairs Act, 1954, and the Housing Act, 1957, provide that local authorities:[68]

May pass a resolution declaring any area to be a clearance area

Shall then proceed to clear the area either by order for demolition or by purchasing the land in the area for demolition by the local authority

May also purchase any other surrounding or adjoining land which is reasonably necessary for the satisfactory development or use of the cleared area

Shall pay compensation for land in any clearance area, including any buildings thereon, based upon the valuation of the land as a site cleared of buildings

May, after fourteen days' notice, take possession of any land to be appropriated without previous consent, subject to payment of compensation for the land taken and proceed with the clearance

These legislative sanctions were a potent force making it possible

[68] *Housing Act, 1957*, 5 & 6 Eliz. 2, chap. 56 (London: H.M.S.O., July 31, 1957), Part III.

for local authorities to move aggressively in slum clearance. The major contributing factor which accounted for the notable progress in slum clearance, however, was the presence of competent staffs in active local authority housing programs. The organization, experience, and know-how developed in public housing construction provided a springboard for slum clearance programing.

Postwar housing programs in the United Kingdom illustrate the implications of housing as a political problem and the difficulties of altering the basic tenets of government housing policy in the short run. The decision by the Labour party at the conclusion of World War II to place primary reliance upon publicly initiated, subsidized, and owned housing, to maintain control over rents, and to nationalize the development value of land relegated the private investor, housebuilder, and private house financing institutions to relatively unimportant positions in the housebuilding economy. Under this system the provision of housing at prewar levels of costs became a public obligation. The Conservative government has made some progress in shifting this responsibility back to the individual and to the private housebuilding industry, but the tradition of public intervention in housing dies very slowly. The measure of success achieved in the over-all provision of housing during the entire period can be attributed to the relatively high standards of public administration in the housing program. The competence of national and local public officials, and the flexibility with which basic adjustments in housing policy and program were effected, testifies to the basic strength of the civil service in the United Kingdom. The legacy of rent controls, and of public responsibility and domination of housebuilding, promises to haunt the political arena for many years and will deter the early revival of a vigorous and healthy private housebuilding industry in the United Kingdom. The implications of this for housing standards is less clear in view of the impressive record of public programs of slum clearance and public housing construction.

IV Sweden

During the nineteenth century the only housing measures enacted in Sweden were concerned with safety and health regulations in an economy dominated by laissez-faire political and social philosophy. Rapid population growth and urbanization contributed to the critical housing shortage before World War I. In the census of 1912–14, it was estimated that more than three fourths of the Swedish people were living in dwellings smaller in size than two rooms and a kitchen.[1] The predominant type of dwelling in Sweden at that time consisted of one room and kitchen. Extensive overcrowding, dilapidation, and the lack of modern conveniences added to the severity of the housing situation.

During and immediately following World War I, with the emergence of the Social Democratic party as a force, the Swedish government assumed a major role in housing. The entrance of the government into the housing field has been attributed to the stagnation of speculative residential construction during the years of World War I and the subsequent inflation, while the population of Swedish cities was increasing rapidly.[2]

As a result of the acute wartime housing shortage in Sweden, the government acted to control rents in May, 1917, and to increase the supply of housing through a subsidy program. The subsidies were primarily for the construction of apartment houses and usually amounted to about one third of the building costs. The national government provided two thirds of the subsidy and the local community one third. The granting of these subsidies was conditional upon the acceptance by the building society of state and local building controls,

---

[1] Leonard Silk, *Sweden Plans for Better Housing* (Durham, N. C.: Duke University Press, 1948), p. 20. The author has drawn extensively from this work in the review of Swedish housing policy before World War II.

[2] *Ibid.*, p. 31.

TABLE IV–1

SWEDISH HOUSING PRODUCTION, BUILDING COSTS, VACANCIES, AND RENTS, SELECTED YEARS, 1915 TO 1950

Year	Total production of dwelling units		Urban housing production by size of dwelling (percentage distribution)					Per cent of dwellings vacant	Rent index (1914 = 100)	Index of building costs (1914 = 100)
	Entire county	Urban areas	Single room	One room and kitchen	Two rooms and kitchen	Three rooms and kitchen	Four or more rooms and kitchen			
1915	n.a.	5,132	14.6	28.6	25.8	10.7	20.3	3.91	100	120
1920	n.a.	4,524	13.5	26.2	33.1	12.1	15.1	.09	155	325
1925	n.a.	13,042	12.8	24.0	32.1	15.2	15.9	—	186	219
1930	n.a.	21,785	20.7	33.4	25.0	10.6	10.3	—	204	208
1935	n.a.	27,303	15.2	31.0	29.8	14.3	9.6	—	199	193
1940	26,000	18,667	16.7	26.7	30.1	16.8	9.8	—	198	272
1941	17,000	11,943	19.7	27.3	27.5	16.5	9.0	—	202	281
1942	29,500	20,552	16.0	21.1	38.5	17.3	7.2	—	201	295
1943	39,500	29,050	13.3	20.0	39.1	20.8	6.8	—	202	322
1944	45,000	35,648	9.6	17.9	41.3	23.0	8.2	—	202	323
1945	49,500	36,931	10.7	12.2	37.4	28.3	11.4	—	202	325
1946	58,000	42,344	11.2	11.9	36.8	28.1	12.1	—	—	—
1947	58,000	37,507	12.4	10.0	35.3	29.2	13.2	—	—	—
1948	48,000	37,063	13.2	10.2	36.9	26.9	12.9	—	—	—
1949	41,551	32,885[a]	11.8	7.8	39.3	28.7	12.5	—	—	—
1950	43,935	35,133[a]	11.7	6.6	37.2	29.4	15.1	—	—	403[b]

Sources: 1915 to 1930—Size of dwellings, rent and building cost indices, and vacancy percentages: Leonard Silk, *Sweden Plans for Better Housing* (Durham, N. C.: Duke University Press, 1948), pp. 117–120. 1935 to 1950—Size of dwellings: *Bostadsbyggandet i Sverige 1956* (Stockholm, 1956), p. 35, Table R.

[a] Only additions because of new building included.

[b] Building costs for Stockholm only, from Svenska Handelsbanken, *Index* (Stockholm, March, 1957).

rent controls, and limitations on profits.[3] Although national production figures are not available up to 1938, it can be seen by Table IV--1 that this program was relatively ineffective in increasing the volume of residential building in urban areas before 1920—primarily because building costs continued to rise. Following the deflation of 1921, when conditions again became favorable for speculative building, the government subsidy program was dropped, and rent controls were repealed in 1923.

The housing shortage following World War I was intensified by a sharp increase in the number of new Swedish households and in consumer incomes. As a result of strong demand influences and a sharp fall in interest rates, coupled with free rental markets and high profit expectations, residential building experienced a relatively unbroken expansion in the period from 1920 to 1938. Lundberg has called attention to this unbroken expansion of housebuilding and to its relative stability, even during 1931 and 1932. He cites the data in Table IV–2

TABLE IV–2

INDICATORS OF ECONOMIC CHANGES IN SWEDEN, 1920 TO 1938
(In percentage of change)

Indicator	1920–21	1925–29	1928–30	1929–32	1932–34	1936–37	1937–38
Investments:							
Total value of gross investments	−40	+28	+14	−27	+28	+23	+11
Machinery (production + imports − exports)	−43	+46	+27	−40	+47	+26	+11
Housebuilding (number of rooms)	+38	+9	+28	+28	+7	+1	+13
Consumption:							
Value of total consumption	−29	+11	+4	−8	+5	+7	+6
Consumption of durable consumers' goods	−39	+22	+5	−21	+22	+19	+15
Incomes:							
National income (gross)	−27	+16	+6	−13	+10	+11	+6
Agricultural income (total sales of produce)	−43	−7	−16	−20	+18	+11	+4
Total industrial wages	−30	+27	+13	−19	+15	+13	+6
Average hourly earnings in industry	±0	+7	+7	−1	−1	+4	+6

Source: Erik Lundberg, *Business Cycles and Economic Policy*, trans. J. Potter (Cambridge, Mass.: Harvard University Press, 1957), p. 43.

in support of his conclusion that housebuilding had a decisive influence upon the stability of total investment in Sweden in the decades pre-

[3] *Ibid.*, p. 33.

ceding World War II. The interest rate for mortgage loans declined from 5 to 5.5 per cent in the 1920's to about 3 per cent from 1933 to 1935. Lundberg attributes the decline in housebuilding in 1936 and 1937 to the sharp rise in building costs and to poorer prospects for employment and incomes, the latter reflected in some decline in rents.[4]

Swedish residential building rose by approximately 50 per cent from 1924 to 1931, and, following a brief and relatively moderate decline from 1932 to 1934, rose to a record high of 59,000 dwelling units in 1939. During this period rents and building costs were maintained at relatively stable levels. Government participation in the housing market was limited to the improvement of mortgage credit facilities and, following the depression, to the improvement of housing for low-income families.

The State Housing Loan Bank was established in 1930 as a semipublic institution for the purpose of issuing second mortgage loans up to a total of 75 per cent of value or first mortgage loans up to 60 per cent of value for periods varying from twenty to forty years. Interest charges were equal to the selling price of the bank's bonds, plus administration expenses and reserves. Individual cities were also authorized to make mortgage loans to stimulate ownership of small homes during this period.[5]

Housing coöperatives had a considerable share in urban residential building from 1924 to 1933, and accounted for approximately 10 per cent of urban residential construction.

The Royal Commission on Housing and Redevelopment was appointed in 1933 and has since been a key factor in the formulation of Swedish housing policy. Acting upon the view that "Few works are more suited to counteract a depression than are building construction projects," [6] the Social Democratic government embarked upon a program of loans and grants for the construction and improvement of rural dwellings from 1934 to 1939. To aid urban housing, the government also provided credit at favorable terms for construction of dwellings by private builders.

Public concern over the declining birth rate focused attention in the depression years upon the housing problems of low-income families. Loans were granted to local authorities and to coöperatives for the construction and conversion of dwellings for families with at least three

---

[4] Erik Lundberg, *Business Cycles and Economic Policy*, trans. J. Potter (Cambridge, Mass.: Harvard University Press, 1957), pp. 42–48.

[5] Silk, *op. cit.*, pp. 37–38.

[6] Alf Johansson, "Social Housing Policy in Sweden," *Annals of the American Academy of Political and Social Science*, CXCVII (May, 1938), 164–165.

children under sixteen years of age. These government loans were amortized over a thirty- or forty-year period at interest rates of 3.25 per cent, the cost of borrowing to the state. Local authorities were required to contribute the costs of preparing sites, provide the balance of loan capital above the state loan, and rent the apartments at rents based upon costs. For those occupying these dwellings, the government at the same time initiated a program of family rental subsidies varying with the size and income of the family.

Housing Policy During World War II

With the outbreak of World War II, Swedish housing production began to fall off rapidly from the record level of 1939. Shortages of materials, the rapid rise in building costs and interest rates, and the general uncertainty brought about by the occupation of Norway and Denmark all contributed to the sharp decline in residential building between 1939 and 1942. Meanwhile, the housing shortage became more severe, and the government took steps in 1942 to reduce mortgage interest rates on new construction and to control rents. In 1942 the Riksdag adopted a new subsidy program, based upon the granting of so-called "supplementary loans" which bore no interest or redemption charges for ten years, after which, if the level of rents had not risen, they were to be written off. If, however, after ten years rents had risen to a point where the owners of the property built with such loans were receiving "extra" profits, the government could require the payment of interest and amortization of the original loan.[7] In addition, the 1942 housing program provided for the granting of third mortgage loans by the government at low interest rates to public, nonprofit, and private builders. Municipal and nonprofit builders could borrow up to 95 per cent of the value of the property; private builders were limited to 90 per cent. Third mortgage loans were also granted for owner-occupied single-family dwellings, up to a maximum total loan of 85 per cent of value. As a general rule, the local communities were expected to contribute 20 per cent of the supplementary loan subsidy and, in addition, were responsible for any losses on loans to enterprises operating in their communities.

It can be seen from Table IV–1 that this program was effective in doubling dwelling unit construction in 1942 over the previous year and in stimulating a continued rise in residential construction during World War II. More than 80 per cent of all dwelling units built from 1943 to 1945 received state aid in some form of loan or subsidy, and in

[7] Silk, *op. cit.*, p. 55.

TABLE IV-3

CHARACTERISTICS OF SWEDISH DWELLINGS

Year(s)	Size of dwellings and percentages (49 urban districts, 1912–1945)[a]							
	One room and kitchen, or less		Two rooms and kitchen		Three rooms and kitchen		Four or more rooms and kitchen	
	Number o dwellin s	Per cent	Number of dwellings	Per cent	Number of dwellings	Per cent	Number of dwellings	Per cent
1912–1915	114,754	56.3	46,345	22.7	19,338	9.5	23,482	11.5
1920	132,524	55.6	56,776	23.8	22,907	9.6	26,300	11.0
1924	136,796	53.7	62,407	24.5	25,816	10.1	29,978	11.7
1933	175,338	53.2	85,236	25.9	33,884	10.3	35,298	10.6
1939	218,110	52.4	115,370	27.7	44,364	10.7	38,248	9.2
1945	246,571	49.0	149,342	29.7	59,900	11.9	47,212	9.4

Year(s)	Swedish housing stock by age (1945 and 1955)[b]													
	Undetermined		Before 1881		1881–1900		1901–1920		1921–1935		1936–1940		1941–1945	
	Number of dwellings	Per cent	Number of dwellings	Per cent	Number of dwellings	Per cent	Number of dwellings	Per cent	Number of dwellings	Per cent	Number of dwellings	Per cent	Number of dwellings	Per cent
1945	262,209	12.5	376,492	17.9	246,184	11.7	392,937	18.7	419,162	19.9	231,191	11.0	174,224	8.3
	Before 1903	1903–1921	1921–1935	1935–1947	1947–1955									
1955	20%	20%	20%	20%	20%									

Year(s)	Percentage of dwellings with selected conveniences[c]												Total number of dwelling units in Sweden
	Central heat				Bath or shower				Inside toilet				
	Stockholm	Malmö	Gotebörg	Entire country	Stockholm	Malmö	Göteborg	Entire country	Stockholm	Malmö	Göteborg	Entire country	
1920	12.7	7.7	8.5	....	10.4	7.4	9.2	....	....	....	....	....	....
1933	61.2	35.2	35.5	....	47.4	24.7	21.5	....	....	....	....	....	....
1939	75.7	59.8	61.7	....	57.9*	31.4*	34.4*	....	....	....	....	....	....
1945	79.1	66.3	66.9	45.5	55.2*	38.0*	37.0*	21.3*	90.0	64.4	66.4	35.6	2,101,790
1955	82.5	66.3	71.6	....	59.2	44.8	42.7	....	96.5	64.4	62.2	....	....

[a] Kungl. Socialstyrelsen, *Bostäder och Hushåll* (Stockholm, 1950), p. 68, Table 50.

[b] 1945: Statistiska Centralbyrån, *Statistisk Arsbok för Sverige, 1957* (Stockholm, 1957), p. 211, Table 244; 1955: Per Holm, *Swedish Housing* (Stockholm: The Swedish Institute, 1957), p. 55.

[c] 1920–1945: Kungl. Socialstyrelsen, *Bostäder och Hushåll* (Stockholm, 1950), p. 88, Table 59, and p. 82, Table 58; 1955: Alvar Westman, "Dwelling Standard in Western Europe," *Building-Forum* (Göteborg, February, 1957), p. 6, Table 3.

* Category definition changed to "private bath."

1945 more than 90 per cent of all new residential construction received financial assistance from the government.[8]

Swedish housing standards had improved substantially by the end of World War II, compared to the situation in 1939 and during the depression years. Approximately 50 per cent of Sweden's urban dwelling units had two rooms and kitchen or were smaller in 1939, and densities of two persons per room or higher still prevailed in approximately 50 per cent of urban dwellings. It was estimated that by the end of World War II only about 30 per cent of Sweden's urban population lived in crowded homes with two or more persons per room. Approximately 40 per cent of new urban dwellings constructed during World War II was in units of three or more rooms and kitchen and more than three quarters in units of two rooms and kitchen or larger. While only 28 per cent of the apartment units in Sweden had a private bath in 1939, practically all of the new urban dwellings added during the period from 1939 to 1945 were equipped with modern conveniences.[9]

Table IV–3 shows the gradual change in the characteristics of the Swedish housing stock from 1915 to 1948.

Post-World War II Housing Policies

Sweden's post-World War II housing policy was essentially an extension of the measures which had been employed in World Wars I and II, combined with a major expansion of the social welfare housing measures which had been inaugurated on a limited scale during the depression years. As the policies of the Social Democratic party evolved over the postwar period, the housing subsidies which were originally developed for low-income and special occupational and social groups were extended to encompass virtually the entire housing market, and the government gradually assumed control over the planning, financing, and construction of Swedish housing. In order to provide a central agency for coördinating the efforts of the national and local authorities in the housing field, the Royal Housing Board (Kungl. Bostadsstyrelsen) was created in 1948 by the reorganization of the State Building Loan Office, which had been established in 1933. The Royal Housing Board coördinates housing activities through a system of provincial housing boards.[10] The organization of the board is set forth in Chart IV–1. It can be seen that the provincial housing

---

[8] *Ibid.*, p. 57.

[9] Harald Dickson and Paul F. Wendt, "Housing Characteristics of the United States and Sweden: 1930–1946," supplement to *Land Economics*, Monograph Series 1 (May, 1950), p. 1.

[10] Social Welfare Board, *Social Sweden* (Stockholm, 1952), chap. xi. See also Silk, *op. cit.*

CHART IV-1
The Organization Of The Royal Housing Board

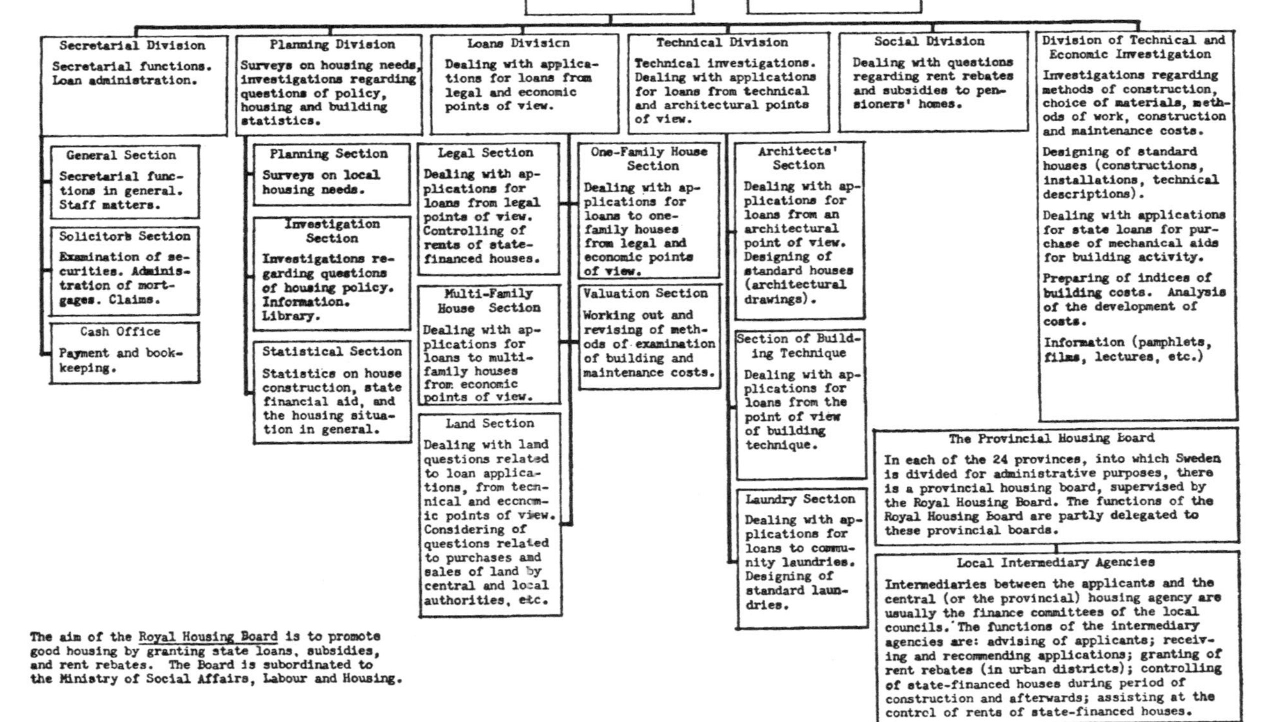

Director-General
The Board
Secretarial Division
Secretarial functions. Loan administration.
General Section
Secretarial functions in general. Staff matters.
Solicitors Section
Examination of securities. Administration of mortgages. Claims.
Cash Office
Payment and book-keeping.
Planning Division
Surveys on housing needs, investigations regarding questions of policy, housing and building statistics.
Planning Section
Surveys on local housing needs.
Investigation Section
Investigations regarding questions of housing policy. Information. Library.
Statistical Section
Statistics on house construction, state financial aid, and the housing situation in general.
Loans Division
Dealing with applications for loans from legal and economic points of view.
Legal Section
Dealing with applications for loans from legal points of view. Controlling of rents of state-financed houses.
Multi-Family House Section
Dealing with applications for loans to multi-family houses from economic points of view.
Land Section
Dealing with land questions related to loan applications, from technical and economic points of view. Considering of questions related to purchases and sales of land by central and local authorities, etc.
One-Family House Section
Dealing with applications for loans to one-family houses from legal and economic points of view.
Valuation Section
Working out and revising of methods of examination of building and maintenance costs.
Technical Division
Technical investigations. Dealing with applications for loans from technical and architectural points of view.
Architects' Section
Dealing with applications for loans from an architectural point of view. Designing of standard houses (architectural drawings).
Section of Building Technique
Dealing with applications for loans from the point of view of building technique.
Laundry Section
Dealing with applications for loans to community laundries. Designing of standard laundries.
Social Division
Dealing with questions regarding rent rebates and subsidies to pensioners' homes.
Division of Technical and Economic Investigation
Investigations regarding methods of construction, choice of materials, methods of work, construction and maintenance costs.
Designing of standard houses (constructions, installations, technical descriptions).
Dealing with applications for state loans for purchase of mechanical aids for building activity.
Preparing of indices of building costs. Analysis of the development of costs.
Information (pamphlets, films, lectures, etc.)
The Provincial Housing Board
In each of the 24 provinces, into which Sweden is divided for administrative purposes, there is a provincial housing board, supervised by the Royal Housing Board. The functions of the Royal Housing Board are partly delegated to these provincial boards.
Local Intermediary Agencies
Intermediaries between the applicants and the central (or the provincial) housing agency are usually the finance committees of the local councils. The functions of the intermediary agencies are: advising of applicants; receiving and recommending applications; granting of rent rebates (in urban districts); controlling of state-financed houses during period of construction and afterwards; assisting at the control of rents of state-financed houses.

The aim of the Royal Housing Board is to promote good housing by granting state loans, subsidies, and rent rebates. The Board is subordinated to the Ministry of Social Affairs, Labour and Housing.

boards operate through the local councils as intermediaries in receiving application for government aid.

The Royal Commission on Housing and Redevelopment, in a report which was adopted by the government as the basis for post-World War II housing policy in 1946, defined the aims of Sweden's postwar housing policy as follows:[11]

To overcome the housing shortage and stabilize new production at a level that, with due regard for the steady growth in number of households, will also meet the need for improved dwelling standards and redevelopment of urban areas.

To raise the space standard by increasing the production of units consisting of at least two or three rooms and kitchen. The one-room flat is condemned as a family dwelling.

To raise the equipment standard through new production and improvement of old units. The standard of rural dwellings is to be brought up to the level of urban dwellings.

To keep down the rent level, partly through public measures, so that modern, spacious family dwellings are also within easy reach of average wage earners. An industrial worker should pay no more than 20 per cent of his wages for a fully modern flat of two rooms and kitchen.

To encourage public financing of residential construction.

To activate the role of local authorities in housing.

To encourage nonspeculative building by offering favorable loan terms.

To achieve the above objectives, the Swedish national and local governments developed an elaborate system of income, mortgage financing, and building subsidies, combined with governmental controls over rents, interest rates, and building activity. The continued development of coöperative and other nonprofit institutions in the residential investment and construction field has also been fostered. Since World War II, Swedish housing policy has assumed that the local governments have the primary responsibility for initiating the planning and construction of housing, aided by over-all planning, coördination, and financial assistance from the national government. As in England, local governments have been granted increased powers to carry on these expanded functions.

Rent Control

It may be said that rent control was of key importance in Sweden's post-World War II housing policies. This is true in spite of the fact

[11] Owe Lundevall, *Swedish Housing Market* (Stockholm: Hyresgästernas Förlags AB, 1957), pp. 7–8. The original wording of Point 7 cited by Lundevall was, "To discourage speculative building by offering favourable loan terms," but Swedish reviewers have suggested the change as shown here.

that the Rent Control Act of 1942 was intended as an emergency measure to remain in force for only one year, for it has since been extended from year to year and is still substantially in effect. At the time of enactment it was generally assumed that the wartime inflation in prices and building costs would be followed by a postwar recession and that the control of rents would assure that wartime inflationary costs would not be "built into" the housing market. The major objective of rent control was to stabilize housing and building costs at the 1939 level. Added objectives, of course, were to control landlords' profiteering and reduce housing expenses for the working classes. Building subsidies were employed to encourage residential construction under conditions of rising costs. It was planned to use these subsidies in combination with rent controls to maintain rents on newly constructed as well as older houses at the 1939 level. According to experts who were active in the development of housing policies, it was expected that the inflationary wartime conditions would be followed by a post-World War II deflation and that at that time rent controls and building subsidies could be eliminated.

Because of the omission of the housing census in 1955 and the manner in which rents are controlled, accurate current rental data are not available on a national basis for Sweden.[12] For purposes of rent controls, Swedish housing is divided into two classifications, houses built before January, 1942, and those built subsequently. For dwellings in the first classification, rents in 1958 were fixed at 129 per cent of the 1942 level within Stockholm and at approximately 139 per cent of the 1942 level outside Stockholm.[13] A system of 565 rent courts and one upper court in Stockholm act upon special cases or appeals for rent increases for new equipment, alterations, etc. The combination of rent controls and high occupancy rates has greatly limited mobility in Sweden's housing inventory. Tenants cannot be removed unless the landlord secures another flat for the occupant at about the same price and location and appeals first to the rent court. Exchanges of living accommodations are frequent and often involve complex multiple moves. Not only do present tenants have occupancy rights, but their children have such rights in the event of the parents' death, with the result that turnover of the housing inventory is very limited.

Fixed rents on houses built after 1942 were based on a formula of 7 per cent on the owner's equity investment, plus an allowance for heat-

[12] The contention by some liberals and conservatives that the Swedish rental policies had resulted in inequities prompted a request by a 1957 parliamentary committee for an investigation of rents in Sweden. This had not been initiated in June, 1958.

[13] Statens Hyresråds, *Cirkular,* No. 94 (Stockholm, 1957). The increases include allowances of 7 per cent for additional heating costs.

ing costs. Annual questionnaires are filed by a sample of owners on operating costs as a basis for adjustments in allowances for these items. Rents for apartments built with the aid of government loans are fixed by the Housing Board, which grants the supplementary loans. The general standard of rents for houses started after January 1, 1958, is approximately a 4.6 per cent return on the total approved loan value plus 6.85 per cent on additional investment without government aid. Varying percentage increases in rents have been allowed for houses built from 1942 to 1953 to offset increasing operating costs. These increases vary from 15 per cent plus increased heating allowances for houses built in 1952 and 1953 to 17 to 21 per cent for houses built from 1942 to 1947.[14]

As a result of the recommendations of a parliamentary committee in 1957, rent controls after January 1, 1958, apply primarily to privately owned dwellings. Community-owned dwellings are exempted from all rent controls; coöperatives are exempt from government fixing of rents at time of construction, but not from general rent controls.

Since building costs have been rising steadily since 1942, and since the subsidies to builders have not kept pace with the rise in costs, rents on houses built since 1942 have increased successively with each rise in costs. Although data are not available for the entire period, statistics developed for dwellings built with government financial assistance from 1954 to 1957 illustrate this trend. The 1957 data represent only a small percentage of the total dwellings built in that year with government aid. It can be seen from Table IV–4 that average approved rentals in privately owned housing, per square meter of floor area, increased from 30 Swedish kronor per year in 1954 to 34.37 in 1957, an increase of 14 per cent for government-assisted rental housing. Actual apartment rents increased more than this, since the average apartment unit increased in size from 56.5 square meters in 1954 to approximately 65 square meters in 1957. The new tenant in 1957, therefore, paid an average rental of 2,236 kronor per year, as compared with 1,695 kronor per year in 1954, an increase of approximately 32 per cent. Of course, the 1957 new tenant received more for the higher rent.

The data for the nation as a whole obscure important regional differentials. Average rents for privately owned dwellings constructed in Stockholm rose from 32.85 kronor per square meter in 1954 to 35.71 in 1957, an increase of only 6 per cent, while rentals in privately owned dwellings in the surrounding communes rose from an average of 34.42 kronor per square meter in 1954 to 41.06 in 1957, an increase of 20

[14] *Ibid.* It was reported in 1960 that rent controls were being abandoned in many smaller towns and communities where housing shortages had ceased to exist.

TABLE IV–4

AVERAGE NEW SWEDISH APARTMENT RENTALS FINALLY APPROVED BY THE ROYAL HOUSING BOARD, 1954 AND 1957, EXCLUDING HEATING

Area and period	Number of dwelling units approved	Average dwelling area (square meters)	Average annual rent per square meter (in kronor)
Stockholm:			
1st half, 1954	3,386	52.4	32.85
1st half, 1957	300	60.8	35.71
Communes around Stockholm:			
1st half, 1954	1,183	62.7	34.42
2nd half, 1957	70	71.3	41.06
Göteborg:			
1st half, 1954	987	56.8	34.95
1st half, 1957	354	64.7	38.54
Skåne:			
1st half, 1954	2,617	59.8	24.77
1st half, 1957	295	61.7	29.62
Northland, excluding Gävleborgs Province:			
1st half, 1954	1,327	56.4	34.69
2nd half, 1957	38	67.7	42.46
All of Sweden:			
1st half, 1954	19,813	56.5	30.08
2nd half, 1957	581	64.9	34.37

Source: Tabulation dated May 16, 1958, prepared by the Royal Housing Board (Kungl. Bostadsstyrelsen). [Mimeographed.]

per cent. Average rents rose more in northern Sweden than in the south, perhaps because of the differences in incomes and in building technology and the shortages of labor in certain areas.

As noted above, rents for new dwellings built with government aid are fixed by the government on the basis of a 4.6 per cent net over-all return on the approved loan value. This return is usually calculated on a basis to provide a 7-per-cent return on the owner's equity. Since financing costs are higher for homes built without government loans, rents on these dwellings have been substantially higher than for similar dwellings built with government aid. According to government officials, rents on privately financed apartments built in Stockholm during the past few years have been as high as 55 to 60 kronor per square meter, without heating costs.

In view of the above description of Sweden's rent controls, it can be seen that no single rent index can accurately portray the movements of rents in the post-World War II period. Although rent control authorities appear to have been successful in maintaining some degree of uniformity in rent levels for housing of similar amenities built with government assistance since World War II, wide disparities appear to exist between rent levels for the older dwellings in Sweden, for those more recently built, and for dwellings built without government aid.[15] The most serious consequence is that the rent control legislation favors those who were occupants of rental housing in 1942 or who have been fortunate enough to secure accommodation in such houses. Newly married couples, unless they "inherit" the tenancy rights in an old apartment from their relatives, are forced to pay the higher rents in newly built apartments or houses. If they cannot wait for an apartment in a government-financed project, they must pay still higher rentals in a privately financed unit. An added problem for those entering the housing market in recent years is that rents are lower in the center of Swedish cities and graduate to higher levels on the outskirts, since most of the older buildings constructed before 1942 are situated near the center. Those unfortunate enough to enter the housing market in the post-World War II years must therefore not only pay a higher rent, but must accept a location more distant from the city, which adds to travel costs.

An additional and expected result of the rent differentials between the older and the more recently contructed housing is that a part of Sweden's housing inventory is not being used to the best advantage. Low rents in some of the larger and older units deter one- and two-person families from moving to smaller units, since the latter frequently command higher rentals and occupy poorer situations. As a result of the low level of controlled rents, some persons maintain two apartments, even though waiting lists for low-rent–controlled units are long. Government officials express the view that black-market operations in housing are not prevalent, although fairly extensive subletting of controlled rental units at rents above ceilings was observed by the author in some of the larger cities. The use of many legal and quasi-legal devices to evade rent controls makes it difficult to measure the actual extent of black-market operations.

A further result of Sweden's rent control policies has been to cause a decline in the attractiveness of real estate as an investment in Sweden. The Swedish landlord has virtually relinquished control of his property

---

[15] A sample study of rent levels in nine principal Swedish cities for a special parliamentary committee in 1951, by Mrs. Stina Thornell, of Statens Nämnd för Byggnadsforskning (Federal Board for Building Research), showed that rent levels were only slightly lower for dwellings built from 1936 to 1940 than for those built from 1942 to 1947 or from 1948 to 1950, although relatively wide differentials were revealed in rents among the various cities studied. Unfortunately, older houses were not included in the sample.

to his tenants and to the state. He has little incentive to improve his property, since Swedish rent courts are generally reluctant to grant increases in rents which more than barely cover increased operating costs. As a result, the landlord is often completely indifferent to the needs and desires of his tenants. Although quantitative data are not available, government officials and private investors acknowledge that a deterioration is taking place in the quality of the privately owned housing inventory in Sweden as a result of undermaintenance during rent controls. This is of further consequence when it is realized that much of this housing is situated in urban areas which are subject to deteriorating influences of other sorts resulting from the growing use of the automobile and consequent congestion. Experts in the field of housing management also point out that many municipalities and small coöperatives have fixed dwelling rents so low that adequate maintenance funds are not available.

Perhaps the most enduring effect of Swedish rent controls has been their effect upon consumer expenditure patterns. Increases in rents since 1939 of approximately 30 per cent can be compared with increases of more than 100 per cent in the general cost of living and building cost indexes, and with increases of more than 400 per cent in the average hourly wage for men. The result has been that, for a newly built two-room flat, the ratio of rent to the average industrial wage in Sweden fell from 35 per cent in 1939 to 25 per cent in 1945, 21 per cent in 1950, and 17 per cent by 1955.[16] Owing to the diversity in rent levels for housing of similar quality in Sweden, it is impossible, of course, to describe changes in rents generally with any degree of accuracy. This is one of the unhappy results of the abandonment of a free housing market under national controls.

The 1950 sample housing census for Stockholm showed that the combination of rent controls and rising consumer incomes resulted in a downward adjustment in over-all rent-income ratios in that city from 17 per cent in 1945 to 13.1 per cent in 1950. It can also be noted from Table IV–5 that rent-income ratios ranged between 12 and 15 per cent for both large and small families. They were, of course, substantially higher in all cases for families with only one adult. Family

[16] Per Holm, *Swedish Housing* (Stockholm: The Swedish Institute, 1957), pp. 66–67. See also Ragnar Bentzel, "Consumption in Sweden 1931–1965," *Skandinaviska Banken, Quarterly Review,* XXXIX (Stockholm, January, 1958), 10–20. The figures cited include heating costs, which account for about 30 per cent of total housing expenditures. Computations made from the Swedish national income statistics show the following rent-income ratios: 1938/39, 12.2 per cent; 1946, 9.0 per cent; 1950, 8.8 per cent; 1955, 8.6 per cent; and 1958, 9.5 per cent. See Meddelanden Fran Konjunkturinstitutet, *Konjunkturlaget Hosten 1959,* Series A–32 (Stockholm, 1959), Tables S II–6 and S II–7.

TABLE IV–5

PERCENTAGE OF RENT TO INCOME IN A SAMPLE CENSUS OF STOCKHOLM HOUSING BY NUMBER OF CHILDREN AND ADULTS, 1950

Number of children	Number of adults					Total families in sample
	1	2	3	4	5	
None	16.9	12.3	10.4	9.4	7.6	12.8
1	21.4	13.5	10.8	8.4	9.1	13.1
2	22.0	13.9	11.2	9.1	10.7	13.6
3	28.8	14.1	12.5	10.8	11.0	14.0
4	29.3	15.9	15.8	16.3	11.0	15.8
Totals by number of adults:						
1950	17.3	13.1	10.7	9.2	8.3	13.1
1945	20.9	17.7	15.3	13.8	11.7	17.0

Source: Stockholm Office of Statistics, *Housing Census of Stockholm, 1950* (Stockholm, 1956), p. 130, Table 100.

Note: It can be seen from the close similarity between the rent-income ratio for families with two adults and for the total of families in the sample that families with two adults are most typical, and that the rent-income ratios for families with one, three, four, and five adults are relatively unimportant in their total influence.

income and housing subsidies, which had the effect of leveling incomes, were an important factor in accounting for the uniformity in rent-income ratios indicated in the table.

The rise of other consumption expenditures in the postwar years leads to the conclusion that one effect of rent controls was to finance the purchase of automobiles, television sets, foreign travel, and other types of consumer expenditures. Although this trend seems to be consistent with one of the objectives of Swedish housing policy cited above, and may be considered in some degree to be a "normal" consequence of the increase in real incomes, it has undoubtedly altered the views of Swedish consumers as to the appropriate percentage of income to be paid for housing and may react unfavorably against the longer aims of Swedish housing policy, which seek to improve the quality, size, and amenities of dwellings.[17] These long-run unfavorable effects of rent controls, and the inequities and maldistribution of the housing stock which have resulted, have already prompted some initial steps by the government to relax rent controls, as pointed out above. A special parliamentary commission, with representatives of the various political parties, recommended in October, 1956, that average rents for newly

[17] United Nations Economic Commission for Europe, *European Rent Policies*, E/ECE/170 (Geneva, August, 1953), p. 25.

constructed multi-family dwellings should be increased by about 15 per cent in 1957 and by another 5 per cent in 1959. In order to compensate families with children for these rent increases, at least in part, the commission recommended increases in family housing allowances. These recommendations were not accepted by the Swedish Parliament, however, and rents were increased by only 6 per cent in 1957. It seems to be largely a political question in Sweden of when, if, and how it will be feasible to restore a free rental market, as has been the case in France, England, and other countries which have experimented with rent controls over a long period of years.

Housing Finance

Mortgage and interest rate subsidies and capital grants were key elements of Sweden's postwar housing policy. The principal government housing subsidies employed in Sweden during the post-World War II years were the following:

Mortgage loan and interest rate subsidies to builders and municipalities
Capital grants (supplementary loans) to builders and municipalities
Homeownership loans and grants
Annual family income subsidies
Subsidies to municipalities and nonprofit builders to provide old-age homes

Swedish housing is typically financed by a system of multiple mortgages held by a variety of government, semiofficial, coöperative, and private institutions. Among the most important semiofficial lending institutions are the Urban Mortgage Bank of Sweden (Konungariket Sveriges stadshypotekskassa), which was founded in 1909 and restricts its financing to first mortgages; The Swedish Housing Loan Bank (Svenska bostadskreditkassan), which was established in 1929 to provide second mortgage loans and first mortgages on one-family houses in urban areas; and the Swedish Mortgage Bank (Sveriges allmänna hypoteksbank), which serves rural areas. The government originally underwrote the initial capital of these institutions. They are conducted as coöperatives under the management of elected representatives from among the owner-borrowers. Funds are raised by the sale of bonds, which usually command favorable interest rates. The interest rate paid by the borrowers is equal to the net interest of the bonds plus a fee for administration.

The National Union of Tenants' Savings Bank and Building Associations, a coöperative organization originally founded in 1924 and known as the "HSB," has assumed an increasingly important role in Swedish housing during the past decade. The national HSB organization is supported by loans and share purchases made by local HSB associations. Although the national HSB does not own houses, it has initiated construction of more than 150,000 flats for local member associations and municipalities in its thirty-year existence and has accounted for between 20 and 25 per cent of apartment construction in Sweden in recent years. An important feature of local HSB association policies has been the "bostadsrätt" or freehold lease, which gives the apartment dweller in an HSB coöperative apartment complete security of tenure and a right which he can sell or otherwise dispose of at will. This technique has undoubtedly been an important factor in encouraging coöperative apartment-house construction in Sweden, since it gives the occupant of coöperative units security of tenure and a financial equity in the unit represented by the lower rental in comparison with units built at higher cost. Subject to certain restrictions which the coöperative may impose, he is free to dispose of this interest. This advantage has been particularly evident during the post-World War II years of rising building costs; it probably would disappear during deflation.[18]

In addition to these institutions, insurance companies, savings banks, and others extend loans secured by first mortgages, usually up to a maximum of 60 per cent of the value of the property. A few private mortgage loan banks financed by bond issues grant first as well as second mortgage loans up to 70 or 75 per cent of the value. Private mortgage loans are typically extended for terms of ten or fifteen years at a rate of interest determined by the lending institution, with the proviso that after the expiration of the period of the loan, it may be continued in effect but will bear the current open market rate of interest. Usually, the first mortgage loan is not amortized over its term.

The Royal Housing Board has been the key governmental organization in residential financing in the post-World War II years, since it has granted so-called "tertiary" or third mortgage loans, subject to first or second mortgage loans held by private lenders. By virtue of its control over such loans, it has been able to control dwelling characteristics and rents of units constructed with government financing aid as well as interest rates on private loans for such dwellings.

Until 1957, government third mortgage loans were granted for forty years at 3 per cent interest. As a result of recommendations of a special parliamentary committee, the rate of interest on these loans was raised to 4 per cent effective January 1, 1958, and the amortization period

---

[18] "Thirty Years of Co-operative Housing," *Att bo,* English edition (Stockholm: HSB, 1955), pp. 32–48.

reduced to thirty years. The interest rates permitted on private first and second mortgages were also raised one half of a percentage point, to 3.5 and 4 per cent respectively, effective July 1, 1957. The technique for fixing rates to be paid for private loans provides that the borrower pay the open market rate of interest to the private lenders and receive in turn an annual payment from the government representing the difference between the open market rate and 3.5 or 4 per cent. The difference in rates represents a direct government subsidy to the owner or builder and to the lending institutions. In the case of rental units, the government subsidies are passed on to the tenant through controlled rents.

In the granting of so-called tertiary loans to builders of apartment houses, the government gives preference to municipalities and nonprofit builders, since such loans can be approved for amounts not covered by first and second mortages up to 100 per cent of approved value for municipalities, up to 95 per cent for coöperatives, and up to only 85 or 90 per cent for private builders. Government officials rationalize this policy by arguing that municipalities could issue their own obligations up to 100 per cent of their credit needs and that, therefore, it makes little or no difference whether the national government advances 100 per cent of the funds or the local government raises the funds through its own financing. Critics of the government's housing policies have maintained, however, that this discrimination against the private builder has reduced the role of private enterprise in Swedish housing.

The Swedish government also granted "supplementary" loans for multi-family dwelling construction varying from 10 to 40 kronor per square meter, in order to equalize the gap between the level of controlled rents and building costs. Since these loans run without interest or amortization, they really amount to a subsidy.[19] Beginning in 1957, these loans or capital grants were limited to specific localities and the government sought to discourage such loans, since the program had resulted in excessive demand for housing credit, rising interest rates, and government costs.

The government also grants homeownership loans on second mortgages to encourage owner-builders, which, added to the customary 50 per cent first mortgage loans from private sources, cover up to 90 per

[19] According to an interview with Harry B. Bernhard, vice-president of the Royal Housing Board and director of the Loan Division, about 30 per cent of the supplementary loans granted during the 1940's has been written off and about 70 per cent has been converted to real loans. Increased rentals have been permitted in the apartment buildings where the supplementary loans have been converted to offset the landlords' increased financing costs. Supplementary loans for homeowners have been written off.

TABLE IV-6

RESIDENTIAL FINANCING IN SWEDEN: CAPITAL COST ESTIMATES APPLICABLE JANUARY 1, 1958

		Weighted average
1. *Public agencies* (government does not fix rents):		
Primary loan (1st mortgage)	60% loan value @ 3.5%	= 2.10
Secondary loan (2d mortgage)	10% loan value @ 4%	= 0.40
Tertiary loan (3d mortgage)	30% loan value @ 4%	= 1.20
		3.70
Over-all percentage return on capital including amortization = 4.6% (raised from 3.85%)		
Return on equity = 6.85% (estimated)		
2. *Coöperative societies financed by state loans* (government does not fix rents):		
Primary loan (1st mortgage)	60% loan value @ 3.5%	= 2.10
Secondary loan (2d mortgage)	10% loan value @ 4%	= 0.40
Tertiary loan (3d mortgage)	25% loan value @ 4%	= 1.00
Own contribution	5% loan value @ x%	=
Over-all percentage return on capital including amortization = 4.6% (raised from 3.85%)		
Return on equity = 6.85% (estimated)		
3. *Private builders financed by state loans* (Bostadsstyrelsen fixes rents):		
Primary loan (1st mortgage)	60% loan value @ 3.5%	= 2.10
Secondary loan (2d mortgage)	10% loan value @ 4%	= 0.40
Tertiary loan (3d mortgage)	15% loan value @ 4%	= 0.60
Own contribution	15% loan value @ x%	=
Over-all percentage return on capital including amortization = 4.6%		
Estimated return on equity = 6.85%		

Attention: The foregoing estimates under items 1 to 3 concern *only* that part of the costs which refers to dwellings. For land purchase financed through state loans the corresponding over-all percentage return = 6.2%.

4. *Private builders financed without state loans:*

Primary loan (1st mortgage)	60% appraised value @ 5.35% (x)	= 3.21
Secondary loan (2d mortgage)	15% appraised value @ 5.85% (x)	= 0.88
Own contribution, balance of total cost @ 7% (x)		
Amortization is 0.75% of the building cost		

(x) If the appraised value is estimated at 90% of total costs, the total financing is obtained by using the following formula:

Primary loan	55% of total cost @ 5.35%	= 2.94
Secondary loan	15% of total cost @ 5.85%	= 0.88
Own contribution	30% of total cost @ 7%	= 2.10
		5.92

Amortization is 0.75% of the building cost

Source: Information supplied by Stina Thornell, Statens Nämnd för Byggnadsforskning, Stockholm, May 30, 1958.

cent of the construction costs for homes of certain prescribed maximum sizes. A part of the second mortgage loan by the government (4,000 kronor) is a subsidy like the "supplementary" loan discussed above for apartment construction, since it runs without interest or amortization. The interest rate on the rest of the loan from private sources is guaranteed by the government at 3.5 per cent.

Table IV–6 illustrates typical financing plans for dwellings constructed during the post-World War II period.

Up to the year 1950, the Sveriges Riksbank continued to support quotations for government bonds to prevent yields from rising above the fixed level of 3 per cent, and the yield on government loans was permitted to rise only gradually to 3.30 per cent by the end of 1953. One of the main purposes of this policy was to make funds available at relatively low rates for the building industry, although the maintenance of full employment certainly played a part in the policy. The Swedish Debt Office issued a 4-per-cent sixteen-year loan in October, 1954, which represented the first major break in the low interest rate policy and was taken as an indication that the low rate policy of the Riksbank was having an inflationary effect.[20] In January, 1955, investment duties were introduced—one for different types of capital expenditure by companies and one for purchase of motor cars. At the same time a more restrictive construction policy and a more austere fiscal policy were announced, representing a further departure from Sweden's post-World War II expansionist fiscal policies.[21]

The continued and rapid rise in building costs which started with the Korean war was an important factor furthering moderately restrictive measures in the field of housing finance. Table IV–7 shows the percentage rise in an index of construction costs for a standard multi-family house in Stockholm, with January 1, 1939, costs as a base. It is, of course, an imperfect measure of the actual change in building costs, since changes have occurred in the type of structure and since no allowance is made for premium payments to labor and other extra costs incurred in actual building operations. The persistence of increasing costs in the face of government subsidies designed to maintain costs at the prewar level was the occasion for a reappraisal of certain features of Swedish housing finance policy by the Parliament.

---

[20] *Skandinaviska Banken, Quarterly Review,* XXXVI (January, 1955), p. 3. The official discount rate of the Riksbank was maintained at 2.5 per cent from 1946 to 1950 and was raised in December, 1950, to 3 per cent. Following a drop to 2.75 per cent in 1953, it was raised to 3.75 per cent in April, 1955, to 4 per cent in November, 1956, and to 5 per cent in July, 1957. In May, 1958, it was reduced to 4.5 per cent.

[21] Investment duties were abolished as of January 1, 1958. *Ibid.,* April, 1958, p. 60.

TABLE IV–7

INDEX NUMBERS OF THE COST OF CONSTRUCTION FOR A MULTI-FAMILY APARTMENT BUILDING IN STOCKHOLM, 1950 TO 1957
(January 1, 1939 = 100)

Cost index as of January 7	Total cost	Labor	Material
1950	159	131	183
1951	209	155	259
1952	220	174	262
1953	213	175	247
1954	210	175	243
1955	217	177	250
1956	225	184	260
1957	230	187	265

Source: Magnus Elison, "Statliga lån och subventioner till bostadsbyggandet," *Ekonomisk Revy,* Häfte 5 (May, 1956), 233–242. Data were corrected and brought up to date by the Royal Housing Board in June, 1958.

The first major step was the imposition of loan ceilings effective January 1, 1956. Before this date, the government appraised properties for loan purposes by the replacement cost method, with an allowance of 5 per cent profit plus an allowance for overhead depending on the size of the project. This method of fixing the value and the determination of rents on the basis of 4.6 per cent of the appraised value furnished an inducement to builders to increase the quality and size of dwellings and to add as many items as the public would accept into the construction. This naturally resulted in higher costs and valuations and higher government supplementary and tertiary loans. Since certain commercial facilities were permitted to be added to the housing facilities for government loans, the percentage of such facilities and their size and quality also increased. The inflationary effects of this system were apparent to most observers and government officials. The loan ceilings apply in such a manner that the government limits the amount of its loans to a percentage of a maximum appraisal value. The builder may elect to build a higher cost dwelling, but he must finance any additional cost privately, and he is allowed a return of 6.85 per cent on this additional part of his investment in the fixing of rents. This is to compensate the builder for the higher financing costs on the additional costs. Although the new regulations appear to have had the desired effect in eliminating unnecessary or particularly high-cost items in new construction, some critics are fearful that the result will be that the squeeze between government loan ceilings and rising costs will force builders to construct mere "shells" without the amenities the public expects to have.

The second major change toward a more restrictive financing policy was the virtual elimination of the so-called supplementary loans or capital grants for multi-family construction, effective January, 1957. Partly as a result of these grants, the percentage of units built without state aid had declined from approximately 20 per cent before the Korean war to less than 5 per cent in 1957. (See Table IV–12.) It had become increasingly difficult for the Royal Housing Board to turn down projects, since practically all building was wholly dependent upon government financing aid. Although the elimination of this special subsidy necessitated a slightly higher level of rents for newly built apartments, the rise in consumer incomes had, in the judgment of the parliament, eliminated the need for it. Because of the widening gap between the rates of interest on government housing loans and mortgage loans available in the open market, however, the reliance of the housebuilding industry upon the government has not decreased since the elimination of the supplementary loan.

The third major change in government financing policy was the increase in interest rates on government tertiary housing loans from 3 to 4 per cent effective January 1, 1958, and the shortening of amortization periods from a maximum of forty years to thirty years. Previously, interest rates had also been fixed at 3 per cent on first mortgages and 3.5 per cent on second mortgages, and these rates were also raised to 3.5 and 4 per cent. As pointed out earlier, these rates also applied to the private loans on houses built with government aid, since the government paid to the owner a subsidy for the difference between the official government rates and the rates paid in the open market. Before the Korean war, open market rates were at the same level as the rates on government loans; however, open market rates for first mortgage loans up to 60 per cent of value had risen to 3.6 per cent by 1953 and to 5.75 per cent in June, 1958, after reaching a high of 6.25 per cent in 1957.[22] Rates for second and third mortgage loans were substantially higher, of course. The combined effect of the increase in interest rates and shortening of maturities on government mortgage loans is not fully reflected in building statistics as yet, but it will undoubtedly add to the level of annual housing costs and rents and widen the difference in rentals between old and new housing. The wide gap which continues to exist between open market and government rates, however, indicates that the state will continue to be the major factor in mortgage credit through its interest subsidy policies.

The expansion of government lending for housing in Sweden has

[22] "Interest on Housing Credits in Different Countries," *Skandinaviska Banken, Quarterly Review*, XXXIV (October, 1953), 98. Current rates obtained by personal interview of the author with bank officials in June, 1958.

resulted in important structural changes in institutional participation in the Swedish mortgage loan market. Table IV–8 shows that state loan funds are gradually supplanting funds previously supplied by other financial institutions. The reasons for this are quite evident, since the government has controlled interest rates in the mortgage loan market, while interest rates on industrial loans and bonds have risen substantially.[23] The loans for commercial banks in Table IV–8 are primarily

TABLE IV–8

VOLUME OF CREDIT FOR BUILDING OPERATIONS AND THE FINANCING OF HOUSING IN SWEDEN, 1944 AND 1957 (DIRECT LOANS)

Type of institution	1944 Million kronor	1944 Per cent	1957 Million kronor	1957 Per cent
Commercial banks	1,661	20.7	731	2.4
			3,919[a]	13.1
Savings banks	2,501	31.2	8,420[b]	28.1
Post office	92	1.1	2,083	6.9
Mortgage banks	1,485	18.5	4,630	15.4
Mortgage investment companies	448	5.6	891[c]	3.0
Insurance companies	1,437	17.9	3,157	10.5
State loan funds	400	5.0	6,184[d]	20.6
Total	8,024	100.0	30,015	100.0

Sources: For 1944, "The Economic Situation," *Skandinaviska Banken, Quarterly Review*, XXXIX (Stockholm, April, 1958), 67; for 1957, estimates by Bengt Senneby, *Skandinaviska Banken*, June, 1958.

[a] All obligations other than government bonds—primarily bonds of mortgage institutions.

[b] Estimated as same percentage as for the year 1956.

[c] 1956.

[d] Preliminary estimate.

for construction loan credit during the period of construction and prior to final approval by the Royal Housing Board. In addition to their direct loans, the commercial banks participate in housing finance indirectly through the purchase of the housing bonds issued by local

[23] The average yield on industrial bonds rose from 2.92 per cent in 1938 to 3.72 per cent in 1953 and to 5.12 per cent in 1957, while the yield on government bonds rose from 2.32 per cent in 1938 to 3.30 per cent in 1953 and to 4.41 per cent in 1957. The rates of interest on mortgage loans with government aid were maintained at 3 and 3.5 per cent until 1957, when the rates were raised to 3.5 and 4 per cent. Interest rates on construction loans have risen from 3.5 per cent in 1945 to 5.25 per cent in 1955 and to 5.75 per cent in 1958. An additional 1 per cent service charge is also made for construction loan credit.

communities and government mortgage banks and through their advances to the national government.

Family Income and Other Subsidies

In addition to loan subsidies, family housing allowances were paid in 1956 to about 140,000 Swedish families with two or more children, having modest incomes, and living in dwellings larger than fifty square meters and constructed since 1941. In 1956 the families receiving these rent allowances—which amounted to 150 kronor per child annually, plus 270 to 330 kronor per family, depending on locality of residence—constituted 30 per cent of all Swedish families with two or more children.[24] The housing allowances are taken as a deduction from mortgage payments to the government by homeowners or in the form of reductions in rent and paid to the landlord for renters. These payments are in addition to general family allowances.

The Swedish government also grants subsidies to municipalities and to nonprofit builders to encourage the building of homes for the aged or to provide pensioner units in ordinary apartment houses. The rents for these units are often fully covered by national and municipal rent allowances supplemented by old-age pensions.

Post-World War II Housing Production

Sweden's housing subsidies, combined with record post-World War II prosperity, have resulted in consistently high levels of residential construction in Sweden since the war, as shown by Table IV–9. Although the number of dwellings constructed did not exceed the prewar peak of 59,000 units completed in 1939 until 1957, when 64,000 units were built, the dwellings constructed since the war have been somewhat larger in size and number of rooms and better equipped.

Table IV–9 shows that multi-family housing has continued to dominate Sweden's housing production during the post-World War II period, although a notable increase has occurred in the production of single-family homes since 1955.

Up to World War II, private enterprise completely overshadowed public, coöperative, and nonprofit building in Sweden. It has been estimated that before 1947 about 90 per cent of Swedish housing was built under private auspices either for owner-occupier use or for lease on the open market.[25] As noted earlier, the 1942 housing program

[24] Holm, *op. cit.*, p. 73.
[25] Lundevall, *op. cit.*, p. 35.

TABLE IV–9

HOUSING CONSTRUCTION IN SWEDEN BY TYPE OF UNIT AND OWNERSHIP, 1949–58

Type and ownership	1949	1950	1951	1952	1953	1954	1955	1956	1957	1958
Type of dwelling unit										
One-family houses	8,344	9,494	8,580	6,617	8,027	10,738	13,383	13,350	15,889[a]	15,984[a]
Two-family houses	2,586	2,630	2,222	1,734	1,507	1,762	2,131	1,665	1,231	1,040
Multi-family houses	30,364	31,494	28,637	36,062	42,003	45,348	41,051	41,436	47,012	44,306
Other	257	317	295	323	374	365	405	455	323	535
Total	41,551	43,935	39,784	44,736	51,911	58,213	56,970	56,906	64,455	62,225
Dwellings constructed by										
State/county council	375	572	551	487	513	456	435	545	403	505
Community/utility companies	13,329	14,340	13,545	17,237	19,554	18,299	17,019	16,714	18,985	18,396
Coöperatives	6,560	6,797	5,984	7,879	10,705	14,383	11,557	14,328	17,530	17,319
Employers	2,715	2,548	2,072	3,486	2,686	1,677	2,041	1,971	1,852	1,357
Owner	9,127	10,509	9,332	7,132	8,514	11,762	14,549	13,708	13,994	15,131
Other builders	9,445	9,169	8,300	8,515	9,939	11,636	11,369	9,640	11,691	9,517
Percentage of new units with										
Three or more rooms and kitchen	45.6	48.8	49.2	41.0	37.6	43.2	47.7	50.8	55.2	63.2
Central heating, private bath, and water closet	84.2	87.8	89.1	84.1	84.1	91.0	92.6	94.5	94.6	95.8

Sources: *Sociala Meddelanden, 1957*, Nr. 8, Tables 4, 7, 8, 10, and (for 1958) Statistisk Centralbyrån, *Statistisk Årsbok för Sverige, 1959* (Stockholm, 1959), Table 217.

[a] Including 3,219 in one-family houses in rows in 1957 and 4,390 in 1958.

provided for more favorable loan terms for public and nonprofit builders than for private builders. The post-World War II statement of housing policy of the Social Democratic government indicated clearly the objective of encouragement of public housing. The results of the policies put into effect were to reduce substantially the activities of private firms in the production of Swedish housing, and it was estimated that less than one quarter of the number of dwelling units completed in 1955 were initiated by private firms.

The marked shift in the relative proportion of residential construction initiated by private owners and builders in Sweden can be seen in Table IV–9. Only about 47 per cent of the dwellings constructed from 1949 to 1956 were classified as built by owner-builders or "other" builders. (The latter classification includes some construction by nonprofit builders not otherwise classified.) The share of housing production accounted for by "company housing" declined from between 5 and 8 per cent of production in 1949 to about 3.5 per cent in 1954–55. Municipalities, which accounted for approximately 6 per cent of Swedish housing construction from 1935 to 1940, initiated 32.1 per cent of the dwelling units constructed from 1949 to 1956. Similarly, coöperatives, which accounted for only about 5 per cent of Swedish residential construction from 1935 to 1940, initiated about 20 per cent of total dwelling units constructed from 1949 to 1956 and a higher percentage —22.7 per cent of construction—from 1953 to 1956. The activities of coöperatives, of which the Tenants' Savings and Building Society (HSB) and Svenska Riksbyggen are the largest, have been concentrated in the larger cities, principally Stockholm and Göteborg.[26]

The emphasis in Sweden upon apartment house construction has tended to foster the development of large building enterprises. The national Tenants' Savings and Building Society functions as a general savings bank and as the central house-planning and financing office for all local HSB societies. The national HSB, which employs some six hundred architects, engineers, town planners, accountants, administrators, and financial experts, buys sites and plans, finances, and builds houses. The finished projects are then taken over by a separate subsidiary coöperative society formed by the people who intend to live in the new houses. A management committee elected by the members is in charge of the general administration of the project.[27] Normally the prospective occupier of an apartment or a house must buy shares of the coöperative society amounting to at least 5 per cent of the total cost of the dwelling. The HSB has built 150,000 flats during the period

[26] *Ibid.*, p. 36.
[27] "Thirty Years of Co-operative Housing," *Att bo*, p. 34.

from 1924 to 1959. The organization accounted for between 5 and 10 per cent of urban building during the nineteen twenties, between 10 and 15 per cent in the thirties, about 20 per cent in the forties, and between 20 and 25 per cent during the past decade.

The Swedish building workers' unions founded "Svenska Riksbyggen" (SR) during the 1940's in order to meet the threat of unemployment in the housebuilding industry. In contrast to HSB, which lets contracts to private building firms, Svenska Riksbyggen carries on actual construction of the large annual volume of housing it plans and finances through the "Trade Unions' Building Enterprise" (Fackföreningarnas Byggnadsproduktion) which serves as a general contractor. Other labor union groups in Sweden are active in the housing field, and the Swedish Federation of Labor (Landsorganisation) has made substantial investments in the HSB society and in other coöperative housing enterprises.

The organization of the private housebuilding industry in Sweden also reflects the encouragement of large-scale production of apartment buildings since World War II. Although detailed statistics are lacking, larger firms tend to dominate the housebuilding industry in Sweden. The major building material manufacturers take a leading part in the planning and financing of private housebuilding. In some cases these firms, such as the International Siporex Company, Ltd., develop building plans, estimate costs, finance land acquisition and construction, and furnish virtually all materials required for a housebuilding job. Some of the larger firms specializing in prefabricated individual houses for rural areas coöperate with employers in arranging for self-erected workers' houses. Building firms such as "Rikshus" acquire the land from the employer or local authorities, plan the buildings, secure financing, and ship the materials to the site ready for erection.

The development of a vigorous and active private single-family housebuilding industry in Sweden has tended to be retarded by the concentration upon apartment building and the dominance of public authorities, nonprofit societies, and material suppliers. The implications of this will be explored further, below, when recent changes in housing demand are considered.

Postwar Changes in Property Ownership

The growing importance of public and nonprofit housing in Sweden has resulted in a major shift in the structure of property ownership over the past decade. Table IV–10 shows the distribution of ownership of Sweden's housing stock in 1945, with estimates as of 1957 developed

TABLE IV–10

CHANGES IN OWNERSHIP OF SWEDISH HOUSING STOCK, 1945 TO 1957

Period	Industrial and commercial firms	State, county, and municipal	Coöperatives	Individuals	Real estate companies	Nonprofit firms	Profit-making firms	Total
1945:								
Total	150,000	97,000	90,000	1,600,000	91,000	32,000	20,000	2,080,000
Per cent	7.1	4.6	4.3	77.1	4.4	1.5	1.0	100.0
1946–1957:								
Total	26,500	164,100	119,700	312,700[a]	—	—	—	623,000
Per cent	4.3	26.3	19.2	50.2[a]	—	—	—	100.0
1957 (estimated):								
Total	176,500	261,100	209,700	1,912,700[a]	91,000	32,000	20,000	2,703,000
Per cent	6.5	9.7	7.8	70.8[a]	3.4	1.2	0.7	100.1

Sources: For 1945, Lundevall, *op. cit.*, p. 34; for 1957, estimated by author, based on Swedish building statistics 1946 to 1956. Changes in ownership were estimated by applying average percentages of new building accounted for by the various ownership classifications to total new building from 1946 to 1956. No allowances were made for demolition or losses by fire and other causes or for transfers of ownership during the period among the various groups.

[a] Includes individuals, real estate companies, nonprofit firms, and profit-making firms.

by the author from official building statistics. The data for the nation as a whole do not adequately reflect the marked variations in the patterns of ownership among individual cities and regions in Sweden. For example, 89 per cent of all units in rural areas were owned by individuals in 1945, while only 46 per cent of Stockholm dwellings were individually owned. Employer-owned housing accounted for 16 per cent of all dwelling units in the smaller manufacturing towns in 1945. Real estate companies, which are included in the private sector, were substantial owners of property in the larger cities, accounting for ownership of 22 per cent of the dwelling units in Stockholm and about 6.5 per cent of dwellings in cities with 30,000 to 100,000 inhabitants in 1945.[28]

The estimates shown for the year 1957 were made by applying average percentages of new building accounted for by the various ownership classifications to total new dwelling construction from 1946 to 1956 and making adjustments therefrom in the 1945 figures. The estimates are rough approximations only, since they make no allowances for demolitions, losses by fire or other causes, or changes in ownership of the existing housing stock during the period. Since building statistics do not segregate building by real estate companies and by nonprofit and profit firms or foundations, the estimates for these groups are lumped together as of 1957. Since the activities of nonprofit firms, such as savings banks, are known to have increased markedly during the period, it is judged that the increase in the share of ownership by these three groups together may be accounted for largely by increases in the nonprofit sector.

The estimates of occupancy of dwellings in Sweden by type of tenure have been made in a similar manner by adjusting the 1945 census data for new production from 1946 to 1956. In making the estimates for 1957, the author assumed that coöperatives and owner-built dwellings each accounted for approximately 20 per cent of total new dwelling construction from 1946 to 1956. Table IV–11 reveals a marked increase in the proportion of occupancy by members of coöperatives, offset by declines in owner occupancy and occupancy by renters. It must be recognized that the estimates in Tables IV–10 and IV–11 probably underestimate the extent of individual private ownership and occupancy of Swedish housing, since no allowance has been made for dwellings constructed by private builders for sale to owner occupiers. Offsetting this, there have been transfers from private owners to coöperatives and governmental units.

---

[28] Lundevall, *op. cit.*, pp. 35–37.

TABLE IV–11

CHANGES IN SWEDISH HOUSING OCCUPANCY, 1945 TO 1957

Period	Rented on the open market	Company-owned workers' housing	Government-owned housing[a]	Coöperatives	Owner-occupied	Social welfare housing	Other tenure[b]	Total dwelling units in Sweden
1945:								
Total	737,203	219,458	34,083	89,726	801,319	31,266	188,735	2,101,790
Per cent	35.1	10.4	1.6	4.3	38.1	1.5	9.0	100.0
Additions, 1946–1957	154,000	26,500	164,100	119,700	158,700	n.a.	n.a.	—
1957, estimated:								
Total	891,203	245,958	198,183	209,426	960,019			2,703,000
Per cent	35.0	9.0	7.3	7.7	35.5	7.5		100.0

Sources: For 1945, Kungl. Socialstyrelsen, *Bostäder och Hushåll* (Stockholm, 1950), p. 74, Table 53; for 1957, estimated by author, based on Swedish building statistics, 1946–56—see Table IV–10.

[a] State, county council, and municipal.

[b] Includes farm workers' housing, union-owned housing, and substandard dwellings.

Dominance of Multi-Family Dwellings

Table IV–9 indicates the relative degree to which the apartment house structure has consistently dominated Swedish housing construction during the post-World War II years. This has resulted from government policies encouraging the building of these types of structures, combined with climatic, topographic, institutional, and economic considerations. The long and cold winter season in Sweden results in high costs of heating, and both fuel costs and costs of maintenance are higher in single-family than in multi-family units. Relatively high foundation costs owing to the character of the soil and the climate are another factor encouraging multi-unit construction. The relatively severe winters also heighten the importance of close proximity to the central area in most Swedish cities. Most of the land area within close proximity to the cities was preëmpted for apartment dwellings during the past two decades of rapid growth, and single-family homesites are usually quite distant from the centers. As a result, housing subsidy and land use policies have encouraged the construction of multi-family units. This emphasis has led to the development of relatively greater efficiency in Sweden in the construction of apartment units than of single-family housebuilding. The adage that a country builds best what it builds most is demonstrated in Sweden.

It is interesting to observe, however, that increasing numbers of people are demanding single-family homes in Sweden today. According to one authority on Swedish housing, this is a natural consequence of rising incomes and the spread in the use of automobiles, and may bring about a "shattering" of the dominance of the multi-family apartment structure within twenty or thirty years. It has been observed, however, that the development costs for single-family homes are three or four times as high as for multi-family units in Sweden.[29] Two other important factors appear to be influencing the production of single-family homes at present. The first is the scarcity of apartment units of adequate family size, owing to government rent controls and other

[29] Holm, *op. cit.*, p. 51.

A series of studies carried out by Lennart Holm, a Swedish economist, from 1951 to 1958, indicated that substantial numbers of Swedish families living in small flats in the larger cities desired to move to larger units, preferably single-family houses. Recent studies in Malmö revealed that 33 per cent of those wishing to move desired a single-family house, and that approximately one half of those desiring to move to single-family houses were willing to pay more for such accommodations. Malmö is an area with ideal land conditions for development of single-family houses.

The following estimates of the differences in land and development costs for a dwelling unit of 22 square meters in 1953 indicate that units in multi-family

factors. Government rent policies virtually force younger married couples with children to go on the waiting list for a new apartment unit at rentals of 55 to 60 kronor per square meter. (Older units might rent for as low as 25 to 30 kronor per square meter, but are available only to selected families and usually after waiting periods as long as five years; some new flats in coöperatives are available in 1960 for immediate occupancy, but require high down-payments.) The alternative is to enter the new home market. Although the annual costs in the latter are very high in proportion to average incomes, many young couples are purchasing new homes in Sweden today on the calculated risk that inflation will continue and that their incomes will rise, and hence that the burden of the housing expense will lessen over the years.

The technique through which the owner of a coöperative apartment in Sweden retains the right to sell his financial equity provides a desirable element of mobility within the Swedish housing inventory. The use of the so-called freehold lease by the apartment dweller in Swedish coöperatives affords some of the advantages of homeownership, since thrift is encouraged in order to secure the initial financial equity and security of tenure is assured. This feature of coöperative occupancy should permit movements to larger apartment units or owner-occupied, single-family dwellings with greater ease.

Any prediction of future demand for owner-occupied homes in Sweden must necessarily be highly speculative. Government taxation policies have thus far been less favorable to homeowners than in the United States or West Germany, since the homeowners must add to their earned income an imputed income at the rate of 2.5 per cent of the value of an owner-occupied home in determining individual tax-

---

structures can be produced at lower costs to the municipalities than for comparable units in row houses or in single-family structures:

ESTIMATED DEVELOPMENT COSTS PER DWELLING UNIT IN STOCKHOLM IN 1953, BY TYPE OF STRUCTURE
(In Swedish kronor)

	Multi-family	Row-chain	Single family
Streets	360	675	1,300
Sewers	150	325	900
Electricity, gas	15	35	90
Foundation	100	200	400
Open land other than parks	47	87	226
Water	8	20	43
Total, excluding land costs	680	1,342	2,959
Estimated land costs—reflecting local price policies, not actual costs. (The city does not sell land, ground rent)	250	250	290

The estimated ratio (square meters of dwelling-unit space for one square meter land) is 0.56 for multifamily, 0.33 for row-chain, and 0.10 for single-family structures.

able income. Although it is reported that this tax provision will be eliminated within the next few years, other reports are that the Social Democratic government is considering a proposal to appropriate the increments in assessed value of owned residences financed with government aid. Enactment of such a proposal would undoubtedly dampen any growing enthusiam for owned homes in Sweden. Offsetting the special tax on imputed income, homeowners are permitted to deduct a part of the interest on borrowed capital from earned income.

In evaluating Per Holm's prediction, quoted above, concerning the "shattering" of the dominance of the multi-family unit in Sweden, it must be recognized that many Swedish apartment dwellers have a summer cottage in the country. This is frequently little more than a one- or two-room wooden shack, but it serves as a means of escape from the city during the summer months. It would seem more likely to the author that the influence of the automobile might give impetus to a further expansion of vacation housing. The degree to which this form of family housing or any other will continue to expand in Sweden depends in the last analysis, of course, on trends in the national real income. Another factor which might tend to limit the expansion in demand for single-family homes is the fact that a large percentage of Swedish housewives work and find that a flat near the place of work is more convenient to maintain for that reason. A further important consideration is the fact that municipalities generally are expected to finance necessary improvements to raw land, such as sewers, water, and roads. Since the finances of many communities have already been strained during the postwar building boom, it seems unlikely that they will regard favorably the increased costs necessary to improve lots for single-family home development. If the communities are unable or unwilling to meet the higher costs of land development for single-family homes, it can be expected that housebuilders will have difficulty in passing on such costs to home buyers in the purchase prices of lots. The real "bottleneck" in the market for single-family homes may be the unavailability of improved lots at prices permitting economical development. Some observers point out the possibility that employers may assume these costs in order to provide housing as a means of attracting and holding labor. The extent to which this can be expected to take place, however, seems unlikely to be great.

Costs of Postwar Government Housing Programs

The postwar expansion in state housing subsidies in Sweden and the important influence of the so-called supplementary loans or capital

TABLE IV–12

FINANCIAL ARRANGEMENTS FOR NEW RESIDENTIAL CONSTRUCTION IN SWEDEN, 1949 TO 1958

Year	Total number of units constructed	Units built with state aid				
		Total	Home-ownership loans	Third mortgage or supplementary loans	Subsidies to pensioners' homes	Other forms of aid
1949	41,551	32,432	5,909	23,665	1,646	1,222
1950	43,955	35,001	8,575	25,152	1,259	215
1951	39,784	31,722	7,890	23,049	756	27
1952	44,736	38,657	6,135	31,561	951	10
1953	51,911	47,925	7,774	39,028	1,081	42
1954	58,213	54,998	11,098	43,233	544	12
1955	56,970	53,121	13,924	37,891	1,280	26
1956	56,906	53,976	13,774	39,300	892	10
1957	64,455	60,715	14,415	44,845	1,443	12
1958	62,225	58,355	15,007	41,714	1,269	365

Sources: *Sociala Meddelanden, 1957,* Nr. 8, Table 6; Statistisk Centralbyrån, *Statistick Årsbok för Sverige, 1959* (Stockholm, 1959), Table 219.

grants is illustrated by Table IV–12. It can be seen that more than 90 per cent of the total number of new dwellings constructed in Sweden in recent years benefited by capital grants from the state. By virtue of the government's financial assistance to this large proportion of total new housing production, the Royal Housing Board has been in position to approve the mortgage terms and rentals on the bulk of Sweden's post-World War II housing.

Public expenditures for housing in Sweden have increased rapidly with the expansion of government subsidies. Lundevall's summary of Sweden's post-World War II expenditures for housing is shown in Table IV–13. Administrative costs of the government housing agency, interest guarantee payments, family housing rebates and subsidies, building improvements, and pensioner housing subsidies are included in Column 1, showing the growth in expenditures for housing reported in the operating budget. The increase of more than 600 per cent in housing expenditures in the operating budget during the period from 1946 to 1957 is primarily the result of an increase of 80 million kronor in annual family housing rebates during the period, and of the guarantee by the government of fixed interest levels during the period of rising market rates of interest, which occasioned an increase of 20 million kronor in annual government expenditures.

TABLE IV–13

STATE EXPENDITURES DEVOTED TO HOUSING IN SWEDEN, 1946–47 TO 1957–58
(In millions of kronor)

Budget year	Housing expenditure reported in operating budget (1)	Total state expenditures in operating budget (2)	Housing advances reported in capital budget (3)	Portion of Column 3 devoted to supplementary loans and non-interest portion of homeownership loans (4)	Total state expenditures in operating and capital budget (5)
1946–47	30	3,155	205	25	3,816
1947–48	36	3,971	221	25	4,345
1948–49	30	4,643	199	29	5,113
1949–50	61	5,002	197	52	5,265
1950–51	54	5,449	302	75	6,018
1951–52	68	6,423	419	79	7,199
1952–53	87	7,647	614	164	8,667
1953–54	112	8,130	650	163	9,164
1954–55	132	8,619	807	259	9,696
1955–56	157	9,691	1,085	345	10,719
1956–57	211	10,978	879	224	11,621
1957–58	239	12,120	1,103	473	13,324

Sources: 1946–47 to 1951–52: "Budgetredovieningen," *Byggforum* 4 (1957), as cited in Owe Lundevall, *Swedish Housing Market* (Stockholm: Hyresgästernas Förlags AB, 1957), p. 70. See also Arne Karlsson, "Swedish Housing Policy Expenditures During the Last Decade," *Building-Forum* (Göteborg, January, 1957), p. 31. 1952–53 to 1957–58: Statistiska Centralbyrån, *Statistisk Årsbok för Sverige, 1959* (Stockholm, 1959), Tables 376, 380, 386.

Notes: Column 1 includes the following: administration costs, interest rebates, rent rebates, improvement loans, subsidies for old age housing for pensioners. Column 3 includes tertiary loans and supplementary loans.

The largest portion of housing advances reported in the capital budget (Column 3) represents long-term loans on houses and apartments. As of June 30, 1956, state loans amounted to about 4,640 million kronor, or 635 kronor per capita.[30] The portion of housing expenditures in the capital budget which can be considered as capital grants is shown in Column 4. It will be seen that these increased by more than fifteen times over during the period from 1946 to 1956, but were sharply reduced in the fiscal year 1956–57, when the granting of supplementary loans was virtually stopped. The rapid rise in the costs of this phase of the Swedish housing program from 1952 to 1956 undoubtedly influenced the decision to limit such subsidies to particular localities in 1957 and to eliminate this form of state subsidy entirely in 1959.

It can be seen from Table IV–13 that total government expenditures for housing in Sweden which should be classed as operating costs of the program (including supplementary loans and the non-interest part of homeownership loans) equaled about 5 per cent of total state expenditures in the operating budget in 1955–56. These estimates do not include local government expenditures for housing purposes, which have undoubtedly increased substantially during the postwar period of family and child welfare allowances. Total expenditures of rural communes, borroughs, and towns in Sweden in 1956 for "administration of real estate" were 540.4 million kronor. These expenditures were offset by revenue of 281 million kronor, leaving a net expenditure of 259.4 million. This total, which included expenditures of 27.9 million kronor on current account and 231.5 million on capital account, represented approximately 8 per cent of total local-government expenditures in 1958.[31]

Review and Evaluation

Sweden has made notable progress in the achievement of the housing objectives adopted in 1946. Before World War II, approximately one

---

[30] Lundevall, *op. cit.*, p. 43.

[31] Statistisk Centralbyrån, *Statistisk Årsbok för Sverige, 1959* (Stockholm, 1959), Table 402. The expenditures in Table IV-13 exclude family and child welfare allowances paid by central and local governments, which rose from 600,000,000 kronor annually in 1948 to approximately 1,000,000,000 kronor from 1954 to 1958. Such payments have accounted for over 6 per cent of total current expenditures of the Swedish national government since 1952. Total expenditures of the Ministry for Social Affairs have accounted for approximately a third of current central government expenditures and 11 per cent of the national income since 1955. *Ibid.*, pp. 226, 300.

half of Swedish apartment units had only two rooms (one room and kitchen) or were smaller, and more than 40 per cent of new production was of units of this size.[32] It can be noted in Table IV–9 that more than 40 per cent of the newly constructed dwelling units in each year since 1949 (excepting 1953) have had three or more rooms and kitchen. The proportion of new construction in units of this size rose to 50 per cent in 1956 and to 55.2 per cent by 1957. During the period from 1954 to 1957 the average size of new dwelling units rose from 56.5 to 64.9 square meters. The equipment standards of the new dwellings constructed in the post-World War II period also represented a marked improvement over prewar levels. More than 90 per cent of the new dwelling units produced since 1954 had central heating, private bath, and water closet. Although density figures will not be available until the 1960 census, it will probably be revealed that the high levels of dwelling construction relative to population growth have reduced average dwelling densities in Sweden.

Lundevall has prepared estimates showing the improvement which has resulted in the characteristics of the Swedish housing stock as a result of the production from 1946 to 1955, which are reproduced in Table IV–14. It can be seen that the percentage of urban dwelling units with central heat rose during the decade from 62 to 72 per cent, the percentage with private bath rose from 34 to 46 per cent, while the percentage of urban dwellings with private water closet rose from 57 to 68 per cent. Even more striking improvements are shown in the percentages of rural units with these amenities over the period.

Another major objective of the 1946 statement of policy has been achieved, since it has been seen that the average rent level for a modern two-room-and-kitchen flat is today probably less than 15 per cent of an industrial worker's wages. This is confirmed by a study of changes in consumption expenditures in Sweden cited earlier which showed that, on the average, consumption expenditures for housing had declined from about 22 per cent of consumer incomes in 1932 to approximately 13 per cent in 1955.[33]

The fifth and sixth objectives of the 1946 statement, to encourage public financing and the role of local authorities in housing, have been achieved with much to spare. It will be noted below that more than 95 per cent of Sweden's new dwelling construction in recent years was built with state financing aid. Meanwhile, the share of Swedish housing construction initiated by municipalities and other public bodies rose

---

[32] Dickson and Wendt, *op. cit.*, p. 3.

[33] Bentzel, *op. cit.*, p. 11.

TABLE IV–14

CHARACTERISTICS OF SWEDISH HOUSING STOCK, 1945 TO 1955

Category	Number of units	Units with Running water	Central heat	Bath	Water closet
Urban:					
Number of units, 1945	1,180,808	88%	62%	34%	57%
New units, 1946–55	383,364	100%	98%	85%	98%
Rebuilt and improved units, 1946–55	—	3,350	7,900	4,600	8,000
Estimated housing stock, January 1, 1956	1,550,000	1,423,000	1,117,000	726,000	1,062,000
Estimated percentages, 1956	—	91%	72%	46%	68%
Rural:					
Number of units, 1945	920,982	37%	24%	7%	8%
New units, 1946–55	125,442	97%	97%	79%	95%
Rebuilt and improved units, 1946–55	—	44,400	33,200	17,700	33,500
Estimated housing stock, January 1, 1956[a]	1,041,000	505,000	378,000	184,000	224,000
Estimated percentages, 1958	—	48%	36%	18%	22%

Source: Owe Lundevall, *Swedish Housing Market* (Stockholm: Hyresgästernas Förlags AB, 1957), p. 32. Percentages as of 1956 calculated by the author.

[a] The estimated housing stock as of January 1, 1956, makes provision for partial removal of older dwellings from the market from 1946 to 1955. The number of such units is computed at 17,000 in urban areas, of which 5,500 had running water in the structure, the figure for rural areas is 5,000 units, of which 1,200 had running water in the structure.

from 6 per cent of the total construction from 1935 to 1940 to more than 32 per cent from 1949 to 1956 (Table IV–8). It has also been seen that government mortgage-financing policies have resulted in maintaining low interest rates and favorable loan terms for residential construction during the post-World War II years.

The so-called supplementary loan was a notable feature of the Swedish government's postwar housing policy. As noted above, these loans, designed to equalize the gap between controlled rents and building costs, bore no interest or amortization. Provision was made, however, for their conversion to real loans, since increased rentals were permitted and part were actually converted. The supplementary loan afforded a flexible and successful subsidy device for encouraging rental housing construction in the immediate postwar period and, at the same time, provided for some recoupment of government outlays as rents rose. It was used with some variation for encouraging single-family home construction also, but in this case no provision was made for its conversion to a real loan and it operated as an outright subsidy. The inflationary effects of supplementary loan-subsidies under conditions of rising consumer incomes and full employment forced their abandonment in 1957. As noted above, these loans represented a growing burden of financial cost to the government.

Eliminating the Postwar Housing Shortage

For reasons following, stemming from the nature of government programs, the accomplishments of Swedish housing policy in eliminating the housing shortage and stabilizing residential building have been less impressive. The extent of the housing shortage which exists in any country depends, of course, upon whether a market concept of shortage is employed, which takes into consideration the public's ability and willingness to rent or buy housing, or whether the housing shortage is to be measured in terms of some criteria of housing need, based upon certain assumptions concerning appropriate housing standards. It is virtually impossible to appraise accurately the extent of any *market shortage* of housing in Sweden today because of the existence of rent controls and the division of the market into various subclasses of subsidized and nonsubsidized housing. Because of the omission of the housing census in 1955, it will be necessary to await the results of the 1960 census to assess the extent of the remaining *housing need* which exists, given certain assumptions as to appropriate standards.

Professor Alf Johansson, secretary of the Social Housing Committee which prepared the general directions for the future housing policy of the Swedish government in 1946, and at present the director of the Royal Housing Board, estimated in February, 1946, that Sweden had a shortage of 50,000 urban dwellings in 1946 and that the production of 45,000 urban dwellings annually from 1946 to 1950 would end the Swedish housing shortage in urban areas by 1950.[34] The report of the committee made the following estimates of the future increase in urban households in Sweden and of the levels of urban housing production necessary to allow for the elimination of the shortage of 50,000 dwellings and the removal of urban housing units classified as uninhabitable or substandard by 1960.[35]

[34] Silk, *op. cit.*, pp. 77–78, quoting an interview with Dr. Johansson on February 13, 1946.

[35] *Ibid.*, pp. 78–79.

Period	Estimated increase in urban households	Urban dwelling units to be built, allowing for expected increase in households, eliminating of shortage, demolition and removal of uninhabitable and substandard units by 1960[a]	
		Total production	Annual production
1946–50	130,000	225,000	45,000
1951–55	105,000	200,000	40,000
1956–60	95,000	190,000	38,000

[a] Estimates of production include allowance for removal of 75,000 units classed as uninhabitable and 160,000 units classed as substandard by 1960.

High postwar marriage rates and establishment of separate households by many of Sweden's unmarried men and women under the stimulus of postwar prosperity resulted in rates of household formation which far exceeded the above estimates in the period from 1946 to 1955. In addition, the doubling of the divorce rate from 1946 to 1955, as compared with the previous decade, resulted in the establishment of separate living quarters by a large proportion of the 60,000 couples obtaining divorces in urban areas from 1946 to 1955.[36] Added to these elements was the increase in urban in-migration and immigration which took place during the period. More than 250,000 persons migrated from the countryside to Sweden's cities from 1946 to 1955, four fifths of whom were concentrated in the marriageable age groups of fifteen to twenty-five years of age. In addition, more than 70,000 foreigners immigrated to Sweden's cities, principally from northern European countries.[37] Undoubtedly, rising incomes and acute labor shortages in many cities were the principal factors encouraging these high rates of migration. The Royal Housing Board estimated in 1955 that 31 per cent of unmarried men over twenty years of age and 45 per cent of unmarried women over twenty years of age had established separate homes.[38]

It will be noted from Table IV–9 that 383,364 new dwelling units were added in urban areas from 1946 to 1955, approximately 40,000 less than the quotas established by the 1946 report. It can be noted from this table, however, that the number of demolitions for urban areas is estimated to have totaled only 17,000 from 1946 to 1955, while the Social Housing Committee estimates allowed for removal of 75,000 units classed as uninhabitable and of 160,000 units classed as substand-

[36] Lundevall, *op. cit.*, p. 49.
[37] *Ibid.*, p. 47.
[38] *Ibid.*, p. 50.

ard before 1960. It can be concluded from the above data that the net increase in supply of dwelling units in Sweden far exceeded the increase of 235,000 households estimated for the years 1946 to 1955. Actual urban household formation probably exceeded the 1946 estimates by 100 per cent, or more. It is not surprising, therefore, that a housing shortage of the magnitude of 100,000 units is still estimated to exist in Sweden.[39] It is quite clear, in retrospect, that the fundamental error of the Social Democratic government was its assumption that the demand for housing was inelastic with respect to income.

A study by the Royal Housing Board of the waiting lists for housing accommodations in sixty-five urban communities with a total population of more than three million persons as of January 1, 1957, revealed a total of 258,746 applicants, of whom 116,693 were without homes of their own. The others already occupied homes and were waiting for homes of different size, type, or location.[40] Only 33,742 of the total of 116,693 persons without homes of their own were married or had dependents. The rest were persons who intended to marry or have families in the future, or desired separate living quarters as single persons. It would seem from these statistics that the current housing shortage in Sweden is somewhat less than the total number of persons on so-called waiting lists for housing. Lundevall and others have pointed out that the rapid population growth and the shortages of the immediate post-World War II years have encouraged many persons to file applications well in advance of their actual need for housing.[41] It is probably true that many persons file applications in the hope of getting a housing unit which might be situated closer to the center of the city or command a lower rent than newly built units. In assessing the degree of housing shortage in Sweden, it is also necessary to consider the extent to which the present housing inventory could accommodate additional family units if housing space were more efficiently rationed. The housing shortage under free market conditions would, of course, differ greatly from that under the present structure of rent controls. This emphasizes the difficulty of measuring the adequacy of the housing supply under rent controls.

Swedish housing market experts expressed the opinion in June, 1958, that an adequate supply of dwellings was available in most communities at present costs and rental levels.[42] This can be taken as

[39] Svenska Handelsbanken, *Index* (Stockholm, December, 1957).

[40] Kungl. Bostadsstyrelsen, Planeringsbyrån, *Om Bostadsmarknadsläget i Början av År* 1957 (Stockholm, April 16, 1957).

[41] Lundevall, *op. cit.*, pp. 52–53.

[42] Interview with officials of the National Association of Tenants' Savings and Building Societies (HSB), June 13, 1958.

an indication that from a market-demand point of view no extensive housing shortage existed in 1958 in most Swedish cities. They point out, however, that an unsatisfied demand exists for smaller and cheaper units at lower rents or selling prices.

In evaluating Sweden's housing program in 1950, this author and his Swedish co-author concluded as follows:

> Because of the stimulation to family incomes through subsidies and the maintenance of low rents [through] controls, a housing shortage continues in Sweden, since the demand for housing at current costs exceeds supply and will probably continue so for several years as long as subsidies are maintained.[43]

Although these conditions persisted for some time, the relatively rapid rise in housing costs in the period since 1950 (brought about by some relaxation of rent controls and by sharply rising building costs not offset by increased subsidies) and the competition of automobiles and other items for consumer expenditures have combined to reduce substantially the persistent housing market shortage experienced in Sweden since World War II.

Achieving Stability in Housing

As noted above (Table IV–1), residential construction in Sweden was characterized by marked instability prior to World War II. After rising to a record high of 59,000 units in 1939, national production dropped to 26,000 units in 1940 and to 17,000 in 1941. The uncertainty as to future political and economic events associated with the Nazi invasion of Norway and Denmark was undoubtedly the most important factor in this precipitate drop, although sharp increases in building costs and in interest rates on building loans were contributing factors.[44] The post-World War II record in Swedish housing construction must be viewed, therefore, in comparison with the prewar instability which characterized the housing economy. Residential construction, which had risen to 58,000 units annually by 1946, declined by about 30 per cent to approximately 40,000 units in 1951. Housing production, however, soon recovered. After remaining at levels of 57,000 units annually from 1954 to 1956, it rose to 65,000 units in 1957, surpassing any previous year's total. Production was maintained at approximately 62,000 units in 1958, and rose to approximately 69,000 units in 1959.

Critics point to the postwar monetary and fiscal policies of the Riksbank as the major reason for the lack of stability in Swedish hous-

[43] Dickson and Wendt, *op. cit.*, p. 28.
[44] Silk, *op. cit.*, pp. 50–51.

ing production.[45] The cheap money policies of the Riksbank, which had been followed since 1945, were modified in 1950 with increases in discount rates, reserve requirements, and government bond yields. Discount rates were again increased in 1955 and 1957, and an extremely restrictive monetary policy was pursued in those years. It has been seen that these steps were followed by increases in private mortgage-loan interest rates, by the application of "loan ceilings," and by the virtual elimination of the so-called supplementary loan (effective January 1, 1957), and finally by increases in interest rates on the government's tertiary loans in 1958. Notwithstanding these measures, a recent review has pointed out that the policies of the Riksbank consistently gave priority to public investment and housebuilding throughout most of the post-World War II period, with the result that monetary and fiscal policies had their principal effects upon private business investment and private consumption.[46] Support for this assertion is found in the fact that business capital and some types of consumers' durable expenditures were restricted by investment duties in 1955 and by a "general ceiling" placed upon commercial bank advances from 1955 to 1957. In addition, interest rates in the housing sector were maintained below other interest rates. Supporters of the programs of the Royal Housing Board argued that continued high production of housing was required if rents were to be controlled. They viewed the government's policies in limiting housing production in 1956 and 1957 through monetary and fiscal controls as inconsistent with the goals of over-all housing policy. Supporters of the government's restrictive policies argued in turn that the loan priorities granted to the housing sector served to restrict unduly other business and private investment.

Table IV–15 confirms the relative stability in housing investment as a percentage of total investment in Sweden during the post-World War II years relative to private investment and consumption. As will be noted in more detail in the final chapter, the increase in the proportion of the gross national product accounted for by the public sector, including housing, is a major feature of postwar economic development in Sweden.

It must be concluded that greater stability has been achieved in Swedish residential construction since World War II than was evident during the prewar decade. The prewar period, however, included the years of the Great Depression and the initial phases of World War II,

---

[45] *Bygg-industrin och Kreditmarknaden,* second report from the Research Institute of the Swedish Building Trades Union (Stockholm, 1958).

[46] Bengt Senneby, "The Swedish Credit Market During the Nineteen-Fifties," *Skandinaviska Banken, Quarterly Review,* XLI (January, 1960), 18–23.

TABLE IV-15

THE PERCENTAGE SHARE IN THE SWEDISH GROSS NATIONAL PRODUCT OF VARIOUS SECTORS

Sector	1949	1952	1955	1958	1959[a]
Private investment	11.3	11.8	12.0	12.7	12.6
Housing	6.2	5.8	6.6	6.6	6.5
Central government investment	5.4	7.2	7.0	7.4	7.9
Local government investment	3.1	3.7	4.2	4.4	4.5
Total investment	26.0	28.5	29.8	31.1	31.5
Central government consumption	4.7	5.0	4.8	5.1	5.2
Local government consumption	5.6	6.3	6.9	7.7	8.0
Private consumption	61.4	57.5	57.2	56.8	55.3[b]
(Private consumption, durables)	(6.2)	(6.5)	(6.8)	(7.0)	(7.0)
Total consumption	71.7	68.8	68.9	69.6	68.5
Public sector (including housing)	25.0	28.0	29.5	31.2	32.1
Private sector	72.2	69.3	69.2	69.5	67.9

Source: Bengt Senneby, "The Swedish Credit Market During the Nineteen-Fifties," *Skandinaviska Banken*, XLI (Stockholm, January, 1960), 18–23.
[a] Preliminary figures.
[b] With correction for the effects of the introduction of the general sales tax.

and present government policies have not stood tests of like magnitude. More important questions appear to be (1) at what level and at what cost to the government can Sweden maintain a high and stable level of new housing production, and (2) what will be the effect of these decisions upon the total Swedish economy and over-all economic stability? In this connection, it is important to examine more closely the estimates of Swedish housing needs from 1956 to 1965 which were included in the long-term economic plan for Sweden published in 1956, as shown in Table IV–16.[47]

This housing program of 65,000 units annually, recommended by the Royal Housing Board, was adopted by the Parliament in 1959. It is of interest to consider the implications of such a program in terms of stability in housing production and general economic stability. Although the program recommended was expected to shift the emphasis further toward single-family homes and larger units, it has been reported that the average size of apartment dwellings erected declined by 4 per cent bteween 1957 and 1959.

Obviously, speculation concerning the effects of any future housing

[47] Statens Offentliga Utredningar, Finansdepartementet, *Balanserad Expansion, Betankande avgivet av 1955 Ars Langtidsutredning, 1956:53* (Stockholm, 1956).

TABLE IV-16

CALCULATION OF SWEDISH HOUSING NEEDS, 1956 TO 1965
(In number of dwelling units)

Increase in urban households		290,000
Household formation as result of natural increase and urban migration	140,000	
Immigration	20,000	
Changes in marital status (divorce, etc.) of population	10,000	
Elimination of housing shortage, increased household quotas	120,000	
	290,000	
Increase in households in suburban areas		115,000
Vacancy reserve		45,000
Elimination of substandard dwellings, including planned redevelopment		100,000
Rural housing requirements		100,000
Total dwelling units needed		650,000

Source: Statens Offentliga Utredningar, Finansdepartementet, *Balanserad Expansion,* Betankande avgivet av 1955 Ars Langtidsutredning, 1956:53 (Stockholm, 1956).

program upon the Swedish economy must require many assumptions concerning government fiscal and monetary policy and the ever present specter of increased pension costs. It is apparent, however, that if Swedish housing policy is inextricably linked with social and family welfare schemes, it is just as closely linked with general economic policy and must be consistent with the latter.

The broad economic implications of Swedish housing policy may be inferred from the following opinion, published in December, 1957, commenting upon the government's proposed program of building 65,000 dwellings annually from 1960 to 1965:

> Even though the immediate prospects are relatively favourable there are also certain disquieting aspects. Housing production during the past few years could not have been maintained at the achieved level were building credits not exempted from the general credit squeeze. As a result, certain other sectors—especially industry—had to be satisfied with a smaller slice of the cake. There is every indication that capital will remain scarce during the next few years and it seems likely that building credits will have to enjoy continued priority if the programme is to be completed. The basic question is how far this priority policy can be stretched without causing harmful repercussions in other sectors of the economy.[48]

The same note of caution concerning the impact of high levels of investment in housebuilding upon other sectors of the Swedish economy

[48] Svenska Handelsbanken, *Index,* December, 1957.

is found in a discussion of the savings shortage in Sweden in mid-1959.

> . . . Yet if we look at the distribution of capital formation among various sectors we find that Sweden, as compared, for example, with West Germany, has a relatively low share which goes to production in industry and agriculture, and a relatively high share in the public sector and housebuilding.
>
> It can be argued—though of course nothing definite can be proved—that investment requirements in Swedish production and trade will be growing briskly during coming years because of the rapid technical developments and structural changes in foreign competition. . . .
>
> Sweden's relatively high wage (and thus wage-cost) level can only be defended and maintained in the future if Swedish firms in different sectors are in a position to retain their relative technical advantage, which among other things necessitates rapid replacement and expansion of machinery and other capital equipment. A necessary condition is that the supply of savings for the private sector is adequate, and presumably considerably larger on a per capita basis than in competing countries. In these respects Sweden's position has, as mentioned above, hardly been specially favourable in recent years. There is therefore a risk that her advantage in productivity cannot be maintained, if and when the supply and distribution of savings evinces tendencies which are unfavourable from this point of view.[49]

Considering the background of postwar inflation in Sweden, it can be argued with some justification that further expansion of housing production in Sweden under present conditions of full employment may be at the expense of industrial investment. Also, it seems probable that the maintenance of an annual level of production of 65,000 units over an extended period may require the renewal of the supplementary loan subsidies which were eliminated in 1957. This would have further implications for controlling inflation in Sweden, which will be considered in the final chapter. It may be possible, of course, that continued expansion of the total labor force and technical innovations in the Swedish building industry may make it possible to achieve the production goals without either increased inflation or renewed subsidies.

Evaluation of Sweden's post-World War II housing policies must recount the losses as well as the gains, since these policies have wrought fundamental changes in housing ownership, market structure, financing methods, institutions, and costs.

The undesirable effects of rent controls in Sweden are clearly evident. Lacking inducements in the form of increased rents, landlords have limited incentive to maintain rental properties. The quality of the

[49] Erik Lundberg, "Capital Formation and the Savings Shortage," *Skandinaviska Banken, Quarterly Review,* XL (July, 1959), 85.

privately owned sector of the rental market is undoubtedly deteriorating. Further, lack of knowledge and experience, together with political considerations, seem to have led many municipalities and some coöperatives to fix rents at a level too low to assure proper maintenance, and hence a part of the publicly owned inventory of housing may also be suffering from undermaintenance.

Since rents are determined according to the time of construction, varying rent levels exist for similar properties. A continued rise in building costs, coupled with reductions in government subsidies, would magnify these differences over time. Rent differentials tend to lower the degree of mobility within the housing inventory, since families are naturally reluctant to move from a unit with a lower rent even though one differing in size or location might suit them better. As can be expected, the subdivision of the rental market into subgroups of dwellings having substantially similar amenities, but differing rents, has led to familiar black-market operations in some controlled rental units.

Government rent policies have restricted the rise in the level of consumers' expenditures for housing relative to total consumption. Consumers' expenditures for housing rose 200 per cent from 1938/39 to 1958, while total consumers' expenditures rose by 300 per cent. Rent controls and housing subsidies have thus made it possible for Swedish families to expand their purchases of consumption goods. Sweden's rent policies have also resulted in an increasing reluctance of working-class families to rent or buy unsubsidized housing built at current costs which meets the government standards of size and quality; they tend to demand, instead, the smaller two-room flats which the government seeks to eliminate for family units. Assuming that the government will continue to impose higher housing standards nationally, a major political task appears to lie ahead in reëducating Swedish families to spend *higher* proportions of family income for housing.[50] As in other countries which have experimented with rent controls and housing subsidies over long periods, these lessons will be less easily learned than the more popular lessons of the 1940's and 1950's.

The achievements referred to earlier in expanding public investment and the role of local authorities in the housing field must be balanced against the costs of these programs and the virtual elimination of rental housing as a field for private investment in Sweden. Government loan and other subsidies have consistently favored public and other types of nonprofit investors since World War II. Rent controls have further

---

[50] Current statistics of national income in Sweden reveal that the proportion of income spent for housing has risen slightly since 1955. As noted above, rent-income ratios in Sweden vary widely among individual groups.

heightened the unattractiveness of rental property for the private investor, although the rather severe inflation has worked in the opposite direction. Municipalities, which control land planning and improvements for residential development, consistently favor the nonprofit investor, according to private developers.

The coöperative movement has undoubtedly been the strongest element in the postwar housing market in Sweden. The national HSB organization and other coöperative groups have helped to sponsor improvements in house planning, design, and construction. Further, coöperatives have been instrumental in stimulating savings for coöperative house purchase. The freehold lease, or *bostadsrätt,* has proven a highly successful instrument for permitting the transfer of interest in coöperative housing units and has permitted the owner of a coöperative dwelling unit to take advantage of increases in values much as a homeowner does in a free market.

It can be argued that the decline of speculative building in Sweden has been offset by the rise of this new type of private investment, using the coöperative form of organization. The implications of this development will vary with the views of the reader as to the relative value of private competition in the housing field.

It is appropriate to consider whether the present organization for housebuilding in Sweden, under the leadership of municipalities and coöperative organizations, will prove responsive to changing demands for housing in Sweden. It has been seen earlier that dwellings built since World War II in Sweden have been predominantly in multi-family structures.

It is not surprising to find that these buildings have been erected with considerable efficiency. Many observers have raised the question, however, of the types of structures which will be demanded in the future, with the expected increase in automobile transportation and urban spread. Since 1955, government policies have tended to encourage a higher proportion of single-family dwelling units. It has not yet been demonstrated that public bodies and coöperatives can operate as efficiently as private builders in this sphere. Sweden's residential construction industry is far behind American industry in its organization for land subdivision and for the financing and construction of single-family homes. As a result, the single-family home, which many forecast will be in demand in Sweden in the years to come, is relatively more expensive than its counterpart in other countries and considerably more expensive than dwelling units in multi-family structures. Part of this difference is explained by climatic and topographical features in Sweden, but part is undoubtedly the result of government policies that have consciously directed building activity to the multi-family dwelling unit since World War II.

The monotonous exterior appearance and design of Sweden's government-approved flats is a more serious shortcoming of post-World War II housing policy. The more recent development of multistoried apartment buildings and of neighborhood units such as the Vällingby Center, outside Stockholm, has done little to relieve the overwhelming impression of sameness in Swedish postwar housing. As a price for government financing subsidies, the typical Swedish consumer has virtually abdicated the right to choose a dwelling of individual design and characteristics. These he must seek elsewhere—in his automobile, boat, or perhaps in his country villa.

Happily, this review and evaluation of Sweden's post-World War II housing policies can end on a note of praise. The results of government housing policies are under continuous review by competent and experienced public officials in the Royal Board of Housing and under the constant watchful eyes of the Parliament. The penetrating character of much of the criticism of government housing policies coming from within the Parliament is well illustrated by the recommendations of a government commission in 1956, including representatives of various political parties, that general housing subsidies should be gradually abolished in favor of special state housing allowances to those in special need, that general housing subsidies should not be used as a permanent feature of government policy, and that rent controls should be substantially altered to permit more realistic levels of rents.

It is generally recognized that the administration of the government housing program on a national and a local level is efficient and lacking in the endless red tape and corruption which characterize so much of governmental activity in the economic field in many countries. Residential development has been carefully and, on the whole, well integrated with regional and local land-use planning. The result has been that the sameness in Sweden's housing has not become drabness, because of the wise provision of open spaces and the preservation of natural beauty.

V West Germany

The year 1870 marked the beginning of a period of rapid increase of population in Germany, and of commercial and manufacturing activity. High rates of urbanization and a shift of population from rural to urban areas accompanied the political and economic unification of Germany.[1]

In the latter quarter of the nineteenth century Germany dealt rather successfully with the imposing problems created by an explosion of economic activity. This success may be attributed in part to the fact that German industrial growth came later than that of the other important European powers of the period, particularly England, France, and Belgium. German cities were not so chaotically constructed as those of other countries, and the flimsy shacks and alley slums common in other countries were the exception rather than the rule in Germany.[2] The efficiency of the early German system of municipal government seems to have contributed to the elimination of many of the evils connected with urban living, and to have contrasted favorably with contemporary municipal efforts in the United Kingdom.[3]

---

[1] For a summary of this activity see Robert A. Brady, "The Economic Impact of Imperial Germany," *Journal of Economic History,* III (December, 1943), 108–123. See also W. O. Henderson, *The Zollverein* (Cambridge, England: University Press, 1939).

[2] Catherine Bauer, *Modern Housing* (Cambridge, Mass.: Riverside Press, 1934), pp. 270–271.

[3] For example: " . . . the Town Councils of nearly all German towns are showing far greater energy in combating this evil [of overcrowding] than our [British] Town Councils are showing, and the methods which they have adopted to remove it, appear much more likely to be successful than the methods adopted by the few English Town Councils which are making serious attempts to lessen overcrowding in their towns. It is, however, chiefly by their remarkable success in making full and healthy life possible in all parts of all towns for those persons, of all classes, who earn enough to be able to obtain an adequate amount of house room, that German Town Councils show that their system is very greatly superior to ours." T. C. Horsfall (compiler), *The Improvement of the Dwellings and Surroundings of the People—The Example of Germany,* supplement to the report of

The typical nineteenth-century residential construction in Germany was a six- or seven-story tenement with two or three "back-buildings," firmly constructed and usually supplied with water. A picture of the density pattern in various cities in Germany in the latter part of the century is given in Table V–1. The data illustrate the predominance of

TABLE V–1

AVERAGE NUMBER OF OCCUPANTS PER STRUCTURE FOR SELECTED CITIES IN GERMANY, 1880 AND 1890

City	Inhabitants		Households, 1890
	1880	1890	
Berlin	44.9	52.6	12.3
Breslau	33.2	35.4	8.2
Königsberg	27.7	29.5	6.4
Chemnitz	32.1	29.1	6.7
Stettin	30.7	27.6	5.6
Dresden	32.6	27.4	6.3
Magdeburg	26.7	27.4	6.0
Leipzig	38.6	25.4	5.4
Munich	19.2	22.4	5.1
Cologne	13.5	13.9	3.0
Bremen	7.1	7.6	2.2
Average	27.8	27.1	6.1

Source: Eugen Jaeger, *Die Wohnungsfrage*, Vol. II (Berlin, 1903); also quoted in T. C. Horsfall (compiler), *The Improvement of the Dwellings and Surroundings of the People—The Example of Germany*, supplement to the report of the Manchester and Salford Citizens' Association for the Improvement of the Unwholesome Dwellings and Surroundings of the People (Manchester: University Press, 1905), p. 3.

multi-family dwellings in Germany and suggest that the housing densities did not improve significantly between 1880 and 1890.[4]

A good part of the success of the German municipal governments in the late nineteenth and early twentieth centuries in alleviating the imposing housing problem can be laid to the fact that the German town councils were allowed to assess vacant construction sites and regulate the prices for which they could be sold.[5] These early achievements were, in part, possible because the German town governments

the Manchester and Salford Citizens' Association for the Improvement of the Unwholesome Dwellings and Surroundings of the People (Manchester: University Press, 1905), p. 24.

[4] *Ibid.*, p. 5.

[5] *Ibid.*, p. 30. The German Communal Rating Act of July 14, 1893, left to each town council the decision as to the manner in which land would be rated. When the Prussian government recommended the adoption of the system of rating land on its selling value, it prepared bylaws for the guidance of communities which desired to accept its advice.

owned considerable amounts of land during this period. In 1901 the Prussian government issued directions to the governors of the twelve Provinces to induce all Prussian towns to buy as much land as they could obtain, and to retain possession of all land they held.[6]

Some evidence exists that in the very early part of the twentieth century some German town councils stimulated private-enterprise housing supplies by leasing parts of government-owned town land to building societies at below-market rental rates and by lending money on easy terms to building societies.[7] However, the over-all importance of national and local government intervention in the private housing market was small until the post-World War I period.

The German cities, in addition to buying large areas of land and exercising some control over land-use patterns, engaged in a variety of public utility activities. Probably the most important of these were efforts directed at low-cost housing. As early as 1889 some legislation granted certain favors to coöperative housing societies, and by 1914 there were about 1,400 of these small coöperative societies in existence. Most were formed by prospective tenants who had little or no equity capital, and the majority of the dwellings they built remained in collective ownership.

The Prussian decree of 1901 led to the imposition of the ministerial recommendations as statutory obligations by several of the provincial governments, and by 1909 at least half of the larger German cities were providing assistance in the construction of low-cost public utility housing.[8] In addition to social insurance funds, which were officially encouraged to make loans on public utility housing, and those funds provided by the town councils, some funds for housing were provided after 1911 out of the proceeds of a land-value increment tax and by some newly formed semiofficial savings banks.[9]

World War I and Its Aftermath

The period between the two World Wars was characterized by great fluctuations in housing activity and by an almost chronic shortage of

[6] *Ibid.*, p. 36. A joint decree on the housing question was issued by the Prussian Ministers of State and Commerce, of the Interior, of Religion, and of Agriculture on March 19, 1901.

[7] For example, the Frankfurt town council offered to lend nine tenths of the cost of dwellings for "workpeople" and lease part of the town land to building societies of public utility and private builders at low rentals for terms of about eighty years. *Ibid.*, p. 26.

[8] Bauer, *op. cit.*, p. 272. "By the end of 1913, the insurance foundations had invested some $114,000,000 in housing, a sum which probably produced a good 150,000 dwellings."

[9] *Ibid.*, pp. 272–273.

dwellings. The greatest obstacle to housing construction was the scarcity and high cost of capital. A first mortgage which would have been granted at a rate of 4 per cent before the war was 10 per cent or higher after it, if the money was available at all, and was still 8.5 per cent in 1929.

The postwar rent for a privately financed new house in 1927, based on construction costs, would have been about four times the prewar rent for the same dwelling. Meanwhile, wages had increased by only 50 per cent, and unassisted private enterprise was relatively ineffective in financing the great mass of housing required.[10] As a result, large-scale government intervention in the housing market began to manifest itself immediately after World War I.

Residential construction declined from 200,000 new units annually in 1913 to less than 3,000 units in 1918. A rapid increase in postwar marriages, coupled with a large influx of refugees, resulted in an extreme shortage of housing. Table V–2 indicates that new construction

TABLE V–2

HOUSING CONSTRUCTION IN GERMANY, 1919 TO 1938
(In number of dwelling units)

Year	New construction	Rebuilding	Total	Rebuilding as per cent of total
1919	35,596	25,265	60,861	41.5
1920	75,928	32,379	108,307	29.9
1921	108,596	32,902	141,498	23.3
1922	124,273	30,697	154,970	19.8
1923	100,401	25,539	125,940	20.3
1924	94,807	20,569	115,376	17.8
1925	164,437	27,375	191,812	14.3
1926	199,084	21,445	220,529	9.7
1927	284,444	22,390	306,834	7.3
1928	306,825	23,617	330,442	7.1
1929	315,703	23,099	338,802	6.8
1930	307,933	22,327	330,260	6.8
1931	231,342	20,359	251,701	8.1
1932	131,160	27,961	159,121	17.6
1933	132,870	69,243	202,113	34.3
1934	190,257	129,182	319,439	40.4
1935	213,227	50,583	263,810	19.2
1936	282,466	49,904	332,370	15.0
1937	308,945	31,447	340,392	9.2
1938	276,276	29,250	305,526	9.6

Source: Deutscher Verein für Wohnungsreform E.V., *Wohnungsbau in Reich und Ländern, 1933–1937* (Berlin: Ernst Wasmuth, 1939).

[10] See Table V–4, below, for detailed data in this respect.

and rehabilitation of older and damaged housing units added only about 120,000 units annually to the housing stock between 1919 and 1924. Many of these units were added by remodeling military barracks for civilian occupancy.[11]

The low level of construction between 1919 and 1924 can be accounted for, principally, by the postwar German inflation.[12] Rents were frozen at prewar levels while inflationary pressures were rapidly pushing up construction costs. During the war the entire housing complex had been regulated by a series of legislative enactments. All rents were officially fixed, private renting contracts were outlawed, and tenants were accorded a permanent right of tenure for their dwellings, provided they paid the set rent. In the last resort, the public authorities took over the function of the renting agent. It can be stated generally that the government intervened at several points to prevent a catastrophic situation in the housing market during the breakdown of the capital market under the strain of the German inflation. The Housing Shortage Law of 1923 (Reichswohnungsmangelgesetz) permitted the government to provide dwellings for the homeless by various methods; the Tenant-Protection Bill of 1923 (Mieterschutzgesetz) was a guarantee to tenants that they could not be forced to leave dwellings except under certain prescribed conditions, and the Rent Act of 1922 (Reichsmietensetz) prevented rent increases except by official permission.

The German government undertook to cover the difference between actual cost price and what was considered a "normal" cost, on the assumption that the rise in building costs was only temporary. This was done either by government construction with a write-off of part of the investment or by granting outright subsidies to public utility societies. But, as it became evident that prewar conceptions of normality were not realistic, it became necessary to replace temporary measures by long-run policies.[13]

Several measures were taken to reorganize the capital market by the establishment of mortgage loan banks with the assistance of public

---

[11] It should be noted that all of these early figures relate to Germany as a territorial entity after World War I and not to the present German Federal Republic. Paucity of data forces consideration of the entire area during this period.

[12] The "German inflation" is usually thought of as a postwar phenomenon. Inflationary pressures during the war were hidden by measures of war economy. The German statistical bureau computed, after the war, that the average level of German wholesale prices had increased 130 per cent during the war; but this computation took into account only the legal official maximums, not the prices really paid. Only when the war economy with all its comprehensive restrictions had broken down did the real extent of the disturbances and dislocations become evident.

[13] Bauer, *op. cit.*, p. 273.

funds. The establishment of the Deutsche Bau und Bodenbank in 1923 was a particularly important step in improving the flow of capital into housing investment. Residential construction did not start in earnest however, until after the stabilization of the currency in 1924. The continued scarcity of capital and accompanying high interest rates prompted the enactment of special government subsidies for housing construction. The funds for government aid were secured from the proceeds of the house-rent tax, or *Hauszinssteuer,* which was levied in 1924, rather than out of borrowed funds. The rationale for this tax was that all pre-inflation-era houses were free of interest costs, since the owners had been able to pay off mortgage debt at the height of the inflation. During this period, houseowners netted handsome revaluation profits, since they were mortgage debtors and mortgages were revalued by only 25 per cent after the stabilization of the currency.[14] This unfair advantage was equalized by the imposition of special taxes on such houses.

The period from 1924 to 1930 became known as the "era of the Hauszinssteuer." During this period the volume of new housing construction increased threefold. As supplements to the rent tax, government loans were made to builders and to government employees at low rates of interest, and private employers were encouraged to construct homes for workers or to offer building loans at low rates of interest.

Throughout this period, public financing accounted for between 50 and 60 per cent of total new investment in housing. The heavy dependence of the housing market upon public financing served to aggravate the severity of the decline when the depression set in between 1930 and 1931. The decline in tax revenues necessitated a drastic reduction in public funds for housing construction and was matched by a similar decline in the amount of credit available through the organized capital markets. As a result of these and other factors, residential construction declined by over 50 per cent between 1929 and 1932.

Housing under the Nazi Government

When the Nazi regime came to power in May, 1933, most phases of economic life, including the housing sector, were brought under a rigid and centralized control. A complex of laws and decrees concerning housing was fitted into the general framework of two four-year plans.

[14] Gustav Stolper, *German Economy, 1870–1940: Issues and Trends* (New York: Reynal and Hitchcock, 1940), pp. 204–205.

The First Four-Year Plan (1933 to 1936) had as its main purpose a revival of the German economy, and during the first two years of this plan great emphasis was placed on rebuilding. The achievement of this plan can be noted by the fact that, in 1933, of all additions to the German housing stock, 34.3 per cent was the result of rebuilding, while in the following year rebuilding accounted for 40.4 per cent of the additions to the housing stock. Table V–3 gives a general picture of the

TABLE V–3

NEWLY BUILT DWELLINGS IN GERMANY, BY TYPES OF BUILDER, 1927 TO 1935

Year	Private builders	Per cent of total	Nonprofit societies	Per cent of total	Public authority	Per cent of total	Total
1927	169,395	60.3	78,426	27.9	33,269	11.8	281,090
1928	180,900	59.6	90,889	30.0	31,538	10.4	303,327
1929	173,139	55.5	109,121	34.9	30,010	9.6	312,270
1930	156,764	51.3	121,394	39.8	27,148	8.9	305,296
1931	118,749	51.7	92,587	40.3	18,492	8.0	229,828
1932	91,672	70.4	27,282	20.9	11,337	8.7	130,291
1933	99,660	75.4	19,546	14.8	12,986	9.8	132,191
1934	133,542	70.5	30,187	15.9	25,760	13.6	189,489
1935	154,845	73.0	40,050	18.9	17,127	8.1	212,022

Source: Heinz Umrath, "Activities of the European Labor Movement in the Housing Field" (unpublished report, Amsterdam, December, 1952), p. 28. This report was prepared in connection with other work done for the Standing Housing Committee of the European Regional Organization of the International Confederation of Free Trade Unions. Hereafter cited as Umrath, "Activities of the European Labor Movement in the Housing Field."

amount of housing construction before and during the First Four-Year Plan, together with the relative importance of the public and private sectors over this period. It should be noted that the changes in the

TABLE V–4

FINANCING OF HOUSING CONSTRUCTION IN GERMANY, 1924 TO 1939

Type of financing	Period under consideration	
	1924–1931	1932–1939
Public funds	51%	14%
Real estate credit institutions	37	46
Other private sources	12	40

Source: United Nations Economic Commission for Europe, *Methods and Techniques of Financing Housing in Europe*, E/ECE/IM/HOU/38 (Geneva, March, 1952), p. 111.

relative importance of private as compared with public construction were in good part induced by the changes in the sources of housing finance that were made by the Nazi government. The shift of financing from public funds to private capital after 1933 is shown in Table V–4. Rebuilding had been encouraged by the pre-Nazi government in 1932,[15] since a considerable surplus of large apartments which had been constructed during the previous boom was available for remodeling to offset a severe shortage of smaller apartments. The tendency throughout the period of the First Four-Year Plan, however, was for the proportion of larger to smaller residential dwellings to increase.

Table V–5 indicates that the percentage of total construction repre-

TABLE V–5

German Residential Dwelling Construction: Size Distribution, 1933 to 1936

Year	Total residential construction	Small houses		Medium-sized houses		Large houses	
		Number	Per cent	Number	Per cent	Number	Per cent
1933	91,909	81,450	88.7	2,887	3.1	7,571	8.2
1934	128,574	113,291	88.1	4,228	3.3	11,055	8.6
1935	134,185	115,705	86.2	5,307	4.0	13,173	9.8
1936	155,112	129,512	83.3	6,600	4.3	19,000	12.4
Total	509,780	439,959	86.3	19,022	3.7	50,799	10.0

Source: Helwig Stern, *Die Bedeutung des Wohnungsbaues im ersten Vierjahresplan* (Würzburg-Aumuhle: Konrad Triltsch, 1940), p. 30.

sented by small houses declined from 88.7 per cent in 1933 to 83.3 per cent three years later.

The law for the encouragement of housing construction,[16] passed in 1935, placed a greater emphasis upon new construction. The percentage of total additions to the housing stock represented by new construction increased to 80.8 per cent in 1935, with a further increase to 85 per cent in 1936. As shown by Table V–2, construction continued to expand during the 1930's and the 1929 high was exceeded in 1936 and 1937. A slight decline in construction occurred in 1938 and reflected a growing shortage of labor and materials owing to increased allocation of economic resources to the military sector of the economy. During this period a serious housing shortage existed, however, despite the

[15] Emergency order, September, 1932.

[16] Reichsgesetz zur Forderung des Wohnungsbaues.

considerable increase in residential construction. Although about 300,000 dwellings a year were added to the housing stock from 1927 to 1930, the shortage increased rapidly because of the more rapid rate of population growth.[17] According to the census of 1933, more than a million households had no separate home, as compared with 600,000 in 1927.[18] Although most of the new construction was in lower-income housing, there was still much construction of dwellings with rentals too high to find tenants in the period before 1933. Fey notes:

> At the end of 1932 more than one million households had no home of their own in Germany. The fact that not even 10 per cent, nay, apparently not a single one of these families disposed of enough purchasing power to rent one of the [150,000] empty apartments clearly shows the wrong relation between rent and income. But the outside impression was that there was no housing shortage in Germany.[19]

The Second Four-Year Plan, which was interrupted by the war, began in 1937 and was designed to overcome the more critical aspects of the housing problem discussed above, although it was almost impossible to close the gap between supply and demand. In contrast to the First Four-Year Plan, increased emphasis was placed upon the construction of smaller apartments and upon rural workers' homes. German rent policy in this period was placed in the hands of a "Reichskommissar für die Preisbildung," who was responsible for the control of prices for goods and production of any kind, in particular, the necessities of life. All rents were frozen, and throughout this period every effort was made to keep rentals at a low, stabilized level.

Armed conflict broke out in Europe soon after the inception of the Second Four-Year Plan, and the allocation of German economic resources was diverted primarily to military activities. After 1938 there was relatively little effort devoted to housing activities per se until after World War II.

Housing Policy During World War II

It is quite difficult to trace in any detail the developments in German housing through the course of World War II. In 1939 the housing stock in the area which has now become West Germany consisted of

[17] See Tables II–1 and II–2 for the relationship between population growth and the amount of new housing construction.

[18] Heinz Umrath, "Activities of the European Labor Movement in the Housing Field" (unpublished report, Amsterdam, December, 1952), p. 2. (See source note to Table V–3.)

[19] W. Fey, *Leistungen und Aufgaben in Deutschen Wohnungs und Siedlungsbau* (Berlin: Duncker & Humblot, 1936).

approximately ten million dwellings serving a population of 39.4 million persons. Over the course of World War II, one quarter of the dwelling units in existence in 1939 were destroyed by bombing and other war action.[20]

In spite of the tremendous war losses suffered by Germany, the population of the country continued to increase. Table II–1 indicates that the population in the territory of West Germany rose by approximately 25 per cent from 38.5 million persons in mid-1937 to 47.9 million at the end of 1952. Since 1952 the population has increased a further 7.5 per cent, to 51.5 million at the end of 1958. The rapid postwar increase in the total population may be attributed more to the heavy influx of refugees from the East than to large changes in the birth or mortality rates. It is estimated that net immigration into West Germany in the period from October, 1946, to December 31, 1951, totaled about 2.1 million persons, with an additional 1.3 million entering West Germany between 1952 and 1958. The total net immigration between 1950 and 1958 is estimated at approximately 2.5 million.

An estimate of the extent of the housing shortage in Germany can be gained from a report of the United Nations which estimated that the number of households in West Germany in September, 1950, totaled approximately 15.2 million (out of a population of 47.7 million) and exceeded the number of available dwellings by about 5.75 million. It was also estimated that about 40 per cent of the German households did not share their dwellings, and that if separate dwellings were to have been provided for all married men and for half of the widowed, divorced, and unmarried persons above thirty years of age the housing stock in West Germany would have fallen short of requirements by almost 4.5 million units in 1950.[21] The housing census taken in Germany in 1950 determined that 6.5 million dwellings or 425,000 dwelling units per year would have to be constructed until 1965 to eliminate the most urgent housing shortage within that period. Even then, an extensive slum-clearance program was regarded as necessary, since many of the existing houses were far below minimum standards.[22]

---

[20] Robert G. Wertheimer, "The Miracle of German Housing in the Postwar Period," *Land Economics*, XXXIV (November, 1958), 338. See also Umrath, *op. cit.*, p. 34.

[21] United Nations Economic Commission for Europe, *The European Housing Situation*, E/ECE/221 (Geneva, January, 1956), p. 18. According to this report, the interpretation given the concept of a "household" in the West German housing census of 1950 included as households some classifications, such as student and apprentices, who do not ordinarily require a separate dwelling. For this reason, the estimates cited may exaggerate somewhat the extent of the housing shortage in Germany in 1950.

[22] Umrath, *op. cit.*, p. 34.

POST-WORLD WAR II HOUSING SITUATION

The emergency nature of the immediate post-World War II housing problem placed emphasis upon the shelter requirements of refugees and those whose homes had been demolished by bombing and other military activities. Scarcely any use was made of temporary housing. In urban areas many people were housed in air-raid shelters, and in the other areas people were housed in available undamaged dwellings. Emergency repair work in the first winter after the war rendered half a million dwellings habitable again, but the shortage of new materials caused the deferment of new construction on any scale until after the currency reform of 1948. During this period directly following the war, first priority went to the repair of damaged but habitable accommodations. In view of the problems of removing rubble and repairing more extensively damaged houses, the provision of dwellings in the early postwar years moved slowly. Hence the main effort from 1945 to June, 1948, was toward the restoration of housing and industrial capacity, the removal of debris, and political reorganization.[23] It was obvious to the Occupying Powers that, whatever the success of these emergency measures, the basic industries of coal and steel must be swiftly restored if, in accordance with the principles of the Potsdam Agreement, the German people were to be enabled to subsist without external assistance.[24] In step with restoring the distribution of available food and finding shelter for the homeless, work was begun on restoring coal and steel output. Initially, coal was more important and priority was given to housing for miners. Within the framework of the Marshall Plan, a special project for miners' houses was developed by the organizations of employers and employees in the Ruhr coal industry. A premium of DM 2 was paid on every ton of coal and DM 100,000,000 was supplied from counterpart funds.[25] The latter amount fully financed the net construc-

[23] Central Mortgage and Housing Corporation, *Housing Progress Abroad,* VII, No. 2 (Ottawa, June, 1952), 6. See also Robert George Wertheimer, "Tax Incentives for Savings and Investments in the German Federal Republic, 1948–1954" (doctoral dissertation, Harvard University, 1956), pp. 4–8.

[24] After the German surrender in 1945, supreme authority in Germany had been vested in the British, United States, Soviet, and French commanders-in-chief, each in his own zone of occupation, and also jointly—as the Allied Control Council—in matters affecting Germany as a whole. It was fundamental to the conception of the purposes of the Occupation, as set out in the Potsdam Agreement, that Germany should be treated as an economic unit, and that required imports should be paid for out of current production, with reparations relegated to second place.

[25] Hermann Wandersleb, "Idea, Planning and Execution of the MSA/FOA Coal Miner's Housing Program," *Eigenheime für den Bergmann* (Bonn: Ministry of Housing, December, 1954). Realizing that any sizable increase in the construction of coal miners' housing would leave the current housing program with a critical

tion costs, of which DM 8 million went for site-improvement costs. The later policies, applying to homes for miners, will be discussed in more detail below; however, these initial steps brought coal from an output of a few thousand tons a week immediately following the war to over 300,000 tons daily within two years.[26] Whereas at least 400,000 miners had no homes at all in 1945, the shortage of miners' dwellings was reduced to 90,000 in 1953 and "probably totally eliminated in 1955." [27]

Currency Reform and Governmental Reorganization

Expectations of reform had inhibited financial undertakings prior to the currency reform of June 20, 1948, and it was only after the reform that any serious approach to the housing problem became possible and that attempts were made to tackle the housing problems of the larger cities. The monetary disorder of the country was recognized as a major impediment to progress. The reichsmark had become almost worthless long before the end of the war; the magnitude of the chronic inflation to which Germany had been subject was concealed by the intricate and pervasive network of controls created by the National Socialist war bureaucracy; currency payments were useless and black-market barter spread to every trade and form of manufacture. Industrial output suffered severely, and only through barter could materials be obtained at all.[28] Although the *Länder* (states) of the German Federal Republic did everything possible from the time they were founded in 1945 to further the repair and construction of dwellings, actual construction was possible only in the rural areas where the country population was in a position to feed construction workers and

---

shortage of funds unless it were possible to tap other sources, the German Congress unanimously adopted a new law, dated October 23, 1951, under which the Federal Republic introduced a levy of DM 2 per ton of bituminous coal and DM 1 per ton of brown coal, to be used exclusively for financing the construction of coal miners' housing. An amendment to this law, dated October 29, 1954, provided for an extension of this financing method through 1957, but reduced the levy to one half the original amount.

These housing programs were originally ECA (Economic Cooperation Administration) projects in 1948; they later shifted to the MSA (Mutual Security Agency) in 1951. The intention of the MSA Mission was to make available DM 100 million of counterpart funds to promote the idea of homeownership and to raise the standard of housing for coal miners represented. Houses built under the MSA Miners' Program were constructed for homeownership in the nine projects.

[26] Great Britain Board of Trade, Commercial Relations and Export Department, *The Federal Republic of Germany: Economic and Commercial Conditions in the Federal Republic of Germany and West Berlin*, Overseas Economic Survey Series (London: H.M.S.O., March, 1955), p. 2.

[27] Umrath, *op. cit.*, p. 38.

[28] Great Britain Board of Trade, *The Federal Republic of Germany*, p. 5.

to barter foodstuffs for building materials through the "gray" and "black" markets.[29] The task of rebuilding many of the rural areas was thus largely completed when the larger cities were only beginning to take on the problems of reconstruction and planning. As in the period following World War I, the revival of urban residential construction had to wait for the currency reform, which came into effect under laws promulgated by the British, French, and American occupation authorities. By 1948 the basis for further expansion had been laid, as the reichsmark was replaced by a new currency controlled by a bank of issue with authority throughout the three Western zones, and the Deutsche mark was established as legal tender.[30] In addition to the currency reform, other programs established were of great assistance in shaping the pattern of future German economic development.[31] The establishment of a stable currency, the prospect of increased imports following from large-scale American aid, and the psychological effect of the association of West Germany with the western European countries in a concerted drive toward economic recovery laid the groundwork for the West German recovery under the Federal Republic established in 1949. The ministers and civil servants in the new government included many who had worked closely and effectively with the Allied authorities.[32] The erection of new dwellings was constituted as one of the foremost tasks of the new Bonn government, according to its policy statement of September 20, 1949, and this was reiterated in the policy statement issued by the second government when it took office in the latter part of 1953.

Housing Policy and the First Housing Act of 1950

When the federal government took office in 1949, a major problem was the provision of the necessary financing at interest rates low enough to enable rents to be controlled at a modest level. The problem was solved by subsidizing housing construction on a large scale from

---

[29] German Federal Republic Press and Information Office, *Germany Reports* (2d. ed.; Bonn, 1955), p. 4.

[30] German citizens received 60 of the new Deutsche marks in exchange for 60 of the old reichsmarks, and all wealth above that figure was converted at the rate of 10 RM = 1 DM.

[31] Particularly the Economic Cooperation Administration (ECA), the Mutual Security Agency (MSA), and the Foreign Operations Administration (FOA) under the framework of the Marshall Plan and the Office of European Economic Cooperation.

[32] Especially important were Professor Erhard, Minister of Economics since 1949 and in charge of economic affairs since 1948, and Herr Schaeffer, Minister of Finance during the same period.

public funds, especially from the funds of the federal and *Länder* budgets, and by making provision for generous income tax relief on nonpublic funds invested in housing.[33]

The federal government's social housing program and the means of financing it were set out in the First Housing Act of 1950, which provided the legislative basis for implementation of the German Federal Republic's housing plans. The Act was amended in certain respects in August, 1953,[34] and further amendments were incorporated in 1955 and in the Second Housing Act of 1956 to give greater encouragement to homeownership. It distinguished three types of housing:

Social housing enjoying subsidies and loans at low rates of interest from public funds

Other housing construction aided by tax concessions and tax exemptions

Housing financed entirely from private funds and enjoying no financial privileges

The subsidized social-housing projects were intended primarily for the broad masses of individuals in the lower income groups. Projects of this type were financed by public loans at a low rate of interest, were limited as to the size of the dwellings constructed, and were subject to strict limitations on the level of rents and the maximum levels of income which could be received by tenants.[35]

Other housing projects utilizing tax exemptions and concessions were also limited as to the size of the dwelling, although they generally provided for homes larger than those considered in the subsidized projects, as will be noted in detail later.

The First Housing Act of 1950 established as a goal the production of 1.8 million new social-housing dwellings over a six-year period. Table V–6 shows that this goal was reached by 1956, although social housing declined to less than 50 per cent of total dwellings completed in 1956 and 1957. As will be noted presently, the elimination of special Section 7*c* income tax concessions in 1955 and 1956, combined with generally restrictive credit measures by the central bank to combat inflationary trends in the economy, probably accounted for the sharp decline in social-housing production in 1957. Tax concessions were reintroduced at the end of 1956, and this development, together with measures through which the federal government provided special finan-

---

[33] Detailed analysis of financing is given later in this chapter.

[34] Restrictions on the sizes and rents of social-housing project dwellings set up in the original Act of 1950 were modified in 1953 to induce private capital into this area of investment.

[35] Great Britain Board of Trade, *The Federal Republic of Germany*, p. 137.

TABLE V-6

DWELLING CONSTRUCTION IN THE FEDERAL REPUBLIC OF GERMANY, 1950 to 1959 (EXCLUDING WEST BERLIN AND THE SAAR)

Year	Total number of dwellings completed	Social housing	
		Number	Per cent
1950	360,000	261,000[a]	73[a]
1951	410,300	293,000[a]	71[a]
1952	443,100	275,000[b]	62[b]
1953	518,400	286,700	55
1954	542,900	284,800	52
1955	541,700	269,400	50
1956	558,900	276,000	49
1957	528,900	211,000	41
1958	486,400	295,000	61
1959	550,000[c]	300,000[c]	55

Sources: Walter Fey, "Umfang und Merkmale des Wohnungsbaues in der Bundesrepublic Deutschland im Jahr 1958," *Bundesbaublatt*, May, 1959, p. 235, and *Housebuilding and Finance of Housing in the Federal Republic of Germany in 1956* (Bad Godesberg: Federal Ministry of Housing, 1957), Table 1. Additional sources indicated by superior letters.

[a] Umrath, "Activities of the European Labor Movement in the Housing Field," p. 36.

[b] Estimated by the author based upon averages of authorizations in 1951 and 1952.

[c] Bundesministerium für Wohnungsbau, *Jahresbericht 1959*, extracted from *Deutschland im Wiederaufbau 1959*.

cial assistance to the *Länder* for providing refugee housing, resulted in a large increase in social-housing production in 1958.

It can be noted that total dwelling-unit completions rose from 360,000 in 1950 to a record total of 558,900 in 1956. This production record is impressive when it is compared with the highest building total for the pre-World War II years—339,000 units in 1929, of which 197,000 units were completed in what is now the German Federal Republic.

Table V–7 shows that from 1950 to 1954 rents for all income groups showed a similar trend, but lagged substantially behind rising building costs in the period. The increase in the average cost per dwelling reflects increases in the size and quality of dwellings as well as the rise in building costs. Recognizing that existing rent restrictions tended to keep rents at an uneconomic level, the federal cabinet approved a rent law in September, 1954, that provided for:[36]

An increase of 10 per cent in rents for all dwellings constructed prior to the currency reform. Increases of 15 per cent and 20 per cent

[36] *Ibid*

TABLE V-7

COMPARISON OF CHANGES IN BUILDING COSTS AND RENTS IN WEST GERMANY, 1950 TO 1958

Year	Estimated cost of an average dwelling	Prince index for dwelling construction (1950 = 100)	Rent index for upper- and middle-income groups (1950 = 100)	Rent index for lower-income groups (1950 = 100)
1950	n.a.	100	100	100
1951	n.a.	116	102	101
1952	n.a.	123	104	103
1953	DM 14,130	119	107	107
1954	15,460	120	107	107
1955	17,020	129	110	110
1956	18,800	133	117	117
1957	21,200	140	119	119
1958	23,000	145	120	120

Sources: Estimated costs from Walter Fey, *Housebuilding and Finance of Housing in the Federal Republic of Germany in 1956* (Bad Godesberg: Federal Ministry of Housing, 1957), Table 5; see also *Annual Report of the Federal Ministry of Housing for 1958* (Bad Godesberg: 1959), p. 5. Price and rent indexes from Statistisches Bundesamt, *Statistisches Jahrbuch für die Bundesrepublik Deutschland, 1959* (Stuttgart: W. Kohlhammer, 1959), pp. 428 (prices) and 431–433 (rents).

were permitted where these dwellings had central heating and other amenities.

Supplementary charges for heating, water supply, and subletting in certain cases for dwellings that had been ready for occupation before December 31, 1949. These charges, however, were not to be included in the standard rent on which the permanent increases were to be calculated.

The charges to tenants with respect to repairs were increased on older buildings to take account of the increase in repair costs since 1936. The purpose of this legislation was to prevent the dilapidation of older buildings.

As a result of these changes, the index of residential rents for all income groups, which had changed little from 1945 to 1950, and had risen by only 7 per cent from 1950 to 1954, rose more rapidly to 120 per cent of the 1945–50 level by 1958.[37] Changes in rents during the postwar period reflect in part improvements in quality of dwellings built during the postwar period. Although the index of rents paid showed a similar trend for all income groups from 1950 to 1958, rents per square meter of floor area in state-assisted dwellings for low-

[37] Statistisches Bundesamt, *Statistisches Jahrbuch für die Bundesrepublik Deutschland, 1959* (Stuttgart: W. Kohlhammer, 1959), p. 431. See Table VII–7 for a comparison of changes in rents and cost of living.

income persons were approximately 15 per cent below the average for all other renters in 1957 and 1958.[38] This reflects the granting of capital and loan subsidies for social housing.

A new rent regulation made effective on August 1, 1958, codifies and simplifies former rent restrictions on approximately nine million existing dwellings. This represented a further step toward the gradual restoration of free competitive market conditions in privately owned rental housing.

The distinguishing features of West Germany's post-World War II housing policies have been the maintenance of tax and loan subsidies designed to encourage private housing investment in social housing, the encouragement of owner-occupied dwelling construction through tax and loan subsidies, and the gradual elimination of government controls over housing and rents. The following sections will examine specific aspects of West German housing policy in greater detail.

Housing Finance

The general financing of housing in West Germany typically involves a system of multiple mortgage loans and this framework of finance is typical of many European nations. Generally, the capital raised to finance housebuilding in the post-World War II period came from four different sources. A first mortgage was provided from private financial institutions; second mortgage loans were obtained from loans and advancements by commercial banks, employers, and tenants, and from other private sources; some capital was raised from the proprietor's own capital resources; and the remainder was provided by public funds from the federal government, the *Länder* and communes, and by the Office of the Equalization of Burdens. Tables V–8 and V–9 show the sources of housing finance in West Germany between 1950 and 1958.

An important aim of government housing policy has been to ensure that the cost of funds for building provided by the capital market should be kept low, relative to the normal cost of long-term capital. This was accompanied by forcing the institutional sources of credit to devote a fixed proportion of their funds to housing construction at a maximum interest rate of 6 per cent. Moreover, under the First Law for the Promotion of the Capital Market (December, 1952), interest on mortgage banks' bonds was made tax free, provided 90 per cent of the lending capacity was used for housing under the social-housing program.

[38] *Social Housing in 1958*, a special report prepared by the Federal Ministry of Housing (Bad Godesberg, 1959), p. 18.

TABLE V-8

FINANCING OF DWELLING CONSTRUCTION IN THE FEDERAL REPUBLIC OF GERMANY: MAJOR SOURCE AS A PERCENTAGE OF TOTAL INVESTMENT, 1903 TO 1959

Source	1903–1911	1924–1931	1932–1939	1950	1951	1952	1953	1954	1955	1956	1957	1958	1959
Financial institutions (including ERP funds):													
Savings banks	...	...	...	13.4	6.2	5.6	9.1	11.2	12.3	10.5	7.7	9.3	...
Mortgage bond institutes													
a) Public	...	...	...	2.4	2.8	3.4	4.7	6.1	7.8	7.3	4.6	5.4	...
b) Private	...	...	...	4.0	3.2	3.8	5.6	9.7	10.5	7.5	6.0	6.9	...
Social insurance (employers' contributions)	...	...	...	6.1	5.0	4.3	4.4	4.5	3.9	4.3	4.7	3.9	...
Building savings associations													
a) Public	...	...	...	5.4	3.8	2.9	3.4	5.0	5.8	6.8	7.2	6.9	...
b) Private	...	...	...	5.2	4.2	3.5	4.2	5.9	7.4	8.4	9.2	9.8	...
ERP Funds	...	...	...	4.8	4.1	1.4	0.5	0.1	0.0	0.0	0.0	0.0	...
Total	54.0	37.0	46.0	41.9	29.8	25.6	32.4	43.0	48.3	46.2	42.0	44.2	54.0
Public sources:													
Federal budget funds													
a) General dwelling construction, including resettling	...	...	...	8.1 (*a* and *b* combined)	4.6	6.4	5.9	5.9	3.3	3.8	3.7	4.7	...
b) Individual special actions, including Soviet zone refugees	...	...	...		2.7	2.7	2.6	2.1	2.0	2.4	4.2	6.7	...
Funds from settlement of expenses (or charges), including loans for construction													
a) Equalization of Burdens fund	...	...	...	9.7	8.8	4.0	10.4 (*a* and *b* combined)	11.7	10.0	9.0	7.8	6.2	...
b) Same, reconstruction loans only	...	...	...	7.9	12.8	6.3		5.3	5.8	5.2	4.3	4.1	...

TABLE V-8 (*Continued*)

Source	1903–1911	1924–1931	1932–1939	1950	1951	1952	1953	1954	1955	1956	1957	1958	1959
Allocations made by the *Länder*	...	...	...	{18.2	{15.2	12.7	9.0	7.8	6.9	8.2	7.0	6.5	...
Allocations made by the communes	...	...	...			6.4	4.5	3.6	3.5	3.4	2.8	2.6	...
Coal levy for miners' housing	...	...	...	n.a.	n.a.	3.8	2.4	1.7	1.3	1.5	1.4	1.8	...
Contributions made by the railway and postal administrations (without 7c Funds)	...	...	...	n.a.	n.a.	0.8	0.5	0.7	0.7	0.7	0.8	0.8	...
Total	3.0	51.0	14.0	43.9	47.1	43.1	35.3	33.6	27.6	29.9	27.7	29.3	25.0
Other funds:													
Proprietor's own capital; self-help; common help; loans and advances made by employers; private mortgages; loans and advances made by tenants; loans made by relatives; accommodation loans; payment of purchase price by instalments; interim credits and outstanding claims, etc.													
Total	43.0	12.0	40.0	14.2	23.1	31.3	32.3	23.4	24.1	24.8	30.3	26.5	21.0
Grand total	100.0	100.0	100.0	100.0	100.0	100.0	100.0	100.0	100.0	100.0	100.0	100.0	100.0

Sources: 1903–1939: United Nations Economic Commission for Europe, *Methods and Techniques of Financing Housing in Europe*, E/ECE/IM/HOU/38 (Geneva, March, 1952), p. 111. 1950–1958: Photostated table enclosed in a letter to the author from Dr. Walter Fey, Federal Ministry of Housing, Bad Godesberg (Mehlem), May 13, 1959. 1959: Bundesministerium für Wohnungsbau, *Jahresbericht 1959*, from *Deutschland im Wiederaufbau 1959*. (Pages unnumbered.)

Note: Only total figures are available for the period 1903 to 1939 and the year 1959. Any discrepancies in the above are due to the rounding-off of figures.

TABLE V–9

FINANCING OF DWELLING CONSTRUCTION IN THE FEDERAL REPUBLIC OF GERMANY, 1950 TO 1958—ACTUAL EXPENSES (PAYMENTS OR TRANSFERS)
(In millions of Deutsche marks)

Source	1950	1951	1952	1953	1954	1955	1956	1957	1958
Financial institutions (including ERP Funds):									
Savings banks	507	290	355	707	1,009	1,246	1,140	885	1,148
Mortgage bond institutes									
a) Public	92	132	214	369	552	787	796	526	665
b) Private	152	149	239	434	878	1,063	816	689	849
Life insurance companies	233	236	269	345	402	396	470	538	474
Social insurance (employers' contributions)	24	23	44	45	42	61	151	299	243
Building savings associations									
a) Public	205	182	184	268	450	584	745	830	855
b) Private	198	197	220	330	532	743	917	1,063	1,209
ERP funds	181	192	89	37	12	1	0	0	0
Total	1,592	1,401	1,614	2,532	3,878	4,881	5,035	4,830	5,443
Public sources:									
Federal budget means									
a) General dwelling construction, including resettling	308 (*a* and *b*)	216	404	464	532	334	413	424	581
b) Individual special actions, including Soviet zone refugees		130	167	200	185	200	264	486	826
Funds from settlement of expenses (or charges), including loans for construction									
a) Equalization of Burdens fund	370	415	251	809 (*a* and *b*)	1,050	1,009	983	896	761
b) Same, reconstruction loans only	300	600	400		479	586	564	494	509
Allocations made by the *Lander*	690 (Länder and communes)	855 (Länder and communes)	800	700	700	700	900	800	800
Allocations made by the communes			400	350	340	350	370	320	310
Coal levy for miners' housing	n.a.	n.a.	241	189	157	128	157	159	223
Contributions made by the railway and postal administrations (without 7c funds)	n.a.	n.a.	50	35	63	68	80	96	95
Total	1,668	2,216	2,713	2,747	3,027	2,789	3,167	3,181	3,596
Other funds:									
Proprietor's own capital; self-help; common help; loans and advances made by employers; private mortgages; loans and advances made by tenants; loans made by relatives; accommodation loans; payment of purchase price by instalments; interim credits and outstanding claims, etc. Total	540	1,083	1,973	2,521	2,095	2,430	2,698	3,489	3,261
Grand total	3,820	4,700	6,300	7,800	9,000	10,100	10,900	11,500	12,300

Sources: Walter Fey, ***Housebuilding and Finance of Housing in the Federal Republic of Germany in 1956*** (Bad Godesberg: Federal Ministry of Housing, 1957), Table 13; also, photostated table enclosed in a letter to the author from Dr. Fey, May 13, 1959.

Tables V–8 and V–9 reveal the gradually declining importance of public mortgage financing in the postwar period as a percentage of total mortgage lending. Public loans by the *Länder* and by local communes accounted for the largest proportion of public loans, although the federal government was active in making loans for housing refugees from the Soviet zone.

Increasing proportions of mortgage funds are shown to have been made available through private financial institutions. Savings banks, special mortgage banks, and construction loan banks accounted for the largest expansion during the period. As will be seen presently, government tax concessions were an important factor in this expansion. Although the percentage of total funds representing "other funds" has remained about constant since 1950, the total amount of funds made available annually, shown in Table V–9, has increased more than three times over.

The effects of elimination of special tax exemptions for private savings deposited in mortgage institutions, and of generally restrictive central bank credit measures, is reflected in the relative decline in mortgage lending by private savings institutions in 1956 and 1957. Some increase in public loans and in the contribution of private loans and equity capital offset this decline. These trends were reversed to a degree in 1958, when the full effect of the reinstatement of tax exemptions for savings, reënacted at the end of 1956, became operative.

Low-Income "Social Housing"

Public assistance to low-rent housing in West Germany comes in the form of low-rate or interest-free loans which are distributed either by the *Länder* or, in certain circumstances, by the communes, but not by the Federal Republic.[39] The First Housing Act of 1950 empowered the *Länder* to make loans for low-rent social-housing dwellings. Under the provisions of the act as it was initially set up, the *Länder* and local authorities were responsible for obtaining building sites and for submitting prospective one-year social-housing programs to the Federal Minister of Housing annually. These plans were coördinated and integrated by the Ministry of Housing into a six-year plan for the years 1950 to 1956. Municipalities and other public housing authorities, public and private housing associations, and private builders were eligible for loans under the Act, provided they complied with speci-

[39] The *Länder*, or states, of the Federal Republic are Bavaria, Bremen, Hamburg, Hessen, Lower Saxony, North Rhine–Westphalia, Rhineland-Pfalz, Schleswig-Holstein, and Württemberg-Baden. The latter was formed in 1952 when the *Länder* of Baden, Württemberg-Baden, and Württemberg-Hohenzollern merged. From that time the Federal Republic of Germany has comprised nine *Länder*, not including the western sector of Berlin. (From a political viewpoint, West Berlin is generally regarded as the tenth member state.)

fied conditions established to control the type of housing constructed with assistance from public funds.[40]

Before September, 1957, when the maximum income was raised to DM 9,000 annually, owners of these social dwellings were required to choose their tenants from a list, submitted by the local housing authority, of those whose incomes did not exceed DM 600 per month.[41] Provided the conditions with respect to both housing site and tenant are complied with, public funds are made available by the governments of the *Länder*, or by bodies appointed by them for that purpose, in the form of mortgage loans.[42] These loans from the state or from credit organizations are usually obtainable for about 60 per cent of the cost of the prospective dwellings at nominal interest rates. Based upon the amounts which can generally be raised on first and second mortgage loans from private sources, the builder invests the remainder of the necessary funds.[43]

First mortgage loans through private sources are usually granted for minimum periods of ten years and require payments of interest rates of 6.5 to 7.5 per cent, plus amortization charges of 1 to 1.5 per

---

[40] To meet the prescribed conditions, the habitable area of a dwelling must not exceed 65 square meters (702 sq. ft.), nor be less than 32 square meters (345 sq. ft.). Rents vary slightly according to local building costs and amenities offered, but the Act limited the rent charged on social housing to a maximum of DM 1, or, in exceptional cases, DM 1.10 per square meter (10.8 sq. ft.) per month. This was subsequently raised to DM 1.20 per square meter. Rents for low-income persons in state-assisted housing averaged DM 1.21 per square meter in 1958. This compared with a rent level of DM 1.28 per square meter for low-income persons in all other rented dwellings and with an average rent level of DM 1.45 per square meter for all other persons. (See *Social Housing in 1958*, p. 18.) A more detailed description of required specifications can be found in United Nations Economic Commission for Europe, *Methods and Techniques of Financing Housing in Europe*, E/ECE/IM/HOU/38 (Geneva, March, 1952), pp. 102–103, 190–191.

[41] International Federation for Housing and Town Planning, *News Sheet*, No. 21 (The Hague, August, 1951), p. 16. In towns of fewer than 100,000 inhabitants, the list for a particular dwelling must contain not less than three names, and in towns of 100,000 and over at least five prospective tenants are submitted to the owner; priority is given to refugees and to those who lost their homes in the war.

[42] In some *Länder* the communes are themselves authorized to grant loans from funds made available to them for the purpose, while in others the communes merely receive the applications and forward them with their recommendations. United Nations Economic Commission for Europe, *Methods and Techniques of Financing Housing in Europe*, p. 108.

[43] *Ibid.*, p. 110. This can be clarified by a typical example: "In 1950 the average estimated cost of production of a dwelling was 10,000 DM, of which 9,000 DM was assumed to represent building costs and 1,000 DM the cost of the site. Assuming the builder to put up 1,000 DM and a first mortgage loan of 3,500 DM to have been obtainable, the remainder, i.e., 5,500 DM, had to be furnished from public funds . . ."

cent annually. However, West Germany's postwar income tax laws permitted any private employer to deduct an amount up to one third of his taxable income, provided this amount was made available for low-cost housing at no interest, with an amortization of 2 per cent annually.[44] During the postwar years these private funds were usually made available to nonprofit building associations in order to avoid abuses, and also to avoid investment of these funds for purposes other than housing. Building-savings banks provided second mortgage loans to homeowners, under condition that 50 per cent of the required loan had been accumulated in a savings account.[45] Alternatively, second mortgage loans could be secured from commercial banks bearing interest rates of 4.5 per cent; these, however, required higher rates of amortization (5 to 7 per cent) and were less frequently used.[46]

Funds resulting from special taxes, paid by those whose property remained undamaged following the war (*Lastenausgleichschmittel*) were used as grants up to DM 4,000 per dwelling unit to aid housing for bombed-out people and for refugees. The owner's equity must have amounted to a minimum of 10 per cent of the total construction cost, and could have been provided as cash, or costed as self-help labor.[47]

According to the Housing Act of 1950, loans from public funds can only be given if other funds from private sources have been secured first.[48] Owing to the complexity of housing finance in West Germany, it was usually necessary for a prospective houseowner or builder to secure construction loan credit in addition to that initially secured, since only 50 per cent of the "7c" and public funds was given at the time of construction. In order to encourage homeownership, half of the federal loan funds for housing in West Germany were reserved for the financing of owner-occupied homes.[49] Public funds, however, as noted earlier from Table V–8, have played a diminishing role in the financing of housebuilding in West Germany.

---

[44] Treatment of the details of tax exemptions will follow.

[45] Bernard Wagner, "Financing of German Housing" (Essen, Germany, September, 1953), p. 2. [Mimeographed.] For example, a borrower could secure a second mortgage loan of DM 10,000, bearing an interest rate between 4 and 5 per cent, if he had accumulated DM 5,000 in a savings account.

[46] *Ibid.*, p. 4.

[47] *Ibid.*

[48] Exceptions can be made for temporary financing of first mortgages out of public funds if no private capital is available.

[49] United Nations Economic Commission for Europe, ***European Housing Progress and Policies in 1953***, E/ECE/189 (Geneva, August, 1954), p. 32.

Tax Incentives for Housing

Tax incentives to aid private housing investment must be viewed against the background of general postwar tax policies in West Germany. The Occupation Powers had imposed a steep personal income tax structure on the German economy in 1946 to control the inflationary tendencies which threatened to hinder economic recovery. The provisional West German government objected to these high personal income tax rates and introduced tax concessions for saving in the Tax Reform Law of 1948. The official position of the German government was that this measure was necessary because the high income tax rates imposed by the Occupation Powers could not be reduced directly and that these stiff tax rates were hurting incentives to work. R. G. Wertheimer notes that in 1956 the German government continued to take the official position that the introduction of saving concessions was forced by the income tax burden imposed by the Occupation, but that the Allies really favored the saving concessions because of their anti-inflationary nature.[50] In any case, the 1948 tax law reëstablished the traditional income deductions for insurance premium payments and contributions to building and loan associations. The stimulation of investment by tax concessions was so successful in the early postwar period that they were continued even after the German government regained its authority to set all taxes at its own discretion.[51]

The Income Tax Law of April 20, 1949, provided further tax incentives for contractual saving by permitting the deduction from taxable income of expenditures for the contributions to housing finance. Two main provisions in this tax law stimulated housing construction. One provision provided for moderately accelerated write-offs for expenditures on newly constructed dwellings, and another, mentioned earlier, permitted deductions from taxable income as business expenses for interest-free loans for social housing.

The first provision allowed 10 per cent of the cost of dwelling units repaired, expanded, or newly constructed to be written off for each of two years following the date of the expenditure, and 3 per cent of the original cost to be written off annually for ten years thereafter, with remaining costs charged off by normal depreciation. Actually, this boiled down to a reduction of taxable income for twelve years of

[50] Wertheimer, "Tax Incentives . . . ," pp. 47–50.

[51] *Ibid.*, p. 56. The Tax Reform Law of June 22, 1948, not only restored traditional deductions, but contained provisions such as accelerated depreciation allowances, special expense deductions, etc., which tended to stimulate investment through self-finance.

amounts deductible in excess of normal write-offs. This provision of the 1949 tax law stimulated expenditures for new and rehabilitated housing and also acted as an inducement to social-housing construction and homeownership.[52]

Section 7*c* of the tax law was of greater importance as an influence on the pattern of German housing, and played a major role in channeling interest-free funds into social housing for use as second mortgages at times when other sources of long-term private capital were fairly limited.

These interest-free loans could be fully deducted as business expenses from the taxable income in the year in which they were made, and were used by both corporate and unincorporated firms and individual taxpayers. The tax deductions were initially unlimited, but were later restricted to DM 7,000 for each dwelling unit and, for firms, up to 30 per cent of annual profits.[53] Through the arbitrary shifting of loan repayments into periods of lower annual income, individuals could reduce their effective income tax payments, and firms could utilize loans for social housing as a device to strengthen their collective bargaining position. These possibilities, coupled with the initial lending of borrowed funds and ability to recall loans at any time, tended to detract from their use as long-term capital, and by 1953 Section 7*c* of the 1949 tax law gave rise to much dispute. Although 7*c* loans represented the heart of West Germany's incentive scheme for aid to housing, abuses such as those mentioned above led to the termination of the system at the close of 1954, since it was found that individuals who least needed these funds found it easy to arrange loans on favorable terms and could indulge in luxury building. Business firms also misused the system by obtaining tax deductions on amounts which were derived from loans rather than from profits.[54] Abuses tended in general to discredit the system of incentive taxation, and the general program was terminated in 1955; however, this was not to be a permanent cessation of tax concession utilization. Special income tax concessions for the stimulation of private savings were reinstated toward the end of 1956.

The amendment to the tax law of October 5, 1956, was designed to stimulate the utilization of savings deposits, which had decreased

---

[52] *Ibid.*, pp. 65–66. For a detailed breakdown one may refer to the Income Tax Law (*Einkommensteuergesetz*) of April 20, 1949, Section 7*b*.

[53] *Ibid.*, p. 67. Until 1953, these loans could be financed from any funds, owned or borrowed, and could be recalled at any time; after 1953, funds had to come from owned assets and were "sunk" for a period of three years.

[54] Wertheimer, "The Miracle of German Housing . . . ," *Land Econ.*, p. 344, and "Tax Incentives . . . ," p. 68.

owing to the inflationary impact of the currency reform and subsequent credit restrictive measures by the German central bank. These forces had led to difficulty in the procurement of first mortgages for social housing. About two months later, on December 19, 1956, the "New Taxation Act" came into force, providing a limited extension of tax concessions for certain savings contracts.[55] Tax concessions related to housebuilding were continued until 1961 in the Income and Profit Tax Amendment of July 18, 1958.

A set of new tax concessions very much different from those so far mentioned was introduced in 1952. The First Capital Development Law of 1952 provided for the development of the German capital market. Section 3*a* of that law set up exemptions from both personal and corporate income taxation on interest income from mortgages paying between 5 per cent and 5.5 per cent interest, if at least 90 per cent of these mortgages were utilized in the financing of social housing.[56] This concession, however, was relatively ineffective for promoting social housing, for it discriminated among types of interest income, and its technique of splitting the capital market issues into taxable and tax-exempt issues was strongly attacked. More important was the fact, however, that the needed social-housing funds had been successfully raised from 1950 to 1955 by the before-mentioned Section 7*c* of the 1949 tax law. There was also much conspicuous abuse of the law of 1952 similar to that which took place under the 7*c* legislation, and it was terminated at the close of 1954.[57]

Wertheimer has estimated that tax incentives were responsible for half of all private savings used in the mortgage market in West Germany from 1950 to 1956, and identifies three ways in which these incentives aided housing finance:[58]

They encouraged personal saving at credit institutions which would use these savings in extending mortgage loans.

They attracted private funds of individuals and businesses for the purpose of tax-exempt mortgage and communal bonds.

They provided large personal or corporate income tax savings for individual or business firms which extended housing loans.

Estimates of the amount of private mortgage funds generated for use in residential construction from 1950 to 1956 are shown in Table V–10.

---

[55] *Annual Report of the Federal Ministry of Housing for 1957* (Bad Godesberg, 1958), p. 6; *ibid., 1958*, p. 29.

[56] Wertheimer, "Tax Incentives . . . ," pp. 103–104.

[57] *Ibid.*, pp. 105–108. Wertheimer expressed the view that the First Capital Development Law increased the supply of low-cost funds for housing, but he asserted that social housing would not have run out of funds without it.

[58] Wertheimer, "The Miracle of German Housing . . . ," *Land Econ.*, p. 342.

TABLE V–10

SOURCES OF PRIVATE FUNDS USED IN PRIVATE RESIDENTIAL CONSTRUCTION IN WEST GERMANY BY USE OF TAX INCENTIVES AND ALSO WITHOUT AID, 1950 TO 1956 (In billions of Deutsche marks)

Sources	By tax incentive	Without aids	Total
Savings banks	2.6	2.9	5.5
Life insurance companies[a]	0.8	1.7	2.5
Building and loan associations[a]	1.7	3.3	5.0
Mortgages and communal obligations	8.8	3.4	12.2
Loans made by business from profits[b]	4.3	0	4.3
Free funds of builders, owners, and others[c]	0	5.6	5.6
Total	18.2	16.9	35.1

Source: Robert G. Wertheimer, "The Miracle of German Housing in the Postwar Period," *Land Economics*, XXXIV (November, 1958), 342.

[a] One quarter of total saving in this form was credited to incentive saving which authorized larger than normal deductions from taxable income for these purposes.

[b] Interest-free loans under Section 7*c* of the Income Tax Law.

[c] Including mortgage loans by social security institutions and the Reconstruction Loan Corporation.

Although the data are not strictly comparable, it can be noted from comparison with Tables V–8 and V–9 that tax incentives were an important factor in stimulating the increased flow of private capital into the mortgage market from 1950 to 1956.

In contrast to the above legislation, the Homebuilding Premium Law of 1952 took the form of a direct subsidy to encourage the private ownership of housing. Under this law, instead of deducting allowable expenses from their taxable income, individuals could demand federal premium payments. These premium payments, however, were limited to a maximum of DM 400 annually (about $24) and graduated according to the family status of the taxpayer. Owners were required to raise funds through private sources for homebuilding, and the extent of use of the subsidy was rather small, although it served as a substitute for the interest-free loans of Section 7*c* during the period from the end of 1954 to October, 1956.[59]

The Second Housing Act, passed in June, 1956, provided a comprehensive plan for social dwelling construction over the six-year period between 1957 and 1962. Its main emphasis was upon the promotion of house ownership and the satisfaction of the housing requirements of the lower income groups of the population. The quantitative objectives of the Second Housing Act were quite similar to those of the First Act

[59] Wertheimer, "Tax Incentives . . . ," p. 109.

of 1950, and the Second Act provided for 1.8 million dwellings (the same number of social dwellings as the First Act) to be constructed over a six-year period.[60] Some of the qualitative aspects of the 1956 act were different. Increased emphasis was placed upon the construction of low-priced owner-occupied houses and upon quality of the dwelling units. Larger floor areas were specified and, relative to the First Act, more detailed prescriptions with respect to minimum standards were made.[61]

Modification of the Housing Act of 1956 became necessary to establish a new income ceiling for social housing tenants after experience in the first year of the Second Housing Act resulted in such a large number of applications for public building loans that they could not all be processed. An amendment to the Act, on September 27, 1957, provided that the dwellings constructed under the state-assisted social housing scheme would be allocated only to individuals whose annual income did not exceed DM 9,000.[62] To this basic amount were added payments for dependents and for individuals with war-inflicted disabilities.[63]

Postwar Housing Production

The effect of the Federal Republic's post-World War II housing policies has been dramatic, as shown by Table V–11. West Germany has shown the most rapid recovery in housing investment of any western European nation, and production of over ten dwellings per 1,000 of population from 1952 to 1958 has exceeded that for Europe as a whole and for either Sweden or the United Kingdom.[64]

This very rapid increase in housing production has resulted in sharp reductions in density of housing occupation since 1950 and improved the relationship between dwellings and population to a level approximating that in 1939, notwithstanding West Germany's high rate of

[60] See p. 124 ff. for a discussion of the First Housing Act of 1950.

[61] *Annual Report of the Federal Ministry of Housing for 1957*, pp. 4, 18; *ibid., 1958*, pp. 5–6.

[62] This DM 750 per month contrasts with the income ceiling of DM 600 per month as set up by the First Housing Act.

[63] *Annual Report of the Federal Ministry of Housing for 1957*, p. 19.

[64] United Nations Economic Commission for Europe, *European Housing Progress and Policies in 1955*, E/ECE/259 (Geneva, August, 1956), Table 1; *ibid., 1956*, E/ECE/292 (Geneva, July, 1957), Table 1; and *Quarterly Bulletin of Housing and Building Statistics for Europe*, VII, No. 2 (Geneva, 1959), Table 1. From 1954 to 1956 the average level of housebuilding for Europe as a whole was 6.1 per 1,000 population; for Sweden, 8 per 1,000; and for the United Kingdom, 6.4 per 1,000. Production in 1958 was 8.5 per 1,0000 in Sweden, 5.5 per 1,000 in the United Kingdom, and 9.5 per 1,000 in West Germany.

TABLE V–11

DWELLINGS COMPLETED BY SIZE, METHOD OF FINANCING, AND TYPE OF STRUCTURE, WEST GERMANY, 1952 TO 1958
(Excluding West Berlin and the Saar)

Year	Total number of dwellings completed (000's)	Total number of dwellings completed, per 1,000 of population[a]	Percentage of total dwellings completed—state-assisted social housing[b]	Percentage of total value of dwellings completed		Percentage of total dwelling construction in one-family houses[d]
				Financed from public sources[c]	Financed from 7c funds	
1952.....	443.1	9.1	62	43	n.a.	14
1953.....	518.4	10.6	55	35	4.4	19
1954.....	542.9	11.0	52	34	5.8	25
1955.....	541.7	10.8	50	28	4.9	27
1956.....	558.9	11.0	49	30	4.5	25
1957.....	528.9	10.5	41	28	2.7	29
1958.....	486.4	9.5	61	29	1.4	31

[a] Walter Fey, "Umfang und Merkmale des Wohnungsbaues in der Bundesrepublic Deutschland im Jahr 1958," in *Bundesbaublatt,* May, 1959, Übersicht 1.

[b] Table V–6, per cent of social housing in total of dwellings construction.

[c] Table V–8, per cent of public sources in total monetary volume of financing.

[d] Percentages of number of dwellings constructed calculated by the author from *Annual Report of the Federal Ministry of Housing for 1956* (Bad Godesberg: 1957); *ibid., 1957* (1958); *ibid., 1958* (1959). The following percentages of the number of single-family houses constructed were state-assisted social housing: 1953, 43.2; 1954, 42.7; 1955, 38.3; 1956, 38.8; 1957, 39.4.

population growth.[65] It was estimated that at the 1954 level of housing production West Germany was reducing the housing shortage by approximately 300,000 units annually, and that the shortage, estimated at 2.5 million dwellings at the end of 1956, would be eliminated by 1960.[66] Because of a continued influx of refugees from the east, however, it was estimated in 1958 that a basic shortage still existed and that 500,000 dwellings would need to be added annually in the years ahead in order to permit the elimination of 500,000 emergency dwellings and take care of expected population increases.[67]

Prior to 1953, West Germany's new housing production was con-

[65] *Quarterly Bulletin of Housing and Building Statistics for Europe,* V, No. 3 (February, 1958), Table 1. West Germany showed an average population increase of 10.7 persons per 1,000 inhabitants from 1952 to 1956, compared with an increase of 3.8 per 1,000 for the United Kingdom and 6.7 per 1,000 for Sweden.

[66] United Nations' Economic Commission for Europe, *The European Housing Situation,* p. 19. See also W. Fey, "Die Fortschritte in der Abdeckung des Wohnungs-Defizits," *Bundesbaublatt,* May, 1955.

[67] *Annual Report of the Federal Ministry of Housing for 1958,* p. 5.

centrated in small apartment units. By a series of steps, increasing emphasis has been placed upon the construction of larger units and of single-family homes for owner occupancy. This trend, shown in Table V–12, has been encouraged by more generous mortgage credit

TABLE V–12

SIZES OF NEW DWELLINGS AS A PERCENTAGE OF TOTAL DWELLINGS COMPLETED IN WEST GERMANY, 1952 TO 1959

Size of dwellings	1952	1953	1954	1955	1956	1957	1958	1959
One and two rooms.....	16.1	14.3	11.6	10.4	9.8	9.1	8.9	8.8
Three rooms...........	46.8	44.4	39.4	35.6	33.3	30.0	26.7	23.7
Four rooms............	28.0	31.8	37.5	40.0	41.1	42.6	42.7	43.8
Five rooms and over....	9.1	9.5	11.5	14.0	15.8	18.3	21.7	23.7
Habitable floor area per dwelling, square meters	55.2	55.7	58.0	60.5	61.7	63.5	66.0	68.0

Source: Bundesministerium für Wohnungsbau, *Jahresbericht 1959*, from *Deutschland im Wiederaufbau 1959.*

terms, tax concessions, and other subsidies granted by the government for these types of dwellings.

High rates of postwar housing production have also been effective in reducing the average age and improving the condition of the housing stock in the Federal Republic. Based upon the results of the census of 1956, the following breakdown of the housing stock by age has been estimated by the Ministry of Housing as of the end of 1958.

Building year	Number of dwellings (in millions)	Per cent
Before 1918...........	6.25	45
1918 to 1945..........	3.03	21
After 1945............	4.63	34

Because of the intensive new building activity between 1950 and 1958, the proportion of dwellings built before 1918 decreased from 65 to 45 per cent, while the proportion of those erected after 1945 increased from 5 to 34 per cent of the total. The average age of all existing dwellings declined from fifty-five years in 1950 to forty-five years in 1958.[68]

[68] Letter from Oberregierungsrat Dr. Klemt, Federal Ministry for Dwelling Construction, Bad Godesberg (Mehlem), March 3, 1960.

It is estimated by officials of the Federal Ministry of Housing that, as of the autumn of 1956, of the total of 12.7 million dwellings in the territory of the Federal Republic 160,000 were of limited habitability (136,000 of these were so-called temporary homes of 30 or more square meters, and 24,000 were in danger of falling down). In addition, about 484,000 emergency dwellings were classed as ripe for demolition.[69]

A special "housebuilding industry," as it exists in the United States, has not developed in West Germany. Private investors (this includes private households and other individual investors) have accounted for approximately 60 per cent of the total number of dwellings licensed in West Germany since 1954. Nonprofit housing societies have initiated a large but declining share of dwelling construction since 1953. Table V–13 illustrates the gradual expansion in private building since 1953,

TABLE V–13

PERCENTAGE DISTRIBUTION OF DWELLINGS LICENSED IN WEST GERMANY BY TYPE OF CONSTRUCTOR, 1953 TO 1958

Type of constructor	Percentage of total dwellings licensed					
	1953	1954	1955	1956	1957	1958
Nonprofit housing enterprises and rural coöperatives	35.6	30.2	29.0	28.4	30.4	30.5
Public authorities	4.3	3.4	2.8	2.7	2.5	2.6
Independent housing contractors	4.2	4.2	4.1	3.8	3.6	4.1
Business and industrial enterprises (company housing investment)	2.5	2.6	4.2	4.5	3.2	3.9
Private individual builders	53.4	59.6	59.9	60.6	60.3	58.9

Source: Walter Fey, "Umfang und Merkmale des Wohnungsbaues in der Bundesrepublic Deutschland im Jahr 1958," *Bundesbaublatt*, May, 1959, Übersicht 7.

which has been paralleled by a decline in both nonprofit and public housing. The latter accounts for the smallest proportion of total production.

Table V–11 shows that the role of the federal government in housing was gradually reduced from 1952 to 1957. This was reflected in a smaller proportion of total production receiving special aid from the state or local governments as "social housing," as well as by the gradual reduction of government financing of housing in West Germany. It is also significant to note that special Section 7*c* income tax subsidies accounted for a reduced share of total funds used in financing housing in 1957 and 1958. As will be noted in further detail in the final chapter,

[69] *Ibid.*

the proportion of government expenditures devoted to housing was also gradually reduced from approximately 5.5 per cent in 1955 and 1956 to approximately 4 per cent in 1957. During this period the federal government was successful in promoting an increasing emphasis upon single-family house construction, which rose from 14 per cent of total production in 1952 to 31 per cent in 1958.

Review and Evaluation

West Germany had the most severe housing shortage of any western European nation at the end of World War II. Primary reliance was placed upon the encouragement of private investment in housing through the granting of low-interest-rate loans and tax incentives. The interest rate on public second mortgage loans for "social housing" was fixed at one half of one per cent; income tax savings encouraged some lenders to make loans at no interest cost.

The stimulation of private savings for housing by the Federal Republic served a dual purpose, since it restricted consumption and aided in the control of inflation. As will be noted in more detail in the final chapter, West Germany was more successful than either Sweden, the United States, or the United Kingdom in controlling inflationary pressures during the postwar years.

High levels of postwar construction have effected substantial improvements in the quality and age structure of the housing inventory in West Germany. Continued high rates of construction are making it possible to gradually bring about the removal of emergency and other substandard housing accommodations.

Although rent controls have been in effect throughout the postwar period in West Germany, attempts have been made to bring rents gradually into line with building costs.

It is difficult to appraise the cost of West Germany's housing subsidy program, owing to the nature of the subsidies employed. It was noted earlier that part of the private funds which have been invested in housing in Germany would have been paid as tax to the government if it were not for the tax exemption regulations in effect. However, it cannot be reasoned from this fact that these foregone taxes represented a net cost to the government, since the rise in employment and incomes resulting from the expanded housing investment most certainly added to government revenues. (This would not be true if it could be argued that West Germany would have achieved full employment without the additional housing investment.) It is important to recognize that West Germany has consistently maintained a balanced budget and accumulated a surplus while at the same time encouraging housing and other capital investment by tax subsidies.[70]

Direct public lending at nominal interest costs exceeded DM 25 billion from 1950 to 1958. Wertheimer estimates that the federal government and the *Länder* lost DM 1.5 billion in potential tax revenues, and that local authorities lost DM 3.7 billion as a result of temporary exemptions from real estate taxes from 1948 to 1957.[71] In addition, tax deferrals by faster write-off and by the granting of mortgage loans by business firms were estimated to total DM 9 billion through 1957.

In addition to these costs, direct subsidies for homebuilding, estimated at DM 400 million, and other subsidies through sale of land for housing must also be recognized.

Although the costs to the government of the direct lending program are substantial, it is important to note that the share of public lending has declined from almost 50 per cent of total mortgage lending in 1951 to approximately 25 per cent in 1959. The stimulation of privately owned single-family homes has proven effective and accounted for almost a third of annual production in 1957 and 1958.

West Germany's postwar housing policies have been a reflection of the basic economic choices made by the new government after the currency reform and the granting of substantial autonomy in 1948. In contrast to the economic policies followed by most western European countries, West Germany chose to rely upon the stimulation of private investment instead of upon public investment.[72] The record in housing production has been impressive. It seems more impressive when it is recognized that high levels of production have been achieved without heavy government outlays or long-term commitments for housing subsidies.

It can be argued that Germany's success in housing has to some extent been bought at a price which is hard to estimate. In contrast to the clear-cut budget allocations and subsidies in the United Kingdom and in Sweden, German housing was financed to an important degree by funds provided through granting generous tax incentives to the business sector. The true cost of this capital to society cannot be exactly estimated, is not directly or immediately felt by anybody, and is largely beyond the grasp of the voter and the politician. Only the future can tell the extent to which the great improvement in terms of

---

[70] David McCord Wright, *Postwar West German and United Kingdom Recovery* (Washington: American Enterprise Association, Inc., 1957), p. 3.

[71] Wertheimer, "The Miracle of German Housing . . . ," *Land Econ.*, p. 345, n. 24.

[72] Wright, *op. cit.*, p. 7.

human welfare, represented by the huge addition to Germany's housing stock, may have been offset in welfare terms by the resultant financial strengthening of the large German industrialists and capitalists. Conversely, one could argue that the tax subsidies for housing have contributed not only to the solution of Germany's acute housing problem, but also to a needed financial strengthening in the corporate sector.

VI The United States

As in other countries, the federal government was slow to enact housing legislation in the United States. Regulation of housing in the United States before World War I was largely confined to municipal or state tenement house codes. The New York Tenement House Law, enacted in 1867, was the prototype for municipal restrictive legislation in the field of housing. Following the amendment of the New York law in 1901, a number of cities and a few states enacted similar laws establishing minimum standards of light, air, sanitation, and safety in city housing. A "model housing law," setting forth recommended minimum standards, was drafted by the National Housing Association in 1914 and served as the basis for state and municipal housing laws which were enacted in Michigan, Illinois, Pennsylvania, Massachusetts, Iowa, California, Kentucky, and other states during the years immediately preceding World War I.[1]

The sharp decline in residential construction which began in 1917 resulted in critical housing shortages in many war-affected communities. As a result, rent control legislation was enacted in Connecticut, Maine, Massachusetts, New Jersey, Virginia, and Nevada early in World War I, and in other states from 1918 to 1921. Municipal rent committees were organized in many cities during World War I, some relying upon city ordinances and others relying upon publicity to control rent increases.

The first action by the Congress of the United States in the housing field was the appropriation of $20,000 to finance a survey of slums in large cities in 1892. Basing its findings upon a 1916 survey of the existing housing supply in two hundred cities, the Council of National Defense reported that the provision of housing for workers in the new wartime industries would prove too great a task for private enterprise.

[1] Edith Elmer Wood, *Recent Trends in American Housing* (New York: Macmillan, 1931), pp. 114–116.

It recommended, therefore, that the federal government should take steps to provide new permanent housing of good quality for workers in war industries. The National Housing Association forwarded a similar recommendation to President Wilson in November, 1917.

Housing Policy During World War I

Direct intervention by the federal government in the housing field was initiated in 1918, when Congress authorized the United States Shipping Board and the Emergency Fleet Corporation to provide housing for employees in the shipyards. Government loans were advanced to real estate companies organized by the shipbuilding companies; as a result, a total of approximately 10,000 houses and apartments, 19 dormitories, and 8 hotels were constructed in twenty-four localities.[2] The Bureau of Industrial Housing and Transportation was established in the Department of Labor in 1918, and through the newly organized United States Housing Corporation, built and managed housing projects in twenty-five communities; these comprised over 5,000 single-family dwelling units, in addition to apartments, dormitories, and hotels. The United States Housing Corporation also considered and handled rent grievances during World War I. Following the war, with the exception of some dwelling units transferred to other government agencies, all government housing was sold to private owners.

Housing Policy During the 1920's

Following World War I, the initiative in government housing legislation passed from the federal government back to the individual states. In many states, postwar housing legislation provided for a continuation of emergency rent controls until shortages were eliminated, while a few states enacted laws providing for state loans for housing purposes or for tax exemption on new residential construction.

Legislation in New York State in 1920 extended rent controls and permitted local governmental units to exempt from local property taxation all new dwellings begun prior to April 1, 1923. New York, the only city which took advantage of the tax exemption provisions of the law, experienced between 1922 and 1924 a rapid increase in apartment-house construction which was attributed largely to the tax exemption provisions.[3] Subsequently, the New York State Housing Law of 1926

---

[2] Jack Levin, *Your Congress and American Housing—The Actions of Congress on Housing from 1892 to 1951*, U.S. 82d Cong., 2d sess, H. Doc. 532 (1952), p. 2.

[3] Wood, *op. cit.*, pp. 101–102.

provided for exemption from state and municipal taxes of limited-dividend housing corporations. These corporations were required by the legislation to limit themselves to a return of 6 per cent and to accept limited rents, and in turn were granted certain rights of condemnation and tax exemption.[4] Participation under the New York State program was limited to six corporations—three coöperatives, two private commercial enterprises, and one sponsored by the Brooklyn Chamber of Commerce. Nine projects were completed under the program, furnishing housing for approximately 1,700 families and representing an investment of $9,000,000.[5]

In 1921 California initiated a program which authorized twenty-year low-interest-rate loans for the purchase of farms or homes by veterans. The program has since been extended to include veterans of World War II and the Korean war. Self-liquidating loans financed by state bond issues are granted to eligible veterans.[6] Wisconsin passed legislation during the 1920's permitting municipalities to lend funds to housing corporations, and the North Dakota legislature authorized direct home-building by the state. Between 1915 and 1931, central mortgage banks of various types were established in New York, California, Florida, Massachusetts, and Ohio.

Groping for a Long-Range Federal Housing Policy

A select committee of the United States Senate, appointed in 1920 "to inquire into the general building situation and to report to the Senate before December 1, 1920, such measures as may be deemed necessary to stimulate and foster the development of construction work in all its forms," recommended that the solution of the housing shortage must come through private business initiative and rejected the idea of direct federal government interference in housing.[7] As a result of the committee's recommendations, however, the Division of Building and Housing was established in the Department of Commerce. Other recommendations of the committee, designed to improve the availability of mortgage funds, undoubtedly had an influence upon later legislation.

As the emergency features of the federal government's housing policy receded in importance, attention was increasingly drawn to the need

[4] *Ibid.*, pp. 261–263.

[5] *Ibid.*, p. 264.

[6] State of California, Division of Real Estate, *Reference Book* (Sacramento, 1959), p. 247.

[7] *Reconstruction and Production*, U.S. 66th Cong., 3d sess., S. Rpt. 829 (Washington, March 2, 1921).

for a long-term federal housing policy. Many of the key features of federal housing policy of the 1930's originated in the recommendations of the "President's Conference on Home Building and Home Ownership," held in December, 1931. President Hoover emphasized one of the major recommendations of this conference in his address at the opening meeting:

> I am confident that the sentiment for home ownership is so embedded in the American heart that millions of people who dwell in tenements, apartments, and rented rows of solid brick have the aspiration for wider opportunity in ownership of their own homes.

The thirty-odd fact-finding and correlating committees participating in this conference formulated recommendations on virtually every aspect of the housing problem. Among the key recommendations which were influential upon federal housing policy were the following:

Replacement of the short-term by the long-term amortized mortgage

Provision of more certain and regular flow of long-term housing credit at lower interest costs

Supplementation of private enterprise with governmental aid in solving the housing problems of low-income families in blighted areas

Cost reduction in housebuilding through encouraging large-scale operations.

Federal Housing Programs in the Great Depression

Table VI–1 shows how the vast private-enterprise building boom of the 1920's collapsed in 1929 and 1930, bringing residential building to a virtual standstill in 1933 and 1934. The Great Depression marked the entry of the federal government into the housing picture as a full-fledged participant, since the provision and improvement of housing soon became recognized as ideal means for combating unemployment.

The rising tide of foreclosures on farms and urban properties following the stock market crash in 1929–30 brought about a gradual weakening of mortgage lending institutions and soon resulted in a situation with which existing federal agencies could not cope.

The creation of the Federal Land Bank System in 1916 had already established as a principle the direct use of federal funds and the extension of Treasury aid to privately owned mortgage lending institutions. Bills had been introduced in Congress during the 1920's and 1930's providing for the establishment of a central mortgage bank. The Federal Home Loan Bank System was finally created in 1932, based upon the recommendations of the Conference on Home Building and Home Ownership called by President Hoover in the previous year. The Home Owners' Loan Corporation, the Federal Farm Mortgage

TABLE VI-1

Total Private and Public Permanent Nonfarm Dwelling Units Started in the United States, 1900 to 1959
(In thousands)

Year	Total private and public permanent nonfarm dwelling units started	Privately owned permanent nonfarm dwelling units started				Publicly owned permanent nonfarm dwelling units started				Total number of starts under FHA inspection
		Total	One-family	Two-family	Multi-family	Total	One-family	Two-family	Multi-family	
1900	189	189	123	31	35	–	–	–	–	–
1901	275	275	177	32	66	–	–	–	–	–
1902	240	240	171	32	37	–	–	–	–	–
1903	253	253	174	30	48	–	–	–	–	–
1904	315	315	207	45	63	–	–	–	–	–
1905	507	507	336	64	107	–	–	–	–	–
1906	487	487	316	69	103	–	–	–	–	–
1907	432	432	291	59	82	–	–	–	–	–
1908	416	416	286	65	65	–	–	–	–	–
1909	492	492	328	73	91	–	–	–	–	–
1910	387	387	251	58	79	–	–	–	–	–
1911	395	395	249	62	84	–	–	–	–	–
1912	426	426	259	71	97	–	–	–	–	–
1913	421	421	263	72	85	–	–	–	–	–
1914	421	421	263	72	87	–	–	–	–	–
1915	433	433	262	73	97	–	–	–	–	–
1916	437	437	267	69	101	–	–	–	–	–
1917	240	240	166	32	43	–	–	–	–	–
1918	118	118	91	13	15	–	–	–	–	–
1919	315	315	239	36	40	–	–	–	–	–
1920	247	247	202	24	21	–	–	–	–	–
1921	449	449	316	70	63	–	–	–	–	–
1922	716	716	437	146	133	–	–	–	–	–
1923	871	871	513	175	183	–	–	–	–	–
1924	893	893	534	173	186	–	–	–	–	–
1925	937	937	572	157	208	–	–	–	–	–
1926	849	849	491	117	241	–	–	–	–	–
1927	810	810	454	99	257	–	–	–	–	–
1928	753	753	436	78	239	–	–	–	–	–
1929	509	509	316	51	142	–	–	–	–	–
1930	330	330	227	29	74	–	–	–	–	–
1931	254	254	187	22	45	–	–	–	–	–
1932	134	134	118	7	9	–	–	–	–	–
1933	93	93	76	5	12	–	–	–	–	–
1934	126	126	109	5	12	–	–	–	–	–
1935	221	216	182	8	26	5	1	0	4	14
1936	319	304	239	13	52	15	5	1	9	49
1937	336	332	266	15	51	4	1	1	2	60
1938	406	399	317	18	65	7	1	0	6	119
1939	515	459	373	20	66	56	26	9	21	158
1940	603	530	448	26	56	73	38	12	23	180
1941	706	620	533	29	58	86	70	6	10	220
1942	356	301	252	18	31	55	40	3	12	166
1943	191	184	136	18	30	7	7	0	0	146
1944	142	139	115	11	13	3	3	0	0	93
1945	209	208	185	9	15	1	1	0	0	41
1946	671	662	590	24	48	9	0	0	9	69
1947	849	846	740	34	72	3	0	0	3	229
1948	932	914	763	46	104	18	3	1	14	294
1949	1,025	989	792	35	162	36	2	1	33	364
1950	1,396	1,352	1,151	42	159	44	3	3	38	487
1951	1,091	1,020	892	40	88	71	8	0	63	264
1952	1,127	1,069	939	46	84	58	3	0	55	280
1953	1,104	1,068	932	42	94	36	6	0	30	252
1954	1,220	1,202	1,078	34	90	18	1	0	17	276
1955	1,329	1,310	1,190	33	87	19	4	0	15	277
1956	1,118	1,094	981	31	82	24[a]	9	0	15	189
1957	1,042	993	840	33	120	49[a]	32	0	17	168
1958	1,209	1,142	933	39	170	68[a]	43	0	25	295
1959	1,379	1,343	1,079	49	215	36[a]	16	3	17	332

Sources: 1900–1938: U.S. Housing and Home Finance Agency, *Eleventh Annual Report, 1957* (Washington, 1958), Tables A-1, A-3, and A-5. 1939–1957: U.S. Housing and Home Finance Agency, *Housing Statistics, Historical Supplement* (Washington, December, 1958), pp. 7–10. 1958, 1959: *Ibid.*, June, 1960, pp. 1–30.

Note: Data for publicly owned starts are available beginning with 1935. Although 55,998 units were completed in 1918 and 1919, the dates for supporting starts are not available.

[a] Armed services housing starts included as follows: 1956—3,900; 1957—23,600; 1958—34,700; 1959—14,300.

Corporation, and the RFC (Reconstruction Finance Corporation) Mortgage Company were created during 1933 and 1934 to arrest the foreclosure trend and bolster weakened mortgage lending institutions.

The National Housing Act of 1934 established the Federal Housing Administration, designed to stimulate new mortgage lending by insuring private lenders against loss on new mortgage loans, and the Federal Savings and Loan Insurance Corporation, modeled after the Federal Deposit Insurance Corporation.

The purpose of the National Housing Act was "to improve nationwide housing standards, provide employment and stimulate industry; to improve conditions with respect to home mortgage financing, to prevent speculative excesses in new mortgages investment, and to eliminate the necessity for costly second mortgage financing by creating a system of mutual mortgage insurance." [8] Other objectives of this Act were the "realization of a greater degree of stability in residential construction" and the "promotion of a freer flow of mortgage funds into and out of securities based on residential properties." [9]

The Farm Security Administration, established in the Department of Agriculture in 1936, provided for the granting of forty-year loans at 3.5 per cent interest for tenant purchase of farms. The program of its predecessor, the Resettlement Administration, which had undertaken the development of garden-city communities for urban workers, was soon abandoned by the Farm Security Administration.

Direct federal aid for residential construction was provided in the Emergency Relief and Construction Act of 1932, which empowered the RFC to make loans to state-regulated limited-dividend corporations. Although Knickerbocker Village in New York was the only project actually authorized within the first year, several states passed legislation providing for participation in the program.

The National Recovery Act of 1933 provided for the "construction, reconstruction, alteration or repair under public regulation or control of low-rent housing and slum clearance projects" and transferred the housing powers of the RFC to the new Public Works Administration.

The PWA attempted to operate through granting twenty-five to thirty-five-year loans up to 85 per cent of value at 4 per cent interest to limited-dividend corporations. When only seven projects were under way at the end of a year's time, the PWA abandoned this scheme of operation in favor of a plan under which the federal government

---

[8] Lawrence N. Bloomberg, "The Role of the Federal Government in Urban Housing," *American Economic Review,* XLI, No. 2 (May, 1951), 591.

[9] William H. Husband and Frank Ray Anderson, *Real Estate Analysis* (Chicago: Richard D. Irwin, Inc., 1948), p. 410.

acquired land and retained title to the housing. From the date of the start of this policy (February, 1934) to November, 1937, when the Housing Division of the PWA was succeeded by the United States Housing Authority, 49 developments, comprising 21,441 dwelling units and costing $129.5 million, were initiated by the PWA. During this period the improvement of housing was an objective secondary to the use of housebuilding as a cure for the depresson. As a result, long-term plans were constantly in conflict with short-run goals for stimulation of employment. Critics of the program pointed to the relatively high unit costs for PWA housing and attributed these to a "mania for durability."

Following the passage of the United States Housing Act in 1937, the functions of the Housing Division of PWA were transferred to the United States Housing Authority. According to the provisions of this legislation, construction, ownership, and operation of public housing properties were to be under the jurisdiction of local housing authorities. The USHA was empowered to make loans to these authorities representing 90 per cent of the cost and to pay annual subsidies which were usually sufficient to meet the carrying charges on the loans. Local governments were required to contribute annual amounts equal to 20 per cent of federal contributions, which were usually in the form of property tax abatement. Because obligations of local housing authorities were exempt from federal income taxation, local housing authorities were able to offer their own obligations, secured by a virtual federal guaranty of principal and interest, at rates lower than those at which the federal government could borrow.[10]

The present structure of federal agencies and policies in the housing field was virtually complete by 1937. World War II and its postwar period were to witness a broadening of the federal government's powers and an extension of its activities within this basic framework established during the depression years. The federal housing policy which had evolved since the 1930's has been based upon the following principles.

Basic recognition of housing as a problem of federal government concern

Acceptance of the ideal of individual homeownership as a major goal of federal housing policy

Emphasis upon mortgage finance terms and mortgage institutions as principal avenues to the wide achievement of homeownership

Acceptance of slum clearance as a coöperative venture by federal and local governments

[10] Robert Moore Fisher, *Twenty Years of Public Housing* (New York: Harper, 1959), pp. 25–27.

Provision of public housing for low-income groups as an aid in clearance of slums and as a useful employment stimulus

Housing Policies and Programs in World War II

Observers have pointed out that by 1940 improved economic conditions had dulled the demand for further federal intervention in the housing field and that a trend toward withdrawal of government influence in real estate finance was evident. The Federal Land Bank System and the Federal Home Loan Bank System were achieving status within the framework of private financial enterprise. The FHA was operating without further direct federal appropriations and was looked upon as an instrumentality of government designed to serve the private mortgage lenders. The Home Owners' Loan Corporation and the Federal Farm Mortgage Corporation were in the process of liquidation, while the ambitious housing programs of the PWA and the Resettlement Administration during the mid-depression years were looked upon as unnecessary and visionary. Meanwhile, private interests in the mortgage finance, building, and real estate fields had organized in opposition to the threat of public housing and Congress had refused requests for additional authorizations for the United States Housing Authority to expand its program.

War preparations in 1941 and 1942 caused a rapid reversal in these trends. On January 11, 1941, the President of the United States created by executive order the Division of Defense Housing Coordination, with the responsibility for preventing any letdown in the national defense program resulting from any serious lack of housing.

Three major developments in national housing policy were initiated during World War II:

Federal housing agencies were consolidated under the National Housing Agency.

The federal government embarked on a large-scale program of construction of war housing.

National rent controls were enacted, which were to be continued for several years after the end of hostilities.

In response to widespread criticism of the confusion and delays caused by the many overlapping agencies engaged in the production of war housing and dissatisfaction with the policies of the Defense Housing Coordinator, on February 24, 1942, the President created the National Housing Agency, which consolidated the functions of sixteen federal housing agencies into one, abolishing the Division of Defense Housing Coordination. The organization of the National Housing Agency is shown in Chart VI–1.

CHART VI-1

Organization of the National Housing Agency, 1942 to 1947

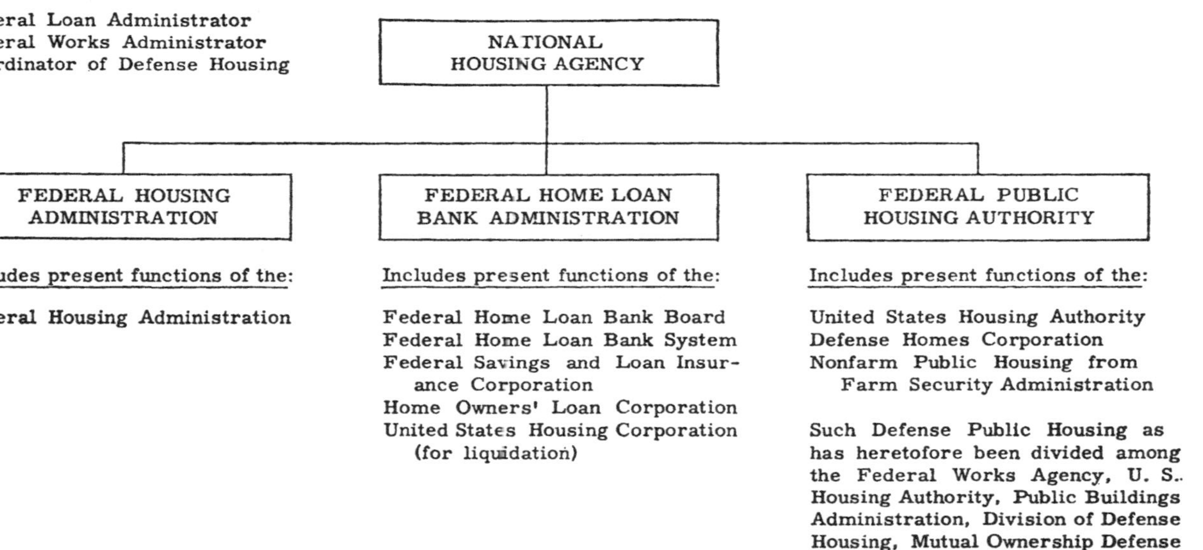

Source: Paul F. Wendt, *The Role of the Federal Government in Housing* (Washington: American Enterprise Association, 1956), p. 6.

The National Housing Agency administered its wartime program through regional offices which investigated local housing needs, authorized additional war housing as required, and served as homes registration centers for the purpose of helping war workers find homes in existing dwellings.

War Housing

Congress, through the Lanham Act and in other ways, had made a total of $440 million available for defense housing before the entry of the United States into the war. These funds were to be expended through a number of government agencies, including the Public Building Administration (PBA), the United States Housing Authority (USHA), the Farm Security Administration (FSA), and the Tennessee Valley Authority (TVA). During the weeks immediately preceding the attack on Pearl Harbor, legislation was pending in Congress to provide an additional $300 million for Lanham Act defense housing.

From 1940 to 1947 approximately one million units of war, emergency, and defense housing were completed under the Lanham Act and other legislation.[11]

The United States Housing Authority (which became known as the Federal Public Housing Authority by executive order on February 24, 1942, and later became the Public Housing Administration) was given jurisdiction over all public war housing except that built by the War or Navy departments on military posts. Congress amended the Lanham Act in July, 1943, to require that all temporary war housing should be disposed of within two years after the President should declare that the war "emergency" was at an end. Although the original intention of Congress was to demolish temporary war housing, the Public Housing Administration was later authorized by law to dispose of emergency war housing through demolition or sale to educational institutions and other nonprofit organizations, authorities, or individuals, with veteran occupants given first preference. Approximately one third of the Lanham Act war housing units were classified as "permanent," and many of these units were offered for sale to local authorities, veterans' coöperative organizations, or other nonprofit institutions, or put up for sale to private investors on a competitive bid basis. By December 31, 1959, all but 5,376 of the total of one million war, emergency, and defense hous-

[11] This included 625,505 units authorized by the Lanham Act (Public Law 849, 76th Congress, approved October, 1940), 266,926 units of Veterans re-use housing, and 83,007 units under related statutes.

ing units had been disposed of by sale, demolition, or other means prescribed by law.[12]

Rent Control

Federal rent control was introduced in the United States by the Emergency Price Control Act of 1942, which authorized the federal administrator to establish maximum rents for housing accommodations in defense rental areas. In 1942 rents were fixed at the levels of April 1, 1941, in cities with severe housing shortages; by 1943 rental housing in all the larger cities and many smaller towns was controlled at rent levels prevailing in 1942 or 1943.

By 1946 about 16 million dwelling units were controlled, which compared with a total of 16.2 million renter-occupied dwelling units in 1940. Until 1947 increases in legal rents were limited to cases where landlords could prove financial hardship or loss, or where services or facilities were improved. Federal legislation in 1947 and 1948 extended rent controls, and the Housing and Rent Acts of 1949 and 1950 gave increasing responsibility for maintenance or termination of rent controls to state and local governmental units. As a result, seven states and many cities had completely removed controls by the end of 1950. Federal rent control was terminated June 30, 1951. Nine states enacted stand-by legislation providing for state control of rents on the termination of federal rent controls—New York City, a few other cities in New York State, and Hawaii have continued to control rents up to the present date.[13]

Table VI–2 summarizes the changes in the U.S. Bureau of Labor Statistics consumer price and rent indexes from 1913 through 1958. Differences in the trend in rents relative to other prices during World Wars I and II are evident. The rent index rose less than 5 per cent from 1940 to 1946, while the consumer price index increased by approximately 40 per cent. Rents increased more rapidly after the war, and by 1950 the rent index had risen to 131 per cent of the 1935–39 average. Several factors lead to the conclusion that the rent index is an inadequate measure of the actual rise in rents during the period from 1940 to 1950. *First,* the rent index does not allow for the shifting of repair costs to tenants or for the loss of rent concessions frequently granted

[12] U.S. Housing and Home Finance Agency, *Thirteenth Annual Report, 1959* (Washington, 1960), p. 213.

[13] State of New York, Temporary State Housing Rent Commission, *Report on Rent Control in New York State, 1955* (New York, 1956), pp. 10–13.

TABLE VI-2

COMPARISON OF U.S. BUREAU OF LABOR STATISTICS CONSUMER PRICE INDEX AND RENT INDEX, 1913 TO 1958
(1947–49 = 100)

Year	Consumer Price Index	Rent Index	Total Consumer Housing Expenditures Index[a]
1913	42.3	76.6	—
1918	64.3	78.8	—
1920	85.7	100.2	—
1925	75.0	126.4	—
1930	71.4	114.2	—
1935	58.7	78.2	—
1940	59.9	86.9	—
1941	62.9	88.4	—
1942	69.7	90.4	—
1943	74.0	90.3	—
1944	75.2	90.6	—
1945	76.9	90.9	—
1946	83.4	91.4	—
1947	95.5	94.4	95.0
1948	102.8	100.7	101.7
1949	101.8	105.0	103.3
1950	102.8	108.8	106.1
1951	111.0	113.1	112.4
1952	113.5	117.9	114.6
1953	114.4	124.1	117.7
1954	114.8	128.5	119.1
1955	114.5	130.3	120.0
1956	116.2	132.7	121.7
1957	120.2	135.2	125.6
1958	123.4	137.7	127.7

Sources: 1913–1957: U.S. Bureau of the Census, *Statistical Abstract of the United States: 1958* (79th ed.; Washington, 1958), Table 419, p. 332. 1958: *Economic Report of the President Transmitted to the Congress January 20, 1959* (Washington, 1959), Table D–38, p. 184.

[a] Includes "other shelter" (home purchase and other home-owner costs—rent, gas and electricity, solid fuels and fuel oil, house furnishings, and household operations).

in 1940. *Second,* the index does not allow for the existence of a black market or for additional costs to renters in the forms of "extras" during the period of war housing shortages.[14] *Third,* the rent index does not allow for the effect upon average rents of adding new units at higher

[14] Sherman J. Maisel, "Have We Underestimated Increases in Rents and Shelter Expenditures?" *Journal of Political Economy,* LVII, No. 2 (April, 1949), 106–117. During the war years the author experienced the influence of some of the factors mentioned in various communities. It was common practice to pay a "reward" for finding a rental unit, to agree to buy "furnishings" from the landlord as a premium for occupancy, or to agree to make certain repairs or alterations.

rents. *Fourth,* the index is designed primarily to measure the change in rents for moderate-income families and hence does not reflect changes in all segments of the market. *Fifth,* the thirty-four large cities used by the Bureau of Labor Statistics for their sample have not had rent movements typical of the country as a whole. The shortcomings of the index are of lesser consequence for the postwar years.

In retrospect, it can be concluded that federal rent controls in the United States during World War II had the following effects upon the housing market:[15]

Restricted the rise in residential rents for existing properties, particularly for established prewar tenants in the larger cities, relative to the rise in other consumer prices

Reduced the proportion of housing expenditures to total consumption expenditures for those segments of the population who were fortunate enough to be protected by rent control

Encouraged the transfer of rental properties to the status of owner-occupied units

Tended to reduce maintenance expenditures by landlords to a bare minimum and thus to reduce the quality of rental housing between 1940 and 1947

Encouraged evasion of rent controls by many landlords through the "black market" or other unlawful means

Encouraged small family units and single persons to occupy more space than they would have occupied in the absence of controlled rents

Discouraged the construction of private rental units

Resulted in substantial inequities among tenants and landlords because of administrative procedures

Although general agreement exists concerning most of these conclusions, it should be pointed out that Grebler and others have maintained that rent controls had no direct and observable influence upon the construction of private rental units. It is the author's view, however, that rent controls will inevitably deter private investment in rental property, unless offsetting incentives to such investment are offered.

TRENDS IN U.S. HOUSING PRODUCTION AND CHARACTERISTICS

Long-term trends in the number of new permanent nonfarm dwellings constructed in the United States from 1900 to 1958 are shown in Table

[15] *Ibid.;* Leo Grebler, "Implications of Rent Control Experience in the United States," *International Labour Review,* LXV, No. 4 (April, 1952), 1–24; Paul F. Wendt, "Effects of Federal Rent Control," *Appraisal Journal,* XVIII (January, 1950), 17–28; State of New York, Temporary State Housing Rent Commission, *People, Housing and Rent Control in Buffalo* (New York, April, 1956).

VI–1. The data underestimate the actual volume of housing construction in the United States for three major reasons:

They exclude farm dwelling construction.
The data are based upon building permits issued, and comparisons with census data indicate that the permit series understate actual volume of construction.[16]
They exclude federal and other temporary war housing production.

Notwithstanding these limitations of the data, they provide a fair indication of long-term changes in volume of production. The sharp declines in residential building experienced during World War I, the Great Depression, and World War II are evident. The low levels of new housing production during these periods were followed by sustained periods of relatively high volume of production. Influence of the federal war housing programs is not reflected in Table VI–1 because the dwellings constructed in these programs during the war years were almost entirely classed as "temporary housing."

Before the Great Depression of the 1930's, approximately two thirds of newly constructed dwelling units were one-family houses, as shown by Table VI–1. Multi-family housing accounted for higher proportions of total dwelling construction during the apartment house building boom of the 1920's. Since the depression it can be noted that over 85 per cent of new residential construction has been in one-family units. Partial explanation of the rise in single-family home construction since the 1930's is found in government loan guaranty and insurance policies, which through the Federal Housing Administration and other programs have tended to encourage owner occupancy. The encouragement of suburban living by increased use of the automobile has represented an underlying factor influencing this trend. The growing importance of

[16] The Bureau of the Census presented revised estimates of housing starts in the United States for the year 1959 and for the first four months of 1960. U.S. Bureau of the Census, *Construction Reports—Housing Starts,* C20–11 (supplement), May, 1960. The revised annual total for the year 1959 was 1,553,100 units, as compared with the old (nonfarm) series total of 1,378,500. The most important reason for the difference was more nearly complete coverage, although the definition of a dwelling unit was also revised to include farm construction. According to the Bureau of the Census, the available evidence indicates that the old Bureau of Labor Statistics series for housing starts is too low, extending back one or more decades, and the upward revision for years prior to 1959 may be greater than 13 per cent. In the above report attention is called to the fact that the 1956 National Housing Inventory indicated that "the number of nonfarm dwelling units (excluding trailers on wheels) built between 1950 and 1956 was some 24 percent higher than the number shown by the the old monthly series now being replaced." The Bureau of the Census reported that its new estimates for 1959 and 1960 may still be too low because of sampling error or the difficulty of finding all new construction. *Ibid.,* pp. 3–4.

government loan insurance programs is shown by the relatively high and increasing proportion of government-insured and government-guaranteed loans in recent decades.

Statistics concerning the changing characteristics of the housing stock of the United States over time are incomplete. The 1940 census of housing was the first census in which detailed information concerning the characteristics of American housing was gathered. Estimates of the numbers of dwelling units for previous years were secured in the censuses of population and agriculture. Problems of comparability also arise, because the concepts and definitions used and the information collected in the 1950 housing census differed from those of the 1940 census of housing.[17] Although the coverage was less complete, the 1956 National Housing Inventory which was based upon a sample survey of 59,600 dwellings, employed concepts and definitions which were almost identical with the 1950 census.[18]

Table VI–3 shows the growth in the number of dwellings in the United States from 1890 through 1956, classified according to nonfarm and farm dwellings by tenure of occupancy. The division of the housing stock into farm and nonfarm classifications represents a difficult statistical problem. Scholars have concluded that the number of nonfarm dwellings in the United States probably exceeded the estimates in Table VI–3 from 1930 on.[19]

The proportion of owner-occupied homes has risen gradually in the United States since 1890, and by the end of World War II it exceeded 50 per cent. The effect of the Great Depression with its high levels of foreclosures is noted in the rise in the proportion of rental occupancy for the year 1940, as compared with 1930. Following the depression, however, the trend toward owner occupancy was resumed. The sharp decline in the proportion of nonfarm rental housing from 1940 to 1947 is attributable in large measure to federal rent controls. Since the selling prices of existing houses were not controlled, owners of rental property were able to evade rent controls to some degree by

---

[17] U.S. Bureau of the Census, *Census of Housing: 1950,* I, *General Characteristics,* Part I, "United States Summary" (Washington, 1953), xii.

[18] U.S. Bureau of the Census, *1956 National Housing Inventory,* I, *Components of Change, 1950 to 1956,* Part I, "United States and Regions," and III, *Characteristics of the 1956 Inventory,* Part I, "United States and Regions" (Washington; 1958, 1959).

[19] Leo Grebler, David M. Blank, and Louis Winnick, *Capital Formation in Residential Real Estate—Trends and Prospects* (Princeton, N.J.: Princeton University Press, 1956), p. 65. See also Sherman J. Maisel, "Importance of Net Replacements in Housebuilding Demand," in *Study of Mortgage Credit,* U.S. Senate Committee on Banking and Currency, Subcommittee on Housing, 85th Cong., 2d sess. (Washington, 1958), p. 34.

TABLE VI–3

TENURE OF HOMES, NONFARM AND FARM, UNITED STATES, 1890 TO 1956

Year	Occupied dwelling units or households	Per cent of total dwellings vacant[a]	Population per occupied dwelling unit	Owner-occupied		Rented	
				Number	Per cent	Number	Per cent
Total:							
1956......	49,873,923	5.8	3.0	30,120,509	60.4	19,753,414	39.6
1950......	42,826,281	3.3	3.5	23,559,966	55.0	19,267,315	45.0
1947......	39,016,000	2.5	3.6	21,347,000	54.7	17,669,000	45.3
1940......	34,854,532	3.3	3.8	15,195,763	43.6	19,658,769	56.4
1930......	29,904,663	—	4.1	14,002,074	47.8	15,319,817	52.2
1920......	24,351,676	—	4.3	10,866,960	45.6	12,943,598	54.4
1910......	20,255,555	—	4.5	9,083,711	45.9	10,697,895	54.1
1900......	15,963,965	—	4.8	7,205,212	46.7	8,223,775	53.3
1890......	12,690,152	—	5.0	6,066,417	47.8	6,623,735	52.2
Nonfarm:							
1956......	43,912,463	—	—	26,118,497	59.5	17,793,966	40.5
1950......	37,105,259	—	3.4	19,801,646	53.4	17,303,613	46.6
1947......	32,354,000	—	3.7	17,025,000	52.6	15,329,000	47.4
1940......	27,665,684	—	4.0	11,358,218	41.1	16,307,466	58.9
1930......	23,235,982	—	4.2	10,503,386	46.0	12,351,549	54.0
1920......	17,600,472	—	—	7,041,283	40.9	10,188,111	59.1
1910......	14,131,945	—	—	5,245,380	38.4	8,426,664	61.6
1900......	10,274,127	—	—	3,566,809	36.5	6,213,170	63.5
1890......	7,922,973	—	—	2,923,671	36.9	4,999,302	63.1
Farm:[b]							
1956......	5,961,460	—	—	4,002,012	67.1	1,959,448	32.9
1950......	5,721,082	—	4.0	3,758,320	65.7	1,962,702	34.3
1947......	6,662,000	—	4.1	4,322,000	64.9	2,340,000	35.1
1940......	7,188,848	—	4.3	3,837,545	53.4	3,351,303	46.6
1930......	6,668,681	—	4.6	3,498,688	54.1	2,968,268	45.9
1920......	6,751,204	—	4.7	3,825,677	58.1	2,755,487	41.9
1910......	6,123,610	—	—	3,838,331	62.8	2,271,231	37.2
1900......	5,689,838	—	—	3,638,403	64.4	2,010,605	35.6
1890......	4,767,179	—	—	3,142,746	65.9	1,624,433	34.1

Source: 1890–1947: *Housing Study and Investigation*, Part 2, "Statistics of Housing," Final Majority Report of the Joint Committee on Housing, U.S. 80th Cong., 2d sess., H. Rept. 1568 (Washington, 1948), p. 7. 1950: U.S. Bureau of the Census, *Census of Housing: 1950*, I, *General Characteristics*, Part 1, "United States Summary" (Washington, 1953), Table 5. Population per dwelling unit, 1890–1950: *Ibid.* 1956: U.S. Bureau of the Census, *1956 National Housing Inventory*, III, *Characteristics of the 1956 Inventory*. Part 1, "United States and Regions" (Washington, 1959), Table 1. Number of farm dwellings estimated by the author.

[a] Habitable and nonseasonal.

[b] It has been estimated that approximately 90,000 dwelling units annually have been subtracted from the farm and added to the nonfarm classification since 1940. Cf. Sherman J. Maisel, "Importance of Net Replacements in Housebuilding Demand," in *Study of Mortgage Credit*, U.S. Senate Committee on Banking and Currency, Subcommittee on Housing, 85th Cong., 2d sess. (Washington, 1958), p. 34.

the sale of houses. Similarly, persons unable to secure adequate rental housing resorted to the purchase of houses in the open market.

Table VI–3 also shows that the number of persons per occupied dwelling has shown a consistent decline in the United States since 1890. Table VI–4 illustrates the parallel trend toward smaller houses since 1920.

These trends are a reflection of the rise in real family incomes, the tendency for the establishment of smaller individual households, and

TABLE VI-4

MEDIAN NUMBER OF ROOMS FOR URBAN AND RURAL-NONFARM OCCUPIED DWELLING UNITS, BY YEAR BUILT, 1950

Year built	Total	Urban	Rural-Nonfarm
1945 or later	4.26	4.35	4.16
1940 to 1944	4.39	4.43	4.30
1930 to 1939	4.56	4.80	4.12
1920 to 1929	4.81	4.87	4.47
1919 or earlier	4.76	4.63	5.29

Source: Louis Winnick, *American Housing and Its Use—The Demand for Shelter Space* (New York: John Wiley & Sons, 1957), p. 72, Table 28.

improvements in space planning in American homes.[20] Winnick concludes that between 1900 and 1950 the average nonfarm household size declined by about 20 per cent and that during the same period the median number of rooms per dwelling declined by about 10 to 15 per cent.[21] The United States Census of 1950 showed that more than two thirds of the nonfarm owner-occupied units and more than half of the renter-occupied units had densities of less than 0.75 persons per room, while 90 per cent of the nonfarm owner-occupied units and 78 per cent of the rented units had densities of less than one person per room.[22]

The proportion of dwellings in the United States with private bath, toilet, and other conveniences has risen substantially since 1900 as a reflection of the high levels of new construction with such conveniences and the alteration and conversion of older structures. Comparable census data with regard to toilet and bathing facilities are available only since 1940 and are summarized in Table VI–5.

Approximately nine million dwellings in the United States lacked inside plumbing facilities in 1956. It can be noted that dwellings without private bath and toilet facilities are concentrated in the rural farm areas. In the 1956 national housing inventory about four million dwelling units were classed as dilapidated.[23] Approximately 770,000 of these

[20] Louis Winnick, *American Housing and Its Use—The Demand for Shelter Space* (New York: John Wiley & Sons, 1957), pp. 71–72.

[21] *Ibid.*

[22] *Census of Housing: 1950,* I, Part I, Table 10.

[23] *Ibid.*, p. xviii. A dwelling was classified as dilapidated in the 1950 and 1956 censuses of housing when it had serious deficiencies, was run-down or neglected, or was of inadequate original construction, so that it did not provide adequate shelter or protection against the elements, or endangered the safety of the occupants. A dwelling unit was reported as dilapidated if, because of either deterioration or inadequate original construction, it was below the generally accepted minimum

TABLE VI-5

SELECTED CHARACTERISTICS OF U.S. HOUSING STOCK FOR THE YEARS 1940, 1950, AND 1956

Subject	1956 total	1950				1940 total
		Total	Urban	Rural, nonfarm	Rural, farm	
All dwelling units	55,341,611	45,983,398	29,569,073	10,056,382	6,357,943	37,325,470
Toilet Facilities:						
Number reporting	54,041,074[a]	45,261,040	29,204,261	9,802,878	6,253,901	36,769,610
Flush toilet inside structure, exclusive use	44,970,691	32,334,831	25,363,475	5,239,674	1,731,682	21,966,878
Flush toilet inside structure, shared	1,394,376	1,839,352	1,654,570	160,374	24,408	1,826,962
Other, or none	8,036,007[b]	11,086,857	2,186,216	4,402,830	4,497,811	12,975,770
Per cent:	100.0	100.0	100.0	100.0	100.0	100.0
Flush toilet inside structure, exclusive use	82.7	71.4	86.8	53.5	27.7	59.7
Flush toilet inside structure, shared	2.6	4.1	5.7	1.6	0.4	5.0
Other, or none	14.8	24.5	7.5	44.9	71.9	35.3
Bathing Facilities:						
Number reporting	54,329,619[a]	44,776,197	28,919,792	9,669,405	6,187,000	36,649,481
Installed bathtub or shower, exclusive use	43,807,024	31,022,259	24,164,843	5,012,816	1,844,600	20,606,386
Installed bathtub or shower, shared	1,322,981	1,733,952	1,560,315	150,758	22,879	1,722,576
No bathtub or shower	9,199,614	12,019,986	3,194,634	4,505,831	4,319,521	14,320,519
Per cent	100.0	100.0	100.0	100.0	100.0	100.0
Installed bathtub or shower, exclusive use	80.6	69.5	83.6	51.8	29.8	56.2
Installed bathtub or shower, shared	2.4	3.9	5.4	1.6	0.4	4.7
No bathtub or shower	16.9	26.8	11.0	46.6	69.8	39.1
Number substandard	13,092,000	16,944,000	—	—	—	18,364,000
Per cent	23.7	36.8	—	—	—	49.2

Sources: 1940, 1950: U.S. Bureau of the Census, *Census of Housing: 1950*, I, *General Characteristics*, Part 1, "United States Summary" (Washington, 1953), Table P. 1956: U.S. Bureau of the Census, *1956 National Housing Inventory*, III, *Characteristics of the 1956 Inventory*, Part 1, "United States and Regions" (Washington, 1959), Table 1.

[a] 899,344 or 1.7 per cent of the total dwelling units reporting in 1956 with private toilet and bath were dilapidated.

[b] 3,155,499 lacked hot water, private toilet, or bath, and also were dilapidated; in 1,960,849 of these dwelling units the plumbing and condition were not reported.

were found in the central cities; 530,000 were inside metropolitan areas, but not in the central cities; and 2,750,000 were outside metropolitan areas. Although the data with respect to substandard units are not

standard for housing and needed to be torn down or extensively repaired and rebuilt. Some of the dwellings classified as lacking plumbing facilities in Table VI-5 were also dilapidated. Dilapidated units and those lacking inside private plumbing facilities are usually represented as "substandard"; the total of such units was estimated at approximately three million in April, 1956. See Table VI–6.

strictly comparable from 1940 to 1950, it can be noted from Table VI–5 that the number of dwellings so classified and the percentage of the total have declined from almost half the total housing stock to less that one quarter by 1956. Even more impressive is the decline in the number and per cent of *occupied* substandard units.

The over-all statistics concerning the condition of the housing stock in the United States tend to obscure the deficiencies of particular segments. While almost all urban units had running water and a kitchen sink in 1940, less than half (43 per cent) of the rural farm units had inside piped running water, and little more than half (55 per cent) had a sink. Approximately 42 per cent of farm dwellings in 1950 had neither a kitchen sink nor inside piped running water. Owner-occupied housing is generally of better quality than rented housing. Approximately 13 per cent of renter-occupied housing was classified in 1950 as dilapidated, while only 6 per cent of owner-occupied housing was so classified. Similarly, the proportion of renter-occupied nondilapidated dwellings with private toilet, bath, and hot running water was only 64.1 per cent compared with 69.1 per cent for owner-occupied housing.[24] Generally, dwellings occupied by nonwhite households are of much poorer quality than those occupied by whites. Approximately one third of the 3,782,686 dwellings occupied by nonwhite families in 1950 were owner-occupied. Approximately 30 per cent of the units occupied by nonwhites were classified as "dilapidated" in the 1950 census. In addition, approximately 36 per cent of those classified as "not dilapidated" lacked either running water or private toilet and bath.[25]

The Housing Situation Following World War II

A critical housing shortage existed in the United States at the end of World War II. In 1944 Congress had passed the Servicemen's Readjustment Act, which provided for guaranty by the Veterans Administration of loans to veterans to buy, build, or improve homes. The National Housing Agency published on January 1, 1946, estimates that (*a*) 1,200,000 American nonfarm married couples were already living "doubled up" with others in October, 1945, while (*b*) 1,600,000 married veterans would be discharged by January 1, 1946, and (*c*) 1,300,-000 single veterans would marry by the end of 1946. This situation was the basis for the government sponsored Veterans Emergency Housing

[24] *Ibid.*, Table 7.

[25] *Ibid.* The 1950 Census of Housing adopted the definition of "substandard" to include all "dilapidated" units plus nondilapidated units lacking inside flush toilet, private bath, or running water.

Program, calling for the addition of 2,700,000 low- and moderate-cost homes by the end of 1947. It was planned to start 1,200,000 homes, of which 700,000 were to be conventional houses and the rest prefabricated or temporary units, during 1946, and 1,500,000 in 1947, of which 900,000 were to be conventional houses.

According to National Housing Agency plans, this ambitious program, calling for production exceeding the largest volume of any previous year on record, was to be achieved through:[26]

Expanded production of materials through federal aid

Control over and postponement of nonessential construction and channeling materials into low-cost housing

Rapid expansion, with federal assistance, of prefabrication

Continuance of rent controls

FHA insurance of mortgages on low-cost housing up to 90 per cent of current costs, with firm mortgage commitments to builders

The appropriation of $250,000,000 for temporary reuse war housing, in addition to $191,000,000 already appropriated

Events of the next few years were to show that the estimates of housing needs by the NHA were much too low. The program was given up as a failure after a year. It can be seen in Table VI–1 that total production of nonfarm dwellings totaled only approximately 1,500,000 units in the first two years after the war's end and did not exceed 1,000,000 units annually until 1949. Meanwhile, under the stimulus of rapid expansion in employment and incomes, family formation continued to rise, exceeding 1,400,000 annually from April, 1947, to April, 1950.[27] The Bureau of the Census estimated that 2,282,000 nonfarm married couples were living "doubled up" in April, 1947, equaling 7 per cent of the estimated total number of nonfarm families on that date.

As a part of a general government reorganization and also in response to widespread criticism of the program of the National Housing Agency, particularly the attempts to control and direct housing production and the use of government funds to encourage prefabrication, the federal agencies in housing were reorganized as the Housing and Home Finance Agency in 1947. In the same year the Congress reaffirmed the declaration in the Price Control Extension Act of 1946 that "it is its purpose to terminate at the earliest practicable date all Federal restrictions on rents on housing accommodations."[28]

---

[26] U.S. National Housing Agency, *Housing Facts* (Washington, January, 1956), p. 2.

[27] U.S. Bureau of the Census, *Current Population Reports—Population Characteristics*, Series P-20, No. 94 (Washington, August 24, 1959).

[28] U.S. Office of the Housing Expediter, *The Housing and Rent Act of 1947, as*

The structure of the Housing and Home Finance Agency as it had evolved by 1953 is shown in Chart VI–2. The significant fact which emerges from Chart VI–2 is that the federal government emerged from World War II with a comprehensive organization and broad responsibilities for financing, administering, and providing housing. The Veterans Administration was a key organization in housing finance which retained its independence throughout the postwar period. This was of particular importance during periods when the Administration sought to control the over-all levels of housing production, as will be noted below.

In December, 1954, the Office of the Administrator was reorganized, following closely recommendations made by the President's Advisory Committee on Government Housing Policies and Programs in its report of December, 1953. The present organization of the Housing and Home Finance Agency includes the following constituent agencies: Community Facilities Administration, Urban Renewal Administration, Federal Housing Administration, Public Housing Administration, and Federal National Mortgage Association.[29]

In his "state of the Union" message to Congress on January 5, 1949, President Truman called attention to the fact that "five million families were still living in slums and firetraps" and "three million families shared their homes with others." The Congress set forth in the Housing Act of 1949 as a national housing objective "the realization as soon as feasible of the goal of a decent home and a suitable living environment for every American family," and described the policy to be used in attaining that objective as follows:[30]

Private enterprise shall be encouraged to serve as large a part of the total need as it can.

Governmental assistance shall be utilized where feasible to enable private enterprise to serve more of the total need.

Appropriate local public bodies shall be encouraged and assisted to undertake positive programs of encouraging and assisting the development of well-planned, integrated residential neighborhoods, the development and redevelopment of communities, and the production, at lower costs, of housing of sound standards of design, construction, livability, and size for adequate family life.

Amended, a collation of Public Laws 129 (Housing and Rent Act of 1947), 422, and 464 (Housing and Rent Act of 1948), 80th Congress, and Public Law 31 (Housing and Rent Act of 1949), 81st Congress (Washington, April 1, 1949), Sec. 201.

[29] U.S. Housing and Home Finance Agency, *Twelfth Annual Report, 1958* (Washington, 1959), p. vii.

[30] Public Law 171, 81st Cong. 1st sess. (July 15, 1949), Housing Act of 1949, Sec. 2.

CHART VI-2

MAJOR HOUSING PROGRAMS ADMINISTERED IN 1953 BY THE HOUSING AND HOME FINANCE AGENCY

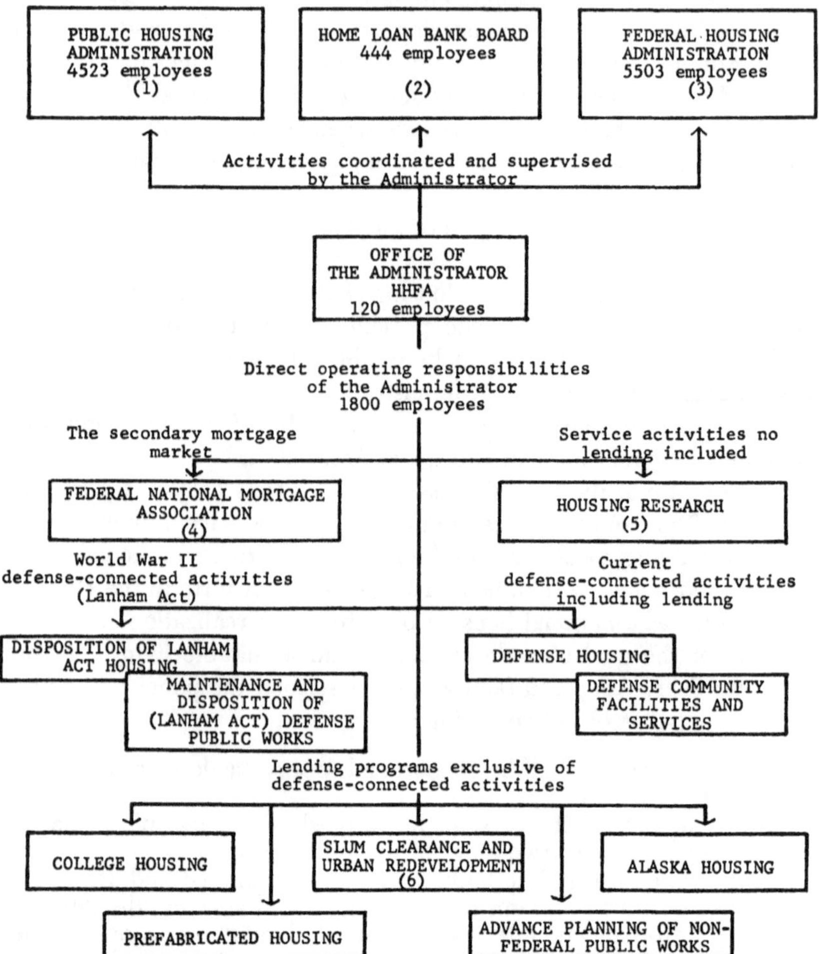

SOURCE: Paul F. Wendt, *The Role of the Federal Government in Housing* (Washington: American Enterprise Association, Inc., 1956), p. 16.

[1] PHA makes loans and grants and provides services to local public housing agencies to assist in providing low-rent dwellings for low-income families. There were about 319,000 PHA public housing units and about 75,000 more were under construction at June 30, 1953.

PHA held about $587,357,000 of obligations of local public housing agencies and it guaranteed about $1,746,088,000 held by others. Grants of $116,243,037 had been made. PHA has $1,000,000 of capital and it may borrow up to $1,500,000,000 for lending. Grants are financed by appropriations.

Although the statement of national housing policy emphasized the role of private enterprise, it is significant that the Housing Act of 1949 made provision for large-scale direct federal and local government participation in two important areas of housing:[31]

The Act programed federal subsidized public housing construction designed to provide a maximum of 810,000 subsidized low-rent dwellings over a six-year period.

The Act provided under Title I for federal loans of $1 billion and capital grants of $500 million for local slum clearance and redevelopment projects over a five-year period.

[31] U.S. Housing and Home Finance Agency, *Third Annual Report, 1949* (Washington, 1950), pp. 2, 40.

PHA also manages and conducts the disposition of housing acquired under the Lanham Act.

[2] HLBB supervises the 11 Federal Home Loan Banks, and it has chartered and regulates 1,597 privately-owned federal savings-and-loan associations.

It supervises Federal Savings and Loan Insurance Corporation which insures about $18,000,000,000 of investors' accounts.

It has been responsible for liquidation of Home Owners Loan Corporation, now completed.

At present all activities of HLBB are financed by the collection of fees and insurance premiums.

[3] FHA conducts programs of loan and mortgage insurance on residential properties. It had authority to issue insurance up to a total of about $20,287,000,000 and had used all but about $1,086,000,000 of this total at June 30, 1953.

The present activities of FHA are financed entirely by fee and premium collections. However, the government guarantees about $79,011,000 of FHA debentures issued in payment of claims on defaulted mortgages, and it will guarantee further issues as they occur.

[4] FNMA buys and holds or sells mortgages insured by FHA or guaranteed by VA.

Its authority to buy amounted to $3,650,000,000 and its portfolio contained 349,153 mortgages with balances of over $2,500,000,000 at June 30, 1953. It was committed to acquire $467,000,000 more.

Investment funds are borrowed from the Treasury. Expenses are paid out of interest collections. Reported accumulated net income was $128,236,174, including $35,682,506 set aside as a loss reserve.

[5] At June 30, 1953, HHFA was conducting research activities on behalf of people and institutions engaged in the construction or financing of residential property.

Although statutory authority for the program extends indefinitely, no funds have been appropriated for periods following April 30, 1954.

[6] Under this program loans and grants are made to municipalities for slum clearance and urban redevelopment. For this purpose HHFA may borrow up to $1,000,000,000 from the Treasury. The authority to make grants is limited to $500,000,000.

At June 30, 1953, outstanding loans amounted to $22,036,000 and grants of $7,818,000 had been made. Undisbursed commitments were $33,901,000 for loans and $70,574,000 for grants.

In its report to President Eisenhower in December, 1953, the President's Advsory Committee on Government Housing Policies and Programs expressed general agreement with the broad housing policies established in the Housing Act of 1949 and recommended that housing objectives be realized through long-established federal housing programs. Among the more significant of the recommendations of this committee, which included strong representation from the mortgage finance and homebuilding industries, were the following:[32]

Increased federal grants and loans to local communities for slum clearance and extension of FHA loan insurance to older areas

Continuance of federally subsidized low-rent public housing with specific provisions for priorities in occupancy for low-income families displaced by slum clearance, rehabilitation, or public works

Liberalization of terms (increase term of loan and maximum amount of loans) for FHA Title I loans for modernization or repair to existing houses

Formation of a privately owned National Mortgage Marketing Cor-

---

[32] The President's Advisory Committee on Government Housing Policies and Programs, *Recommendations on Government Housing Policies and Programs* (Washington, December, 1953).

Among other specific recommendations were: that the FHA and VA work out an interagency agreement for FHA to take over technical functions of VA home loan guaranty program, including valuation and appraisal, market analysis, property inspection, construction standards, etc.; that a Federal Home Loan Board be newly established in place of the present Home Loan Bank Board, responsible for the Federal Home Loan Bank System, the Federal Savings and Loan Insurance Corporation, and the newly recommended National Mortgage Marketing Corporation; elimination of a number of federal programs administered by the Housing and Home Finance Agency, including Housing Research, Prefabricated Housing Loans, College Housing and School Construction programs, Programming of Defense Housing, Federal National Mortgage Association, International Housing Activities, Alaska Housing Program, and others; merger of the group insurance accounts now maintained under the FHA mutual mortgage insurance system into a single insurance fund.

Most of the recommendations of this committee were enacted into law by the Housing Act of 1954. Maximum terms of loans, however, were restricted to 95 per cent and thirty years. In addition, the provision for the formation and capitalization of the Federal National Mortgage Association in the Housing Act of 1954 differed from the recommendations in that the Secretary of the Treasury was authorized to subscribe to $21,000,000 of preferred stock, with the remainder of capital funds accumulated by requiring each mortgage seller to make capital contributions. The control of the Federal National Mortgage Association was vested by the Act of 1954 in a board of directors headed up by the Housing and Home Finance Administrator, and provision was made for a gradual redemption of Treasury-held stock and a shift to private stock ownership and operation as an independent secondary mortgage facility. After 1954 the Slum Clearance and Urban Redevelopment Agency became known as the Urban Renewal Administration. It remained for the Housing Act of 1955 to provide for the separation of the Home Loan Bank Board from the jurisdiction of the Housing and Home Finance Agency and a change in its name to the Federal Home Loan Bank Board.

poration with original capital stock of $50 million subscribed by lenders eligible to use its facilities (the rest of the subscription required to be subscribed by the Federal Home Loan banks)

Two-year experimentation with 100-per-cent forty-year FHA loans up to limited dollar amounts

Reorganization of federal housing activities under a single administrator with clear supervisory authority

Post-World War II housing progress in the United States is reflected in the production of new dwellings and in changes in the characteristics of the housing stock as influenced by new production, demolitions, conversions, and improvements to existing structures. The improvement in selected characteristics of the United States housing stock has already been noted in Table VI–5. The combined influence of high rates of new construction, rehabilitation of housing formerly classed as substandard, and removal of substandard units resulted in a decline in the number of substandard units in the United States from 16,400,000 to 13,092,000 by 1956. It has been estimated that the total of such units will have declined further to 11,500,000 by 1960.[33]

The contribution of new production, net conversions, and other factors to the changes in the United States housing inventory from 1950 to 1956 was summarized in testimony before the Senate Banking and Currency Committee, as shown in Table VI–6.

It is apparent from these data, abstracted from the 1956 National Housing Inventory, that almost five million substandard units were eliminated from the inventory by repairs and rehabilitation, conversions, and other net losses between 1950 and 1956. Maisel estimated that approximately 11,646,000 of 16,400,000 total substandard dwellings as of December, 1950, were nonfarm dwellings and that the total number of nonfarm substandard units would decline to 9,000,000 by 1960. These developments reflect significant housing progress in the United States since the end of World War II.

It is more difficult to assess the relative contribution of government housing policies to this record of accomplishment. The achievement of

[33] Reinhold P. Wolff, "Substandard Dwelling Units and Their Replacements, 1961–70," in *Study of Mortgage Credit,* p. 45.

A critic of these estimates maintains that Wolff overstates the National Housing Inventory 1950–56 figure for "substandard units rehabilitated and now standard" by 1.1 million units and that as a result Wolff's projection of the number of units to be shifted from substandard to standard during the 1960's (4,600,000 units) is "too optimistic." He expresses the view that "if this gross figure reaches three million the nation would be fortunate." See Frank S. Kristof, "Components of Change in the Nation's Housing Inventory in Relation to the 1960 Census," a paper presented at the annual meeting of the American Statistical Association, December 28, 1959, p. 10.

TABLE VI–6

FACTORS OF CHANGE IN THE UNITED STATES HOUSING INVENTORY, 1950 TO 1956
(In thousands of dwelling units)

Condition	1950 units	Change in 1950 inventory				1950 inventory in 1956	New construction	1956 inventory
		Change in same units	Net conversions and mergers	Net other losses	Total			
Total for United States:								
Standard	28,102	+2,754	+391	−143	+3,002	31,104	9,649	40,753
Substandard	16,400	−3,187	−299	−1,268	−4,754	11,646	983	12,629
Not reported	1,481	+433	−56	−190	+187	1,668	288	1,956
Total	45,983	......	+36	−1,601	−1,565	44,418	10,920	55,338
Inside standard metropolitan areas:								
Standard	19,314	+1,110	+272	−206	+1,176	20,490	6,389	26,879
Substandard	5,565	−1,099	−178	−517	−1,794	3,771	257	4,028
Not reported	747	−11	−32	−121	−164	583	117	700
Total	25,626	......	+62	−844	−782	24,844	6,763	31,607
Outside standard metropolitan areas:								
Standard	8,788	+1,644	+119	+63	+1,826	10,614	3,260	13,874
Substandard	10,835	−2,088	−121	−751	−2,960	7,875	726	8,593
Not reported	734	+444	−24	−69	+351	1,085	171	1,256
Total	20,357	......	−26	−757	−783	19,574	4,157	23,723

Source: Sherman J. Maisel, "Importance of Net Replacements in Housebuilding Demand," in *Study of Mortgage Credit*, U.S. Senate Committee on Banking and Currency, Subcommittee on Housing, 85th Cong., 2d sess. (Washington, 1958), Table 18, p. 40.

national housing objectives during the postwar years in the United States has been sought through federal programs in three major areas: mortgage finance, public housing, and slum clearance and urban removal.

In the sections to follow, the accomplishments of government programs in each of these areas will be appraised and an attempt will be made to evaluate their over-all influence upon housing production, costs, and standards.

Mortgage Finance

The encouragement of homeownership through improving the availability of long-term mortgage funds at low interest rates has been the foundation of United States housing policy since the 1920's. Table VI–7

TABLE VI–7

Mortgage Status of Owner-Occupied Dwelling Units, 1890 to 1950

Census year	Total owner-occupied dwelling units	Reporting mortgage status	Mortgaged		Not mortgaged
			Number	Per cent	
1950	19,801,646	17,795,844	7,825,116	44.0	9,970,728
Urban	14,376,594	13,296,133	6,429,743	48.4	6,866,390
Rural–nonfarm	5,425,052	4,499,711	1,395,373	31.0	3,104,338
1940	11,413,036	10,611,259	4,804,778	45.3	5,806,481
1930	10,549,972	n.a.	n.a.	n.a.	n.a.
1920	7,041,283	6,867,546	2,735,668	39.8	4,131,878
1910	5,245,380	5,109,916	1,701,062	33.3	3,408,854
1900	3,566,809	3,394,967	1,086,605	32.0	2,308,362
1890	2,923,671	2,923,671	809,933	27.7	2,113,738

Source: Richard U. Ratcliff, Daniel B. Rathbun, and Junia H. Honnold, *Residential Finance* (New York: John Wiley & Sons, 1957), Table 1, p. 5.

Note: For 1950 and 1940, the mortgage statistics are for owner-occupied dwelling units in one- to four-dwelling-unit structures without business. For 1920 and earlier, the mortgage data are for owner-occupied units in all types of structures. Although the types of units for which mortgage data were reported are not the same for all censuses, the differences are not large enough to invalidate comparisons.

shows the long-term trend in mortgage status for owner-occupied dwellings in the United States.

The objectives of government housing policy have been to promote greater stability in the flow of residential mortgage funds, longer terms of loans, higher loan-value ratios, and lower interest rates. Government housing loan programs have been implemented through four principal agencies:[34]

The Federal Home Loan Bank System (FHLB), established in 1932 to provide a reservoir of reserve credit which would be available for savings and loan associations and other institutions investing mainly in residential mortgages

The Federal Housing Administration (FHA), established in 1934 to insure residential loans on new and existing dwellings made by private lenders

The Veterans Administration (VA), authorized by the Servicemen's Readjustment Act of 1944 to guarantee private lenders against losses on housing loans to veterans of World War II

The Federal National Mortgage Association (FNMA), first organized in 1938 as the "National Mortgage Association of Washington" to aid in the establishment of a secondary market for FHA-insured mortgage and to make loans on large-scale rental housing projects under the National Housing Act, and to offer its own obligations for investment by individuals and institutions.

Federal Home Loan Bank System

The Federal Home Loan Bank Act of 1932 provided for the establishment of eleven regional Home Loan Banks authorized to make advances to federal-government- and member-state-chartered savings and loan institutions. Originally financed by government capital, the Federal Home Loan Banks have been owned by member institutions since 1951. Borrowing member institutions are required to purchase Home Loan Bank stock and the Federal Home Loan Banks are authorized to sell their obligations in the open market. The Federal Savings and Loan Insurance Corporation, an associated agency, insures savings deposits with insured member institutions and has been an important factor aiding in the expansion of individual savings deposits with local savings and loan institutions.

Savings deposits and mortgage loans of member institutions of the Federal Home Loan Bank System have expanded rapidly during the postwar period. Assets of member institutions increased from $10.4 billion in 1947 to approximately $53 billion in 1958. Savings deposits with savings and loan associations increased from $9 billion in 1947 to $48 billion in 1958, while savings deposits in mutual savings banks, which also participate in the mortgage loan market, rose from $17.7 billion in 1947 to $34 billion in 1958.[35] Advances by the Federal Home

[34] William H. Husband and Frank Ray Anderson, *Real Estate* (rev. ed.; Homewood, Ill.: Richard D. Irwin, 1954), chap. xxii.

[35] United States Savings and Loan League, *Savings and Loan Fact Book* (Chicago, 1959), Table 2, p. 13.

TABLE VI–8

MORTGAGE DEBT ON NONFARM HOMES, BY TYPE OF LENDER, AT YEAR END, 1940 TO 1959
(In millions of dollars)

Year	Savings and Loan associations	Life Insurance companies	Commercial banks	Mutual savings banks	FNMA	Individuals and others	Total volume
1940	$ 3,919	$ 1,803	$ 2,363	$ 2,162	$ 178	$ 6,966	$ 17,391
1941	4,349	1,969	2,672	2,189	203	6,969	18,351
1942	4,349	2,241	2,752	2,128	206	6,536	18,212
1943	4,355	2,386	2,706	2,033	60	6,271	17,811
1944	4,617	2,435	2,703	1,937	50	6,182	17,924
1945	5,156	2,306	2,875	1,894	7	6,353	18,591
1946	6,840	2,545	4,576	2,033	6	7,034	23,034
1947	8,475	3,497	6,303	2,283	4	7,637	28,199
1948	9,841	4,943	7,396	2,835	198	8,066	33,279
1949	11,117	6,093	7,956	3,364	806	8,283	37,619
1950	13,116	8,478	9,481	4,312	1,328	8,455	45,170
1951	14,844	10,610	10,275	5,331	1,818	8,833	51,711
1952	17,645	11,757	11,250	6,194	2,210	9,444	58,500
1953	20,999	13,195	12,025	7,373	2,358	10,144	66,094
1954	25,004	15,153	13,300	9,002	2,328	10,890	75,677
1955	30,001	17,661	15,075	11,100	2,444	11,969	88,250
1956	34,004	20,130	16,245	12,990	2,866	12,802	99,037
1957	37,996	21,441	16,385	14,110	3,777	13,908	107,617
1958	42,890	22,374	17,628	15,640	3,580	15,574	117,686
1959[a]	49,727	23,622	19,240	16,868	4,938	16,749	131,144

Source: United States Savings and Loan League, *Savings and Loan Fact Book, 1960* (Chicago, 1960), Table 41, p. 60.
[a] Preliminary figures.

Loan Banks to member institutions have exceeded $1.2 billion since 1955.

As a result of their more rapid growth, savings and loan associations have gradually increased their share of residential mortgage lending from approximately 30 per cent of total annual dollar volume in the period preceding World War II to more than 38 per cent in 1958 and to 40.6 per cent in 1959.

Table VI–8 shows the expansion in nonfarm mortgage debt by type of lending institutions from 1940 to 1958. It can be noted that savings and loan associations held approximately 36 per cent of the outstanding total home mortgage debt in 1958, compared with approximately 22 per cent in 1940.

Between 85 and 90 per cent of the dollar volume of mortgage lending by savings and loan associations has been in the form of so-called "conventional" loans, as distinguished from government insured (FHA) or guaranteed (VA) loans. Conventional mortgage loans by savings and loan associations typically bear interest rates above those for government-insured or government-guaranteed loans. A study of interest rates on conventional loans by savings and loan associations in the spring of 1959 revealed that 55 per cent of the number of loans then being advanced carried an interest rate of 6 per cent, while 29 per cent were at 5.5 per cent. The median purchase price of single-family homes conventionally financed at savings and loan associations in 1957 was $17,107. At the same time the median loan was $11,131, with a median loan-to-price ratio of 67.3 per cent. This is substantially lower than the loan-to-price ratio for FHA-insured loans, shown in Table VI–2 to exceed 80 per cent. Higher ratios of mortgage loan to purchase price for government-insured and government-guaranteed loans were also observed in the results of the 1950 census of housing.[36]

Federal Housing Administration

Before World War II, the Federal Housing Administration was the principal federal agency insuring residential mortgage loans, and it can be noted from Table VI–1 that insured loans under its programs ac-

[36] Richard U. Ratcliffe, Daniel B. Rathbun, and Junia H. Honnold, *Residental Finance* (New York: John Wiley & Sons, 1957). Table 37 of this study showed that the median ratios of mortgage loan to purchase price in 1950 were: FHA-insured, 79 per cent; VA-guaranteed, 91 per cent; conventional, 66 per cent. Table 34 of the same study showed that the median terms of first mortgage loans on single-family, owner-occupied units were twenty years for FHA and VA loans and only eleven years for fully amortized conventional loans. The median interest rate on conventional first mortgage loans on single-family, owner-occupied units was 5 per cent.

TABLE VI–9

MORTGAGES AND LOANS INSURED BY U.S. FEDERAL HOUSING ADMINISTRATION, 1934 TO 1959

Year	Total—all programs	Home mortgage programs		Project mortgage programs		Property improvement loans		Manufactured housing loans	
	Amount	Number	Amount	Units	Amount	Number	Net proceeds	Number	Amount
1934	$ 27,406	—	$ —	—	$ —	72,658	$ 27,406	—	$ —
1935	297,495	23,397	93,882	738	2,355	635,747	201,258	—	—
1936	532,581	77,231	308,945	624	2,101	617,697	221,535	—	—
1937	489,200	102,076	424,373	5,023	10,483	124,758	54,344	—	—
1938	671,593	115,124	485,812	11,930	47,638	376,480	138,143	—	—
1939	925,262	164,530	694,764	13,462	51,851	502,308	178,647	—	—
1940	991,174	177,400	762,084	3,559	12,949	653,841	216,142	—	—
1941	1,152,342	210,310	910,770	3,741	13,565	680,104	228,007	—	—
1942	1,120,839	223,562	973,271	5,842	21,215	427,534	126,354	—	—
1943	933,986	166,402	763,097	20,179	84,622	307,826	86,267	—	—
1944	877,472	146,974	707,363	12,430	56,096	389,615	114,013	—	—
1945	664,985	96,776	474,245	4,058	19,817	501,441	170,923	—	—
1946	755,778	80,872	421,949	2,232	13,175	799,304	320,654	—	—
1947	1,788,264	141,364	894,675	46,604	359,944	1,247,613	533,645	—	—
1948	3,340,865	300,034	2,116,043	79,184	608,711	1,357,386	614,239	3	1,872
1949	3,826,283	305,705	2,209,842	133,135	1,021,231	1,246,254	593,744	196	1,466
1950	4,343,378	342,582	2,492,367	154,597	1,156,681	1,447,101	693,761	175	569
1951	3,219,836	252,642	1,928,433	74,207	583,774	1,437,764	707,070	131	560
1952	3,112,782	234,426	1,942,307	39,839	321,911	1,495,741	848,327	85	237
1953	3,882,328	261,541	2,288,626	30,701	259,194	2,244,227	1,334,287	40	221
1954	3,067,250	214,237	1,942,266	28,257	234,022	1,506,480	890,606	115	356
1955	3,806,937	318,500	3,084,767	9,431	76,489	1,024,698	645,645	11	36
1956	3,460,468	253,300	2,638,230	11,177	130,247	1,013,086	691,992	—	—
1957	3,716,980	202,400	2,251,064	43,609	597,348	1,111,962	868,568	—	—
1958	6,328,597	389,400	4,551,483	64,953	908,671	1,038,315	868,443	—	—
1959	7,740,742	505,500	6,069,400	43,976	674,700	1,096,635	996,642	—	—
Total	$61,074,823	5,306,285	$41,430,058	841,488	$7,268,790	23,356,575	$12,370,662	756	$5,317

Sources: 1934 to 1958: U.S. Housing and Home Finance Agency, *Twelfth Annual Report, 1958* (Washington, 1959), Table III–1. 1959: U.S. Housing and Home Finance Agency, *Housing Statistics, Annual Data, March 1960* (Washington, 1960), Tables A–46, to A–48.

counted for approximately 35 per cent of recorded loans on new dwellings constructed from 1938 to 1941. During the war years the proportion rose considerably higher because virtually all new private residential construction was under materials and priorities control administered through the Federal Housing Administration. Since World War II, FHA loan insurance programs have accounted for between 25 and 35 per cent of the number of new private housing starts. All classes of mortgage lending institutions originate and hold in their portfolios residential loans insured by the Federal Housing Administration. Over the years, however, life insurance companies, savings banks, and commercial banks have been the principal holders of loans insured by the FHA. As of December 31, 1959, life insurance companies held approximately 28.4 per cent of the total amount of FHA-insured mortgages outstanding, commercial banks held 23.8 per cent, and mutual savings banks held 21.3 per cent. The remainder was held by mortgage companies, savings and loan associations, and federal agencies (FNMA).[37] As will be noted below, the volume of mortgage insurance under the FHA and other government programs has varied with changes in the interest rate structure and with the market operations of the Federal National Mortgage Association, in large part because maximum interest rates are established by law for government loans insured or guaranteed by the government.

Table VI–9 shows the range of the FHA's loan insurance activities since 1934. It will be seen that over 4.5 million units have been financed since 1934 in FHA home mortgage programs, while so-called project mortgage programs (those with eight or more units per project) accounted for approximately 750,000 dwelling units. The number of property improvement loans rose substantially following World War II and has exceeded 1,000,000 per annum in each year since. The dollar amount of the individual loans for property improvement was small as can be seen, averaging less than $500 per loan.

It is more difficult to assess the specific influence of the FHA's mortgage insurance programs than to recite their volume. Before the mid-1930's, when FHA was established, the average mortgage loan covered about 50 per cent of the value of the house, with a few savings and loan associations lending as high as 75 per cent. Bank and insurance company conventional loans approximated three to six years in duration, while savings and loan companies and mutual savings banks extended mortgage loans to six to twelve years. A study of typical mortgage terms on new homes in fifteen metropolitan areas during the

[37] U.S. Housing and Home Finance Agency, *Housing Statistics, Historical Supplement* (Washington, June, 1960), p. 141.

last half of 1949 revealed that mortgage loans had an average duration of twenty-two years, with the initial equity averaging about 26 per cent of the average loan of $8,410. One quarter of the loans required no down payment.[38] Although the data do not permit accurate statistical comparison, it is generally acknowledged that interest charges on first mortgage loans thirty years ago ranged from 6 to 8 per cent, as compared with average terms of 5 to 6 per cent in most areas in the years since World War II.[39]

Further evidence of the trend toward liberalizing mortgage credit terms is found in the results of the census of housing for 1950, which revealed:[40]

A long-run decline in mortgage interest rates from an average of 6.2 per cent in 1890 to approximately 5 per cent in 1950

A gradual shift to longer-term amortized loans in urban areas

A long-term rise in the percentage of dwellings mortgaged and in the average ratio of debt to market value

Analysis of the characteristics of FHA single-family home loans insured since 1946, shown in Table VI–10, confirms the fact that the term of loans has been in a gradual up-trend from approximately twenty years for newly constructed homes in the immediate postwar years to over twenty-five years since 1955. Similar trends are evident for loan terms on existing homes. Loan value ratios have remained relatively constant for newly constructed homes at approximately 86 per cent of value, but seem to have risen for existing homes from 78.4 per cent in 1946 to over 90 per cent in 1958. This is a reflection of liberalization of FHA policies with respect to loans for existing homes after passage of the Housing Act of 1954. It is of interest to note that although the estimated value of homes and monthly housing expenses approximately doubled during the period, the ratio of housing expense to income remained virtually constant at about 20 per cent. This was a reflection, of course, of the rise in average annual incomes of borrowers during the period, from slightly over $3,000 in 1946 to

---

[38] Sherman J. Maisel, *Housebuilding in Transition: Based on Studies in the San Francisco Bay Area* (Berkeley and Los Angeles: University of California Press, 1953), p. 366, Table 40.

[39] Albert Heeley Schaaf, "Federal Interest Rate Policy on Insured and Guaranteed Mortgages" (doctoral dissertation, University of California, Berkeley, 1955), chaps. ii–iii; "Federal Influence on the Urban Residential Mortgage Market," Federal Reserve Bank of St. Louis, *Monthly Review*, September, 1953, pp. 121–129; United States Savings and Loan League, *Savings and Loan Fact Book* (Chicago, 1959), pp. 24–25; Richard U. Ratcliff, *Urban Land Economics* (New York: McGraw-Hill, 1949), chap. ix.

[40] Ratcliff, Rathbun, and Honnold, *op. cit.*, chap. ii.

TABLE VI–10

CHARACTERISTICS OF ONE-FAMILY HOME TRANSACTIONS UNDER THE NATIONAL HOUSING ACT, AS AMENDED, SELECTED YEARS

Median	1958	1957	1956	1955	1954	1952	1950	1948	1946
NEW HOMES									
Mortgage:									
Amount	$12,697	$11,823	$11,010	$10,034	$8,862	$8,273	$7,101	$7,058	$5,504
Term in years	27.3	25.5	25.5	25.6	22.9	21.7	24.1	20.1	21.0
Loan-value ratio (per cent)	91.5	85.1	86.6	88.7	85.3	83.7	88.0	81.0	87.0
Total monthly payment	$96.10	$90.29	$81.63	$74.14	$68.62	$64.16	$54.31	$58.08	$46.18
Property:									
FHA-estimated value	$14,207	$14,261	$13,203	$11,742	$10,678	$10,022	$8,286	$8,721	$6,558
Market price of site	$2,223	$2,148	$1,887	$1,626	$1,456	$1,227	$1,035	$1,049	$761
Site-value ratio (per cent)	15.4	14.9	14.1	13.4	13.1	12.0	12.0	11.7	11.5
Per cent with garages	72.7	76.6	72.8	69.8	66.6	53.4	48.7	55.1	58.1
Structure:									
Calculated area (sq. ft.)	1,092	1,105	1,064	1,022	961	923	838	912	n.a.
Number of rooms	5.8	5.8	5.7	5.6	5.4	5.3	4.9	5.4	5.5
Number of bedrooms	3.5	3.5	3.4	3.4	3.3	3.1	n.a.	n.a.	n.a.
Mortgagor:									
Annual effective income	$6,803	$6,632	$6,054	$5,484	$5,139	$4,811	$3,861	$4,000	$3,313
Monthly housing expense	$120.87	$115.17	$104.48	$95.70	$88.91	$83.16	$75.41	$78.64	$62.85
Expense-income ratio (per cent)	20.4	19.7	19.5	19.7	19.6	19.6	21.6	21.7	20.9

TABLE VI-10 (*Continued*)

Median	1958	1957	1956	1955	1954	1952	1950	1948	1946
EXISTING HOMES									
Mortgage:									
Amount	$11,325	$10,498	$10,013	$9,603	$9,030	$8,047	$6,801	$5,969	$4,697
Term in years	24.2	22.5	22.5	22.7	20.1	19.7	20.2	19.3	18.9
Loan-value ratio (per cent)	90.2	84.9	82.9	85.0	78.5	77.9	77.8	77.9	78.4
Total monthly payment	$90.30	$85.54	$78.62	$74.57	$74.34	$65.08	$56.65	$49.76	$40.83
Property:									
FHA-estimated value	$12,778	$12,572	$12,261	$11,555	$11,549	$10,289	$8,865	$7,579	$5,934
Market price of site	$2,150	$2,041	$1,931	$1,707	$1,591	$1,296	$1,150	$970	$833
Site-value ratio (per cent)	16.5	15.7	15.1	14.2	13.3	12.3	12.4	12.0	13.3
Per cent with garages	74.9	78.5	81.1	79.9	79.6	70.7	70.6	70.5	83.4
Structure:									
Calculated area (sq. ft.)	1,053	1,060	1,060	1,030	1,035	992	1,006	972	n.a.
Number of rooms	5.8	5.8	5.7	5.6	5.6	5.5	5.6	5.6	5.9
Number of bedrooms	3.2	3.2	3.2	3.1	3.1	3.1	n.a.	n.a.	n.a.
Mortgagor:									
Annual effective income	$6,502	$6,296	$6,033	$5,669	$5,696	$4,938	$4,274	$3,731	$3,101
Monthly housing expense	$115.31	$110.12	$102.00	$97.34	$97.41	$86.63	$78.99	$71.00	$58.11
Expense-income ratio (per cent)	20.4	19.9	19.2	19.4	19.4	19.4	20.3	20.4	20.3

Source: U.S. Housing and Home Finance Agency, *Twelfth Annual Report, 1958* (Washington, 1959), Table III–37.

about $6,500 in 1958.[41] In this connection, it is of interest to note that mean average personal incomes per family (and unattached individual) before income taxes are estimated to have risen from $4,130 in 1947 to $6,130 in 1957.[42]

It is significant to note that the number of mortgage foreclosures per year has been at relatively low levels during the postwar years. Similar trends are revealed in the fact that defaults on FHA home mortgages, in effect, have not exceeded 20,000 at any one time since 1950, and have equaled less than one per cent of the mortgages in force in every year since 1951.[43] See Table VI–11.

It is clear that FHA policies have encouraged the granting of liberal terms on long-term mortgages in the postwar housing markets and facilitated the major expansion in homeownership which has occurred. It is also evident that these liberal terms have not resulted in any major wave of foreclosures, even during the relatively severe recession of 1958. (The postwar peak in the rate of nonfarm foreclosures was reached in March, 1959, when foreclosures totaled 3,933.) The costs of this program and its effect upon mortgage interest rates, stability in residential construction, and residential building costs will be explored below.

Veterans Administration

Title III of the Servicemen's Readjustment Act of 1944 (Public Law 346) provided for federal government guaranty of up to 50 per cent of loans by private lenders for the purchase or construction of homes by eligible veterans of World War II. The maximum amount of individual home loans guaranteed by the federal government was limited by the 1944 Act to $2,000 or 50 per cent of the loan, but this was increased to $4,000 by amendment in 1945 and to $7,500 or 60 per cent of the loan by Public Law 475, passed in 1950. The maximum maturity on a VA home loan was increased from twenty-five to thirty years by the 1950 law. Up to October, 1950, the Veterans Administration guaranteed so-called Section 505 second mortgage loans which were also secured by a Federal Housing Administration first mortgage. The ex-

[41] U.S. Housing and Home Finance Agency, *Twelfth Annual Report, 1958,* Table III–37. Monthly housing expense includes total monthly mortgage payment and the FHA-estimated cost of monthly maintenance and repair, and heating and utility expenses. Mortgagor's effective income is the FHA-estimated amount of the mortgagor's earning capacity (before deductions for federal income taxes) that is likely to prevail during approximately the first third of the mortgage term.

[42] Selma F. Goldsmith, "Size Distribution of Personal Income," U.S. Department of Commerce, Office of Business Economics, *Survey of Current Buisness,* XXXVIII, No. 4 (April, 1958), 11.

[43] U.S. Housing and Home Finance Agency, *Eleventh Annual Report, 1957* (Washington, 1958), p. 89.

TABLE VI-11

AVERAGE NUMBER OF NONFARM FORECLOSURES FOR FIVE-YEAR PERIODS, 1931 TO 1956, AND ANNUALLY SINCE 1950

Year	Average number of nonfarm mortgage foreclosures
1931–35	230,790
1936–40	126,230
1941–45	31,140
1946–50	14,567
1951–56	23,982
1950	21,337
1951	18,141
1952	18,135
1953	21,473
1954	26,211
1955	28,529
1956	30,963
1957	34,204
1958	42,367
1959	44,075

Sources: Five-year averages, 1931–1956, from United States Savings and Loan League, *Savings and Loan Fact Book, 1957* (Chicago, 1957), p. 29; annual data, 1950–1957, from U.S. Housing and Home Finance Agency, *Housing Statistics, Historical Supplement* (Washington, December, 1958), pp. 140–141, and *ibid.*, June, 1960, p. 143.

tensive use of the Section 505 loan in 1948 and 1949 permitted 100-percent government-underwritten financing on the sale of new tract homes to eligible veteran borrowers. Although the Veterans Administration has no specific dollar limitation on the amount of a loan eligible for government guaranty, loans above $25,000 are required to have regional office approval.[44] The maximum interest rate on VA-guaranteed loans was raised from 4 per cent to 4.5 per cent in May, 1953; to 4.75 per cent in 1958; and to 5.25 per cent in mid-1959.

Up to June 30, 1959, under this program, 5,327,157 home loans to veterans totaling $45.8 billion had been partially guaranteed or insured by the Veterans Administration.[45] The average dollar amount of loans guaranteed up to June 30, 1959, was $8,617; the average size of loans closed in recent years has increased to approximately $13,000.[46]

[44] Willis R. Bryant, *Mortgage Lending* (New York: McGraw-Hill, 1956), chap. x.

[45] The law as amended provides for insurance as well as guaranty of home loans to veterans. Up to June 30, 1959, however, only 0.3 per cent of all loans closed in the program were insured.

[46] *Loan Guaranty Highlights* (Washington: U.S. Veterans Administration), June, 1959, p. 2.

TABLE VI-12

NUMBER AND CHARACTERISTICS OF VA-GUARANTEED LOANS FOR NEW AND EXISTING HOMES, 1946 TO 1959

Year	Section 501, number of loans closed	Principal amount of loans partially guaranteed ($000,000)	Average purchase price	Average loan, as a per cent of purchase price	Per cent of total VA loans with maturity 26–30 years
1946	442,037	2,302	n.a.	n.a.	n.a.
1947	531,217	3,286	n.a.	n.a.	n.a.
1948	349,565	1,881	n.a.	n.a.	n.a.
1949	276,795	1,424	n.a.	n.a.	n.a.
1950	497,596	3,073	n.a.	n.a.	n.a.
1951	447,373	3,614	n.a.	n.a.	n.a.
1952	306,466	2,718	n.a.	n.a.	n.a.
1953	322,053	3,061	11,117	86.4	5.4
1954	410,746	4,256	11,548	90.4	24.8
1955	649,412	7,154	12,026	92.4	44.7
1956	507,500	5,886	12,857	90.8	38.6
1957	306,437	3,758	13,715	90.6	47.3
1958	143,519	1,864	14,034	92.0	61.4
1959	210,511	2,788	13,979	95.0	72.0

Sources: 1946–1957: U.S. Housing and Home Finance Agency, *Housing Statistics, Historical Supplement* (Washington, December, 1958), pp. 195–196, 200. 1958: *Ibid.*, June, 1959, pp. 60–61. 1959: *Housing Statistics*, May, 1960, p. 62; *Housing Statistics, Annual Data*, March, 1960, p. 49.

Table VI–12 shows the expansion in the number of loans guaranteed under the veterans' home loan program in the postwar period, the gradual increase in the average home purchase price with the rise in home prices and building costs, and the lengthening of maturities in recent years. The sharp decline in the number and principal amount of home loans guaranteed in 1948–49, 1952–53, and in 1957–58 was primarily a reflection of the unattractiveness of Veterans Administration–guaranteed loans bearing a fixed maximum interest rate during periods of general credit restrictions.

Up to September 30, 1960, a total of 1,637,162 Veterans Administration home loans amounting to $10.5 billion had been paid in full. Although defaults were reported on 845,269 loans over the period from 1946 to September 30, 1960, these were "cured" without loss to the government in over 86 per cent of the cases and actual guaranty claims were paid by the federal government in only 63,874 cases, totaling $279.8 million—a default percentage representing approximately one quarter of 1 per cent of the original total amount of loans guaranteed and approximately one half of 1 per cent of the original guaranty amount.[47]

The veterans' home loan program, which was originally enacted as a temporary measure to effect the orderly readjustment of veterans of World War II to civilian life, is at present slated for termination on July 25, 1962, for World War II veterans and on January 31, 1965, for veterans of the Korean war. It has been estimated, however, that approximately ten million veterans still remained eligible for benefits under the program.

A special sample study of home loans guaranteed by the Veterans Administration during 1954 and 1955 revealed that the average age of veteran home purchasers was 32.1 years and the average estimated monthly housing expenses for veteran families participating in the program in those years was $96.75 (equivalent to 19.6 per cent of the average monthly income of $493.80).[48] Over 50 per cent of the veterans' home loans guaranteed during these years were to veterans with incomes between $300 and $499 per month, while only between 3 and 4 per cent of the number of loans were to those with incomes below $300 per month. The remainder of the loans were to veterans with incomes above $500 per month. The ratios of housing expense to monthly income varied from approximately 13 per cent for veterans with incomes of $800 per month and over to 29 per cent for those with monthly incomes of less than $300 per month.[49] Similarly, the average purchase prices for veterans with incomes of more than $800 per month were in excess of $16,000, while those with incomes of less than $300 purchased homes averaging approximately $8,300.

The Veterans Administration home loan program has been of broad significance to the postwar housing market. Not only have a large number of veteran home buyers taken advantage of the program to acquire homes, but the generous mortgage credit terms available through this program have been transmitted to the home market generally through resale of homes by veterans, the new purchaser carrying the existing loan on the property. As will be noted presently, the Veterans Administration home loan program, operated in conjunc-

---

[47] *Ibid.*, September, 1960, p. 2. Refunds and recoveries amounted to $237.2 million, leaving a net loss of only $42.6 million as of September 30, 1960.

[48] U.S. Veterans Administration, Department of Veterans' Benefits, Loan Guaranty Service, *Special Study of GI Home Loans Guaranteed by the Veterans' Administration in 1954 and 1955* (Washington, April 25, 1956). Monthly housing expenses include principal and interest repayments on mortgages, the estimated cost of property taxes, insurance, heat, and utilities, and an allowance for maintenance costs.

[49] *Ibid.*

tion with the secondary mortgage market facilities of the Federal National Mortgage Association, provided long-term amortized mortgage credit on low down-payment and monthly payment terms for an important segment of the housing market. The unattractiveness of fixed-interest-rate government-guaranteed or government-insured loans during the period of rising interest rates in recent years has reduced the volume of Veterans Administration–guaranteed loans to a small percentage of former levels, as shown in Table VI–12.

Federal National Mortgage Association

This agency was established in 1938 as successor to the RFC Mortgage Company to provide a secondary market for government-insured mortgage loans. The Federal National Mortgage Association has not functioned exclusively as a secondary mortgage market facility, but rather has served as a flexible instrument for implementing federal mortgage credit policy. Table VI–13 summarizes the annual purchases and sales of mortgages by FNMA and its year-end portfolios from 1948 to 1959. It can be noted that mortgage purchases have been confined to government-insured and government-guaranteed mortgages bearing fixed maximum interest rates. The volume of FNMA purchases of mortgages has varied with the availability of funds in the private lending market. A 1955 report by a nonpartisan task force on government lending agencies concluded as follows:

> In effect, the operations of FNMA have been a form of direct lending of public funds to maintain a par market for FHA-insured and VA-guaranteed mortgages. Private investors have found it profitable to turn over their holdings of such loans to FNMA whenever the fixed interest rate has been less than the comparable return available from other investments. In this way, the borrowers on FHA-insured and VA-guaranteed mortgages have been subsidized to the extent of the difference.[50]

Important adjustments were made in the character of FNMA operations by the Housing Act of 1954, which divided the operations of FNMA into three categories, "secondary market operations," "portfolio management and liquidation," and "special assistance functions." Funds to finance secondary market operations, which were envisaged in the Act as a privately financed activity, are derived from the sale of stock to lenders who sell mortgages to FNMA in the amount of 3 per cent (reduced later to 2 per cent) of the unpaid principal of the mortgages

[50] Commission on Organization of the Executive Branch of the Government, *Task Force Report on Lending Agencies* (Washington: Government Printing Office, 1955), p. 34.

TABLE VI–13

COMBINED PURCHASE AND SALE OPERATIONS OF THE FEDERAL NATIONAL MORTGAGE ASSOCIATION (FNMA), 1948 TO 1959
(In millions of dollars)

Year	Purchases			Sales			Balance of Mortgages Held on December 31		
	Total	FHA	VA	Total	FHA	VA	Total[a]	FHA	VA
1948	$ 197.9	$ 186.8	$ 11.1	$.....	$.....	$.....	$ 199	$ 188	$ 11
1949	672.2	252.7	419.5	19.8	19.4	0.4	828	403	425
1950	1,044.3	49.3	995.0	469.4	261.4	208.0	1,347	169	1,178
1951	677.1	74.3	602.8	111.1	28.2	82.8	1,850	204	1,646
1952	537.9	167.8	370.1	55.9	35.7	20.2	2,242	320	1,922
1953	542.5	355.1	187.4	221.1	32.3	181.4	2,462	621	1,841
1954	658.1[b]	353.6	260.8	525.2	134.3	381.1	2,476	802	1,632
1955	411.4	184.6	226.9	61.8	13.9	46.9	2,656	901	1,714
1956	608.7	153.2	455.6	5.0	2.9	11.7	3,086	978	2,069
1957	1,096.0	313.4	782.7	2.9	2.0	0.8	4,012	1,237	2,737
1958	622.8	469.4	153.4	482.3	155.4	326.8	3,938	1,484	2,418
1959	1,922.4	1,157.3	765.1	4.5	3.5	1.0	5,649[c]	2,713[c]	2,864[c]

Sources: United States Savings and Loan League, *Savings and Loan Fact Book, 1959* (Chicago, 1959), p. 107; U.S. Housing and Home Finance Agency, *Housing Statistics, Annual Data* (Washington, March, 1960), p. 52.

Note: All FNMA activity was with FHA-insured mortgages up to July 1, 1948. The breakdown of purchases and sales between FHA and VA loans as reported in the *Savings and Loan Fact Book, 1959*, does not equal the totals reported in *Housing Statistics* because of rounding and other miscellaneous adjustments.

[a] Total includes direct mortgages and Defense Homes Corporation notes from 1954 to 1959.

[b] Includes a transfer of Defense Homes Corporation notes and Reconstruction Finance Corporation mortgages totaling $43,700,000.

[c] February 28, 1960 (*Housing Statistics*, May, 1960, p. 71).

involved, and from the issuance of obligations of the Federal National Mortgage Association to private holders upon approval of the Secretary of the Treasury. Although obligations of the Association may be issued to the Secretary of the Treasury, they are not guaranteed by the United States Government.[51]

Under its new plan of operation as a secondary market facility, FNMA was directed to purchase only such mortgages as were of a quality to meet the purchase standards required of private investors and to proceed with the general liquidation of its portfolio ($4 billion).

Under the program of Special Assistance Functions, FNMA may purchase, or make commitments to purchase, such mortgages as the President of the United States shall determine to be in the public interest. An original limit of $300 million (raised in 1958 to $500 million) was placed on the total of mortgages held under the program, plus commitments to purchase. Government funds borrowed from the Treasury are used in financing this phase of the program.[52] Emergency housing legislation in 1958 increased the total authorization of funds under the direction of the President for special assistance programs to $500 million and initiated a new program of $1 billion requiring FNMA to buy FHA and VA mortgages up to $13,500 at par under special assistance programs. An additional $25 million was authorized for mortgage purchase by FNMA for military housing and $25 million for housing at research and development centers.[53] Based upon the experience in recent years, the federal government will employ the special assistance program as a means of stimulating the flow of mortgage funds for such special phases as housing for the aged, military housing, coöperative housing, and other housing for low- and moderate-income groups.

Changes in the status of the FNMA in 1954 envisaged the development of this agency as a privately financed secondary mortgage market facility. Experience to date suggests that this function will be overshadowed by use of FNMA by the federal government as an instrumentality for stimulating the flow of credit into residential mortgage markets during periods of credit stringency and as a means of financing special government assisted housing programs.

---

[51] *Ibid.*, p. 35. As of December 31, 1958, the Secretary of the Treasury owned preferred stock in the Federal National Mortgage Association amounting to $143 million. Common stock issued to mortgage sellers totaled $38 million, while funds borrowed from the U.S. Treasury amounted to $1.2 billion and debentures in the hands of the public totaled $797 million.

[52] "The Urban Residential Mortgage Market—Recent Experience," Federal Reserve Bank of St. Louis, *Monthly Review*, November, 1955, pp. 127–129.

[53] *House and Home*, April, 1958, pp. 52–53, and July, 1958, p. 47.

EVALUATION OF FEDERAL MORTGAGE CREDIT PROGRAMS

It was stated earlier that the central and continuing objectives of federal government housing policy have been to promote greater stability in the flow of residential mortgage funds, and to assure liberal credit for residential construction and home purchases. It is evident that mortgage loan credit generally has been available for longer terms and with higher loan-value ratios and lower interest rates during the years following World War II than prevailed in the decades of the 1920's or even in the 1930's. It is more difficult, however, to assess the contribution of federal government programs to these developments, since it can be maintained that more generous credit terms would have prevailed through normal competition among private leaders. There is some basis for contending that the large expansion in individual saving through life insurance companies and savings institutions during and after World War II provided the basis for a large flow of these savings into the residential mortgage market after World War II. It is, however, equally clear that the Federal Housing Administration and Veterans Administration loan insurance and guaranty programs facilitated and encouraged the flow of funds into these markets. Further, it is evident that the operations of the Federal Home Loan Bank System and of the Federal Savings and Loan Insurance Corporation augmented the flow of savings into savings and loan institutions and the ability of these institutions to accommodate the demand for mortgage funds.

It is even more difficult to determine whether the more liberal mortgage credit terms induced by federal loan insurance and guaranty programs resulted in a higher level of housing production during the postwar years than would have otherwise prevailed. Some students of this question have argued that residential construction following World War II was less than might have been expected in view of trends in population and family formation, relative to prewar levels, and that the primary effect of the government's credit liberalization program was to bring about a more rapid rise in construction costs and prices of housing relative to other goods.[54] Although many would agree that one result of federal mortgage finance policies has been to cause a somewhat greater rise in construction costs and home prices than would otherwise have resulted, the evidence marshaled in support of the

[54] R. J. Saulnier, Harold G. Halcrow, and Neil H. Jacoby, *Federal Lending and Loan Insurance* (Princeton, N.J.: Princeton University Press, 1958), pp. 341–347.

conclusion that federal programs failed to stimulate housing production is unconvincing.[55]

In evaluating the effect of government housing credit policies, Grebler concluded that "federal credit aids since the middle thirties have probably accelerated the decline in residential mortgage interest rates and the liberalization of other contract terms," but that "these advantages were at least partially cancelled by price effects."[56] Commenting elsewhere on the contribution of government policies to stability in residential construction, Grebler concluded:

> All that can be said with a degree of confidence is that recent governmental policies have done nothing to prevent fluctuations as great as, or even greater than, those observed in previous periods. They have certainly contributed to the sharp increase in building costs and in prices of new as well as existing houses.[57]

In an analysis of veterans' home loan purchases in the San Francisco Bay area from 1947 to 1949, Rathbun concluded that "over one half of these homebuyers could not have purchased the homes they bought if down payments had not been reduced or eliminated through the veterans' home loan program."[58] Although conceding that the federal

[55] The authors of *Federal Lending and Loan Insurance* present data comparing residential building activity from 1923 to 1925 in comparison with activity from 1948 to 1950 as a basis for the conclusion that "the boom of the late forties proves to be low in comparison with that of the twenties, despite the intervention in the former period of federal programs of credit aid." Although it is clear from the data presented that privately financed nonfarm dwelling production was lower in 1948–50 than in 1923–25, relative to the housing stock and to the increase in population, it does not follow that federal credit aids failed to stimulate housing production. In the first place, if the comparison of production is made over a longer period, e.g., from 1948 to 1957 as compared with 1921 to 1930, production in the postwar decade makes a much more favorable comparison with that of the earlier period. Second, the authors' assumption that, other things being equal, we should expect a higher rate of new building in 1950 than in 1925, assumes away a host of demographic and economic factors which influence the volume of housing production in a given year. Third, in arguing that the federal mortgage finance policies caused a rise in construction costs and home prices rather than a rise in production, the authors fail to recognize that the price and cost effects and the effect on housing construction volume are not unrelated, since the rise in home prices and construction costs has provided a safety cushion for mortgage lenders and also furnished incentive for home purchasers to take advantage of inflationary price increases.

[56] Leo Grebler, *The Role of Federal Credit Aids in Residential Construction* (New York: National Bureau of Economic Research, 1953), p. 53.

[57] Leo Grebler, "Stabilizing Residential Construction—A Review of the Postwar Test," *American Economic Review* September, 1949, p. 909. See also his papers on "The Role of Residential Capital Formation in Postwar Business Cycles," in *Conference on Savings and Residential Financing, 1959 Proceedings* (Chicago: United States Savings and Loan League, 1959).

[58] Daniel B. Rathbun, "The Veterans' Home-Loan Program: Success or Failure?"

home loan guaranty program probably resulted in increases in building costs and home prices and that the excess of market over fixed rates on government-guaranteed loans was added to the price of homes purchased by veterans, Rathbun's over-all evaluation of the program was that it has been successful in broadening the housing demand of low- and middle-income veterans.

It must be acknowledged that any final conclusion as to the effect of government housing finance policies upon the volume of housing production would require substantial additional knowledge concerning the price and income elasticities of housing demand and supply. The weight of evidence would seem to support the view that government loan insurance and guaranty programs have encouraged lenders to extend loan terms that have greatly magnified consumers' purchasing power in the housing market.[59] Some consumers have undoubtedly taken advantage of this expansion in purchasing power to increase expenditures for automobiles, travel, and other goods, since studies have shown wide variations in consumer expenditures for housing.[60] Sustained high levels of single-family housing production suggest that many family groups have taken advantage of generous government loan insurance or guaranty programs to acquire new or used housing since World War II.

Some observers have called attention to the illogic of a dual federal mortgage loan system involving the Federal Housing Administration, with its emphasis upon the security of the mortgage instrument, and the Federal Home Loan Bank System, emphasizing a strong system of home mortgage lending institutions. The Veterans Administration home loan guaranty program must be viewed as a "temporary" government mortgage loan facility. The question at issue is whether the Federal Home Loan Bank System could or should perform the entire function of providing residential mortgage credit.[61] Although this is debatable, it must be agreed that, lacking an effective secondary mortgage market, the Federal Housing Administration has been an effective

Appraisal Journal, July, 1954, p. 408. Rathbun found that 71 per cent of the veterans using Section 501 loans during the years 1947–49 in the San Francisco Bay area had incomes of $4,000 or less and that 75 per cent of them had liquid assets of less than $2,000.

[59] Albert H. Schaaf, "Federal Mortgage Interest Rate Policy and the Supply of FHA–VA Credit," *Review of Economics and Statistics,* November, 1958, pp. 384–389.

[60] Sherman J. Maisel and Louis Winnick, "Family Housing Expenditures: Elusive Laws and Intrusive Variances," a paper presented at the Conference on Consumption and Saving, Wharton School of Finance and Commerce, University of Pennsylvania, March 30–31, 1959.

[61] Husband and Anderson, *op. cit.,* pp. 405–407.

instrument for channeling institutional funds into the mortgage market. Its major shortcoming, as has been observed, has been the instability in the flow of mortgage credit over time.

It can be argued that any major reorganization of the federal mortgage lending program should provide for an improved secondary market facility. This might imply that the operations of the Federal National Mortgage Association should not be confined to FHA and VA mortgage paper, since this excludes the bulk of mortgage paper originated through the Federal Home Loan Bank System. The solution to this problem would appear to require either an extension of FNMA operations to the conventional loan market or the creation of an additional secondary market facility through the Federal Home Loan Bank System. It is the view of many that a new secondary mortgage market facility is needed to compensate for the complexities and rigidities of the present instrumentalities.[62] This would permit FNMA to be used in the implementation of broader programs of federal assistance and might provide a solution for the lack of a secondary market for conventional mortgage paper.

Public Housing

Congress sounded the keynote which continues as the guide for low-rent public housing policy, in the opening section of the Housing Act of 1937:

> It is the policy of the United States to promote the general welfare of the nation by employing its finances and credit to assist the several states and their political subdivisions to alleviate present and recurring unemployment and to remedy the unsafe and unsanitary housing conditions and the acute shortage of decent, safe and sanitary dwellings for families of low income in rural or urban communities which are injurious to the health, safety and morals of the citizens of the nation.

The dire fiscal straits of state and local governments during the depression and the fact that the federal public housing program was conceived primarily as an employment stimulus account for the fact that all but five states enacted legislation to permit municipalities to build and operate public housing with the aid of the federal government during the 1930's.

---

[62] Edward E. Edwards, "Improvement of Federal Home Loan Bank Program," in *Study of Mortgage Credit*, pp. 265–270; Kurt F. Flexner, "A Program for the Federal Home Loan Bank System Designed to Improve the Distribution of the Pool of Credit Available for New Residential Construction," *ibid.*, pp. 271–276; Robinson Newcomb, "Changes in Federal Home Loan Bank Programs," *ibid.*, pp. 277–282; Miles L. Colean, "A More Effective Mortgage Insurance System," *ibid.*, pp. 289–313.

Although it has been recommended that local and state governments assume greater financial responsibility for meeting the housing needs of low-income groups, only a few states in the heavily urbanized areas of the Atlantic coast have initiated programs of state assistance for low-income housing.[63]

Federal public housing legislation, as amended, provides for federal loans up to 90 per cent of construction costs and for annual subsidies to local housing authorities to make up the difference between the level of economic rents based on cost of facilities and the rents which low-income families are able to afford.

Under the 1937 Act the local government was required to contribute 10 per cent of the cost of construction of the project and 20 per cent of the annual subsidy. The former could be borrowed, and subsidy contributions could be in the form of tax exemptions. The upper limit of rentals in public housing was required to be 20 per cent below rents in "recent, safe, and sanitary" privately owned housing units. The Housing Act of 1949 was amended to require only that federally aided low-rent housing projects be exempt from local property taxation. Offsetting this, the law provided for payment by the federal government of a payment in lieu of taxes of 10 per cent of shelter rents provided the local contribution through tax exemption less federal payments in lieu of taxes equaled at least 20 per cent of federal annual contributions to be made. Under the law as amended, local authorities must establish minimum rents at a level high enough to cover all operating expenses and payments in lieu of taxes.

The construction cost limits of $1,000 per room under the 1937 Act were raised to $1,750 per room by the Housing Act of 1949, with a provision for increases of $750 per room where necessary. Maximum costs were increased by an additional $250 per room by the Housing Act of 1957. Original loan amortization periods of sixty years were reduced by the Housing Act of 1949 to forty years. Federal legislation requires that families be living in substandard housing to be eligible for admission, with special preferences given to veterans' families and to those displaced by urban redevelopment projects.

[63] Delmont K. Pfeffer, "Public Housing—History, Present State and Federal Programs," a lecture given at the Graduate School of Banking of the American Bankers Association, Rutgers University, June 20, 1951. Mr. Pfeffer pointed out that Connecticut, New Jersey, Massachusetts, and New York had initiated sizable programs prior to 1951, while Pennsylvania and New Hampshire had more modest programs. California and Texas have statutes requiring local referendum before construction of public housing, while Ohio has resisted public housing and does not exempt public housing from property taxes. Other states which had no laws authorizing the organization of local housing authorities in 1951 were Iowa, Kansas, Utah, Oklahoma, and Wyoming.

Income limits for admission and continued occupancy in public housing are set by local housing authorities, subject to approval by the Federal Public Housing Authority, and vary according to family size and local economic conditions. Local housing authorities select the tenants for low-rent housing, but are required to reëxamine annually the status of each family to determine its eligibility for continued occupancy. Eligibility for continued occupancy is based upon a separate set of income limits which are generally 25 per cent higher than those established for admission. As of December 31, 1959, the median income limit for admission to public housing was $3,000 annually for an average-size family. About 17 per cent of the localities with low-rent public housing programs had limits of $2,500 or less, while about 24 percent had limits as high as $3,500.[64] The median gross monthly rent of families admitted to public housing during the first half of 1959 was $38.

As of December 31, 1959, approximately 1.9 million persons were housed in 585,212 federal low-rent dwelling units. The capital investment of local housing authorities exceeded $3 billion, represented primarily by obligations of local housing authorities in the hands of private investors.[65] During the fiscal year ending June 30, 1959, contributions to local authorities for subsidizing rents totaled over $115 million, and the cumulative deficit in this federally subsidized program totaled over $885 million.

Table VI–1 shows that the volume of construction of public housing reached its peak in 1940 and 1941 as a result of the urgency of housing needs in war-affected communities. It will be recalled that an additional one million units of "temporary" war housing were added before and during World War II. The Housing Act of 1949 reaffirmed the need for federal aid to low-rent public housing and provided that the Public Housing Administration could authorize local authorities to commence the construction of 135,000 units each year in each of the succeeding five years. The Housing Act of 1954 (Public Law 560, 83d Congress) lowered the public housing goals of the 1949 Act and authorized 35,000 low-rent public housing units to be placed under annual contributions contract during the fiscal year 1955, and authorization for the year 1956 were limited by the Housing Amendments of 1955 (Public Law 345, 84th Congress) to not more than 45,000 units. The Housing Act of 1956 authorized the Public Housing Administration

---

[64] U.S. Housing and Home Finance Agency, *Thirteenth Annual Report, 1959,* p. 200.

[65] *Ibid.*, p. 219.

to enter into contracts with local authorities for 35,000 units each during the fiscal years 1958 and 1959.

It can be noted from Table VI–1 that the maximum number of low-rent public housing units started during any postwar year was in 1951, when 71,000 units were started. Under the stimulus of the depression year 1958, Congress extended existing but unused authorizations for one year and authorized an additional 35,000 low-rent units to be put under contract any time prior to July 1, 1962. It will be noted from Table VI–1 that, although 68,000 public housing units were started in 1958, more than half of these were military housing. During the calendar year 1958 local governments asked for authority to build more than 48,000 low-rent public housing units. It can also be seen that military housing accounted for almost half of total public housing construction in 1959.

The failure of the federal low-rent public housing program to make a greater contribution to the nation's housing supply can be attributed to two principal factors:

Many citizens, including influential real estate and construction industry groups, oppose in principle any programs for direct federal subsidies for housing.

Opponents of public subsidies for housing low-income groups view the federal program as a failure and its advocates recognize its basic shortcomings.

Although the opposition of industry groups to federally subsidized public housing has been an important factor, it is probably true that the widespread criticism of the administration and leadership in the federal low-rent program has been the principal factor accounting for its lack of public support. It is notable, for example, that the President's Advisory Committee on Government Housing Policies and Programs, in its 1953 report, recommended a continuation of the public housing program, but recommended changes to alter its institutionalized character.[66] Sociologists have pointed out that the combination of bureaucratization in public housing management, restrictions upon earnings and initiative of occupants, and the fact that "inadequate personalities and problem-type persons tend to accumulate in public housing" supports the view that "public housing has been and is still characterized by a confusion in its basic objectives." [67] One of the

[66] *Recommendations on Government Housing Policies and Programs* (Washington, 1953), p. 16.

[67] H. Warren Dunham and Nathan D. Grundstein, "The Impact of a Confusion of Social Objectives in Public Housing: A Preliminary Analysis," *Marriage and Family Living*, XVII, No. 2 (May, 1955), 103–113.

staunch leaders of the public housing movement in the United States commented in a similar vein in a recent appeal for a fresh approach to the public housing problem:

Life in the usual public housing project just is not the way most American families want to live. Nor does it reflect our accepted values as to the way people should live. . . . Public housing projects tend to be very large and highly standardized in their design . . . their density makes them seem much more institutional . . . [and] any charity stigma that attaches to subsidized housing is thus reinforced. Each project proclaims visually, that it serves the "lowest income group." [68]

Some insight into the attitudes of former public housing residents can be secured from the results of a 1957 survey by the Public Housing Administration of 2,044 families who had recently moved from public housing projects in nine cities:[69]

The "move-out" rate for public housing rose nationally from 13 per cent to 28 per cent per year in 1954 and declined slightly from 1954 to 1957.

With the rise in incomes and more rigid enforcement of income limits upon occupancy, the percentage of families found ineligible to remain in public housing declined from 22 per cent of those re-examined in 1949 to 12 per cent in 1951 and to only 4 per cent in 1956.

Income limits were raised with the increase in the cost of living and wages. Between 1949 and 1956 the median income of *eligible* families in public housing increased from $1,700 to $2,164, a rise of 27 per cent.

Table VI–14 shows a percentage distribution of the major causes of move-outs for the sample families surveyed during the six-month period ending June 1, 1957.

In view of the criticisms of public housing, it is interesting to note that approximately one quarter of those leaving public housing were dissatisfied. It can be surmised that a substantial proportion of those shown as moving for "cause not ascertained" may also have been dissatisfied.

It is of further interest to note that 25 per cent left at the request of the management, with a high and low range of 41 per cent and 13 per cent, and that a substantial proportion of these were evicted because of nonpayment of rent.

In view of the strong arguments referred to below against the use

[68] Catherine Bauer, "The Dreary Deadlock of Public Housing," *Architectural Forum*, CVI, No. 5 (May, 1957), 141–142.

[69] U.S. Housing and Home Finance Agency, Public Housing Administration, *Mobility and Motivations—Survey of Families Moving from Low-Rent Housing* (Washington, April, 1958), pp. 1–66.

TABLE VI–14

WHY FAMILIES MOVE FROM LOW-RENT HOUSING
(In percentages)

Reasons	Mean	Range High	Range Low
Total move-outs	100	—	—
By request of management	25	41	13
Ineligibility	9	20	2
Other reasons	16	24	5
Due to changes in personal circumstances	36	50	27
Left area	18	38	11
Circumstances made move necessary	18	29	8
By choice	26	40	18
Desire for other housing	4	9	1
Dissatisfied	22	35	14
Already returned to public housing	2	3	0
Cause not ascertained	11	17	5
Scattered or no member able to give information	4	12	...[a]
Could not be located	6	10	0
Information refused	1	2	0

Source: U.S. Housing and Home Finance Agency, Public Housing Administration, *Mobility and Motivations . . . Survey of Families Moving from Low-Rent Housing* (Washington, April, 1958), p. 15.

[a] Less than 0.5 per cent.

of a rent certificate plan, it is of extreme interest to note that many needy families are forced to leave low-rent public housing because of nonpayment of rent.

In the author's experience, local housing authorities tend to select public housing tenants much as a private landlord would, seeking the most stable, happily married, educated wage earners who will minimize management problems. This conception of public housing management negates to a degree the basic principle of federal aid to low-rent housing, namely, that it will serve the needy and the indigent.

A former assistant commissioner in the Public Housing Administration recently criticized the federal leadership, holding that the Public Housing Authority is "very largely to blame" for the fact that the "whole public housing program is sick unto death," and that the federal administrators have displayed a "bankruptcy of leadership, inflexible and bureaucratic supervision and a smug and complacent attitude." [70]

The findings of a 1960 conference on "Housing the Economically and Socially Disadvantaged in the Population" emphasized the need

[70] "ASPO Hears Public Housers Blame PHA for Their Troubles," *House and Home*, July, 1958, p. 61.

for improved federal and local administration of the federal public housing program, less institutionalism in public housing, and wider experimentation with rehabilitation and purchase of old and new private projects.[71]

The author of a recent study of public housing in Pittsburgh, Pennsylvania, concludes:

> . . . the public housing program has not made any substantial inroads into the problem of supplying [a] "decent home and a suitable living environment for every American family"—this, despite the addition of 489,744 units of public housing space. The program, to date, has apparently failed to achieve even a temporary solution to the housing problems of the majority of the low-income group, let alone a lasting solution.[72]

As a result of the widespread criticism of the federal public housing program, fundamental changes in its character and operation have been recommended. In another work, the present author recommended experimentation with a variety of alternative solutions to the low-income housing problem, including tax subsidies, family income subsidies, and increased reliance upon locally initiated and controlled programs for renovating existing housing.[73]

In a special report to the United States Housing Administration in January, 1960, Dr. Ernest M. Fisher recommended the development of a single closely knit federal housing agency, the relaxation of federal controls over local housing programs, and the development of integrated, broadened, and diversified housing programs on the local level.[74] The implications of the lack of success of federal programs for improving the housing of low-income groups in the United States will be explored further below.

---

[71] Metropolitan Housing and Planning Council of Chicago, in coöperation with Action, Inc., of New York, The National Council for Good Cities, *Interim Report on Housing the Economically and Socially Disadvantaged Groups in the Population,* proceedings and working papers of a conference held in Highland Park, Ill., February 26–27, 1960 (Chicago: Metropolitan Housing and Planning Council of Chicago, 1960), pp. 2–3.

[72] Robert K. Brown, *Public Housing in Action: The Record of Pittsburgh* (Pittsburgh: University of Pittsburgh Press, 1959), p. 79.

[73] Paul F. Wendt, *The Role of the Federal Government in Housing* (Washington: American Enterprise Association, Inc., 1956), chaps. iii–iv.

[74] Ernest M. Fisher, *A Study of Housing Programs and Policies* (Washington: U.S. Housing and Home Finance Agency, January, 1960), p. v. See also *Views on Public Housing,* a symposium of letters written at the request of Norman P. Mason, United States Housing Administrator (Washington: U.S. Housing and Home Finance Agency, March, 1960).

Causes of Slums and Blight

Cities undergo constant change with growth and shifts in economic functions, obsolescence, and changes in technology. The development of great American cities has resulted from a continuous and dynamic succession of land uses through public and private investment. It is in the nature of this process that segments of cities will be old and worn out at any given time and that inevitably some cities will decline in area and importance. The problem of urban slums and blight arises when the processes of renewal through private investment seem to be permanently interrupted. It has long been recognized that any realistic program for the improvement of urban housing would require a broad attack on this problem.

The problems of urban blight go far beyond the consideration of housing low-income families living in slums, and their causes must be sought in the complexity of factors affecting urban real estate investment. One of the underlying causes of the interruption of private investment in urban real estate is found in the serious financial problems which have plagued American cities and in the fact that cities have relied so heavily upon real estate taxation as the basis for municipal revenues. Allied to this is the cumulative obsolescence which has occurred in streets, transportation services, schools, and other public facilities within cities. Undoubtedly, the tremendous stimulus to homeownership through federal mortgage insurance programs has combined with the forces of industrial and commercial dispersion to direct residential investment to ownership housing in outlying areas beyond the reach of the central city taxes. A third basic cause of slums is to be found in the conditions of housing shortage which have prevailed in many large American cities for almost half a century. These conditions have had particular impact upon racial minorities and low-income groups with less residential mobility than others.

As a result of housing shortages, landlords have received continuous incomes from substandard properties; city officials have failed to establish and enforce minimum housing standards, and the slums endure. The imposition of federal rent controls during World War II and its aftermath, and their continuance in some cities and states, reduced maintenance standards in urban rental housing and probably deterred new investment or renovation of substandard housing. Another obstacle to the functioning of the renewal processes is to be found in the diversity of property ownership in cities and in the fact that owners hold out for high prices in the expectation of the growth of new commercial or residential areas.

The attack on the problem of slums and blight has been complicated not only because of its complexity, but also because of the wide differences in point of view of those concerned with the problem. Professional "housers" view slums primarily as an arena for public housing. ("Comprehensive redevelopment . . . could never become a reality in most localities without a continuous public housing program on a major scale.") [75] Downtown merchants support urban redevelopment in order to draw population and purchasing power back to the central city. Investors and property owners view it as a means of bolstering property values and municipal finances, but are strongly opposed to public housing. City planners look upon urban redevelopment as a golden opportunity to achieve more rational land use in central areas of cities. Recently, homebuilding and real estate groups have mobilized strongly behind urban renewal as a means of revitalizing the "filtering processes" in housing and fore-stalling public housing development. These differences in viewpoints have prompted the comment that "Seldom has such a variegated crew of would-be angels tried to sit on the same pin at the same time." [76]

Federal Aid for Slum Clearance and Redevelopment

It was noted above that the entry of the government into the field of local slum clearance was primarily a depression pump-priming measure and that the accomplishment was negligible. The Housing Act of 1937 approached the problem of urban blight as a housing problem alone and sought to remove slums by requiring that a substandard dwelling be eliminated for every low-rent public housing unit built. This "equivalent elimination" doctrine has served to link slum clearance with federal public housing ever since the passage of the 1937 Act.

In the Housing Act of 1949 the Congress recognized that a comprehensive attack upon the slum problem must be broader than was possible under a public housing program alone, and provided for participation by private enterprise in the redevelopment of slum areas. The Act authorized the Housing and Home Finance Agency to make loans up to $1 billion and grants up to $500 million to localities to

[75] Coleman Woodbury and Frederick Gutheim, *Rethinking Urban Development*, Urban Relevelopment Series, No. 1 (Chicago: Public Administration Service, 1949), p. 13.

[76] Catherine Bauer, "Redevelopment: A Misfit in the Fifties," in Coleman Woodbury (ed.), *The Future of Cities and Urban Redevelopment* (Chicago: University of Chicago Press, 1958), p. 9.

assemble land, clear slums, and make the areas available for redevelopment by either public or private enterprise.

The Housing Act of 1949 continued the former emphasis upon the provision of public housing in redevelopment by requiring that adequate housing be made available to all families displaced by redevelopment projects under the Act. The standards of "adequacy" in terms of quality, location, and rentals were such that they could be satisfied only by public housing in most localities. In order to link public housing more closely with federal redevelopment, the Act required that (except in the case of veterans for a five-year period) admission to low-rent housing should be restricted to families coming from substandard dwellings and that families displaced by redevelopment should be given preference for admission to public housing in each locality.[77]

In setting up an "Urban Renewal Fund," the Housing Act of 1954 liberalized the conditions under which the HHFA could make advances, loans, and grants to communities for planning and carrying out urban renewal, and it also set forth the criteria to be used by the Administrator in determining whether a city had undertaken a "positive program" for the prevention of blight and a "workable program" for dealing with slums and blight.[78] The 1954 Act continued the limitation in former laws that occupancy of new public housing be limited to "displaces" from governmental redevelopment or to families coming from substandard dwellings.[79]

Acting upon the recommendations of the President's Advisory Committee on Government Housing Policies and Programs, Congress also provided for FHA insurance of long-term loans for the rehabilitation of existing dwellings and construction of new dwellings in urban renewal areas in the Housing Act of 1954 (Sec. 220) and for the provision of low cost housing for relocation of families displaced from urban renewal areas (Sec. 211).

The main features of the federal government's current program for aiding in slum clearance and urban renewal are:

Federal capital grants to local redevelopment agencies to aid in the acquisition of land for redevelopment in the amount of two thirds of the difference between acquisition cost of the land and its value for sale for future development (net project cost)

Sale of land acquired by public condemnation to private developers at prices designed to encourage private investment

---

[77] U.S. Housing and Home Finance Agency, *The Relationship Between Slum Clearance and Urban Redevelopment and Low-Rent Housing* (Washington, 1950).

[78] Public Law 560, 83d Congress, 2d session, Secs. 100–101.

[79] "Housing Law: After Long Labor, a Mouse," *House and Home,* September, 1955, pp. 39–40.

Federal loans and technical aid for surveys, plans, and other assistance to local governments in the elimination of slums and blighted areas

Encouragement of the adoption of "positive" and "workable" programs for the prevention and elimination of slums and blight through the requirement of such programs as a condition for receiving federal assistance

Emphasis upon relocation of former slum dwellers as a major feature of any federally aided redevelopment plans.

It was reported as of June, 1955, that 99 urban redevelopment projects had reached the project-execution stage, 104 were in the final planning stages, and 94 were in preliminary planning stages, and that two thirds of the states had enacted legislation authorizing local public agencies to undertake slum clearance and urban redevelopment projects.[80]

By December 31, 1959, the total number of "well advanced" federally assisted urban renewal projects in progress was 437, representing total net project costs in excess of $1 billion, of which the federal share was $853 million. According to the Housing and Home Finance Agency, 186,760 dwelling units were substandard, out of a total of 235,173 reported in 426 of these projects. It was estimated that 106,213 families, out of a total of 187,487, were eligible for public low-rent housing.[81] As a reflection of the slowness with which the urban renewal program has progressed, only 26 projects were completed from 1949 to 1959.

Urban Renewal and Rental Housing

The use of eminent domain to facilitate assembly of land for redevelopment is considered the most important single factor encouraging new private investment in slum and blighted areas. By common agreement, however, the success of urban renewal programs depends upon

---

[80] U.S. Housing and Home Finance Agency, Urban Renewal Administration, *Urban Renewal Project Characteristics* (Washington, June 30, 1955), p. 55, Table 1.

See also U.S. 83d Cong., 2d sess., *Hearings Before the Committee on Banking and Currency, House of Representatives, on H.R. 7839, Housing Act of 1954, Testimony of Hon. James W. Follin,* p. 127. Currently cities are experiencing a surge in public and private investment. It is notable, however, that most of the new investment is in commercial and public buildings rather than in rental housing. Federal loans, grants, and technical aid and local redevelopment agencies have undoubtedly played an important part in encouraging this new investment. Cf. "Rebirth of the Cities," *Time,* December 5, 1955, pp. 25–28.

[81] U.S. Housing and Home Finance Agency, *Thirteenth Annual Report, 1959,* pp. 271–272,

the encouragement of large-scale private investment in rental housing.[82] In the light of this, it is discouraging to note that federal housing policies during most of the postwar period failed to attract large-scale investment in rental properties.[83] This is of significance, not only in connection with the record and prospects for urban renewal, but also in accounting for the predominance of single-family house construction in the United States during the years following World War II.

Any evaluation of national progress in urban renewal must conclude that government-aided programs have been more promising than productive thus far. The long-standing controversy over public housing in urban areas was an important factor in delaying the initiation of renewal in many cities. The failure of government programs to stimulate large-scale private investment in rental housing has been a related and an important influence. A wave of public interest in renewing America's slum areas has been accompanied by vigorous efforts in many cities to accelerate urban renewal programs. The rapid increase in applications for federal aid seem to augur greater progress in the next decade.

Fundamental questions concerning federal urban renewal programs remain unanswered. Why is it particularly desirable to stimulate investment in existing downtown areas? Would it not be more efficient in the long run to rebuild outside existing cities? Can the assembly of land by public agencies for sale to private developers below cost be rationalized as an appropriate use of public funds? Will such a program actually result in any substantial change in the rate of new investment in existing cities? What, if any, is the true relationship between federal housing programs and urban renewal? How effective will code enforcement be in improving housing standards in the absence of programs to stimulate new housing production? What will be the effects on the total housing market and new construction? Is it

[82] The President's Advisory Committee on Government Housing Policies and Programs (in its 1953 *Recommendations* . . . , pp. 110–111) estimated that the cost of removing an estimated 5 million substandard dwelling units requiring demolition would probably equal $15 billion and that at the rate of clearance then current it would take over two hundred years to do the job. In addition to costs of removal, it was estimated that public improvements required would equal $9 billion. These estimates do not include the costs of rehabilitation of old dwellings or construction of new dwelling units to replace those demolished.

[83] Miles L. Colean, "Impotency of FHA Policies on Apartment Finance," *Architectural Forum*, CII, No. 6 (June, 1955), 110: "The whole FHA rental housing experience, including the aftermath of investigation, accusation, black-listing and general hubbub, is a perfect example of missing the main point . . . The problem of equity investment in rental property is not one of getting the money in but of getting it out."

efficient and economical to encourage rehabilitation of slum dwellings? These and a host of similar questions plague the critical analyst of federal urban renewal programs, and may account for some of the delay and confusion that underlies federal urban renewal programs. In addition, they point up the obvious fact that federal urban renewal legislation is only in minor part a housing program.

Costs of Federal Housing Programs

Estimation of the total costs of federal housing programs during the post-World War II period is very difficult. Table VI–15 shows the

TABLE VI–15

Estimated Direct Costs of Federal Government Housing Programs, 1950 to 1958
(In millions of dollars)

Year	Veterans Administration loan guaranty program	Public Housing Administration		Urban Renewal Administration capital grants disbursed	Federal Housing Administration		Total expenses, columns 1–5
		Administrative expenses	Annual contributions		Operating expenses	Total income from fees, premiums, and investments	
	(1)	(2)	(3)	(4)	(5)	(6)	
1950...	$ 59	$ 6.3	$ 5.7	—	$ 27.5	$ 85.7	$ 98.5
1951...	90	9.7	9.1	—	31.3	98.0	140.1
1952...	78	9.3	12.6	—	30.6	103.0	130.5
1953...	66	8.2	25.9	$ 8.7	31.3	115.3	140.1
1954...	45	6.6	44.5	12.6	31.4	125.2	140.1
1955...	29	7.4	66.6	37.6	36.2	138.8	176.8
1956...	40	9.1	81.7	16.1	40.6	145.5	187.5
1957...	60	10.0	90.6	30.2	41.3	147.0	232.1
1958...	80	11.6	98.7	49.7	45.5	157.2	285.5
1959...	121	12.4	115.4	78.5	52.8	181.5	380.1
Total..	$668	$90.6	$550.8	$233.4	$368.5	$1,297.2	$1,911.3

Sources: Col. 1, U.S. Bureau of the Census, *Statistical Abstract of the United States, 1960* (Washington, 1960), p. 252; cols. 2–3, Robert Moore Fisher, *Twenty Years of Public Housing* (New York: Harper, 1959), Table 10; col. 4, U.S. Housing and Home Finance Agency, *Thirteenth Annual Report, 1959* (Washington, 1960), p. 275; cols. 5–6, *ibid.*, p. 151.

administrative and other direct costs of major government housing programs from 1950 to 1958. It will be noted that the income from Federal Housing Administration insurance fees, premiums, and investments of reserve funds approximately offset the administrative and other direct costs of government housing programs from 1950 to 1953. Since that time the income from Federal Housing Administration operations has increased only moderately, while substantial increases have occurred in the annual cost of the federal urban renewal and public housing administration programs. It must be recognized that the cumulative excess in Federal Housing Administration fees over expenses is set aside in reserves of the Title I Housing Insurance Fund, the Mutual Mortgage Insurance Fund, and miscellaneous other funds for the reimbursement of claims made to FHA by lenders. Total reserves in these insurance funds amounted to approximately $643 million on June 30, 1958, of which $406 million was represented by reserves in the Mutual Mortgage Insurance Fund.[84]

It can be noted from Table VI–15 that the operating and administrative costs of federal housing programs rose from $98.5 million in 1950 to $392 million in 1958. It can also be seen that these costs exceeded income from mortgage insurance fees and other premiums by $234 million by 1958.

The indirect costs of federal housing programs are more difficult to determine. The increased interest cost to the federal government on its total debt resulting from the federal guarantee of local housing authority obligations and those of the Federal National Mortgage Association is probably minimal, although the actual effect is indeterminate. The exemption from federal income taxation of local housing authority obligations, which exceeded $3 billion at the end of 1957, undoubtedly results in an undeterminable tax revenue loss to the federal government. The disbursement of payments by the federal government to local housing authorities in lieu of local property taxes represents a cost to the federal government and an offsetting revenue to local governments. A 1952 study by the Public Housing Administration revealed that the federal government made payments in lieu of taxes amounting to $3,398,000 on 412 projects covering 143,430 dwelling units. The dwellings included accounted for somewhat less than one quarter of the total number of dwelling units in the federal low-rent housing program.[85] Operating expenses of the Federal National Mortgage Asso-

[84] U.S. Housing and Home Finance Agency, *Twelfth Annual Report, 1958*, p. 147. As of June 30, 1959, these reserves totaled $758 million, of which $476 million was represented by the Mutual Mortgage Insurance Fund. *Thirteenth Annual Report, 1959*, p. 153.

[85] Robert Moore Fisher, *Twenty Years of Public Housing*, p. 199. It was estimated that the payments in lieu of taxes by the federal government represented approximately 27 per cent of the full taxes which would have been payable if the projects were privately owned.

ciation are omitted from Table VI–15 because the operations of that agency have been required to be self-supporting since its reorganization in 1954.

On the whole it would appear that the total costs of federal housing programs in the United States have risen quite rapidly in recent years, and that this is primarily attributable to rising expenditures for urban renewal and public housing programs.

Total expenditures by state and local governmental units for housing and community redevelopment ranged between $450 and $630 million from 1950 to 1957, and predominantly represented expenditures for provision of local public housing.

Evaluation

It has been seen that postwar housing policy in the United States has been keyed to the following principles:

Primary reliance upon the stimulation of a high volume of privately owned and occupied single-family houses

Federal insurance and guaranty of loans to encourage the granting of loans on generous terms by private lenders

Special interest-rate subsidies for veteran groups

The provision of publicly owned housing at subsidized rents for low-income groups occupying substandard housing

Federal loans and grants for urban renewal and slum clearance

The evidence reviewed above has shown that these programs, aided by a major expansion in family incomes, have resulted in a sustained high volume of new housing production during the postwar years, a large increase in homeownership, and a major improvement in housing standards in the United States.

A review of specific criticisms of federal housing policies provides a suitable framework for evaluation of housing policies in the United States.

Criticism 1. Federal Mortgage Insurance programs have not met the needs of families most in need of housing.

The housing status of nonfarm family units in the United States for selected years is shown in Table VI–16. It can be noted that the percentage of homeownership has increased rapidly during the postwar years for all family income segments except the two lowest-quintile income segments.[86] The relatively high percentage of homeowners in

[86] As of 1957, one fifth of total families had incomes under $2,500 and another fifth had incomes between $2,500 and approximately $4,500. U.S. Bureau of the

the lowest income group can be explained in part by the large numbers of retired family heads typically owning their own homes and reporting minimum incomes. As will be noted presently, data on the number of nonmortgaged homes in the lower price ranges suggest that many of the lowest-income families own their homes free of any mortgage debt. Table VI–16 also reveals the tendency for many low-income families to share homes with others either from choice or necessity. The substantially lower percentage of nonwhite families owning their own homes is indicative of the concentration of such families in the lower income groups. It is important to realize that the percentage data in the table should not be allowed to obscure the fact that large absolute increases have taken place in the number of low-income families owning their own homes in the postwar years.

In considering the impact of government programs on these trends, it should be observed that less than 25 per cent of the total dollar volume of mortgage debt outstanding at the end of 1945 was government insured or government guaranteed. The proportion had increased to approximately 32 per cent by 1950, and by December, 1959, the total amount of government-underwritten mortgage loans totaled $53.8 billion or 41 per cent of the total mortgage debt outstanding in the United States.[87] These trends, of course, provide no conclusive evidence of the particular impact of government loan programs upon homeownership trends for low-income groups.

It is important to observe from Table VI–17 that approximately 45 per cent of the single-family owner-occupied homes were not mortgaged in 1956, and that a substantial proportion of these were homes with relatively low market values and were, presumably, occupied by low-income groups.

The distribution of mortgage loans outstanding on December 31, 1956, by type of loan and income of family, also shown in Table VI–17, reveals that less than a half a million families owning single-family mortgaged homes and having incomes below $4,000 held government-insured or government-guaranteed loans, and that only 1,267,000 home-owning families with incomes under $5,000 held government-insured or government-guaranteed loans. In contrast, 1,260,000 families owning single-family homes and having incomes under $4,000 held conventional mortgage loans, while over two million families with incomes under $5,000 had conventional mortgage loans. These statistics can be compared with the most recent estimates that approximately 16 million

---

Census, *Current Population Reports—Consumer Income,* Series P-60, No. 30 (Washington, December, 1958), p. 21, Table 4.

[87] *Federal Reserve Bulletin,* October, 1960, p. 1163.

TABLE VI–16

HOUSING STATUS OF NONFARM FAMILY UNITS WITHIN SPECIFIED GROUPS
(Percentage distribution)

Group characteristic	All cases	Owns 1959	Owns 1954	Owns 1949	Rents 1959	Rents 1954	Rents 1949	Others 1959	Others 1954	Others 1949
All nonfarm family units[a]	100	58	56	51	35	37	40	7	7	10
Nonfarm family income quintiles:[b]										
Lowest	100	46	45	40	36	34	38	18	22	22
Second	100	42	46	43	48	47	46	9	7	11
Third	100	59	51	47	37	44	45	4	5	8
Fourth	100	63	65	55	34	32	41	4	3	4
Highest	100	79	71	69	20	28	28	1	1	2
Age of head of family:										
18–24	100	16	17	21	57	50	48	26	25	31
25–34	100	42	42	35	52	52	53	6	6	12
35–44	100	63	57	53	33	38	42	5	5	5
45–54	100	64	63	59	31	31	34	5	5	7
55–64	100	69	66	62	25	28	32	6	6	6
65 and over	100	66	63	59	24	23	27	10	14	14
Occupation of head of family:										
Professional and semiprofessional	100	54	58	48	37	36	38	9	6	14
Managerial	100	70	59	66	27	37	30	2	4	4
Self-employed businessmen	100	80	76		19	22		1	2	
Clerical and sales	100	58	55	46	38	37	41	4	8	13
Skilled	100	63	54	52	33	41	44	4	4	4
Semiskilled	100	54			42			4		
Unskilled and service	100	43	41	40	43	42	43	14	17	17
Retired	100	68	65	60	23	21	25	9	14	14
Race of head of family:										
White	100	60	57	53	33	35	38	7	8	9
Nonwhite	100	40	40	31	52	32	31	8	8	18

TABLE VI–16 (*Continued*)

Source: "1959 Survey of Consumer Finances, Housing of Nonfarm Families," *Federal Reserve Bulletin*, September, 1959, p. 1107, Supplementary Table 1.

Note: The data are as of date of interview, early in year indicated. The "Rents" group differs from that in other years because it excludes family units that rent part of another family unit's dwelling. If these units were included, the proportion renting in 1959, 1954, and 1949 would increase by 2, 3, and 4 percentage points, respectively, and the proportions in the "Others" group would decrease correspondingly. The data under "Others" refer to family units that rent part of another family unit's dwelling, receive housing as part of compensation, live temporarily in houses they have sold, etc. Details may not add to totals because of rounding.

[a] A family unit includes all persons living in the same dwelling who are related by blood, marriage, or adoption. Single-person family units are included.

[b] Quintiles were obtained by ranking nonfarm family units according to money income before taxes in the preceding year.

TABLE VI-17

PROPERTY AND MORTGAGE CHARACTERISTICS, PROPERTY WITH ONE DWELLING UNIT, 1956

Subject	Market value of property						
	Total	Less than $8,000	$8,000 to $12,999	$13,000 to $20,000	More than $20,000	Not reported	Median market value
Mortgaged.......	12,713,028	2,541,780	4,422,808	4,005,374	1,688,917	54,149	$12,416
Nonmortgaged...	9,950,333	3,772,289	3,004,615	1,588,535	1,142,362	442,532	$ 9,611

Subject	Type of first mortgage, with no second mortgage				
	Total	FHA	VA	Conventional	Not reported
Owner characteristics:					
Total..........................	12,713,028	1,998,461	2,890,339	5,968,442	989,248
Income of family:					
Less than $2,000..............	442,247	40,341	36,089	269,843	60,288
$2,000 to $2,999..............	493,266	29,397	48,757	306,056	68,910
$3,000 to $3,999..............	1,248,478	113,932	187,242	684,662	159,621
$4,000 to $4,999..............	1,898,220	312,536	498,709	815,966	122,350
$5,000 to $5,999..............	2,110,479	328,037	657,914	855,561	155,210
$6,000 to $6,999..............	1,527,595	348,814	382,314	598,592	95,809
$7,000 to 7,999...............	1,213,346	191,870	391,417	469,363	86,189
$8,000 to $8,999..............	712,770	139,600	158,814	332,765	43,284
$9,000 to $9,999..............	462,910	73,538	102,338	232,245	17,026
$10,000 or more...............	1,326,428	194,678	201,454	746,720	75,287
Not reported..................	1,277,289	225,718	225,291	656,669	105,274
Median income.................	$5,775	$6,178	$5,854	$5,677	...
Property characteristics:					
Median purchase price........	$10,237	$10,894	$11,092	$9,362	...
Median market value.........	$12,416	$13,144	$12,695	$12,360	...
Median loan.................	$7,765	$8,477	$9,879	$6,206	...
New or previously occupied, by year acquired:					
1955 to 1956					
New.......................	1,877,724	304,310	695,474	668,711	82,233
Previously occupied.........	2,186,247	289,675	508,286	992,675	148,626
1950 to 1954					
New.......................	2,656,167	566,729	823,558	1,042,150	115,153
Previously occupied.........	2,918,037	438,713	542,144	1,473,235	240,050
1949 or earlier					
New.......................	288,941	51,514	18,383	159,125	43,287
Previously occupied.........	2,737,739	341,958	300,185	1,611,539	340,703
Not reported..................	48,173	5,562	2,309	21,007	19,196

Source: U.S. Bureau of the Census, "Financing of Owner-Occupied Residential Properties," *1956 National Housing Inventory* (Washington, 1958), II, 17, 20, 22–23.

American families had annual incomes in 1957 of less than $4,000 and that 22,059,000 families had annual incomes of less than $5,000.

The data in Table VI–17 confirm earlier data from the 1950 census of housing which showed that purchases of homes in 1949 and 1950 financed with government-insured or government-guaranteed loans were concentrated in the $6,000-to-$12,000 price classes and that substantially larger percentages of low-priced homes were financed with conventional loans.[88] The evidence would seem to demonstrate that small percentages of low-income families were borrowers under federal loan programs.

It can also be noted from Table VI–17 that the average family income, purchase price, estimated market value, and amount of original loan were lower for borrowers on conventional mortgages than for either FHA or VA borrowers. These differences reflect the influence of several factors:

Greater proportionate volume of government loan activity at the higher postwar price levels.

Greater proportionate volume of government loan activity in the new versus the existing home market.

More generous loan terms in the government sector.

Concentration of low income purchasers on conventional borrowing in the lower priced, older home field. (Many such homes fail to meet minimum construction requirements of FHA and VA.)

The conclusion from the data of Tables VI–16 and VI–17 that low-income home purchasers have been served primarily in the conventional loan market does not establish that government loan programs have had no effect upon the credit terms available to them. To the extent that the government's loan insurance and guaranty programs have actually attracted funds to the residential mortgage market which would not otherwise have been available, it can be argued that government programs have resulted in an increase in the total supply of mortgage funds and hence have improved the general terms of availability to all income groups. Specifically, the program of the Federal Savings and Loan Insurance Corporation has been an important factor undergirdling the expansion in conventional lending. Further, the Federal National Mortgage Association, through its programs of extending loan commitments and purchasing government-insured and government-guaranteed loans in the secondary market has made it possible for conventional and government-insured lending to increase. It can also be argued that more favorable competitive loan terms in the government sector of the market have encouraged conventional lenders to offer credit on more liberal terms than would otherwise have been available. Although it is impossible to measure the indirect effect of government mortgage loan policies upon the terms of lending in the conventional market, it can be assumed to have been substantial.

No conclusive evidence is at hand to determine the proportion of

---

[88] Grebler, *The Role of Federal Credit Aids in Residential Construction,* pp. 24–25.

American families *potentially* assisted by federal mortgage insurance programs, and the views expressed on the question vary widely. One critic pointed out in 1950 that "only about 11 million of the 37 million American nonfarm families (about 30 percent) were within reach of the private builders' market." [89]

In contrast with the above view, another authority argued in 1951 that:

> The generalization that houses can be and are being built only for the upper income groups is incorrect. It is more accurate to state that if existing veteran terms of no or low downpayments, 4 per cent interest rates, and thirty year amortization were made available to all, nearly every family receiving a minimum full-time income could afford to purchase a house if it so desired. This desire would require those lowest on the income scale to spend average or above amounts for housing and to accept a suburban house.[90]

Assuming that families could pay 25 per cent of their income to cover mortgage and tax payments, Maisel concluded that under the above assumptions approximately 80 per cent of all American families with "minimum full-time incomes" could be served by federal loan insurance or guaranty programs.[91]

The difference in these two points of view can be explained in part by differences in definitions and assumptions. Abrams was referring to the percentage of *all* families which would be able to purchase *new* housing under *existing* FHA loan terms. Maisel's estimates excluded family units without full-time incomes and postulated the generous conditions of credit availability under Veterans Administration 100-per-cent thirty-year loans at 4 per cent interest. It should also be noted that Abrams's estimates of median income are lower than the most recent estimates by the Bureau of the Census. The median income of all families in the United States for the year 1957, shown in Table VI–18,

---

[89] Charles Abrams, "The Residential Construction Industry," in Walter Adams (ed.), *The Structure of American Industry* (New York: Macmillan, 1950), p. 131. More recently the same author cited the fact that "half of all spending units in the United States had an income of less than $4,350 in 1957, while less than 6 per cent of all new one-family homes purchased with FHA insurance in the same year were bought by families with annual incomes of less than $4,200" as additional evidence to support his earlier contention. *Study of Mortgage Credit,* pp. 81–82.

[90] Sherman J. Maisel, "Policy Problems in Expanding the Private Housing Market," *American Economic Review,* XLI, No. 2 (May, 1951) 599.

[91] *Ibid.,* pp. 601, 606. If monthly housing expenditures for mortgage payments and taxes were reduced to 20 per cent of family incomes, Maisel estimated that about 10 per cent of those otherwise eligible would be kept from the market.

was estimated to be $4,971. Families with a head shown as a year-round full-time worker had median incomes of $5,718, while urban families had median incomes of $5,359.

Table VI–18 shows the importance of the exclusion of family units without full-time incomes in Maisel's analysis and focuses attention upon the specialized nature of the housing problem for many low-income groups. According to Bureau of the Census estimates, over 20 per cent of the total number of families in the United States in 1957 were classified as "not in the labor force, unemployed, or in the Armed Forces." Of greater significance is the fact that almost half of the families in the lowest one-fifth by income were in these classifications.[92] The exclusion of approximately 4.2 million families without full-time incomes or unemployed represents almost half of the approximate number of 8.7 million families with annual incomes less than $2,500. Further examination of the characteristics of the family structure in the United States, as shown in Table VI–18, reveals that a substantial proportion of the families with incomes below $2,500 are concentrated in rural farm areas, with a similar number residing in rural nonfarm housing. Although it is inappropriate to dismiss the problem of rural housing from consideration in evaluating public policies, it can be argued that the entire structure of incomes, housing standards, and construction costs differs markedly for residents of rural areas and that this aspect of the national housing problem must be considered separately.[93]

Other studies have shown that many of the lowest-income families

---

[92] U.S. Bureau of the Census, *op. cit.* The term "family," as used in the *Current Population Reports,* refers to a group of two or more persons related by blood, marriage, or adoption and residing together. The estimates include money income prior to deductions for taxes. The total number of families was estimated as 43,714,000. Of these, 27,486,000 were classed as urban, 11,418,000 as rural nonfarm, and 4,810,000 as rural farm families. The incomes of an estimated additional 10,313,000 "unrelated individuals" were shown separately. Of the total number of families, 34,496,000 were headed by an employed civilian, 2,341,000 by an unemployed person, 6,077,000 by a person "not in the labor force," and 800,000 by a member of the Armed Forces. *Ibid.,* Table 9.

[93] See Glenn H. Beyer, "Demand and Need Factors—United States Farm Housing 1961–70," in *Study of Mortgage Credit,* pp. 121–129. The author reviews the factors leading to the decline in the number of farm households from 6,275,000 in 1950 to an estimated 5,218,000 in 1957, and forecasts annual net losses of 24,500 to 55,200 in the decade from 1961 to 1970. He draws attention to the higher rates of dilapidation for rural farm and rural nonfarm housing and to the relative lack of facilities in farm housing. He forecasts that the number of substandard units can be expected to remain around four million for the coming decade, and recommends special federal programs for strengthening the economic position and improving the housing and living standards of small-farm families.

TABLE VI-18

Families by Total Money Income in 1957, United States, Urban and Rural, by Region and Color

Total money income	United States			Northeast	North Central	South			West
	Total	White	Nonwhite			Total	White	Nonwhite	
Families									
Total number (000)	43,714	39,692	4,022	n.a.	n.a.	n.a.	n.a.	n.a.	n.a.
Per cent	100.0	100.0	100.0	100.0	100.0	100.0	100.0	100.0	100.0
Per cent under $500	3.0	2.5	7.8	1.5	2.7	5.1	3.7	12.1	2.0
$500 to $999	3.4	2.7	10.8	1.5	2.5	6.8	4.8	16.8	1.7
$1,000 to $1,499	4.0	3.5	9.2	2.9	3.6	6.2	5.0	11.8	2.5
$1,500 to $1,999	4.5	4.1	8.2	3.3	4.3	6.1	5.6	8.8	3.4
$2,000 to $2,499	5.2	4.6	10.3	3.7	4.4	7.5	6.6	11.6	4.6
$2,500 to $2,999	4.4	4.2	7.0	3.6	4.4	5.4	4.9	7.7	4.1
$3,000 to $3,499	5.7	5.5	7.8	4.9	5.3	7.2	7.2	6.9	5.1
$3,500 to $3,999	6.1	6.0	7.0	5.7	6.3	6.7	6.9	5.8	5.0
$4,000 to $4,499	7.3	7.4	5.9	8.0	7.5	6.5	7.1	3.8	7.3
$4,500 to $4,999	6.8	7.0	5.1	7.2	7.0	5.8	6.4	2.8	7.8
$5,000 to $5,999	14.5	15.1	8.8	17.0	14.8	12.5	13.9	5.4	13.9
$6,000 to $6,999	10.3	10.9	4.5	11.1	11.0	8.0	9.0	3.2	12.2
$7,000 to $9,999	16.3	17.4	6.3	19.1	17.4	10.9	12.5	2.9	20.4
$10,000 to $14,999	6.5	7.1	1.2	8.1	6.9	4.3	5.1	0.4	7.5
$15,000 to $24,999	1.4	1.5	...	1.7	1.6	0.8	0.9	...	1.7
$25,000 and over	0.5	0.5	...	0.6	0.5	0.2	0.3	...	0.8
Median income	$4,971	$5,166	$2,764	$5,453	$5,135	$3,925	$4,373	$2,022	$5,468
Head year-round full-time worker									
Per cent of total	65.4	67.2	47.9	67.8	67.9	61.2	64.5	45.1	64.2
Median income	$5,718	$5,836	$3,741	$6,008	$5,769	$4,949	$5,240	$2,764	$6,331
Urban									
Median income	$5,359	$5,557	$3,352	$5,464	$5,556	$4,623	$5,013	$2,622	$5,793
Rural nonfarm									
Median income	$4,894	$5,037	$2,440	$5,626	$4,979	$4,130	$4,449	$2,047	$5,025
Rural farm									
Median income	$2,490	$2,833	$919	$3,535	$3,056	$1,936	$2,259	$906	$3,797

UNRELATED INDIVIDUALS									
Per cent	100.0	100.0	100.0	100.0	100.0	100.0	100.0	100.0	100.0
Per cent under $500	16.8	16.2	20.8	13.5	17.0	24.2	22.7	28.1	11.4
$500 to $999	20.6	19.3	28.9	20.0	21.9	25.1	20.0	39.3	13.7
$1,000 to $1,499	12.7	12.9	11.8	13.4	10.5	10.7	10.2	12.1	17.8
$1,500 to $1,999	8.5	8.7	7.8	8.6	8.6	7.3	8.5	3.9	10.1
$2,000 to $2,499	7.6	7.3	9.2	8.1	7.0	6.3	7.0	4.3	9.2
$2,500 to $2,999	5.5	5.6	5.2	6.1	5.3	5.0	5.4	3.9	5.8
$3,000 to $3,499	5.6	5.6	5.5	7.1	5.4	3.8	4.2	2.8	6.1
$3,500 to $3,999	5.0	5.1	4.5	5.2	4.4	4.6	5.7	1.5	6.3
$4,000 to $4,499	4.7	5.0	3.2	4.8	5.3	3.3	3.5	2.8	5.7
$4,500 to $4,999	3.1	3.4	1.3	4.2	3.7	1.7	2.3	0.2	2.7
$5,000 to $5,999	4.4	5.1	0.8	3.6	5.4	4.4	5.7	0.9	4.1
$6,000 to $6,999	2.1	2.4	0.5	2.0	2.2	2.0	2.7	...	2.2
$7,000 to $9,999	2.0	2.3	0.3	2.4	1.6	1.0	1.3	0.2	3.7
$10,000 to $14,999	0.9	1.0	...	0.7	1.5	0.5	0.7	...	0.7
$15,000 to $24,999	0.2	0.2	...	0.2	0.1	0.1	0.2	...	0.4
$25,000 and over	...	0.1	...	0.1	0.1	...	...	...	...
Median income	$1,496	$1,592	$1,013	$1,680	$1,535	$1,033	$1,358	$779	$1,851
Year-round full-time workers									
Per cent of total	38.8	39.5	34.3	45.3	37.1	34.1	36.3	27.7	38.5
Median income	$3,214	$3,362	$2,251	$2,934	$3,585	$2,877	$3,437	...[1]	$3,448
Urban									
Median income	$1,716	$1,838	$1,256	$1,699	$1,937	$1,338	$1,770	$868	$1,869
Rural nonfarm									
Median income	$1,037	$1,132	...[1]	$1,847	$886	$842	$914	...[1]	$1,647
Rural farm									
Median income	$945	$1,129	...[1]	...[1]	...[1]	$634	...[1]	...[1]	...[1]

Source: U.S. Bureau of the Census, *Current Population Reports—Consumer Income*, Series P-60, No. 30 (Washington, December, 1958), p. 28.

[1] Median not shown where there were fewer than 100 cases in the sample.

are "older person" households with a nonworker or female head, or are nonwhite households.[94] Although annual income may be an unsatisfactory determinant of financial ability for persons in older age groups, it is significant to note that more than half of the 5,818,000 families with the age of the head sixty-five years and older in 1957 were estimated to have incomes below $2,500. Over 87.5 per cent of the 3,419,000 so-called unrelated persons in this age group, i.e., those not living with any relatives, were estimated to have incomes below $2,500 in 1957.[95]

Further evidence of the nature of the low-income housing problem in the United States is found in the observation from Table VI–16 that more than four million nonwhite families reported a median income in 1957 of $2,764, approximately half that for white families.[96] It is also important to note the wide variations which exist in the level of incomes of nonwhite families in different regions of the United States. The median annual income for nonwhite families with a full-time worker as head ranged from $3,352 in urban areas to $2,440 in rural nonfarm areas and $919 in rural farm areas.

These data suggest that a large proportion, probably above 75 per cent, of these families that in terms of income class are in the lowest one-fifth in the United States represent highly specialized housing problems calling for special assistance programs and cannot be served on any extensive basis by existing federal mortgage loan insurance programs designed to aid in promoting homeownership. Indeed, the data suggest that it is unrealistic to expect that large numbers of families in the lowest income group would be homeowners. If the families of this income class (those with incomes in 1957 below $2,500) are excluded from consideration in terms of the effectiveness of federal mortgage loan insurance programs, it can be estimated that homeownership is within the reach of more than 75 per cent of the remaining American families. The rapid postwar increases in homeownership by American families in the income groups earning above $4,500 attest that homeownership had been realized by 60 per cent of the families with median incomes ($4,971) and by substantially higher proportions of those in the upper two-fifths of the income groups.

In summary, it must be concluded with the critics that federal mortgage insurance programs have not specifically met the needs of the families most in need of housing, those with incomes below $2,500.

[94] Goldsmith, *op. cit.*, and "Income Distribution by Size, 1955–58," *Survey of Current Business*, April, 1959.

[95] U.S. Bureau of the Census, *op. cit.*, p. 21, Table 4.

[96] *Ibid.*, Tables 2 and 12.

It has been noted, however, that for many of these homeownership is not practical and that others represent special groups in the population, calling for specialized programs of assistance. Although it has been seen that direct participation in federally insured mortgage lending has been substantially greater by those with incomes of $5,000 and more, substantial proportions of families with incomes below $5,000 have been able to secure mortgage credit and achieve homeownership during the postwar years. To the extent that federal mortgage loan insurance programs have improved the general availability of mortgage credit, they have aided in this development.

It can also be argued that the maintenance of fixed interest rates on government-underwritten mortgages has limited the availability of FHA-insured and VA-guaranteed loans in sections of the United States suffering from a shortage of savings relative to the demand for funds. The secondary market activities of the Federal National Mortgage Association have not been wholly effective in facilitating the flow of funds to areas of shortage. Improved secondary mortgage market facilities for both conventional and government-insured loans are needed, therefore, in order to provide greater stability in the flow of funds into residential mortgage markets.

Criticism 2. Undue emphasis in federal housing policies has been placed upon the stimulation of single-family, owner-occupied home construction.

It can be noted from Table VI–1 that multi-family rental housing construction reached substantial levels only during a brief period from 1948 to 1950 and in 1958 and 1959.[97] The relatively high levels of activity from 1948 to 1950 may be accounted for by the granting of the thirty-year low- or no-equity FHA-insured "608" loans which were based upon 90 per cent of current construction costs, calculated in such a manner that many builders were able to acquire title to apartment properties with little or no equity. Congressional investigations in 1953 and 1954 brought to light that the Federal Housing Administration had guaranteed "608" loans "on more than 700 projects running to millions of dollars in excess of the cost of the projects" and that "unconscionable profits have been made by many in construction projects sponsored by the Federal Government under its housing programs."[98]

[97] For a discussion of this second criticism see Charles Abrams, *The Future of Housing* (New York: Harper, 1946), pp. 224–225.

[98] U.S. 83d Cong., 2d sess., *Hearings Before the Committee on Banking and Currency, United States Senate, on Housing Act of 1954 FHA Insurance Provisions, S 2889, S 2938, S 2949, Part 3, Statement by Senator Harry F. Byrd* (April 13, 1954), p. 1307.

As a result of the "608" scandals, the FHA rental housing program fell into disrepute and the terms and conditions for government loan insurance were so altered as to discourage apartment-house promotion.

A recent analysis of the opportunities for private investment in rental housing in the United States attributes the lack of large-scale apartment-house production during the postwar years to the following factors:[99]

The strong preference of American families for homeownership

A long period of prosperity which enabled most consumers to realize their goal for homeownership

The relatively low returns realized by investors in rental housing since the 1920's, and the consequent disappearance of the small apartment-house investor

Experience with federal rent controls during and immediately following World War II which deterred many individuals and institutions from making long-term capital commitments in rental housing

The failure of government housing programs to attract equity capital to rental housing field

Lessened demand for rental housing as a result of the effectiveness of government programs to stimulate homeownership

The furthering of homeownership by tax benefits available to homeowners

Demographic changes in the postwar period which favored ownership housing

The prospects for rental housing construction in the future, however, as they may influence progress in urban renewal, seem somewhat brighter, as indicated by the substantial revival in rental construction in 1958 and 1959.[100] Winnick points out that the liberalized mortgage lending terms of the Housing Act of 1956 together with the removal of many of the irksome FHA restrictions on the operation of completed projects have increased investors' interest in FHA rental programs. He forecasts that continued prosperity, the growth in small private-housekeeping family units (both young and old) and a "back to the city movement" (encouraged by the growing shortage of land in the suburbs) may result in substantially increased levels of apartment-house construction.[101] Federal and local government subsidies and other aids for urban renewal will undoubtedly encourage this trend.

Recent revivals in rental housing construction lend credence to Win-

---

[99] Louis Winnick, *Rental Housing* (New York: McGraw-Hill, 1958), chap. ix.

[100] According to *Housing Statistics, Historical Supplement*, June, 1960 (pp. 7, 11), a total of 195,400 multi-family units were started in 1958, of which 170,000 were privately owned, and a total of 231,400 multi-family units were started in 1959, of which 214,900 were privately owned. See also Colean, *op. cit.*, p. 110.

[101] Winnick, *op. cit.*, pp. 239–240.

nick's forecast. Privately owned multiple-dwelling construction reached its postwar peak in 1958 at 170,000 units, and reached the highest level since the 1920's in 1959 when 214,900 units were started. It is significant, however, that less than 15 per cent of the total of 170,000 privately owned multi-family dwellings started in 1958 and less than 12 per cent of those started in 1959 were financed through government-insured loans.[102] It was noted earlier that lenders have preferred conventional loan contracts during recent years because of the low fixed-interest rate on government-insured or government-guaranteed loans. There is also some evidence that lenders and some borrowers prefer the flexibility and lack of red tape in conventional loan contracts to government-insured loans. The postwar record would seem to justify the conclusion that government mortgage loan policies *can* be effective in stimulating multi-family residential construction, but that effectively designed federal loan programs to achieve the objective have not been in effect for any sustained period since World War II. The revival of private investment in rental housing in recent years can be attributed in major part to the postwar rise in incomes and the upward movement in rents. It can be expected that this sector of the housing investment market will be highly sensitive to changes in business conditions, population mobility, interest rates, and changes in incomes and rents. After taking into account the greater expected instability in multi-family housing construction, it must be concluded that federal loan programs have been less effective in stimulating the construction of multi-family housing than that of single-family homes. In accepting this conclusion, however, it should be recognized that one of the principal objectives of national housing policy for the past three decades has been to stimulate homeownership in the United States. Viewed in this light, the criticism loses some of its force. As will be noted presently, however, the failure of government programs to stimulate the production of low-rent housing has particular consequence for important segments of the low-income group who are logical occupants of rental housing.

Criticism 3. The federal low-rent public housing program in the United States has failed to solve the housing problems of low income groups and urban renewal programs have done little to aid in their solution

Over 8.7 million families in the United States had incomes below $2,500 in 1957. Approximately 20 per cent of families with incomes

[102] *Housing Statistics, Historical Supplement,* June, 1960, pp. 7, 11, 16.

below $3,000 occupied substandard housing in 1950.[103] As of December, 1957, only approximately one half-million low-income families were housed in federal public housing. Although it is evident that the federal public housing program has not directly affected the housing standards of a large segment of the low-income population, it has been instrumental in effecting the removal of about 400,000 unsafe or unsanitary urban dwellings over a twenty-year period and in providing housing of acceptable physical standards for approximately 500,000 low-income families, most of them with children.[104] Despite this accomplishment, the consensus of views would certainly be that the federal public housing program has not and, as presently conceived, probably will not solve the housing problems of low-income groups. This failure focuses attention upon other recommendations for improving low-income housing standards.

The diversity of the housing problems of special groups suggests that a combination of solutions is required. It is evident that the housing needs of low-income groups should be met in part by ownership and in part by rental housing. The President's Advisory Committee on Government Housing Programs and Policies included the following in its 1953 recommendations:

Grant liberal FHA mortgage insurance for rehabilitation of sound existing structures

Extend forty-year 95-per-cent loans for new, low-cost single-family dwellings for owner occupancy at current interest rates on government bonds

Continue the public housing program as contained in the Housing Act of 1949, with administrative changes to modify the institutional character of public housing, including the use of rehabilitated dwellings and smaller, lower-density projects on scattered sites

Congressional legislation since 1954 has liberalized mortgage insurance terms for rehabilitation and for new construction of low-cost single-family dwellings (Sec. 220), and for low-cost relocation housing (Sec. 221), but mortgage lending under these programs has been limited to less than 18,000 units by December, 1958.

The reasons for the failure of FHA mortgage insurance programs under Sections 220 and 221 of the Housing Act of 1954 are complex. Basically, FHA loans have not been attractive to private lenders during the tight money market conditions which have generally prevailed since 1954. Loans to low-income borrowers are also generally regarded as less attractive to private lenders than loans for middle- or upper-

[103] U.S. Bureau of the Census, *Census of Housing: 1950,* II, Part I, Table B–4.
[104] Fisher, *Twenty Years of Public Housing,* chap. viii.

income housing. Further, the standards of FHA appraisals have resulted in relatively low valuations for properties to be occupied by low-income groups. Controversies over appraisals for Section 220 and 221 loans have frequently resulted in long delays in securing FHA commitments and in additional reluctance by private lenders to make loans.

The recent initiation of special federal mortgage insurance programs for the aged, for coöperatives, and for residents of and those displaced from urban renewal areas is a recognition of the specialized needs of these groups. Investors and private lenders have been reluctant to take advantage of loans under Sections 220 and 221, and the administrative difficulties in gaining FHA approval for such loans have been a further limitation of volume. Good arguments can be made for direct government lending or for outright purchase by the government of housing for resale on favorable loan terms to low-income groups not adequately served by private investors or lenders. The success of California's veterans' home loan program, which provides for the outright purchase and sale of housing to eligible veterans on contracts of sale, illustrates the possibilities of successful state administration of special housing aid programs and provides a useful pattern for special housing subsidies where these are needed.[105]

Direct government lending, however, has significant disadvantages. It would be costly and difficult to make sure that direct government loan subsidies benefited low-income families only. This would be particularly difficult in the use of direct government loans for rental housing. Also, large-scale government lending programs frequently lend themselves to bureaucracy and inefficiency. Another disadvantage is that direct government lending would be in competition, to a degree at least, with private lenders.

In view of these shortcomings, alternative solutions to raising low-income standards should be considered. Improvement in the quality and quantity of privately owned rental housing for low-income groups would seem to depend upon:

Increasing the rent-paying ability of low-income families to the level required by current construction costs

Making production of low-rent housing attractive to investors

Providing for strict enforcement of minimum housing standards

If it is assumed that the present federal low-rent housing program is unsatisfactory, an alternative technique for subsidizing the incomes of low-rent families should be considered. Direct family housing sub-

---

[105] See *Study of Mortgage Credit*, pp. 389–93.

sidies have worked effectively in Sweden for many years and would have many advantages over the present federal system. Variations of direct family rent subsidies have been proposed to the Congress as substitutes for federal public housing programs by several trade organizations active in the real estate, mortgage lending, and home-building industries on several occasions since 1936.[106]

A report prepared by the Legal Division of the Public Housing Administration summarized the objections to family rent subsidy plans by several welfare agencies as presented to the Subcommittee on Housing and Urban Redevelopment in 1947:[107]

1. A large number of individuals would be added to the rolls of the relief agencies.

a. Millions of persons who need improved housing, including many who are otherwise financially independent, would be forced to accept rent relief through welfare agencies in order to pay rents sufficient to obtain housing which meets a minimum standard as defined by the respective municipalities.

b. There would be many complex difficulties in establishing and maintaining the eligibility requirements governing assistance in the form of rent certificates.

2. Local administration of the plan would be costly and complicated.

a. Recurrent inspection of dwellings scattered throughout the city, record keeping, income checks, investigations for millions of families living in substandard housing would involve a vast expenditure of public funds.

b. Local welfare agencies would be able to cope with the administrative problems of this plan only if provided with largely increased appropriations for additional staff and facilities.

c. Local welfare agencies would be forced to engage in the granting of relief in kind, a practice that is now being given up as unsound welfare policy.

---

[106] President's Advisory Committee on Government Housing Policies and Programs, *Recommendations* . . . , Exhibit 21, "Congressional Consideration of Rent Certificate Plans in Developing Legislation on Public Housing for Low-Income Families." Among the private business groups cited as advocating such plans were the National Association of Real Estate Boards, the United States Chamber of Commerce, the United States Building and Loan League, the Homebuilders Association of Metropolitan Washington, and the Producers Council. According to the Committee's report (dated December, 1953), since 1936 no favorable action had ever been taken on such recommendations by any committee of either the House of Representatives or the Senate.

[107] *Ibid.* The statement of objections, according to the report, was approved by the executive committees of the Family Welfare Association of America, the American Public Welfare Association, the American Association of Social Workers, and the National Committee of Housing Associations and by the board of governors of the National Association of Housing Officials.

3. The rent certificate plan would be more costly to the taxpayers than the existing public housing program.

a. The rentals of private housing meeting a minimum standard are about $15 per month in excess of the unsubsidized rents of public housing. Therefore, the rent certificate plan of assistance would necessitate a very great increase in subsidy if the same standards are to be met.

b. Public subsidy to low-income families to enable them to obtain adequate housing would continue. The burden of an increased subsidy, however, would fall on the taxpayers who support local welfare agencies. There is question as to whether sufficient funds would be allocated to welfare agencies for such a program.

4. A needed new supply of low-rent housing would not be provided.

a. The present program of rent allotments by welfare agencies often results in the housing of welfare clients in slum housing.

b. The rent certificate plan would not provide the means for the construction of low-rent housing.

c. Unless the supply of low low-rent housing is increased, progress cannot be made toward solving the problem of providing adequate housing for all families of low income.

5. Substandard housing would not be eliminated.

a. Even with the increased rents paid under the rent certificate plan, the improvement of blighted neighborhoods would not be assured, and there is no positive provision for the redevelopment of the slums.

b. Localities would need improved housing codes and methods of enforcement. The facts are that few localities have adequate housing codes and enforcement experience. It is unreasonable to expect that the housing regulation activities of cities can suddenly be vastly improved and expanded. Vigorous enforcement of adequate housing regulations would result almost immediately in a shortage of housing accommodations. In all areas where the percentage of vacancies of low-rental housing is low, excessive rents would prevail unless effective rent control were established; otherwise, public funds would be paid to the owners of substandard buildings, thus subsidizing and perpetuating poor housing and blighted areas.

The author of a recent study of public housing in Pittsburgh argues that most of the disadvantages stated above may be viewed as advantages, and recommends a rent subsidy program as an alternative to the present federally subsidized low-rent housing program.[108]

In the views of the present author, some of the above objections to adoption of programs of direct family-rent subsidies are unreasoned and others unjustified. *First:* It is probably true that more eligible

[108] Brown, *op. cit.*, chap. ix.

families would actually receive housing subsidies under a direct family income subsidy program since the availability of public housing units acts as a rationing device. This, however, may be viewed as an argument in favor of such subsidies. *Second:* Recurrent inspection of dwellings is a key requirement for the elimination of substandard housing and, as such, should be included in any local housing program regardless of the methods of subsidizing low-income housing needs. As will be suggested below, rent subsidies need not be granted in kind. *Third:* The implication that direct rent subsidies would be "more costly to the taxpayers than the existing public housing program" cannot be established and implies without foundation that private housing cannot be provided at costs competitive with publicly owned housing. Assuming programs of comparable scope, the relative costs to taxpayers would depend in the final analysis upon the relative costs and efficiencies of private and public enterprise in providing housing accommodation. The exemption of local housing authority obligations from income taxation or the granting of federal subsidies to local housing authorities cannot be viewed as a cost advantage to the taxpayer in favor of public housing, because any federal expenditures must be made up for in other taxation. *Fourth:* To argue that a program of family rent subsidies will not provide a new supply of low-rent housing or eliminate substandard housing is not a logical argument against the use of such subsidies in combination with other public measures to accomplish these specific ends. In theory, family rent or income subsidies should provide additional demand for rental housing and stimulate its production. This tendency would be increased under strict code enforcement of minimum housing standards to eliminate substandard housing. The objections to the improvement of housing codes and to the practicality of improving methods of code enforcement sound like voices from the Dark Ages.

It is of interest to note that a group of housing experts recommended a variation of the rent certificate device at a 1960 conference on "Housing the Economically and Socially Disadvantaged Groups in the Population." The three plans recommended for simultaneous experimentation were as follows:[109]

Plan "A"

This approach would provide federal loans for new construction of housing by private builders, for rent or sale, subject to government supervision with the requirement that a given proportion of the occupants hold housing certificates as "disadvantaged" families. Basic rents or sales prices, including a fair profit, would be established subject to

[109] *Interim Report on Housing*, pp. 3–4.

government approval. Specific families, based on their income and ability to pay, would receive "housing certificates." The Federal government would pay a subsidy making up the differential between the established rent or mortgage payment, and the individual family's ability to pay, pursuant to the certificate. If the owner's mortgage were held by the Federal government, the subsidy would be paid by crediting its amount on the payment of debt service next due under the mortgage.

Certificates would be renewed annually with any modifications proper to reflect changes in the family's status, so long as assistance was necessary. It was suggested that Plan A would encourage a democratic admixture of families of various income levels, and result in making available a variety of locations, types, designs, and choices of dwellings in the private housing market.

Plan "B"

While not directly serving the hard core of disadvantaged families, a second approach, by stimulating construction at the intermediate level, would accelerate the filtering down of units for the lower income groups. This program would serve the demand for suburban, single-family detached houses for sale. Any efficient builder would be allowed Federal National Mortgage Association commitments for 25 to 50% of his normal production, at interest rates of from 1% to 4% to families requiring such loans in order to obtain new housing. Each mortgage would be subject to revision of interest rate every 5 years, depending on the family's credit standing at the time.

Plan "C"

A third suggested innovation proposed direct Federal loans to non-profit and cooperative corporations, for 60 year terms, at interest rates comparable to those on loans made under the Rural Electrification Act of 1936. Loans would be limited to housing of sound standard, but subject to suitable cost limitations; and where maximum self-help and maintenance would be required. Structural and exterior maintenance would be the responsibility of the corporation rather than the occupant.

Limitation of loans to non-profit corporations would assure the maximum reduction in monthly charges, but not preclude the full utilization of private builders and private management companies in the construction and management of such projects, for reasonable fees.

It is believed that many of the objections of welfare agencies to "rent certificate" plans as proposed in the past could be overcome by modifications in administration of family housing subsidies. The use of federal income tax credits provides a medium through which low-income housing subsidies could be made available for both rental and owner-occupied housing. The eligibility of families for housing subsidies could be determined by local housing and welfare agencies, based upon standards of federal assistance established by federal law. Federal assistance as a proportion of rents or housing costs would be granted to eligible families by federal income tax credit. Families with incomes below those requiring filing of income tax returns could claim housing allowances on income tax forms as a special credit to be paid directly to them. This method of reporting and granting subsidies would provide a technique for enforcement of legal standards of assistance through coöperation between the Bureau of Internal Revenue and local housing authorities. Families receiving credit for housing subsidies would be required to report rents paid, or housing costs if based upon owned homes. Indigent families with no income would be required to give an accounting of the use of federal housing subsidies to the local relief agency.

This type of housing subsidy program would provide freedom for the low-income family to seek housing in the private rental or ownership market or in existing public housing. It would dispel the present concentration of low-income families in public housing. It would overcome the objections to rent certificate programs as a form of the dole. Family housing subsidies, in combination with federal income tax subsidies to private investors and low-income homeowners, should stimulate private investment in low-rent housing. The enforcement of minimum housing standards, as suggested above, would be a key element in the success of this combined approach to the problem of housing low-income groups. The requirement that families receiving such subsidies occupy housing of minimum standards would do much to encourage private rehabilitation of housing and public enforcement of minimum housing standards.

Under such a family housing subsidy program, increasing reliance would be placed upon the "filtering down" of the existing housing inventory for use by low-income groups. Although Ratcliff and others have argued that filtering is a "totally inadequate remedy for the acute problem of substandard housing," their arguments have leaned heavily upon such critical assumptions as constant family incomes and constant proportions of incomes spent for housing, and upon the assumption that a surplus of housing at any level will serve as a check on new production.[110] Although it is not feasible to explore these arguments in detail here, it is maintained that during the postwar period none of the limiting assumptions in Ratcliff's analysis was present. High levels of new house production have continued in the upper and middle price ranges even though surpluses have been evident in the used house market. High postwar housing production has been accompanied by fairly large-scale removal of the government's temporary

[110] Ratcliff, *Urban Land Economics*, pp. 321–334.

war housing and other marginal housing, and by rising incomes; meanwhile, it has been seen that housing standards have been improved for low- as well as for upper-income groups. The data in Table VI–5 suggest that "filtering" has, to a degree, operated to improve housing standards in the postwar period. Under the program proposed, it would be assumed that the federal government would both continue and expand its programs of special mortgage assistance to private housebuilding, thus encouraging the maintenance of new production. Future improvement in housing standards for low-income groups is much more likely to occur if family incomes continue to rise more rapidly than housing costs and if the amounts spent for housing by low-income groups are increased through a rent certificate plan.

Criticism 4: Federal housing credit policies have led to instability in residential construction, and have contributed to inflationary cost increases in building and in the economy generally.

This criticism, which was touched upon earlier in the evaluation of federal mortgage credit policies, poses the following basic and controversial questions:

> To what extent is stability in residential construction desirable per se? Should it be subject to the overriding objectives of stability in total construction activity or general economic stability?
>
> What should be the criteria for measuring stability in residential construction—stable unit production? a constant dollar volume of expenditures? a constant real volume of expenditures? a constant percentage relationship between residential construction and the gross national product? a constant relationship between new starts and new households established? Or should a level of residential construction be sought which would result in over-all stability in housing prices and rents?

It was noted earlier that the achievement of stability in residential housing production has been a general objective of national housing policy ever since the passage of the National Housing Act of 1934 and was reaffirmed in the statement of national housing policy in the Housing Act of 1949. Federal mortgage credit programs have been designed to provide a continuous flow of mortgage funds to aid in the achievement of this objective.

The arguments in support of the view that stabilization of the total volume of all construction is of key importance have been set forth by Colean and Newcomb as follows:[111]

[111] Miles L. Colean and Robinson Newcomb, *Stabilizing Construction: The Record and the Potential* (New York: McGraw-Hill, 1952), pp. 126–127.

It would encourage the development of stable construction organizations with greater continuity of experience.

It would induce a greater capital investment in such organizations and hence speed the mechanization of construction operations.

It would encourage greater investment in research in design, construction methods, and materials.

By removing the fear of serious depressions, the scramble for higher wages and high profits during a boom period would be lessened.

As a result of all this, the cost of construction might be lowered, the effective demand for it gradually broadened, so that the long-term trend would rise rather slowly.

As a consequence, the intensification added by construction movements to general economic fluctuations would be eliminated and, instead, a stabilizing influence would be introduced into the economy as a whole, with special reference to the savings-investment process.

It is obvious that some degree of stability in the housing market generally is a *sine qua non* to the achievement of stability in residential construction under private enterprise.

In discussing the role of federal housing programs in economic stabilization policy, Grebler has presented in cogent fashion the view that general economic stability is an overriding national objective. His conclusions can be summarized as follows:

Federal housing programs should be used as tools of stabilization policy only sparingly and with great caution.

Temporary relaxation of permanent stimuli to residential construction during periods of general economic prosperity can be justified in the interest of general economic stability.

Occasional restraint of activity in the housing sector can be considered good housing policy as well as a necessary or desirable tool of economic stabilization policy. Maximum output of new residential construction is not the only criterion of good housing policy, at least in the short run. Another valid objective of good housing policy is maintenance of reasonable stability in the housing market itself.

A policy of incessant stimulation of housing may adversely affect the flow of funds into other "high priority" sectors of the economy.

Maintenance of economic stability and growth is an overriding national objective.[112]

---

[112] Grebler, "The Role of Residential Capital Formation in Postwar Business Cycles," *op. cit.*, pp. 76–77. This author has stated more recently that federal policies "geared solely to the objective of a sustainable level of home building would appear to be both fair and feasible, although the determination of sustainable levels at any given juncture would be beset with difficulties. But efforts to support a given volume regardless of effective demand would encounter serious practical difficulties. Thus, he argues, "stability of residential construction in a literal sense is a highly impractical objective." Leo Grebler, *Housing Issues in Economic Stabilization Policy* (New York: National Bureau of Economic Research, 1960), pp. 109–110.

Examination of the record of postwar housing production in Table VI–1 reveals fairly substantial fluctuations in the annual volume of dwellings started, although fairly large percentage errors are implicit in the annual data. Completion data would probably reveal a smaller degree of variation in the annual figures. The data show greater stability of production in the past decade than during any of the three previous decades. Brief reflection suggests, however, that neither unit volume of production or current dollar volume of expenditures can serve as adequate measures of the degree of stability in housing production. Unit production fails to account for differences in size and character of dwellings produced, while current dollar expenditures would reflect changes in the price level.

Expenditures for residential construction in current dollars as a percentage of the gross national product and as a percentage of private fixed capital investment represent more suitable measures of the degree of stability in housing production relative to the economy as a whole. These measures, summarized in Table VII–2 for the United States, reveal considerable stability in residential building over the postwar years. It is also significant to note that comparison with prewar periods indicates that residential construction has been more stable during the postwar years than for any period for which comparable data are available.[113]

Grebler mobilizes some evidence in a recent work to show that during the period from 1953 to 1957 stable or expanding expenditures for residential construction tended to moderate the downward pull of recessionary forces in other sectors of the economy and that on the whole the residential construction industry was no more unstable in the 1953–58 cycle than in earlier postwar cycles.[114] He argues that examination of quarterly changes in gross national product and residential construction expenditures do not reveal a systematic contracyclical behavior of residential construction from 1953 to 1957, and points out that spending on total new construction in the 1955–57 period was in fact highly stable.[115] He implies, however, that during this period any contribution of federal housing policies toward improving stability in residential construction was an unintentional result of the maintenance of fixed-interest-rate policies on government underwritten loans.

It has been argued that in terms of the economy as a whole the

---

[113] Grebler, Blank, and Winnick, *Capital Formation in Residential Real Estate*, p. 134.

[114] *Housing Issues in Economic Stabilization Policy*, pp. 101–105.

[115] *Ibid.*, p. 110.

behavior of mortgage credit and residential construction has exerted a stabilizing influence during the postwar period. The Federal Reserve Bank of New York commented on the postwar trend as follows in April 1959:[116]

> . . . But, in striking contrast to most other industries the surges in residential construction have usually begun during periods of economic recession, and then have moved sideways or declined once the rest of the economy reached levels of high prosperity. Probably the major factor in this contracyclical pattern has been the changing availability of mortgage credit, as competing demands for long-term funds tended to rise and fall with the cyclical swings of the economy. In terms of economic activity as a whole, the behavior of mortgage credit and residential construction would thus appear to have exerted a stabilizing influence.

The author accepts Grebler's views that stability in residential construction in the literal sense is probably an impossible goal. Stability in residential construction must be subject to the achievement of stability in the economy as a whole, and in a private enterprise economy subject to over-all stability in the housing market.

It is the author's conclusion that federal housing credit policies have not led to any greater degree of instability in residential construction than would be expected in the absence of federal programs in the field. It is clear that rapid changes in federal housing credit policies have contributed to some short-run instability during the postwar years and that the major contributions of government policies to stability (the fixed-interest-rate policy) may be construed as unintentional. It can also be argued that under a flexible mortgage interest rate policy the volume of government underwritten loans would probably have been more stable and this *might* have contributed to greater stability in total residential construction. On the whole, however, residential construction has been stable in the post-war period relative to the gross national product and to its prewar record.

It seems virtually impossible to isolate the relative inflationary and deflationary effects of housing credit programs upon building costs and the price level generally from other influences having their origins in monetary and fiscal policy. Although it is evident that federal housing policies and programs have from time to time contributed to price and cost increases in housing, they have also brought about improvements in production, marketing, and designing of houses and, through

---

[116] Federal Reserve Bank of New York, *Monthly Review*, April, 1959, pp. 60–61.

their effect on volume of production, have probably contributed to important cost reductions.[117]

In summary, it would seem that the notable accomplishments of national postwar housing policy in achieving high levels of new housing production, expanding homeownership, and improving housing standards generally must be offset against significant failures. High levels of new house production during the postwar years have undoubtedly made it possible for many low-income families to acquire used housing through the filtering process. However, substantial proportions of low-income and minority groups still lack adequate housing, and the quantity and quality of rental housing available to low-income groups continues to be inadequate. The fundamental problem has been that many families lack sufficient incomes to command housing of acceptable quality. Wartime rent controls resulted in unsatisfactory investment experience for many landlords and contributed to the decline in the quality of rental housing. Federal loan programs in the rental housing field have been characterized by conflicting aims and unsatisfactory results, while programs designed to produce publicly owned low-rent housing have been relatively ineffective and are judged by most to have serious social and economic shortcomings. As a result of these and other factors, private investment in rental housing has been sporadic and, in general, directed toward higher-income families. The lack of progress in slum clearance has impeded the operation of the filtering processes in housing. Although housing production has been maintained at high and relatively stable levels in comparison with the years before World War II, absolute stability in housebuilding probably cannot be achieved. Federal housing policy has also undoubtedly contributed in a measure to the rise in building costs and to the general inflationary tendencies in the economy in the postwar years.

[117] Maisel, "Policy Problems in Expanding the Private Housing Market," *Amer. Econ. Rev.*, p. 603.

VII Evaluation of Post-World War II Housing Policies

The establishment of criteria to be used for evaluating national housing policies is fraught with subjective difficulties. It is possible to evaluate housing policies solely in terms of their relationship to stated housing objectives or their short-run effect upon national housing standards. More broadly, an evaluation might consider the effects of housing policy upon long-run real housing costs, mortgage financing institutions, the housebuilding industry, and the stability of the residential construction industry, or upon the economy as a whole.

Although admittedly ambitious, it is proposed to evaluate from several points of view the housing policies since World War II of West Germany, the United Kingdom, Sweden, and the United States. Initially, the evaluation will include consideration of the objectives of each nation's housing policy, a review of the relationship between policies and stated objectives, and an evaluation of the administration of policies and programs. Consideration will then be given to the effect of policies upon housing standards, stability of residential construction, organization and efficiency of the building industry, strength of mortgage finance institutions, and housing costs. In summary, an attempt will be made to evaluate the influence of housing policies upon postwar national economies and to identify those policies and programs which, in the light of the postwar experience, appear to have been most effective in an over-all sense.

Housing Objectives and Policies

The achievement of a high level of housing production was a common objective of the housing policies of West Germany, the United Kingdom, Sweden, and the United States. It was observed in chapter ii that the immediate postwar housing shortage was more critical in West

Germany than in either Sweden, the United States, or the United Kingdom. Relative to other nations, the ratio of dwellings per thousand inhabitants in the early 1950's was relatively high in the United States and Sweden, about average in the United Kingdom, and low in West Germany. These comparisons are borne out when consideration is also given to the size and quality of the housing inventory in these countries.

West Germany

In the light of her relative housing situation, it is understandable that the housing policies of West Germany should have emphasized more than those of the other countries the early achievement of a high volume of housing production. The objective of realizing the production of 1,800,000 low-income or "social housing" units over a six-year period was clearly established as the central goal of West Germany's housing policy by the First Housing Act of 1950. Further, the emphasis on stimulation of housing production was consistently adhered to as the goal was increased to 350,000 units annually from 1953 to 1956 and maintained at 300,000 units annually until 1962. Total annual housing production rose from 362,000 units in 1950 to 561,000 in 1957. Following a decline to 518,000 units in 1958, housing production reached a new high record of 580,000 dwellings in 1959.

Collateral objectives of West Germany's housing policy were to encourage private investment and private ownership of housing. The latter objectives were consistent with over-all national economic policies during the post-World War II years, which emphasized fiscal control of inflationary tendencies, tax incentives to encourage private saving and investment, and restrictive wage policies.

The most important features of West Germany's postwar housing policies were the granting of low-interest-rate public loans for social housing and the maintenance of tax subsidies designed to encourage the flow of private mortgage funds into social and other housing. Following the passage of the Homebuilding Premium Law of 1952 and the Second Housing Act of 1956, direct subsidies and tax incentives were extended to encourage construction of owner-occupied, single-family homes.

Tax subsidies played a major role in channeling interest-free second mortgage loan funds into social housing when long-term mortgage funds were limited and in great demand. Interest-free loans for mortgage purposes could be fully deducted from taxable income by corporations and individuals in the year in which they were granted, under Section 7*c* of the tax law. Under the First Capital Development Law of 1952, interest income from mortgages paying between 5 and 5.5 per cent for social housing was also exempt from both personal and corporate income taxation.

Although social housing was subject to strict rent controls, rents on other dwelling were gradually increased after 1954, and the privately owned housing market has been gradually freed from rent restrictions. Social housing occupancy was limited to families with basic incomes of less than 6,000 DM until 1957, when the limit was raised to 9,000 DM, with added allowances for dependents and disabled veterans.

It can be argued that West Germany's post-World War II housing objectives not only reflected needs, but were internally consistent and not in conflict with other important national objectives and programs. Housing policies were well designed to meet the established objectives of stimulating a high volume of low-income "social housing" and at the same time encouraging construction of other privately owned rental and owner-occupied housing. Low-interest-rate third mortgage public loans reduced the risks of primary and secondary lenders, and tax subsidies proved a powerful instrument for channeling private funds into the second mortgage market at relatively low interest rates. The encouragement offered to savers through income tax subsidies contributed to the over-all national objective of controlling inflation and provided an indirect form of capital rationing.

The Federal Ministry of Housing exercised a considerable degree of control over the formulation of broad national housing policies designed to achieve housing objectives. The individual *Länder* were directly responsible for drawing up annual programs to be financed in their separate jurisdictions by the *Länder* or the communes. Since the nature of the housing problem varied considerably among the different *Länder,* this provided much needed flexibility in carrying out national objectives, permitting greater emphasis upon social housing in some of the heavily populated industrial centers and upon owner-occupied dwellings in other sectors. Although no extensive research was carried on in the field of public administration of West Germany's housing policies, the author gained the general impression that the basic decentralization of responsibilities among the individual *Länder* resulted in high levels of housing production and, in a broad sense, effective administration of national housing policies.

Table VII–1 shows that West Germany was the only nation of those studied which realized substantially higher levels of housing production in the post-World War II period relative to prewar years. In part, this reflects the limited attention devoted to stimulating prewar housing production in Germany and, to a greater degree perhaps, the

TABLE VII-1

New Dwellings Completed in Four Countries, 1948 to 1958
(In dwellings per thousand persons)

Country	Prewar annual average over four best years	1948	1950	1952	1954	1956	1957	1958
Sweden	9.5	6.9	6.4	6.1	8.2	7.9	8.8	8.5
West Germany	5.1	n.a.	7.7	9.1	10.3	11.0	10.3	9.4
United Kingdom	7.5	4.8	3.9	5.2	7.0	6.1	6.0	5.5
United States	7.7	6.3	9.2	7.2	7.5	6.6	6.1	6.9

Sources: 1948–52: U.S. Office of Information, Research Branch, *Postwar Housing Trends in Seven Countries of Western Europe* (Paris, June 4, 1953). 1954–56: United Nations, *European Housing Trends and Policies in 1956*, E/ECE/292 (Geneva, July, 1957), Table 1. 1957: United Nations, *European Housing Trends and Policies in 1957*, E/ECE/329 (Geneva, 1958), Table 1. 1958: United Nations, *Quarterly Bulletin of Housing and Building Statistics for Europe*, VII, No. 2 (Geneva, 1959), Table 1. 1948–58: Population of United States, end of year (excludes Armed Forces overseas), from U.S. Bureau of the Census, *Current Population Reports*, August 17, 1950, end January 14, 1960. Number of new nonfarm dwellings started, from U.S. Bureau of the Census, *Statistical Abstract of the United States: 1959* (80th ed.; Washington, 1959), p. 761.

severity of the post-World War II housing shortage resulting from war destruction and heavy in-migration from East Germany.

It can also be noted, from Table VII–2, that West Germany, and Sweden to a lesser degree, in relation to the United States and the United Kingdom, devoted higher proportions of the gross national product to fixed capital formation, higher proportions of fixed capital formation to residential construction, and, as would follow, higher proportions of gross national product to residential construction. This, of course, is a reflection of the general investment climate in West Germany and these countries during this period, as well as of national housing policies. Table VII–2 indicates that housing investment was somewhat more stable as a percentage of the gross national product in Sweden than in the other countries studied; but the ratio showed a considerable degree of stability in each of the countries. Reasons for the greater apparent fluctuations in the United Kingdom are found in the shift in housing policies with the change in governments, and in government measures to restrict housing production as a device for control of inflation.

It has been seen that low-interest-rate mortgage loans and income tax subsidies were highly effective in stimulating production of low-

TABLE VII–2

RELATIONSHIPS BETWEEN GROSS NATIONAL PRODUCT, GROSS FIXED INVESTMENT, AND RESIDENTIAL CONSTRUCTION FOR SWEDEN, WEST GERMANY, THE UNITED KINGDOM, AND THE UNITED STATES, 1950 TO 1958

Relationship	1950	1951	1952	1953	1954	1955	1956	1957	1958
Per cent of gross national product at factor costs devoted to gross domestic fixed capital formation:									
Sweden	20.4	19.8	20.3	22.4	22.7	21.9	22.1	22.1	23.2
West Germany	21.8	21.6	22.2	23.4	24.5	26.4	26.7	25.5	25.7
United Kingdom	15.2	15.1	15.3	16.1	16.4	17.0	17.4	17.8	17.8
United States	19.0	17.9	17.3	17.6	18.1	18.8	19.2	19.2	17.9
Per cent of gross domestic fixed capital formation devoted to residential construction:									
Sweden	26.1	24.2	23.2	24.3	25.7	25.7	25.9	26.0	25.1
West Germany	27.1	25.9	24.1	27.2	27.6	25.4	26.1	26.4	n.a.
United Kingdom	19.1	19.7	23.2	26.5	25.0	21.6	19.9	17.9	16.5
United States	30.5	25.9	26.1	25.8	27.4	28.9	25.4	23.5	27.2
Per cent of gross national product at factor costs devoted to residential construction:									
Sweden	5.3	4.8	4.7	5.4	5.8	5.6	5.7	5.7	5.8
West Germany	5.9	5.6	5.4	6.4	6.3	6.7	7.0	6.7	n.a.
United Kingdom	2.9	3.0	3.6	4.3	4.1	3.7	3.5	3.2	2.9
United States	5.8	4.6	4.5	4.5	5.0	5.4	4.9	4.5	4.9

Source: Organization for European Economic Cooperation, *OEEC Statistical Bulletin, General Statistics*, 1960, No. 1, "National Accounts" (Paris, January, 1960).

income or "social" housing. The owners of social housing built with government aid accepted restrictions upon rents charged and eligibility of occupants as a *quid pro quo.* Table VII–3 shows that publicly owned housing represented less than 3 per cent of West German housing production during the years following World War II. In evaluating the data in Table VII–3 it should be emphasized that, as shown earlier in Table V–8, a substantial proportion of Germany's housing production from 1950 to 1958 was financed through direct government loans, or aided through government tax concessions. In addition, it will be noted that housing associations and coöperatives, which are quasi-public organizations, accounted for approximately a third of total housing production. Tax deductions for homeowners and for those depositing savings with mortgage lending institutions proved effective in stimulating housebuilding for higher-income groups not eligible for direct public low-interest-rate loans.

The federal government in West Germany retained control over the volume of housing investment through its power to alter income tax subsidies, which were the most forceful stimulants to housing investment. Permitted income tax deductions for funds deposited without interest in mortgage lending institutions offered an inducement to private saving and made it possible for the West German government to reduce private consumption at the same time that private investment in housing was increased. This was undoubtedly a key factor in aiding the control of inflation in West Germany during the postwar period.

It is not surprising to find that the country which showed the most impressive growth in housing production during the postwar years assumed a relatively high burden of costs by national, state, and local governmental units. It can be noted in Table VII–4 that the costs of its housing programs to the Federal Republic of Germany ranged between 3 and 4 per cent of the total federal government expenditures in recent years. In addition, it was estimated that approximately 8 per cent of the *Länder* government expenditures were for housing purposes (principally loan subsidies), and many local governmental units maintained active loan subsidy programs.

Substantial indirect costs were assumed by the West German government in the postwar years through the granting of income and property tax subsidies. It has been estimated that tax incentives were responsible for over DM 18.2 billion, or over half of all private savings used in the West German mortgage market from 1950 to 1956.[1] Wer-

[1] Robert G. Wertheimer, "The Miracle of German Housing in the Postwar Period," *Land Economics,* XXXIV, No. 4 (November, 1958), 342, 345.

TABLE VII-3

DWELLING CONSTRUCTION COMPLETED BY CATEGORY OF BUILDER IN SWEDEN, WEST GERMANY, THE UNITED KINGDOM, AND THE UNITED STATES, 1954 TO 1958

Country	Category of builder	1954	1955	1956	1957	1958
Sweden	Total number of dwellings (*000's*)	58.2	57.0	56.9	64.5	62.2
	Percentages:					
	State	0.8	0.8	0.9	0.6	0.8
	Municipalities	31.4	29.9	29.4	29.5	29.6
	Coöperatives	24.7	20.3	25.2	27.2	27.8
	Private:[a]					
	Owner-occupiers	20.2	25.5	24.1	21.7	24.3
	Others	22.9	23.5	20.4	21.0	17.5
United Kingdom	Total number of dwellings (*000's*)	354.1	324.4	307.7	307.6	278.6
	Percentages:					
	Local authorities	67.2	60.4	55.5	55.1	51.4
	Other authorities	6.2	3.8	3.4	3.0	1.9
	Private persons[b]	26.6	35.8	41.1	41.9	46.7
West Germany	Total number of dwellings (*000's*)	542.9	541.7	558.9	528.9	486.4
	Percentages:					
	Public authorities	3.4	2.8	2.7	2.5	2.6
	Housing associations and coöperatives[c]	30.2	29.0	28.4	30.4	30.5
	Private:[d]					
	Individuals	59.6	59.6	60.6	60.3	58.9
	Housing corporations	4.2	4.0	3.8	3.6	4.1
	Enterprises	2.6	4.2	4.5	3.2	3.9
United States	Total number of dwellings (*000's*)	1220.4	1328.9	1118.1	1041.9	1209.4
	Percentages:					
	Public authorities	1.5	1.4	2.1	4.7	5.6
	Private owners and housebuilders[e]	98.5	98.6	97.9	95.3	94.4

Sources: United Nations, *European Housing Trends and Policies in 1957*, E/ECE/329 (Geneva, 1958), Table 3. Walter Fey, "Merkmale und Finanziering im Jahre 1958," *Bundesbaublatt*, 1959. United Kingdom: Central Statistical Office, *Annual Abstract of Statistics, 1959*, No. 96 (London: H.M.S.O., 1959), p. 61. Percentages calculated by the author. Sweden, 1957 and 1958: *Statistisk Årsbok för Sverige, 1959* (Stockholm, 1959), p. 185. Percentages calculated by the author.

[a] More than 90 per cent aided by state.

[b] Principally for owner-occupiers.

[c] Almost all with aid.

[d] Individuals partly with and partly without aid; housing corporations and enterprises mostly without aid.

[e] Of the totals the following percentages were constructed with government-insured or government-guaranteed mortgage loans: 1954—47.8 per cent; 1955—50.3 per cent; 1956—41.1 per cent; 1957—44.1 per cent; and 1958—30.7 per cent.

TABLE VII-4

PERCENTAGES OF GOVERNMENT EXPENDITURES DEVOTED TO HOUSING: SWEDEN, WEST GERMANY, THE UNITED KINGDOM, AND THE UNITED STATES, 1950 TO 1957

Country	1950	1951	1952	1953	1954	1955	1956	1957
Sweden[a]	...	...	...	...	4.5	5.4	5.6	4.2
West Germany[b]	...	...	...	...	3.2	2.9	3.2	4.0
United Kingdom[c]	0.7	0.7	0.7	0.8	0.9	0.9	0.9	0.9
United States[d]	...	...	0.2	0.4	0.2	0.3	0.4	0.5

[a] See chap. iv, Table IV-13. Includes total state expenditures in operating budget, plus part of housing advances devoted to supplementary loans and noninterest portion of homeownership loans. Excluding "Supplementary" state loans the percentages would be: 1954—1.7 per cent, 1955—1.7 per cent, 1956—1.4 per cent, and 1957—1.7 per cent. The data do not include family and child welfare allowances which have accounted for over 6 per cent of total current expenditures by the central government since 1952. Total expenditures of the Ministry for Social Affairs have accounted for approximately a third of current central government expenditures and 11 per cent of the national income since 1955.

[b] *Handbook of Economic Statistics, Federal Republic of Germany and Western Sectors of Berlin* (Bonn-Bad Godesberg: Economic Affairs Section, American Embassy, November 1, 1959), p. 35. Includes federal housing construction and settlement.

[c] United Kingdom percentages calculated by the author. See Table III-6, col. 6 for central government grants to local governments for housing by fiscal years. For total central government expenditures, see Central Statistical Office, *National Income and Expenditure, 1959* (London: H.M.S.O., 1959), Table 4. Central government expenditures are for calendar years. These estimates do not include central government administrative expenses for housing.

[d] United States percentages calculated by the author. For total government expenditures see U.S. Department of Commerce, *Statistical Abstract of the United States, 1959* (Washington, 1959), Table 463, "Housing Expenditures," and *supra*, Table VI-14.

theimer estimated that the federal government and the *Länder* lost DM 1.5 billion in potential income tax revenues from 1948 to 1957 and that local governments lost approximately DM 3.7 billion in temporary exemption from real estate taxes. In addition, he estimated that Section 7*c* tax deferrals had equalled approximately DM 9 billion up to 1957. It is difficult to defend the view, however, that the total amount of income tax credits allowed represented a net loss to federal and state governments, since the subsidized housing investment undoubtedly contributed to the total taxable income in the nation.

One authority has advanced the theory that the astounding economic advances in West Germany during the postwar period can be attributed to the fostering of competition in a free enterprise economy.[2] Although this point is arguable, it would seem that West Germany's

[2] Egon Sohmen, "Competition and Growth: The Lesson of West Germany," *American Economic Review*, XLIX, No. 5 (December, 1959) 986–1003.

housing policies were consistently applied over the entire period and that they encouraged competition and private investment in the housing sector.

United Kingdom

The objectives of postwar housing policy in the United Kingdom have undergone important changes with the shift from Labour to Conservative governments. The critical postwar housing shortage dictated that the Labour government take steps to supply the maximum number of houses in the minimum period of time. In order to achieve this objective the Labour government relied primarily upon local authorities to initiate publicly owned rental housing with the aid of Exchequer subsidies and low-interest-rate loans. Rent and price controls of newly built houses were key features of the Labour government's policy. Scarcity of labor and materials, and the serious dollar shortage which plagued England in the immediate postwar years, were factors which necessitated rationing of materials and labor during this period. Inevitably, the Labour government's concern with the nationalization of land development values and with the planning of "New Towns" became intertwined with its housing policies and objectives.

In October, 1951, the newly elected Conservative government assumed a production goal of 300,000 houses a year, or 50 per cent above the production of 1950 under the Labour government. The policies of the Conservative government were to redirect housing policy gradually toward greater reliance upon free markets and the building of houses by private enterprise for owner occupancy. The Conservative government increased Exchequer subsidies initially to encourage production, but these were subsequently reduced and limited after 1956 to housing built in special-needs categories.

Although both the Labour and Conservative governments held as a major objective the production of a high volume of housing, the type of housing encouraged and the policies for achieving high levels of production were quite different. The Labour government relied upon public enterprise through the local authorities and emphasized production of publicly subsidized rental housing. The Conservative government shifted the emphasis in its policies to privately initiated single-family housing for owner occupancy, although it continued to subsidize publicly owned housing for New Towns and other special needs.

Rents of prewar houses, which were generally based upon 1939 levels at the close of the war, were rigidly controlled under the Labour government, and great disparities existed between the rents of new houses and prewar houses when the Conservative government took over. Beginning in 1952, the Conservative government took steps to encourage local authorities to adjust rents upward, and general rent increases were granted by rent tribunals from 1954 to 1956. The Rent Act of 1957 removed over 4.5 million owner-occupied homes from rent controls and was the initial step in the Conservative policy of gradually abolishing rent controls in England.

It was concluded in chapter iii that the housing policies of the Labour government were poorly adapted to the achievement of a high level of housing production, since they excluded private building and were grounded in a maze of bureaucratic rationing and price controls. Defenders of the Labour government's policies have argued that the immediate postwar years necessitated primary reliance upon public housing, rationing, and price controls, and that the policies would have achieved greater success if capital rationing had been extended to all sectors of the British economy. These observations emphasize the fact that housing policy must be consistent with general economic policy and that the lack of this consistency was the key element in the failure of the Labour government's housing policy. The postwar record suggests that, whatever the reasons may be, the Labour government's housing policies fell far short of achieving the objectives of a high level of housing production. Further, the program of subsidies on which they were based added a substantial burden to Treasury and local government expenditures which will continue for many years. In addition, the maintenance of rent controls reduced typical housing expenditures to levels which were too low to maintain the quality of existing rental housing or to induce private investment in rental housing.

The policies of the Conservative government represented a return to the doctrine that the citizen who is able to do so should pay the cost of his own housing and that it is his responsibility and not that of the local authority to arrange for his housing needs. The traditions of homeownership are still strong in England, and thus far the Conservative government's policy of a gradual return to a private-enterprise housing economy seems to have the support of the voters. The Labour government's policies, however, have left a legacy of large annual government subsidy payments, uneconomic rents, and a large segment of the population who regard the provision of housing as an obligation of the local authority. These elements promise to haunt the Conservative government in its endeavors to restore housing to the private sector.

The consistency in policies and success in housing production in West Germany can be contrasted with the shifting policies, relatively mediocre record of housing production, and high long-term costs of housing programs to both central and local governments in the United Kingdom during the post-World War II decade. Housing quality and density compare favorably with West Germany and Sweden. The record of postwar housing production in the United Kingdom in relation to prewar levels and as a percentage of gross national product is, however, relatively unimpressive.

Government subsidies to public authority housebuilding in the United Kingdom resulted in a major increase in the role of local authorities in producing publicly owned housing, but total housing production did not equal the 1937 prewar record level of 347,000 units until 1954. The relatively unfavorable record of total housing production in the United Kingdom shown in Table VII–1, particularly during the years prior to 1953, seems to be most directly attributable to central government cutbacks in total national housing programs, necessitated by critical dollar shortages and by early and sharp increases in building costs and in the general price level. Centralization of public lending authority in the Public Works Loan Board, control of the level of subsidies through the Ministry of Housing, and licensing of private housebuilding made it possible for the central government to exercise control measures as the inflationary conditions in the general economy required.

The rise in housing investment in the United Kingdom as a percentage of gross national product in 1953 and 1954, shown in Table VII–2, resulted from the early action taken by the Conservative government to increase the general-needs subsidies and to free private housebuilding from licensing. The subsequent decline in housing investment can be attributed in part to the gradual reduction and eventual elimination (by the Housing Act of 1956) of the general-needs subsidies for housing and to the exercise of general credit controls via the "bank rate" by the Conservative government. The failure of private housebuilding to increase rapidly enough to offset the decline in public authority housing in more recent years is in part the result of the lack of inducements to private housebuilding throughout much of the postwar period. The most important restraint upon private housebuilding (other than central government subsidies to local authority housing and licensing restrictions upon private housebuilding which were in existence through much of the period) has been the maintenance of rent controls and of low levels of rents in both privately and publicly owned housing before and since World War II. This has undoubtedly made housing investment relatively unattractive in comparison with alternative investments.

Publicly initiated houses accounted for over 85 per cent of total dwelling construction in the United Kingdom from 1945 to 1951 and continued to account for over one half of annual volume through 1958. The abrupt reversal in central government housing policy under the conservative government altered the relative participation of private and public capital in housing, modified antiquated rent controls, and halted the rapid growth in the burden of public housing subsidies. Viewed over the entire postwar period and as an over-all program, however, it is not at all clear that a high level of private unsubsidized housing investment can be maintained in combination with an encompassing program of publicly owned housing at subsidized rentals. Viewed in this light, it can be argued that British postwar housing policy has been relatively ineffective as compared with the more consistent and better integrated policies in Sweden and West Germany.

British housing throughout the postwar period has been subject to a complex structure of national and local governmental controls. Enmeshed in this bureaucracy, postwar achievements in improving housing standards are a tribute to the integrity, skill, and patience of the British civil servants and the housebuilding industry.

Sweden

Sweden's housing objectives following World War II have emphasized stability of housing production and costs, the raising of space and equipment standards, the reduction of family housing expenditures, control of rents, and the activation of the role of local authorities. Higher ratios of dwellings to population reflected a less critical post-World War II supply situation in Sweden and accounted in part for the lesser attention to the stimulation of house production as a goal in itself. The objectives of Swedish housing policy were clearly set forth in 1946 and have been maintained consistently, although a special parliamentary commission recommended a review of basic government rent policies in 1956.

Sweden's postwar housing policies were integrally related to the broad social-welfare programs adopted by the Social Democratic government. The principal features of housing policy were low-interest-rate third mortgage loans extended by the national government, with preference in terms given to municipalities and nonprofit builders; supplementary loans bearing no interest or amortization, granted by the national government to equalize the gap between the level of controlled rents and current building costs; comprehensive family-income subsidies; and rent controls. This policy structure provided a centralization of control over housebuilding in the Royal Housing Board, which was in a position to influence greatly the rents, amount, and characteristics of housing built, as well as the relative participation of public and private enterprise in housebuilding. In view of the over-all objectives of Swedish government housing policy, it can be maintained that policies and programs were reasonably well adapted to their realization. The emphasis upon the control of rents, while other prices were allowed to rise, aided in the achievement of one of the major goals of Swedish housing policy—the reduction of the percentage of income spent for housing. At the same time it created the need for continuously increasing housing subsidies and forced restrictions upon other investment. Meanwhile, the combination of favored loan terms to publicly owned housing and rigid rent controls discouraged broad participation by private builders for profit. One of the unhappy results of rent control in Sweden, of course, has been the virtual abandonment of the market mechanism as a means for resource allocation. Lundberg has concluded that:[3]

> The relatively low level of rents [in postwar Sweden] thus without doubt helped to perpetuate the housing shortage and to prevent the creation of a housing reserve. . . .
>
> Both Swedish agricultural and housing policy thus give examples of social policy which . . . seeks to influence the distribution of income and the direction of consumption, yet by these very means contributes to an inoptimal allocation of the community's productive resources.

Sweden's housing programs and policies have been well administered. The small size of the country contributes to ease of centralized administration. (Total annual national production approximates that of the Los Angeles metropolitan area.) The Swedes are accustomed to extensive government control over economic life. Government housing officials are competent, and decision making has been effectively decentralized.

The record of housing production in Sweden during the postwar years seems to establish that over-all housing standards can be improved markedly by efficient public control over housebuilding and financing, in combination with a vigorous coöperative program and generous state subsidies. The volume of housing investment relative to prewar years and to the gross national product exceeds that for the United States and the United Kingdom, but is less than for West Germany. Although densities are substantially higher and the percentage of the total housing stock with modern conveniences is less than for the United Kingdom and the United States, major improvements have been achieved in over-all standards of convenience and in space

---

[3] Erik Lundberg, *Business Cycles and Economic Policy*, trans. J. Potter (Cambridge, Mass.: Harvard University Press, 1957), p. 330.

standards during the post-World War II years. The improvement in the quality of housing built for the average family can be attributed in large measure to the strict control of dwelling construction standards by the Swedish central government.

A severe climate and traditionally crowded housing conditions underlie the strong housing demand in Sweden. Because Sweden was able to produce a substantial volume of housing during the war years, the housing shortage was less acute at the end of World War II than for other European nations. The combination of rent controls and family housing subsidies has maintaned housing demand at high levels during the postwar decade.

Municipalities and coöperatives have accounted for over half of the total volume of housebuilding in Sweden in the postwar decade. Municipalities occupy a key position in housebuilding in Sweden because of their exclusive control over public improvements for land development. Land use control by municipalities has resulted in rational and economical land use patterns in striking contrast with those in the United States, where local governments have assumed a more passive role.

Coöperatives have accounted for approximately 25 per cent of postwar housing production in Sweden and have been progressive in house planning, construction, financing, and management. Coöperative housing ownership has to a degree provided a substitute for private individual ownership of housing in Sweden because participants in coöperative housing projects have been able to acquire a transferable interest in housing units.

Because of climatic, historical, topographical, and institutional factors, Swedish housing has been dominantly for multi-family rental occupancy. Recent trends indicate a shift in public preference in favor of single-family owner-occupied housing. The reduced importance of the speculative builder in Sweden has eliminated the beneficial effects of competition in furnishing housing accommodation and, it can be argued, has resulted in a degree of unresponsiveness to changes in public demands. It has also been observed that the "institutionalization" of housing in Sweden has left its marks in the sameness of Swedish housing. The type of housing one occupies is not a measure of status to the same degree as in the United States, because of the limited range of housing types available in Sweden and the restrictions upon incomes.

The cost of Sweden's housing programs as a percentage of national and local government expenditures has been greater than that of any of the other countries examined, and it rose steadily in the postwar years until 1957, when subsidies were reduced. It was noted in Table VII–3 that the inclusion of family and child welfare allowances for Sweden, which have exceeded 6 per cent of central government expenditures in recent years, would result in very much higher imputed costs for Sweden's housing program. There is some evidence linking the rise in building costs and in the cost of living generally to the program of housing subsidies in Sweden, although it is difficult to segregate the influence of housing subsidies from the many other family income subsidy programs. Swedish housing policies, unlike those in West Germany, did not provide for tax inducements to encourage private saving or for reductions in private consumption as inflation control devices.

Critics of the government housing policy maintain that direct state loans for housing have restricted the availability of funds for other forms of investment and that these restrictions are having an unfavorable effect upon Sweden's capacity to compete for export markets with West Germany and other nations. More fundamentally, they argue that the government's housing and public investment policies since 1955 have involved a combination of inflationary pressure and government allocation of funds in the capital market and that these trends have tended to destroy the effectiveness of market mechanisms in allocating investment in accordance with profitability. Supporters of the government's program, on the other hand, maintain that any withdrawal of state housing subsidies is unwarranted in view of the continuing need to improve housing standards and that investment in the housing sector should not be evaluated on the basis of profitability.

United States

As in most European countries, the immediate objective of post-World War II housing policy in the United States was to satisfy the emergency housing needs of the veterans. Encouragement of homeownership has been the central objective of federal housing policy since the 1920's. The period of emergency action was followed by the establishment of a statement of national housing policy in the Housing Act of 1949, setting forth both general and specific objectives. The general objective of national policy was established in the Housing Act of 1949 as the achievement of "a decent home and a suitable living environment for every American family." Among the more specific objectives of the Act were the following: elimination of instability in residential construction; reduction in residential building costs; elimination of substandard dwellings; and improvement in housing environment and in the structural amenities of dwellings.

During the postwar period of "emergency" housing action, the Democratic administration sought to achieve high levels of housebuilding rapidly by controlling nonessential construction and channeling materials into low-cost housing, by providing federal assistance for the production of prefabricated dwellings, and by adapting various types of temporary war housing to civilian needs. Federal rent controls were continued during this period. Accomplishments under this program were disappointing, and a major reorganization of the National Housing Agency ensued in 1947. The immediate postwar experience in the United States was somewhat parallel to that in the United Kingdom, inasmuch as the housing programs in both countries bogged down amid detailed and extensive national controls and bureaucracy.

Following the reorganization of the National Housing Agency and the passage of the Housing Act of 1949, federal housing policies were reoriented to provide for more extensive reliance upon free markets and private investment. This reorientation was reflected in the gradual decontrol of rents, congressional limitations upon the volume of publicly owned housing authorized, gradual liberalization of government mortgage loan insurance and guaranty terms, and government support of the market for federally insured or guaranteed mortgages on privately owned single-family units. The combined effect of these policies during the postwar decade was to encourage private homeownership and the extending of more generous loan terms by private lenders.

Although it is evident that federal policies were associated with high levels of housing production, a rapid expansion in homeownership, and an over-all improvement in housing quality during the postwar years, it has been pointed out that the achievement of these objectives was offset by significant failures in accomplishing other objectives of national housing policy, namely, the elimination of instability in residential construction, the reduction in housebuilding costs, the improvement in the general housing environment, and the solution of the problem of housing low-income families. Many would maintain that federal housing policies have not been appropriately geared to the latter objectives. For example, it can be argued that the liberalization of mortgage credit terms during certain years in the postwar period has led to unnecessary cost increases, that the aim of maximizing annual production has resulted in instability in housing produtcion, that federal housing policies have been in general directed toward assistance of higher-income families, and that federal policies and programs designed to stimulate production of privately owned and publicly owned housing for low-income groups have been most ineffective. Some of these shortcomings will be examined in more detail below.

Post-World War II housing objectives and policies have been further criticized on the grounds that at times they have been inconsistent with an overriding objective—over-all economic stability. Defendants of government policies would counter that although liberal housing credit policies may from time to time have a destabilizing short-run influence on the economy, the over-all postwar record indicates that government housing policies have contributed to national economic stability. The evidence cited in support of this position shows that postwar peaks in housing production have been reached in years in which industrial production was declining. For instance, as seen in Table VII–2, residential construction increased its share in the total gross national product during the recession in 1958 in comparison with 1957.

Many lay the blame for shortcomings in national housing policies at the door of the public administration of federal housing policy. Federal organization for administering national housing policies has been much less well integrated in the United States than in the other nations considered. In part this may reflect the greater size and complexity of the task as well as the traditional turnover and general mediocre quality of federal public administration in the United States. Closer study and comparison, however, suggests that the irrational separation of policy-making functions between the Housing and Home Finance Agency and its semiautonomous Federal Housing Administration, the Veterans Administration, the Federal National Mortgage Association, and the Federal Home Loan Bank System has added greatly to the problems of administering long-range housing policies in the United States. Problems of coördinating and integrating federal housing policies were magnified, of course, by the administration of general credit and monetary controls through the board of governors of the Federal Reserve System, which from time to time exercised both direct and indirect controls over federal mortgage lending policies during the postwar years. The attendant problems were the basis for a recommendation in 1953 by the President's Advisory Committee on Government Housing Policies and Programs that federal housing activities be reorganized under a single administrator with clear supervisory authority. This much needed change has not been effected, and federal housing policy in the United States continues to suffer from the lack of centralized authority and an organization well designed for policy implementation.

Postwar residential construction accounted for a higher proportion of total fixed investment in the United States, Sweden, and West Germany than in the United Kingdom, as shown in Table VII–2. The proportion of the gross national product devoted to fixed capital formation was lower in the United States and the United Kingdom as compared with Sweden and West Germany, however, as was the proportion of the gross national product devoted to residenital construction. During the boom years of 1950 and 1955, residential construction in the United States rose to 5.8 per cent and 5.4 per cent, respectively, of the gross national product, but declined in each instance in the years following. Residential construction was also less stable as a percentage of the gross national product in the United States during the postwar years than in West Germany or Sweden. The differences not accounted for by variations in statistical measurement can be attributed to the differences in the nature of the subsidy devices employed and in the degree of central government control over housing investment in the United States as compared with the European countries. Primary reliance in the United States was placed upon monetary policy as a means of controlling the over-all volume of fixed investment, the market was allowed to determine the areas within which reductions in investment should take place. The net result was that housing investment, which has proven to be highly sensitive to changes in credit terms, was reduced during periods of general monetary stringency.

Postwar housing production has been preponderantly single-family, owner-occupied housing initiated by the private housebuilding industry. Government housing programs have concentrated upon aids to the flow of mortgage funds into residential construction.

The degree to which government insurance and guaranty of mortgage loans has increased total postwar housing investment in the United States is arguable, as was noted in chapter vi. The author's conclusion, supported by a priori reasoning and statistical data, is that these programs have resulted in an expanded volume of housing investment during the postwar years coupled with a degree of inflation in building costs and housing prices. Conclusions as to the effects of government housing policies upon the residential construction industry and the economy as a whole will be explored below.

Comparative Changes in Housing Standards

Inter-country comparisons of housing standards are extremely difficult because of differences in climate and customs and because the sources and methods of gathering housing data and their accuracy vary widely between countries. The measures used in comparing the postwar changes in housing standards in the United States with those in the United Kingdom, West Germany and Sweden are:

New dwellings produced per capita
Size of new dwellings produced
Percentages of new production and total housing inventory with modern conveniences

Table VII–1 shows the relative growth in housing production in these four countries in relationship to their population. It is evident that West Germany is the only country of the four included which has shown a notable expansion in the number of dwellings completed per thousand of population as compared with prewar levels. This can be explained in part by the low levels of dwelling construction in Germany, relative to population, before World War II. High dwelling construction in the United States per thousand of population in 1950 reflected the influence of high postwar demand and the Korean war inflation in the United States. The rise in production in the United Kingdom was undoubtedly caused in part by the revival of investment confidence and the impact of housing policy changes instituted by the Conservative government.

In interpreting these figures, it should be recognized that the number of new dwellings constructed provides no indication of the size or quality of housing provided. Table VII–5 reveals that housing production in Sweden and West Germany was concentrated in small flats of three rooms or less from 1948 to 1955. A gradual shift toward construction of larger units is apparent in the years 1956 and 1957 in Sweden and West Germany, reflecting the changes in housing policy discussed above. A trend toward lower space standards in the United Kingdom, noted in chapter iii, resulted in part from specially favorable government subsidies in that country to encourage the construction of small flats.[4]

Housing production in the United States was concentrated in the single-family houses of five rooms or more during the entire postwar decade. A revival in multi-family construction in the United States was started in 1957, and this trend has continued through 1959. The effect of this has been to reduce slightly the relative production of dwellings with five or more rooms in recent years.

It has already been noted that postwar houses in Sweden, West Germany, and the United Kingdom have been constructed with higher standards of conveniences than were typical for the housing stock in the prewar period. Table IV–9 showed that 98 per cent of the new urban dwellings constructed in Sweden in the period from 1946 to 1955 had central heat and private water closet and 85 per cent had private bath. The percentage of new Swedish rural housing units with

[4] See chap. iii, pp. 48–49.

TABLE VII–5

Percentage of Dwellings Completed in Four Countries, by Number of Rooms, 1948 to 1958

Year	United Kingdom					West Germany						Sweden						United States				
	1–2	3	4	5	6 or more	1	2	3	4	5	6 or more	1	2	3	4	5	6 or more	1	2	3	4	5 or more
1948....	...	3	13	81	3	...	...	...	...	...	...	...	...	...	...	...	...	...	...	...	...	...
1949....	...	6	16	75	3	...	...	...	...	...	...	10	9	35	30	11	5	...	...	...	...	...
1950....	...	7	23	66	4	...	...	...	...	...	...	10	7	34	30	13	6	...	...	...	...	...
1951....	...	8	29	60	3	...	...	...	...	...	...	10	8	33	29	13	7	...	...	...	...	...
1952....	...	7	35	55	3	1	15	47	28	6	3	16	8	35	26	10	5	...	...	...	...	...
1953....	...	8	37	53	2	1	13	45	32	6	3	17	8	38	24	9	4	...	...	...	...	...
1954....	...	8	36	54	2	2	10	40	37	7	4	12	9	36	26	11	6	...	...	...	...	...
1955....	10	36		53	2	1	9	36	40	14		11	10	32	25	14	8	...	...	...	...	...
1956....	11	35		55		10		33	41	16		9	9	9	31	28	15	2.7	7.9	14.5	32.3	42.5
1957....	13	36		51		9		31	42	18		11	9	25	31	16	8	...	...	...	...	...
1958....	18	36		46		9		27	42	22		9	8	20	34	20	9	...	...	...	...	...

Sources: 1948–54: United Nations, *European Housing Progress and Policies in 1955*, E/ECE/259 (Geneva, August, 1956), Table 4. 1955–57: United Nations, *European Housing Trends and Policies in 1957*, E/ECE/329 (Geneva, 1958), Table 2. West Germany: See Table V–8. 1958: United Nations, *European Housing Trends and Policies in 1958*, E/ECE/365 (Geneva, 1959), Table 3.

Note: United States urban and rural nonfarm estimates for period 1945 to 1950 based upon unpublished sample from the U.S. Census on Housing. See Leo Grebler, Louis Winnick, and David M. Blank, *Capital Formation in Residential Real Estate* (Princeton, N.J.: Princeton University Press, 1959), Table J–2.

these conveniences was almost as high in the postwar decade. The effect of this has been to increase substantially the proportion of total dwellings with these conveniences in Sweden. It can be seen, however, that the percentages with such conveniences are still low relative to the United States or the United Kingdom, particularly in rural areas. Similar trends are evident in West Germany. Although less than 20 per cent of total dwelling units in West Germany had a private bath in 1950 (see Table VII–6), it is reported that more than 75 per cent of newly constructed dwellings in the postwar decade were equipped with this facility.[5] It was noted in chapter iii that separate inside bathrooms are now recommended in all local authority housing in the United Kingdom and that it is within the discretion of local authorities whether or not to provide a second water closet for houses with three bedrooms.[6] It can be assumed that virtually all new permanent private housing in the United Kingdom and the United States has all of the facilities shown in Table VII–6.

This table indicates in a broad manner the relative quality standards achieved in the four countries under consideration by the early 1950's. The measures shown do not, of course, adequately reflect housing standards; they do not fully reflect the extent of obsolescence in the housing inventory. The data do indicate, however, a relative ranking of housing standards in terms of modern conveniences with West Germany lowest, followed by Sweden, the United Kingdom, and the United States.

The statistical comparison in Table VII–6 is misleading to many observers who regard modern Swedish houses as better planned and constructed and having more modern conveniences than modern houses in the United Kingdom. A Swedish economist has suggested the hypothesis that more resources are employed in the average dwelling in the United States, Sweden, and West Germany than in the United Kingdom.

This hypothesis was tested by dividing the figures in Table VII–2 showing housing investment as a percentage of the gross national product by the "new dwellings per 1,000 persons" shown in Table VII–1. This resulted in indexes which measured the relative investment per dwelling for the four countries. These indexes, which are shown for 1956 and 1957 below, confirm the view that the average housing investment per dwelling in real terms is highest in the United

[5] United Nations Economic Commission for Europe, *The European Housing Situation*, E/ECE/221 (Geneva, January, 1956), p. 19.

[6] See chap. iii, p. 56.

TABLE VII–6

MEASURES OF HOUSING QUALITY IN FOUR COUNTRIES, SELECTED YEARS

Measures of quality	West Germany, 1950			Sweden			United Kingdom, 1951			United States, 1950		
	Total	Rural	Urban	Total, 1954	Rural, 1956	Urban, 1956	Total	Rural	Urban	Total	Urban and rural nonfarm	Rural farm
Per cent with electricity	98.4	97.9	99.1	93.7	96.2	99.6	88.0	...	...	94.0	96.6	77.7
Per cent with inside running water	78.0	66.3	95.6	74.0	48.0	91.0	94.0	79.0	99.0	88.8	96.4	77.9
Per cent with bath	19.7	13.2	29.6	34.0	18.0	46.0	62.0	53.0	65.0	83.0[e]	90.4[e]	65.3[e]
Per cent with central heating	7.0	...	...	45.5[b]	36.0	72.0	1.0	...	...	50.4[h]	55.3	18.1
Average number of persons per room	1.11[a]	...	...	.93	...	...	.77	...	...	.69[f]	.69[f]	.69[f]
Per cent of dwellings with more than two persons per room	10.5[a]	...	8.8[a]	11.0[b]	...	...	3.6	...	...	1.8[f]	1.4[f]	2.7[f]
Per cent of dwellings over 100 years old	...	...	...	17.91[c]	9.99[c]	24.45[c]	20.8	...	...	...	...	...
Estimated per cent of dwellings delapidated or unfit for occupancy	...	...	...	...[g]	...	...	6.5[d]	...	...	9.4	8.2	19.5

Sources: West Germany, Sweden, and United Kingdom: United Nations, *The European Housing Situation*, E/ECE/221 (Geneva, January 1956), Table 13. (See also Table IV–9 for Sweden, 1956. United States: See Table VI–5.) Also U.S. Bureau of the Census, *1956 National Housing Inventory*, III, *Characteristics of the 1956 Inventory*, Part 1, "United States and Regions" (Washington, 1958), Table 1.

[a] Total 1953, urban 1950. [b] 1955, Owe Lundevall, *Swedish Housing Market* (Stockholm: Hyresgästernas Förlags AB, 1957), p. 31.

[c] Per cent over 65 years old, 1945. [d] England and Wales only. [e] Excludes units lacking hot water and private toilet *or* bath and units not reporting.

[f] 1950 nonfarm housing. According to the Census of 1950, 6.2 per cent of all occupied dwellings had over 1.51 persons per room—5.6 per cent of urban and rural nonfarm housing and 10.2 per cent of rural farms had 1.51 persons per room or more.

[g] The Royal Housing Board at the end of 1955 classified 125,000 urban units and 500,000 rural units lacking inside running water as substandard. An additional 350,000 urban dwellings and 300,000 rural dwellings lacked water closet. The total of these represents over 50 per cent of the total housing inventory. Leonard Silk, *Sweden Plans for Better Housing* (Durham, N. C.: Duke University Press, 1948), quoted the Social Housing Committee as estimating that 75,000 *urban* dwellings should be removed between 1946 and 1960 as "uninhabitable" and that another 160,000 urban dwellings should be removed as "substandard" The Royal Housing Board estimated that 100,000 "substandard" dwellings should be removed between 1946 and 1956. (See Table IV–14.)

States, next highest and about the same in Sweden and West Germany, and lowest in the United Kingdom.

	1957	1956
United States	74	74
Sweden	65	72
West Germany	65	64
United Kingdom	53	57

Although the proportion of dwellings over a hundred years old in West Germany is not available, it is estimated to be relatively low, owing to the extent of war destruction and the rapid population growth within the present borders of West Germany during the last one hundred years.[7] It would seem, therefore, that lower densities and higher percentages of dwellings with modern conveniences in the United Kingdom are offset by greater average age of dwellings and by higher proportions of obsolescent dwellings. International comparisons of relative percentages of dwellings viewed as obsolete are particularly hazardous, because standards vary so widely. It was estimated in 1954 that 6.5 per cent of the total number of dwellings in the United Kingdom were "unfit for human habitation."[8] It was noted in chapter vi that an estimated 13 million dwelling units were classified as "substandard" in the United States as of 1956, representing 23.7 per cent of the total number of dwellings in the country. Of these, 3,155,499 dwelling units (5.6 per cent of the national total) lacked hot water, private toilet, or bath and were dilapidated, while 899,344 (1.7 per cent of the total) had private toilet and bath and were dilapidated. It would appear that the total of these dwellings classified as dilapidated should be used as a basis of comparison with those dwellings classed in the United Kingdom as "unfit for human occupancy." Although comparable figures are not available for West Germany and Sweden, it is apparent from Table VII–6 that substantially higher proportions of dwellings in these countries lack inside running water, central heating, and private bath. The availability of central heating, is, of course, an inadequate measure of relative quality owing to the more severe climate in Sweden and the differences in the heating customs in the United Kingdom and the United States. It is also probably true that smaller proportions of dwellings in these countries would be classified by United States standards as rundown, neglected, or providing inadequate shelter against the elements.

---

[7] United Nations Economic Commission for Europe, *The European Housing Situation,* p. 19.

[8] See chap. iii, p. 67.

On the basis of the data reviewed above, it can be concluded that West Germany and Sweden have added the largest number of new dwellings per thousand population during the postwar years. Housing production rose more rapidly in the United States than in the United Kingdom, but production per thousand of population has been roughly comparable since 1954. The higher volume of dwelling construction in Sweden and West Germany was offset in part by the fact that over one half of total production was accounted for by dwellings with three rooms or less before 1956. This factor, together with the serious housing shortages continuing in these two countries, has resulted in a continuance of higher densities measured by persons per room than in the United Kingdom or in the United States.

Although it is difficult to compare standards of housing quality between countries, it seems that standards of convenience in the total housing stock in West Germany and Sweden are relatively low in comparison with those in the United Kingdom and the United States. High rates of new production of dwellings with modern conveniences, however, are bringing about a rapid improvement in the over-all quality of the housing inventory in all of the countries studied. Measured in terms of new production, the improvement has been most rapid in West Germany and least rapid in the United Kingdom. Comparison of the estimated changes in characteristics of the housing stock in Sweden and in the United States over the past decade indicates roughly comparable rates of improvement in both countries. (See Tables IV–9 and V–5.)

Effect of Policies upon the Residential Construction Industry

It is important to view the effects of national housing policies upon the stability of residential construction and upon the organization and efficiency of the housebuilding industry, as reflected in trends in housebuilding costs. Chart VII–1 shows index numbers of the value of dwelling construction, in 1954 constant prices with 1950 as a base year, for West Germany, Sweden, the United Kingdom, and the United States. The lower portion of the chart shows the trends in building costs in these countries over the same period.

The indexes of the value of dwelling construction for the various countries highlight the continually rising level of physical housing output in West Germany in comparison with the other countries. Although the use of the 1950 base year is favorable to the comparative performance of West Germany and both cost indexes and output data for West Germany are under revision, allowances for these factors are

CHART VII-1

TRENDS IN VALUE OF DWELLING CONSTRUCTION AND BUILDING COSTS IN FOUR COUNTRIES, 1950 TO 1958

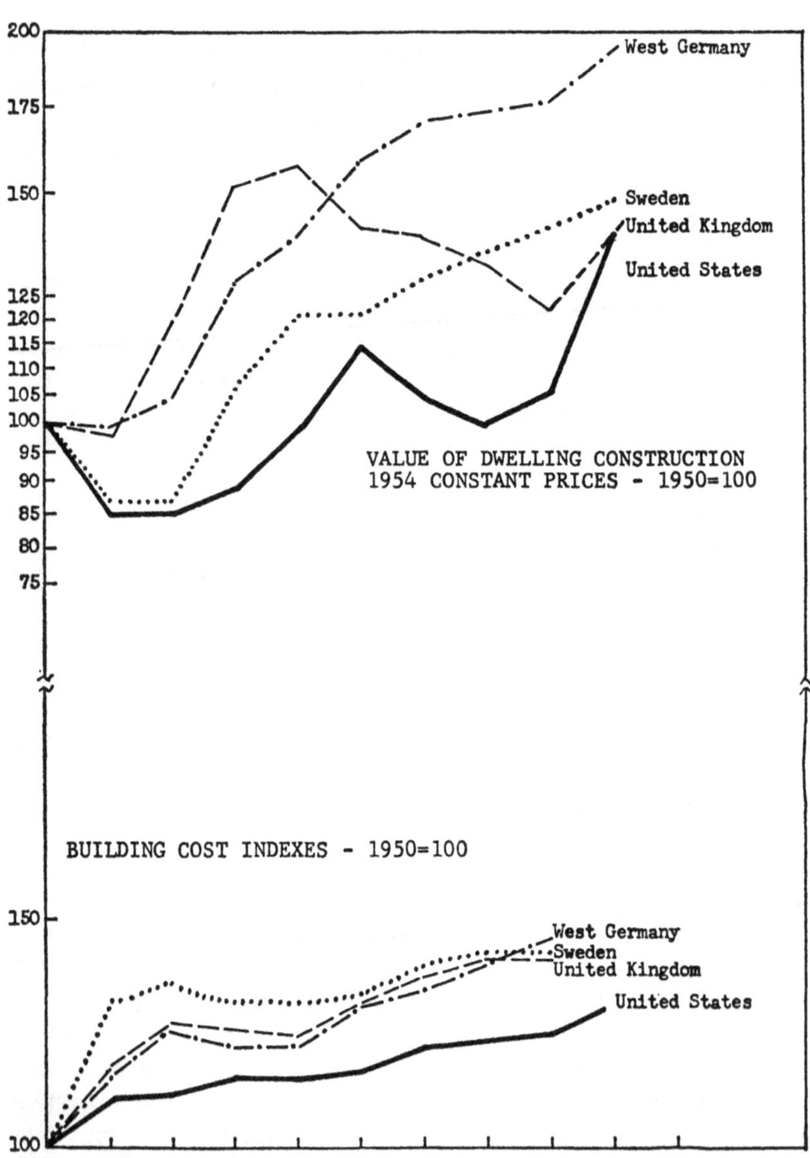

unlikely to modify the basic trends in the data shown. The effect of the shift in housing policies with the election of the Conservative government in 1952 is shown by the sharp rise in housing production in the United Kingdom in 1953 and 1954. It can be seen that physical output has remained relatively stable in both the United States and Sweden over much of the postwar period. Sharp increases in the value of dwelling construction measured in current dollars have occurred in both countries, but, after adjustment for building cost changes, physical output expanded by approximately 40 per cent during the years from 1950 to 1958.

The close similarity in the trend in building costs in the four countries over the past decade is notable. The record of West Germany in expanding physical output with only a moderate rise in building costs is testimony to the efficiency of the housebuilding industry in that country and also to the over-all effectiveness of national housing and economic policies.

Attention was called in chapters iii and iv to the fact that the increasing participation by municipal authorities in the provision of new housing in Sweden and in the United Kingdom during the postwar years had tended to restrict the private sector and to limit the role of the private speculative housebuilding industry in these countries. Table VII–3 shows the comparative participation of major groups in the provision of housing in the four countries under review. It can be seen that West Germany has relied upon the private sector in the provision of housing to a predominant degree, while local authorities continue to dominate new housing construction in the United Kingdom and account for a third of national production in Sweden.

It is not surprising to observe that the private speculative housebuilding industry has been reduced to a relatively minor role during most of the post-World War II years in the United Kingdom and Sweden. In both countries a relatively small number of large building firms seem to account for a large part of publicly initiated construction.

SOURCES: Value of dwelling construction: Table II–3. Building Costs for Sweden, the United Kingdom, and West Germany: 1950–1956, United Nations Economic Commission for Europe, *Quarterly Bulletin of Housing and Building Statistics for Europe*, V, No. 3 (Geneva, 1957), Table 8; 1957–1959, United Nations Economic Commission for Europe, *Annual Bulletin of Housing and Building Statistics for 1958* (Geneva, 1959), Table 14. Building Costs for the United States: U.S. Department of Labor and U.S. Department of Commerce, *Construction Volume and Costs, 1915–1956, A Statistical Supplement to Construction Review*, pp. 54–55; U.S. Department of Commerce, *Construction Review*, VI, No. 9 (September, 1960), 36. The E. H. Boeckh and Associates *Cost Index for Residences* is used for the United States.

As was noted in chapter iv, coöperatives have also assumed an expanding role in Swedish residential construction. Privately initiated housing has accounted for a substantially larger share of total residential building in West Germany and for a predominant share of residential building in the United States. It is, of course, difficult to ascribe particular importance to the influence of the structure of the housebuilding industry upon national housing performance. It would seem significant that expansion in single-family, owner-occupied housing has been accompanied by the vigorous development of the private housebuilding industry in the United States and in West Germany and that this was a characteristic of the housebuilding industry in the United Kingdom in the prewar years.

Effects of Housing Policies upon Postwar Economies

Three facts stand out when the postwar economic development of western Europe and the United States is compared with prewar years:

Rapid rates of postwar economic growth
Low levels of unemployment
Rising price levels

The broad economic objectives of most western European countries and of the United States during this period have been to maintain high and stable employment with high rates of growth and price stability. The attainment of these objectives, of course, would require a high degree of perfection in national economic policy making, which was seldom achieved. In the different countries, different means were chosen for achieving the above objectives, and the constraints acting upon national economic policies also have differed from country to country.

Virtually all western European countries, and also the United States, have passed through four major phases in the postwar period under consideration: the Korean war boom of 1950–51, the post-Korean recession of 1952–53, the 1955–56 boom, and the 1958 recession.

Price stability has been interpreted more literally in West Germany than in either Sweden, the United States, or the United Kingdom. This was undoubtedly owing to the sensitivity of the West German population to inflation. The large labor supply and the concomitant relatively slow wage increases in West Germany rendered possible a rapid expansion with only moderate inflationary tendencies. In addition, the continually rising foreign exchange reserves of West Germany reflected the competitiveness of West Germany's exports and other international factors.

The principal factors responsible for the high rate of growth of the West German economy during the 1950's can be identified. Wartime destruction and postwar dismantling of plants raised the scarcity of and the return to capital. At the same time the rapid growth of population in West Germany both added to capital requirements and provided the basis for an expansion of production. The relatively weak bargaining position of labor moderated the rise in money wages from the levels established at the time of the currency reform, and the rapid increase in productivity as investment and output expanded further strengthened the competitive position of West German industry. Relatively low real wages and high rates of profit favored a high savings ratio, and during most of the period budget surpluses made an appreciable contribution to total savings. In general, West Germany relied primarily upon monetary as opposed to fiscal controls in its countercyclical policy, although income tax exemptions were used to a considerable degree to control the volume of investment in housing and other capital goods.[9]

Government budgetary measures were used only to a limited degree as instruments of countercyclical policy in West Germany during the postwar period. Government budgets were employed to meet the traditional needs of public programs and, predominantly, to provide a favorable framework for the activities in the private sector. As noted in chapter v, tax reductions and incentives were widely employed to direct private investment into housing and other socially desired sectors. The fortunate position of West Germany with respect to its labor supplies and physical resources made unnecessary such governmental policies of over-all restraint as were employed in the United Kingdom and Sweden. To be sure, it has been argued by some that West Germany's budgetary policies "have sometimes run counter to what were considered by the monetary authorities to be the policy requirements of the moment." [10]

It has been observed that the United Kingdom gave first priority in its postwar economic policies to safeguarding the balance of payments.[11] National economic policies were limited by low international liquidity and by a low elasticity of domestic supply, as well as by the large claims of defense upon national resources. The strength of British trade unions and the mechanism of wage settlements in the United

---

[9] United Nations Economic Commission for Europe, *Economic Survey of Europe in 1958*, E/ECE/345 (Geneva, 1959), chap. iii, pp. 24–25.

[10] United Nations Economic Commission for Europe, *Economic Survey of Europe in 1959*, E/ECE/383 (Geneva, 1960), chap. vi, p. 17.

[11] *Ibid.*, chap. vi.

Kingdom acted to make price stability a secondary consideration. The upward pressure on wages associated with virtually full employment in the United Kingdom throughout most of the period complicated the task of reconciling short-term restraint upon aggregate domestic demand with the long-term aim of high and rising investment in housing and other capital goods. High defense expenditures added to the task of achieving stability and growth in the British economy.

Before 1952, the Labour government was absorbed in problems of labor and material shortages and serious foreign exchange difficulties. These problems were complicated by the problems encountered in schemes for nationalization of important sectors of British industry. For the first time since before the war, some slack appeared in the British economy in 1952, and measures were taken in 1953 and 1954 to stimulate domestic demand. The 1953 budget included a 25-per-cent cut in the purchase tax, a reduction in the standard rate of income tax, and the reintroduction of initial depreciation allowances, which had been suspended in 1952. As noted in chapter iii, general housing subsidies were increased by the Housing Act of 1952, and restrictions upon private housebuilding were substantially modified in January, 1953. In addition, the excess profits levy was abolished in January, 1954. The 1954 budget also introduced the device of investment allowances, which constituted a remission rather than a deferment of taxes.[12]

Private consumption and private investment expanded rapidly in the United Kingdom in 1954 in response to the above incentives. Strong expansion in the private sector resulted in a marked deterioration of the balance of payments on current account, and taxes on consumption and profits were raised in October, 1955, and the investment allowances, which had proved a powerful stimulus to private investment, was abolished in 1956. During this period housing subsidies were gradually reduced and, in November, 1956, finally abolished. Another balance of payments crisis in the autumn of 1957 resulted in increases in the bank rate to 7 per cent and cuts in government expenditures. The decline in import prices in 1958 restored the favorable balance of payments for the United Kingdom, government policy shifted in 1958 from restraint to cautious relaxation, and higher public expenditures and investment allowances were restored in the 1958 budget. Energetic steps were taken to promote a renewed expansion in the budget of April, 1959.

Sweden's postwar economic policies emphasized full employment and sustained economic growth. Although price control and price

[12] *Ibid.*

stability ranked high as postwar national economic objectives, and although government regulation of prices was authorized during most of the postwar period, the cost of living in Sweden rose steadily from 1948 to 1958.[13] Continuous shortages of skilled labor under virtual full employment, upward pressure on import prices, and rising incomes under government subsidies were the powerful underlying forces contributing to the rise in the cost of living and in other prices.[14]

Swedish monetary policy during the postwar period moved gradually from early emphasis upon expansion of credit and stabilization of interest rates to the exercise of central bank control over bank liquidity and the money supply. Up to 1952, the Riksbank followed an active policy of maintaining low interest rates and encouraging credit expansion. As inflationary tendencies became marked in the Swedish economy, particularly at the time of the Korean war, the Riksbank had to direct its energies toward a policy of active limitation of credit. In addition, stringent import regulations were put into effect as early as 1948, and some limitations were placed upon the volume of building. During the first half of 1952, the Riksbank endeavored to check credit expansion by limiting the supply of liquid assets in the banking system. As a result of a new wave of credit expansion in 1954–55, the Riksbank finally raised the official discount rate by 1 per cent to 3.75 per cent, at the same time that the government issued a 4.5-per-cent long-term loan. These measures were followed by successive increases in the discount rate to 5 per cent by July, 1957. It has been pointed out, however, that the restrictive credit policies of the Riksbank were somewhat less than fully effective, because building credits and government loans were exempted from direct limitations upon the extension of bank credit.[15]

Sharp declines in national production in 1958, accompanied by a halt in the upward movement of prices, were followed by expansionary Riksbank credit policies in 1959 and by further rises in both production and prices, which were continuing in 1960. Continuous efforts of the Swedish government to maintain full employment resulted in budget deficits in every year of the 1950's except 1951 and 1952. A related factor has been the severe shortage of skilled labor in Sweden during the entire postwar period. The combination of Riksbank and other government policies resulted in an almost continuous rise in price and wage levels during the postwar years.[16]

[13] See Table VII–7.

[14] Lundberg, *op. cit.*, chaps. x-xi.

[15] Svenska Handelsbanken, *Index* (Stockholm, September, 1957).

[16] *Skandinaviska Banken, Quarterly Review*, XL, No. 4 (Stockholm, October, 1959), 133–141.

Since housebuilding accounted for about two thirds of total building activity, government curtailment of housebuilding activity was an important instrument of Swedish postwar stabilization policy in the early postwar years. These controls were exercised through the control of building authorizations as well as through control of the use of labor in the building trades. As housing needs became more acute, however, under the stimulus of rising incomes and expanding population, housing received a higher priority in national programs, and government restrictions were concentrated upon other types of private investment.[17]

As in western European countries, the postwar economic policies of the United States were dominated by concern over maintaining economic growth and full employment, with price stability of secondary importance in the earlier years, but of increasing concern in the period following 1955. With rising employment and production, the gross national product and personal incomes measured in current dollars and in real terms showed a strong secular expansion in the United States during the postwar period. Although cyclical fluctuations were evident in 1953–54 and 1957–58, they were mild in their amplitude and short in duration. Consumer prices and wages rose almost uninterruptedly during the decade of the 1950's. The federal government's expenditures exceeded revenues in seven of the ten years from 1950 to 1959, and the total government debt gradually increased to an all-time high in 1960.

The Treasury–Federal Reserve Accord of March, 1951, opened a new era for United States monetary policy, providing for freely fluctuating short- and long-term interest rates. After a sharp tightening of monetary policy in early 1953, the Federal Reserve banks shifted to a policy of active ease in mid-1953 at the very beginning of the recession, and the mildness of that recession is attributed in part to this prompt action by the monetary authorities. As noted earlier, the permissible terms on government-insured and government-guaranteed loans were greatly liberalized in 1954. Consumer spending, investments, and prices rose rapidly during the 1955–57 boom, but the restraining action by the Federal Reserve Board was handicapped by the great liquidity in the banking system. Interest rates rose to levels equaling those of the 1920's, bank reserves were kept under pressure, and the expansion in the money supply gradually ceased in mid-1957, to be resumed early in 1958. The Federal Reserve System was slow in reversing its policies of restraint following the recession which set in in mid-1957. The first major measure, a cut in the discount rate, was

[17] Lundberg, *op. cit.*, p. 283.

taken in November, 1957, followed by a reduction in reserve requirements early in 1958. It was not until mid-1958 that the monetary expansion was in full swing and business recovery clearly evident. Personal incomes and the gross national product resumed their postwar rise in the last half of 1958, reaching new highs in 1959 and continuing through mid-1960.

It is, of course, exceedingly difficult to separate the effects of government housing policies and programs from the myriad influences acting upon national economic life. It would seem logical to suppose, however, that the degree of influence of housing programs on national economic conditions would depend upon their magnitude in relation to gross investment and gross national product. By the same token, the magnitude and timing of housing construction would be an important factor influencing building costs, general price levels, and interest rates. Government outlays for housing provide a measure of the influence of housing investment on public expenditures and supporting levels of taxation.

Table VII–2 shows that West Germany and Sweden have devoted a higher proportion of the gross national product to residential construction since 1950 than have the United States or the United Kingdom. It can also be noted that higher percentages of the gross national product have been devoted to gross domestic fixed-capital formation in West Germany and Sweden. The percentage of gross fixed investment devoted to residential construction is significantly smaller for the United Kingdom than for the other three countries since 1950.

The data in Table VII–2 are primarily a reflection of the relative severity of the postwar housing shortages which existed in West Germany and Sweden, and of the effectiveness of national housing programs. It has been observed that the proportion of national income devoted to housing may be expected to decline in a country with a rapidly rising standard of living.[18] Observation over a relatively short period cannot, of course, serve as the basis for refuting this proposition, advanced by Grebler, Winnick, and Blank. It is interesting to note, however, that the proportion of the gross national income invested in residential construction has remained relatively stable in all the countries studied during a period in which the standard of living has undoubtedly risen substantially.

The continuing and more consistent expansion of residential construction in West Germany (shown in Chart VII–1) along with general

[18] Leo Grebler, David M. Blank, and Louis Winnick, *Capital Formation in Residential Real Estate—Trends and Prospects* (Princeton, N.J.: Princeton University Press, 1956), pp. 141–142.

expansion in the national product is in marked contrast to the relative instability of the real volume of dwelling construction in the United States, Sweden, and the United Kingdom. In view of this fact, it is noteworthy that West Germany has achieved such an expansion in dwelling construction without experiencing any greater rise in building costs than the other countries. It can also be noted from Table VII–7 that this high level of building has been maintained with a relatively stable general price level. It will be recalled, further, that West German housing production has been consistently higher on a per capita basis than that of the other countries studied (see Table VII–1). The comparative uniformity in the movement of the building materials price indexes over the period is in contrast to the differences in volume of construction noted above. The data would seem to suggest that other factors besides residential construction volume accounted for the changes in building materials prices. This view is confirmed by references to relative changes in the cost of living indexes for the countries studied, shown in Table VII–7.

Comparisons of the volume of housing production and changes in building costs are of greater significance when consideration is also given to the percentage of government expenditures devoted to housing in the various countries. It can be noted from Table VII–4 that government expenditures for housing were higher in each of the three western European countries than in the United States. This can be attributed in part to the characteristics of the national housing programs and to the techniques of measurement employed. The housing expenditures for the United Kingdom represent the total of national subsidies for only one year to local authority housing programs. Since subsidies are granted for sixty-year periods, it can be argued that the true annual costs of government housing programs in the United Kingdom, and, to a degree, in Sweden, represent the present value of all the future obligations incurred, which is, of course, substantially higher than is indicated in Table VII–4. The data for Sweden include housing expenditures reported in the national housing budget plus that part of national housing loans represented by "supplementary" loans bearing no interest or amortization charges. The data for the United States include the direct operating costs of major federal housing agencies.

A more complete picture of government financial aid to housing would include state and local expenditures for housing and the interest cost to the national and local governments of financial aids to housing.

It was noted in Table III–6 that local governments in the United Kingdom showed an annual balance of expenditures for housing rising from £10 million in 1950 to almost £20 million in 1957–58. This represented in excess of 10 per cent of total annual expenditures of local governments in the United Kingdom on revenue account during the post-World War II period. Table V–7 showed that the state and local governments in West Germany accounted for between 10 and 20 per cent of the low-interest-rate financing for social housing from 1950 to 1958. Although detailed comparisons are not available, data for 1953 and 1954 indicate that housing expenditures accounted for approximately 8 per cent of total current expenditures of the *Länder* for those years.[19] For Swedish local government units, data for the year 1954 indicate that net current outlays for housing accounted for 8 per cent of total current expenditures of towns, boroughs, and rural communes. For the same year, real estate investment accounted for approximately 30 per cent of capital expenditures of these same local governmental units.[20] State and local expenditures in the United States for housing programs have ranged between $460 and $630 million since 1950. In 1957 total state and local government expenditures for housing and redevelopment in the United States totaled $460 million and represented approximately 1 per cent of total current expenditures of these governmental units of over $47 billion.[21]

It is evident that the relatively high levels of national government expenditures for housing in Sweden and West Germany are paralleled by high levels of state and local government expenditures for such purposes. Although central government expenditures for housing are relatively low in the United Kingdom as a percentage of total expenditures, they are supplemented by high local-government outlays for housing on current account. Direct governmental outlays for housing in the United States are very low relative to the other countries. This is a reflection, of course, of the structure of government housing aids in the United States, and of the self-supporting financial operations of the Federal Housing Administration and, to some extent, of the Federal National Mortgage Association and other agencies.

Changes in the cost of living in the four countries, shown in Table VII–7, provide some indication of the degree to which the individual countries have experienced general price inflation during the postwar years. Comparing these data with Chart VII–1, it is important to note that the United Kingdom, which showed the smallest relative increase in housing production during the postwar years, experienced the larg-

[19] Statistisches Bundesamt, *Statistisches Jahrbuch für die Bundesrepublik Deutschland, 1956* (Stuttgart: W. Kohlhammer, 1956), p. 397.

[20] Statistiska Centralbyrån, *Statistisk Årsbok för Sverige, 1957* (Stockholm, 1957), p. 345.

[21] U.S. Department of Commerce, Bureau of the Census, *Statistical Abstract of the United States, 1959* (Washington, 1959), p. 408.

TABLE VII–7

COMPARISON OF CHANGES IN THE COST OF LIVING INDEX AND THE RENT INDEX FOR THE UNITED STATES, THE UNITED KINGDOM, WEST GERMANY, AND SWEDEN, 1948 TO 1958

	Cost of living index 1948 = 100				Consumer price index for rent (as quotient of cost of living index)			
Year	United States	United Kingdom	West Germany	Sweden	United States	United Kingdom	West Germany	Sweden
1948......	100	100	100	99	1.00	1.00	1.00	1.00
1949......	99	103	107	100	1.06	.99	.94	1.01
1950......	100	105	100	101	1.08	1.00	1.01	1.00
1951......	108	116	108	117	1.05	.94	.95	.87
1952......	110	126	110	126	1.06	.90	.95	.85
1953......	111	130	108	128	1.11	.93	1.00	.90
1954......	112	132	108	129	1.15	.94	1.00	.93
1955......	111	138	110	133	1.16	.93	1.01	.93
1956......	113	145[a]	113	139	1.17	1.00[a]	1.03	.97
1957......	118	151[a]	115	145	1.15	1.04[a]	1.03	.97
1958......	120	155[a]	119	152	1.15	1.12[a]	1.00	.98

Sources: The Cost of living index is from United Nations Statistical Committee, *Statistical Yearbook, 1958* (New York, 1958), pp. 422 (United States), 425 (West Germany), 427 (United Kingdom, Sweden). It is supplemented by data from U.S. Department of Commerce, Bureau of the Census, *Statistical Abstract of the United States, 1959* (Washington, 1959), p. 333; Statistisches Bundesamt, *Statistisches Jahrbuch für die Bundesrepublik Deutschland, 1959* (Stuttgart: W. Kohlhammer, 1959), p. 431; and Statistiska Centralbyrån, *Statistisk Årsbok för Sverige, 1959* (Stockholm, 1959), p. 171. The base has been shifted from 1953 = 100 to 1948 = 100 by the author.

[a] New indexes and new weights, 1956 to 1958.

est degree of price inflation affecting the cost of living as well. Building materials prices and the cost of living index rose almost as much in Sweden during this period, although the percentage increase in physical output in dwelling construction was greatly exceeded by that in West Germany and was proportionately as great in the United States. In making these comparisons with Sweden, it should be remembered that housing construction was at relatively high levels in 1950 in Sweden and the United States, as compared with West Germany. These data do not, of course, establish any causal relationship between the volume of national housing production and the degree of price inflation. It is of interest to observe, however, that the relatively high levels of postwar housing production in West Germany were not accomplished at the expense of extraordinary cost increases or price inflation.

The relationship between the consumer price index for rent and the cost of living index, also shown in Table VII–7, reveals the impact of rent controls in the western European countries since World War II. In a free competitive market, the ratio of rent increases to changes in the cost of living would reflect the relative degree of efficiency in furnishing housing as compared with other goods. The data for the United States, the only one of the four countries with a free rental market during the period, indicate that rents have increased in price more than the over-all cost of living index. The predominance of owner-occupied housing in the United States since World War II to some degree invalidates the use of rent as a measure of housing costs. Lower ratios for the other three countries reflect the degree to which rents have been controlled in relation to the general cost of living. Although technical differences in the rent index may account for some degree of difference among the individual countries, it seems that rents have been adjusted upwards more in line with cost-of-living changes in West Germany than in the United Kingdom or Sweden. As noted in chapters iii and iv, relatively wide variations exist in the distribution of rents in the United Kingdom and Sweden, with a tendency for newly constructed dwellings to bear high rents in relation to older units.

The data examined in Table VII–2 reveal that dwelling construction has represented an expanding and relatively stable segment of the national economies examined during the postwar years. To an important degree this reflects the fact that residential construction has been employed as a contracyclical device in most of the countries during this period. Although the nature of central government controls over housebuilding has varied among the individual countries, the exercise of government controls over the volume of residential construction has been a potent influence in accounting for the relative stability of construction since 1950. In the United States, control over housebuilding has been effectuated through changes in general monetary policy, which have altered interest-rate structures, while FHA and VA mortgage interest rates have been maintained at relatively fixed levels. This has resulted in short-run changes in the availability of government-insured and government-guaranteed loans under conditions of general monetary stringency. In Sweden, the Royal Housing Board was able to regulate the volume of housing production through its direct control over the granting of third mortgage loans and so-called supplementary loans, which initially bear no interest or amortization. In addition, government controls were exercised over the inflow of labor into the housebuilding industry. In Germany, governmental control over housebuilding volume was exercised through the granting and subsequent adjustment of income tax concessions designed to encourage the flow of savings into mortgages and homeownership. The volume of housebuilding was controlled in the United Kingdom through a combination of adjustable central government subsidies, licensing by the Ministry of Works, and control of local authority borrowing by the Public Works Loan Board. As noted in chapter iii, governmental control of capital expenditure in the United Kingdom is effected through approval by the Ministry of Housing and Local Government of all borrowing by local authorities. The Labour government pursued a policy of low rates of interest on loans to local authorities from 1945 to 1951. The Conservative government has relied upon the use of varying interest rates to control local investment, and since 1952 local authority housing investment has been made subject to this influence. To some degree the decline in annual housebuilding from the high point of 347,000 dwellings in 1954 to 273,000 in 1958 was a product of this influence. Through highly diverse procedures, the volume of housebuilding was subject to a substantial degree of central government control in each of the four countries studied.

The general conditions of sustained economic prosperity and rapid economic growth which prevailed in each country during the postwar years required the use of these controls in varying degrees. Both the structure of controls and the extremities of the dollar shortages resulted in more extensive use of central government controls over the volume of housebuilding in the United Kingdom than in the other countries.[22] It was observed in chapter iv that Sweden made use of central government controls over housebuilding during the export drive in 1948 and again to cushion the price-wage inflation in 1955–57. Housebuilding was stimulated in Sweden in 1958 as a means of counteracting the recessionary tendencies in the economy at that time through reduction of interest rates and relaxation of housing controls. The high social priorities attached to housebuilding throughout the postwar period insulated the industry from drastic cutbacks in production.

In West Germany, modification of the income tax laws in 1953, 1955, and 1956 provided a means through which the government varied inducements to private capital to initiate housing construction. Although the instruments of control in the United States were crude in

[22] "As a consequence of the review of capital investment undertaken by the Government in the early autumn, the Minister told the House of Commons on 11th of November that some slowing-down of housebuilding by public authorities could not be avoided and that the number of houses to be started in 1958 would be adjusted so as to reduce the number of houses completed in 1959 by local authorities and New Towns to 100,000 a year." *Report of the Ministry of Housing and Local Government, 1957,* Cmnd. 419 (London: H.M.S.O., May, 1958), p. 11.

comparison with those in use in Sweden and the United Kingdom, it has been seen in chapter vi that they, in combination with other factors, were effective in imparting a contracyclical trend to the availability of housing mortgage credit in the postwar years.

These observations place national housing policy in perspective as an important sector of both private and public investment, subject to the overriding importance of general national economic stability. It has already been noted that residential construction has represented an important segment of total domestic fixed-capital formation in the countries studied. The rapid growth in output and the high rates of investment activity during the postwar years have necessitated national controls over housing investment as a key segment of national economic policies.

Conclusions

Comparative evaluation of national housing policies which differed so greatly in their objectives and programs is very difficult. In a broad sense, the most significant distinction in postwar housing policies has been between countries with loosely controlled and directed housing economies and those in which free market forces and private enterprise have been dominant. It is not surprising to find that detailed central government controls in the housing sector have usually been paralleled by broad and persuasive general economic controls.

The postwar housing economies of the United Kingdom and Sweden have been subject to relatively high degrees of government control through licensing, credit rationing, rent controls, and other devices. Central governments in these countries have made direct loans, controlled rents, granted housing subsidies on a large scale to families, and encouraged housebuilding by local housing authorities. Contrarily, the housing economies of the United States and, to a lesser degree, of West Germany have been relatively free from central government control and have relied primarily upon private housebuilding. The role of the central government in the latter countries has been generally limited to the granting or insuring of loans and to offering other inducements to private housing investment.

It is natural to observe that national housing policies have been geared not only to national economic programs, but to geographic and national characteristics as well. The central direction of national housing policies and programs is relatively simple to administer in small countries with a uniform climate and topography, such as Sweden or the United Kingdom. Central government is pervasive and relatively efficient in these countries—housing requirements are comparatively uniform, after-tax incomes are distributed relatively evenly, and standardized housing was acceptable as a solution to critical postwar shortages.

It is understandable that central government control of housing production or financing would be much more complex in a country of the size of the United States, with varied climatic, housing, and living standards. The country's size and diversity also account in part for the fact that federal government administration of housing and other programs has been relatively and historically inefficient in the United States. The geographic and economic differences within the different sections of West Germany have called for a relatively high degree of decentralization of policy making and programing in housing. Traditionally, central government administration has been relatively efficient in Germany.

Judged by the most obvious criterion, namely, the relative improvement in national standards, the programs in Sweden and West Germany seem to have resulted in the most rapid improvement in housing standards during the postwar years. This is in part a reflection of the fact that housing standards in those countries were and continue to be below those in the United States and, by some standards, below those in the United Kingdom. It also reflects the magnitude of the national product devoted to housing in those countries. The preoccupation of the United Kingdom with problems of the balance of payments and the severe shortages of labor and materials can account for the notable lag in housing produtcion prior to 1952 in the United Kingdom.

The quality of the housing inventory in the United States has also shown a rapid improvement in the postwar period. This is primarily a reflection of high rates of new construction and of repair and rehabilitation of substantial numbers of existing dwelling units. Although housing standards have been raised in the United Kingdom, the overall improvement in the quality of the national housing inventory has been less notable, owing to the relatively low level of new construction and the undermaintenance associated with low, controlled rents in that country.

The postwar record of West Germany was also outstanding in terms of the magnitude of housing production, its maintenance at high levels, and the accompanying stability in building costs. Residential construction volume was subject to effective central government control in West Germany owing to the extensive use of income and other tax subsidies, and in the United Kingdom and Sweden as a result of the structure of national controls over housebuilding.

Housing policies and programs in Sweden, West Germany, and the United Kingdom were successful in directing public and private investment toward improving the housing standards of low-income groups of the population. Programs in the United States have relied upon high production rates of new housing and the filtering process to improve general housing standards. Programs for direct improvement of the housing status of low-income and other special groups have, for various reasons, exhibited a number of shortcomings and have been, on the whole, relatively insignificant.

Costs of national housing programs have been related to the magnitude of government programs and to the degree to which they have involved direct government subsidies or outlays. Large-scale programs of public housing and government housing subsidies involve high and continuing costs in Sweden and the United Kingdom. Because of the extensive use of income tax subsidies in West Germany and the reliance upon government loan insurance and guaranty in the United States, costs to their governments are much more difficult to assess. Direct governmental outlays were substantially lower relative to the volume of housing production in the United States and West Germany than in Sweden or the United Kingdom.

Specific features of national housing policy deserve mention as having proved outstandingly successful. The use of income tax subsidies as a device to direct private investment into desired types of housing investment was a key feature of West Germany's housing policy which recommends itself to a country such as the United States, which relies primarily upon private housing investment. Rapid amortization for federal income tax purposes of private investments in low-income rental housing should furnish a strong incentive for private investors to build housing for such groups. Because of the strong preference for ownership housing in the United States, provisions for rapid amortization subsidies should be extended to owner occupants unable to afford housing of acceptable standards without subsidy.

Aggressive and effective housing programs of coöperatives and the use of family income subsidies are the most impressive features of postwar Swedish housing policy. Although the coöperative movement cannot be expected to develop to as large an extent in the United States, owing to differences in national characteristics, coöperatives offer an important avenue for improving the housing standards of specific groups. Increased technical assistance for coöperatives through the Federal Housing Administration, combined with an expanded "special assistance" loan purchase program by the Federal National Mortgage Association, would seem to be logical steps to further the expansion of coöperative housing in the United States.

The success with which Sweden has administered family housing subsidies over an extended period furnishes support for the recommendation in chapter vi that family housing subsidies be employed in the United States as an alternative to present federal public housing programs. The administration of such subsidies through federal income tax claims and deductions, with certification by state or local governmental agencies, could ensure rental or ownership housing of acceptable standards for families receiving such subsidies.

Government insurance and guaranty of loans made by private institutions has served as a useful means of encouraging private loans for homeownership in a private enterprise economy such as that of the United States. Loan insurance programs similar to that of the Federal Housing Administration would further homeownership in European countries. The uneven flow of funds into private mortgage lending institutions has from time to time impeded the functioning of the private mortgage market in the United States. Exemption of the interest on individual savings deposits with mortgage lending institutions from the federal income tax, as in West Germany, would undoubtedly improve the availability of mortgage loan funds in the United States and provide a substitute for direct government lending in Sweden and the United Kingdom. Exemption of interest on savings deposits from federal income taxes would also furnish a flexible control instrument for altering levels of savings, consumption expenditures, and the flow of funds into residential construction.

These steps, in combination with improvements in secondary mortgage market facilities and removal of interest-rate ceilings on federally insured and guaranteed loans in the United States, discussed in chapter vi, should assure a larger and more stable flow of funds into residential mortgage markets in the United States. Assuming that improvement in housing standards is an important social objective, such measures seem justifiable and even necessary. The use of flexible-interest income tax subsidies could retain a desirable degree of indirect governmental control over housebuilding. Federally underwritten mortgages constitute by now standardized and attractive investments, and competition for them in the highly organized national securities market renders obsolete the need for consumer protection through control of their interest rates.

The incompatability of maintaining a large program of publicly owned housing controlling rents, and at the same time encouraging private investment in new housing is well illustrated in Sweden and the United Kingdom since World War II. Federal income tax subsidies, to stimulate savings and housing investment, and family housing allowances should provide an effective substitute for federal public housing and a solution to the low-income and minority housing problem in the United States.

The postwar housing record confirms the view that maximum levels of new private housing investment, together with the efficient use of the existing housing inventory and its proper maintenance, can be best achieved through a free rental market. Postwar experience in Sweden and the United Kingdom demonstrates that government fixing of rents below the levels necessary to induce new investment and promote proper maintenance contributes to the deterioration of the quality of the national housing inventory and eliminates the market mechanism as an effective rationing device.

Strict enforcement of minimum housing standards by local governments represents a more direct type of control over the quality of the existing housing inventory, and, in this respect, local communities in Sweden, West Germany, and the United Kingdom seem to have better administered programs than do most cities in the United States. It has also been observed elsewhere that local governments in western Europe exercise more effective control over urban land usage and development than do urban communities in the United States.[23]

Government inducements to housing investment imply some form of government controls over the volume of such investment. It was observed that housing programs in Sweden and the United Kingdom were highly responsive to short-run changes in government policies. It can be expected that such controls would be more effective in nations with a maximum of local and national participation in initiating and financing housing construction. Postwar experience in the United States and West Germany has shown that private housing investment is also responsive to central bank monetary controls and that general credit policy can prove effective in regulating the volume of private housing investment even though it may lack the precision of more direct central government controls. The use of tax incentives modeled after those used in West Germany should provide more direct and effective means through which the volume of housebuilding could be controlled in the United States.

It is, of course, impractical to argue that any particular set of hous-

[23] Paul F. Wendt, "Lessons from the Old World for America's City Builders," *California Management Review*, I, No. 3 (Spring, 1959), 47–55.

ing policies should be adaptable for all countries, since national housing policies must be directed toward appropriate national housing objectives and, at the same time, must be in keeping with over-all economic programs and policies. It is difficult, therefore, to argue that postwar national housing policies in Sweden and the United Kingdom should not have provided for central government control over the type, volume, and financing of new housing production and over rentals for existing housing. It can be argued, however, that over-all results of the housing programs in these countries, which were characterized by extensive central government controls and direct local government participation in the provision of new housing, were not outstandingly and comparatively successful from the viewpoint of the quantity of housing produced, the maintenance of quality of the existing inventory, the efficiency and cost control in building, or economy in governmental costs. In addition, the maintenance of rent controls throughout the postwar period has in a real sense committed the central governments of Sweden and the United Kingdom to a continuation of extensive direct housing subsidies for many years in the future.

Viewed in the same light, the housing program in West Germany was conspicuously more successful in terms of the quantity of housing produced, the improvement of the general housing inventory, and economy of administration. The private-enterprise housing economy of the United States, more nearly similar to that of West Germany than to that of either the United Kingdom or Sweden, can be credited with achieving high levels of production of good-quality housing, fostering a progressive and efficient private housebuilding industry, and improving the quality of existing housing, and with relative economy in national and local housing administration. It is significant to note that the most costly housing programs in the United States in terms of governmental outlays—public housing and urban renewal—were evaluated as the least successful in terms of accomplishment. The shortcomings of the public housing program were attributed to the basic technique and administration of the federal public housing program, and were magnified by a substantial degree of ideological strife. The lack of progress in urban renewal can be attributed to the magnitude and complexity of the urban renewal problem and the difficulties of coördinating federal and local programs.

The foregoing analysis of national housing policies reveals that the core of the post-World War II "housing problem" in the countries examined has been the provision of adequate housing for low-income groups. Although the postwar housing program in the United States has been relatively successful in achieving a high level of new housing production for upper- and middle-income groups, and although over-all housing standards have been raised in the postwar period through a combination of rising incomes and other factors, the rate of improvement in housing standards for low-income families has been slower than is considered socially desirable by many.

Successful programs directed toward the solution of the low-income housing problem in Sweden and West Germany recommend themselves for consideration in the United States. The most important of those identified are: the use of income tax subsidies to encourage investment in low-income housing and a flow of funds into residential mortgage markets, the granting of family housing subsidies for those unable to afford housing of acceptable quality, and the encouragement of housing coöperatives through technical and loan assistance.

The adoption of these recommendations would call for basic changes in present United States government housing programs for low-income groups, and for expanded national, state, and local government assistance in solving the low-income housing problem. In view of the magnitude of the problem in the United States and the lack of success in its solution through present government programs, the need for such an expansion seems inescapable.

Index

Abrams, Charles, 210, 215*n*
Adams, Walter, 210*n*
Agencies, departments, ministries, etc. —Sweden: Royal Commission on Housing and Redevelopment, 65; State Housing Loan Bank, 65; Swedish Housing Loan Bank, 77; State Building Loan Office, 68; Royal Housing Board, 68–69, 78–79, 95, 241–242, 265; Swedish Mortgage Bank, 77; Urban Mortgage Bank of Sweden, 77; Svenska Riksbyggen, 88; Royal Board of Housing, 110; Riksbank, 259
Agencies, departments, ministries, etc. —United Kingdom: Royal Commission on Housing of the Industrial Population of Scotland Urban and Rural, 15; Ministry of Health, 16, 18, 27; Inter-Departmental Committee on the Rent Restriction Acts, 21; Ministry of Agriculture, 27; Ministry of Labour and National Service, 27; Ministry of Town and Country Planning, 27; Ministry of Works, 27, 266; Ministry of Housing and Local Government, 28, 266; Public Works Loan Board, 36, 240, 266; Girdwood Committee, 46–47; Ministry of Housing, 240
Agencies, departments, ministries, etc. —United States: Bureau of Industrial Housing and Transportation, 146; Emergency Fleet Corporation, 146; United States Housing Corporation, 146; United States Shipping Board, 146; Division of Building and Housing, 147; Federal Farm Mortgage Corporation, 148, 152; Federal Home Loan Bank System, 148, 152, 172–174, 187, 189–190, 246; Home Owners' Loan Corporation, 148, 152; Federal Land Bank System, 148, 152; Federal Housing Administration, 150, 152, 158, 165, 168, 172, 174–180, 187, 189–190, 199, 202–203, 210, 215–219 *passim*, 246, 265; Federal Savings and Loan Insurance Corporation, 150, 172, 187, 209; Farm Security Administration, 150, 154; Public Works Administration, 150–151, 152; Reconstruction Finance Corporation, 150, 184; Resettlement Administration, 150, 152; United States Housing Authority, 151, 152, 154; Division of Defense Housing Coordination, 152; National Housing Agency, 152–154, 163–164, 245; Federal Public Housing Authority, 154, 192, 195; Public Housing Administration, 154, 165, 192–193, 220; Tennessee Valley Authority, 154; Veterans Administration, 163, 165, 172, 180–184, 187, 189, 210, 215, 246, 265; Community Facilities Administration, 165; Urban Renewal Administration, 165; Federal National Mortgage Association, 165, 172, 176, 184–186, 190, 203–204, 209, 215, 223, 246; National Mortgage Marketing Corporation, 168–169; Federal Reserve System, 246, 260. *See also* States
Agencies, departments, ministries, etc. —West Germany: Deutsche Bau und Bodenbank, 116; Office of Equalization of Burdens, 127; Federal Ministry of Housing, 131–132, 232. *See also* Länder
Anderson, Frank Ray, 150*n*, 172*n*, 189*n*

Austria, 6–8

Barnes, Harry, 14*n*
Bauer, Catherine, 111*n*, 113*n*, 115*n*, 194*n*, 198*n*
Belgium: war destruction, 4; dwellings-population ratio, 6–7; value of construction, 7–8
Bentzel, Ragnar, 75*n*, 98*n*
Bernhard, Harry B., 79*n*
Beyer, Glenn, 211*n*
Blank, David M., 159*n*, 227*n*, 249*n*, 261
Bloch, Alexander, 22*n*
Bloomberg, Lawrence N., 150*n*
Bowley, Marian, 14*n*, 15*n*, 16*n*, 19, 20*n*, 21
Brady, Robert A., 111*n*
Britain. *See* United Kingdom
Brown, Robert K., 196*n*, 221*n*
Bryant, Willis R., 181*n*
Building and Loan associations, 134
Building Materials and Housing Act of 1945 (U.K.), 27
Building societies. *See* Coöperatives and building societies
Bureau of Industrial Housing and Transportation (U.S.A.), 146
Bureau of Labor Statistics rent index, 155–157

California: standards, 145; central mortgage bank, 147; loans to veterans, 147, 219
Chamberlain Act of 1923 (U.K.), 18, 19
Colean, Miles L., 190*n*, 201*n*, 216*n*, 225
Community Facilities Administration (U.S.A.), 165
Company housing, 87, 90
Conference on Home Building and Home Ownership (1931), 146
Connecticut, 145
Conservative government (U.K.), 31–36, 44–45, 238–241
Construction: production levels achieved and projected, 7–10, 19–20, 27, 28, 49–52, 64–65, 66, 85–88, 103–110 *passim*, 114–116, 118–119, 138–142, 145, 149, 157–163, 164, 192–193, 225–229, 231–233, 236, 238–247, 253–256, 265–266; United Kingdom, 15–21 *passim*, 36–38, 44–45; worker productivity, 29, 45–49 *passim;* quality of, 42–43; Sweden, 62–110 *passim;* by coöperatives, 65, 77–78, 87–88, 243, 256 (*see also* Coöperatives and building societies); multi-family projects, 79, 83, 85, 88, 92–95 (*see also* Public housing); West Germany, 111–144 *passim;* barter and black-market arrangements, 122–123; tax concession stimulus, 134–138, 146–147 (*see also* Finance); United States, 145–229 *passim;* Great Depression programs, 146–152; war housing, 152; impact of federal finance programs, 187–189, 222–223; and "filtering down" of improvements, 224–225; ratio to population, 248–249; public vs. private, 225–256 (*see also* Private construction and ownership; Public housing). *See also* Costs; Housebuilding industry; Maintenance; Rehabilitation; Standards; Subsidies
Coöperatives and building societies; finance by, 38–43 *passim*, 77–78; construction by, 65, 77–78, 87–88, 243, 256; rent control of, 72; government encouragement of, 79; proportion of housing stock, 90; mobility of occupancy, 93; as substitute for private investment, 109; early German movement, 113, 141; federal (U.S.A.) loans to, 233
Costs: trends, 28–29, 64, 65, 66, 81–82, 94–97, 114–115, 253–255; of maintenance, 32, 92 (*see also* Maintenance); and amount of public housing, 36–38, 44–45; Girdwood Committee investigation, 46–47; relationship to rents, 52, 71–72, 114, 125–126; standards and, 73–74, 82, 92, 125; multi-family vs. single-family, 109; impact of federal finance programs, 187–189, 225–229 *passim;* public housing limits on, 191–192; urban renewal, 200; over-financing of, 215; relationship to production, 240, 262–265. *See also* Finance; Public expenditures
Council of National Defense housing report, 145
Cross Act of 1875 (U.K.), 13–14

Denmark, 6–8
Density, 5–7; Scotland, 15; control of, 20–21; Sweden, 68; Germany, 112, 138; United States, 160–161, 194; United Kingdom, 240; construction-population ratio, 248–249
Depreciation incentives, 134–135

Deutsche Bau und Bodenbank, 116
Dickson, Harold, 68*n*, 98*n*, 103*n*
Division of Building and Housing (U.S.A.), 147
Division of Defense Housing Coordination (U.S.A.), 152
Dunham, H. Warren, 193*n*

Economic policies and conditions, 2–3, 231–232, 235, 239; patterns of investment, 10–11, 121, 233–234; relationship to construction level, 28–29, 45–46, 64–65, 103–104, 105–106, 115–116, 245–246, 256–267; interest rate policy, 36–38, 44–45, 81; distribution of family income, 75–76, 108, 177–180, 183, 205–215, 217–218, 233–234, 240, 246–247; and housing preferences, 92–93; and elasticity of demand, 101–102; fiscal and monetary policy, 103–104, 122–123, 131; impact of war production, 118–119, 152; economic reconstruction, 121, 148–152 *passim;* currency reform, 122–123; inflation control, 134, 225–229 *passim,* 231, 240 (*see also* Rent control); and housing standards, 217–218
Edwards, Edward E., 190*n*
Elison, Magnus, 82*n*
Elizabeth I, 13
England. *See* United Kingdom
Emergency Fleet Corporation (U.S.A.), 146
Emergency Price Control Act of 1942 (U.S.A.), 155
Emergency Relief and Construction Act of 1932 (U.S.A.), 150
Erhard, 123*n*

Farm Security Administration (U.S.A.), 150, 154
Federal Farm Mortgage Corporation (U.S.A.), 148, 152
Federal Home Loan Bank System (U.S.A.), 148, 152, 187, 189–190, 246
Federal Housing Administration (U.S.A.), 150, 152, 158, 165, 168, 172, 174–180, 187, 189–190, 199, 202–203, 210, 215–219 *passim,* 246, 265
Federal Land Bank System (U.S.A.), 148, 152
Federal Ministry of Housing (West Germany), 131–132, 232
Federal National Mortgage Association (U.S.A.), 165, 172, 176, 184–186, 190, 203–204, 209, 215, 223, 246
Federal Public Housing Authority (U.S.A.), 154, 192, 195
Federal Reserve System, 246, 260
Federal Savings and Loan Insurance Corporation, 150, 172, 187, 209
Fey, W., 119*n*, 125*n*, 126*n*, 129*n*, 130*n*, 139*n*
Finance: local authorities sources of, 36; building societies, 38–43 *passim;* by local authorities, 43–45; life insurance companies, 43; investment and interest rates, 64–65, 176–177, 215; government role and impact, 65, 66, 83–84, 116, 148–150, 158, 187–189, 204–217 *passim,* 219, 225–229 *passim,* 231, 241–242, 247, 256–261, 265–266 (*see also* Agencies, departments, ministries, etc.; Legislation; Subsidies; Public housing); Sweden, 77–85 *passim;* labor union role, 88; capital availability trends, 103–104, 106–107, 114–116, 122–123, 131, 148, 240 (*see also* Economic policies and conditions); of low-cost and public housing, 113, 191–196 *passim,* 235; under Nazi government, 117–118; Marshall Plan role, 121–122; under Bonn government, 123–138; tax concession schemes, 123, 131, 133, 134–138, 146–147, 203, 231–232, 235–237; depreciation incentives, 134–135; relationship to standards, 82, 124, 139–140, 209, 221, 222, 224, 242–243; for war housing, 146, 154; for veterans, 147, 163, 165, 174–184 *passim,* 219 (*see also* Veterans Administration); foreclosures, 148, 180; and one-family unit preference, 158, 215–217; of slum clearance and redevelopment, 167–168, 198–200; United States policies and programs, 171–190; of private rental housing, 200–202, 215–217; national expenditures on, 202–204, 243–244, 262–263 (*see also* Public expenditures); shortcomings of fixed interest rates, 215; and costs, 187–189, 225–229 *passim,* 240. *See also* Coöperatives and building societies
Finland, 6–7, 10–11
First Capital Development Law of 1952 (West Germany), 136, 231–232

First Housing Act of 1950 (West Germany), 124, 131, 133, 231
First Law for the Promotion of the Capital Market (West Germany), 127
Fisher, Ernest M., 196
Fisher, Robert Moore, 151, 202*n*, 203*n*, 218*n*
Flexner, Kurt F., 190*n*
Florida, 147
France, 4, 6–7

Germany. *See* West Germany
Girdwood Committee investigation, 46–47
Goldsmith, Selma F., 180*n*, 214*n*
Göteborg, 87
Government role, 4–12, 145–146. *See also* Agencies, departments, ministries, etc.; Housing policy; *Länder;* Legislation; Local authorities; Public housing; Public expenditures; States; Subsidies
Great Britain. *See* United Kingdom
Grebler, Leo, 3*n*, 157, 159*n*, 188, 209*n*, 226, 227, 249*n*, 261
Greece, 4, 8–10
Grundstein, Nathan D., 193*n*
Gutheim, Frederick, 198*n*

Halcrow, Harold G., 187*n*
Hawaii, 155
Henderson, W. O., 111*n*
Holm, Lennart, 92*n*, 94
Holm, Per, 75*n*, 85*n*
Homebuilding Premium Law of 1952 (W.G.), 137, 231
Home Owners' Loan Corporation (U.S.A.), 148, 152
Honnold, Junia, 171*n*, 174*n*, 177*n*
Horsfall, T. C., 111*n*, 112*n*
Hoover, Herbert, 148
Housebuilding industry, 45–49, 88, 253–256
Housing Acts—United Kingdom: of 1924, 18; of 1933, 20; of 1936, 21, 38; of 1938, 20–21; of 1949, 38, 57; of 1952, 31; of 1956, 34, 60; of 1957, 60–61. *See also* Legislation
Housing Acts—United States: of 1937, 190, 191, 198; of 1949, 165–167, 191, 192, 198–199, 225, 244, 245; of 1954, 177, 184–186, 192, 199, 218; of 1956, 192–193, 216; of 1957, 191. *See also* Legislation
Housing and Home Finance Agency (U.S.A.), 164–166, 198–199, 246
Housing policy: problems of analysis of, 1–2; pre-World War I United Kingdom, 13–14; Scotland, 15; World War I influence, 15–18, 152–157; interwar problems and programs, 18–21, 146–162; Labour party program, 23–30 *passim*, 238–241; Conservative program, 31–36, 44–45, 238–241; inflation and, 36–38, 44–45 (*see also* Economic policies and conditions); administration and effectiveness of, 61, 246; Sweden, 68–70, 97–99, 241–244; maintenance of financing, 81, 83, 122–123, 127, 131, 225–229; multi-family construction, 92–95 *passim*, 200–201, 215–217; private housing, 93–94, 165–167, 171–190, 215–217, 238, 239; needs and, 105–110; public housing, 108–109, 151, 190–196, 217–225, 231–232, 238, 239 (*see also* Public housing); review by Parliament (Sweden), 110; Bonn government's objectives, 123–127, 231–238; post-World War II United States, 165–167, 204–229, 244–247; slum clearance and redevelopment, 198–200 *passim;* construction stability, 225; comparative evaluation of, 230–272; social welfare objectives, 241–242; impact on construction industry, 253–256; and economic trends, 256–267
Housing and Rents Act of 1949 (U.S.A.), 155
Housing and Rents Act of 1950 (U.S.A.), 155
Housing and Repairs Act of 1954 (U.K.), 60
Housing Repairs and Rents Act of 1954 (U.K.), 34, 57
Housing shortage: United Kingdom, 14–15, 20–21, 66; Sweden, 100–103; West Germany, 113–114, 118–119, 120, 121–122, 139; United States, 145, 159, 163–171, 197; and level of construction, 261. *See also* Density
Housing Shortage Law of 1923 (Germany), 115
Housing and Town Planning Act of 1919 (U.K.), 15–16
Housing of the Working Classes Act of 1890 (U.K.), 14
Howard, D. G., 48
Hungary, 10

Husband, William H., 150*n*, 172*n*, 189*n*

Illinois, 145
Income and Profit Tax Amendment of 1958 (W.G.), 136
Income Tax Law of 1949 (W.G.), 134–135
Industrialization, 13–14
Inflation. *See* Costs: Economic policies and conditions
Iowa, 145
Ireland, 6–8
Italy, 4, 8–10

Jacoby, Neil, 187*n*
Jaeger, Eugen, 112*n*
Jarmain, John Roland, 14*n*, 16*n*, 21*n*
Johansson, Alf, 65*n*, 100

Karlsson, Arne, 96*n*
Kentucky, 145
Klemt, 140*n*
Knickerbocker Village, 150
Kristof, Frank S., 169*n*

Labour government policies, 23–30 *passim*, 238–241
Länder, 130–132 *passim*, 232, 235, 237
Lanham Act (U.S.A.), 154
Legislation—Germany and West Germany: Housing Shortage Law of 1923, 115; Rent Act of 1922, 115; Tenant-Protection Bill of 1923, 115; First Housing Act of 1950, 124, 131, 133; Second Housing Act of 1956, 124, 137–138, 231; First Law for the Promotion of the Capital Market, 127; Tax Reform Law of 1948, 134; Income Tax Law of 1949, 134–135; First Capital Development Law of 1952, 136, 231–232; Income and Profit Tax Amendment of 1948, 136; New Taxation Act of 1956, 136; Homebuilding Premium Law of 1952, 137, 231
Legislation—Sweden, 71
Legislation—United Kingdom: Shaftesbury Act of 1851, 13; Torrens Act of 1868, 13; Cross Act of 1875, 13–14; Housing of the Working Classes Act of 1890, 14; Housing and Town Planning Act of 1919, 15–16; Rent and Mortgage Interest Restriction Act, 15, 16; Chamberlain Housing Act of 1923, 18; Housing Act of 1924, 18; Housing Act of 1933, 20; Housing Act of 1938, 20–21; Housing Act of 1936, 21, 38; Rent Act of 1946, 25; Building Materials and Housing Act of 1945, 27; Housing Act of 1952, 31; Town and Country Planning Act of 1953, 31; Housing Act of 1956, 34, 60; Rent Act of 1957, 34, 239; Housing Repairs and Rents Act of 1954, 34, 57, 60; Public Works Loans Act of 1875, 36; Housing Act of 1949, 38, 57; Small Dwellings Acquisition Act of 1899, 38; Housing Act of 1957, 60–61
Legislation—United States: New York Tenement House Law of 1867, 145; New York State Housing Law of 1926, 146–147; Emergency Relief and Construction Act of 1932, 150; National Housing Act of 1934, 150, 225; National Recovery Act of 1932, 150; Housing Act of 1937, 151, 190, 191, 198; Lanham Act, 154; Emergency Price Control Act of 1942, 155; Housing and Rents Act of 1949, 155; Housing and Rents Act of 1950, 155; Servicemen's Readjustment Act, 163, 180; Price Control Extension Act of 1946, 164; Housing Act of 1949, 165–167, 191, 192, 198–199, 225, 244, 245; Federal Home Loan Bank Act of 1932, 172; Housing Act of 1954, 177, 184–186, 192, 199, 218; Housing Act of 1957, 191; Housing Act of 1956, 192–193, 216
Leigh-Breese, P. L., 13*n*
Lend-lease, 23
Levin, Jack, 146*n*
Life insurance companies, 43
Local authorities: construction by, 15–18; restriction of, 20; licensing of private construction, 31; rent policies and functions of, 33–34, 131–132, 145, 155, 223–224; financing sources of, 36, 79; expenditures of, 38–42, 97, 204, 262–263; support of private construction, 43–45, 65; slum clearance and redevelopment role, 60–61, 187–200 *passim;* role in finance and housing administration, 66, 70, 98–99, 111–113, 131–132, 151, 165, 190–196 *passim*, 238–239, 240, 243, 255–256; role in land improvement, 94; land ownership by, 112–113; control of standards, 145; property tax losses, 203. *See also Länder;* States
London, 13

Lundberg, Erik, 64–65, 107*n*, 242, 259*n*, 260*n*
Lundevall, Owe, 70*n*, 85*n*, 89*n*, 90*n*, 95, 96*n*, 97*n*, 98, 99*n*, 101*n*, 102, 251*n*

Maine, 145
Maintenance: cost of, 32, 155; rent control and, 55–56, 60, 75, 107–108, 126. *See also* Rehabilitation; Slums
Maisel, Sherman J., 156*n*, 159*n*, 160*n*, 169, 170*n*, 177*n*, 189*n*, 210, 211, 299*n*
Marshall Plan counterpart funds, 121
Mason, Norman P., 196*n*
Massachusetts, 145, 147
Michigan, 145
Migration, 101, 120
Ministry of Agriculture (U.K.), 27
Ministry of Health (U.K.), 16, 18, 27
Ministry of Housing (U.K.), 240
Ministry of Housing and Local Government (U.K.), 28, 266
Ministry of Labour and National Service (U.K.), 27
Ministry of Town and Country Planning (U.K.), 27
Ministry of Works (U.K.), 27, 266
Mortgages. *See* Finance
Mutual Mortgage Insurance Fund, 203

National Housebuilders Registration Council (U.K.), 42–43
National Housing Act of 1934 (U.S.A.), 150, 225
National Housing Agency (U.S.A.), 152–154, 163–164, 245
National Housing Association, 145, 146
National Housing Inventory (U.S.A.), 159, 169
National Mortgage Marketing Corporation (U.S.A.), 168–169
National Recovery Act of 1932 (U.S.A.), 150
National Union of Tenants' Savings Bank and Building Associations (Sweden), 77–78
Netherlands, 6–10 *passim*
Nevada, 145
Newcomb, Robinson, 190*n*, 225
New Jersey, 145
New Taxation Act of 1956 (West Germany), 136
New York Tenement House Law of 1867, 145
New York City, 155
New York State Housing Law of 1926, 146–147
Norway, 6–11 *passim*
North Dakota, 147

Office of Equalization of Burdens (West Germany), 127
Ohio, 147

Pennsylvania, 145
Pfeffer, Delmont K., 191*n*
Pittsburgh housing survey, 196, 221
Poland, 4, 10
Population growth, 4–12 *passim;* United Kingdom, 14, 21–22; Sweden, 62, 64, 100–102; West Germany, 114, 119, 120, 138–139; United States, 164; and construction rate, 248–249. *See also* Density
President's Conference on Home Building and Home Ownership, 1931, 148
Price Control Extension Act of 1946, 164
Private construction and ownership: level of, 15–17, 20, 21, 31, 52–54, 64–65, 74–75, 85–87, 90, 108–109, 114–115, 117–118, 131–132; bias for, 18, 23, 31–36 *passim,* 44–45, 79–80, 141, 147–148, 150, 151, 165–167, 231, 238; finance of, 38–45, 136–137, 200–202 (*see also* Finance; Subsidies); local government role in, 38–42; building societies for, 42–43 (*see also* Coöperatives and building societies); company housing, 87, 90; tax policy and, 93–94, 134–138 (*see also* Tax concessions); opposition to, 108–109, 152; of "social housing," 131–132; for war workers, 145–146; role in slum redevelopment, 198–199; potential market for, 210–215; single-family vs. multi-unit, 215–217; limitations of, 255–256
Production. *See* Construction
Public Building Administration (U.S.A.), 154
Public expenditures, 262–263; United Kingdom, 38–42, 237; Sweden, 94–97, 237, 243–244; West Germany, 141–143, 235–237; United States, 151, 202–204, 220–221, 235–237, 243–244. *See also* Finance; Subsidies
Public health, 13, 14
Public housing: policy shifts and shortcomings, 11–12, 23, 190–196, 217–225, 238–240; role of local authori-

ties, 15–21 *passim;* rents, 26*n*, 72; level of, 36–38, 44–45, 54–56, 240–241; standards, 49, 55–56, 132, 199; bias toward, 87, 108–109, 238; maintenance, 108; "social housing," 131–133, 191–192, 232; tax incentives, 135–136; disposal of, 146, 154; U.S.A. programs, 150–151, 154, 167; opposition to, 152, 193; war housing, 154; tenant problems and problem tenants, 193–195 *passim;* slum clearance and, 198–199; lieu-of-taxes payments to local government, 203; state and local expenditures, 204; rent subsidy substitute, 220
Public Housing Administration (U.S.A.), 154, 165, 192–193, 220
Public Works Administration (U.S.A.), 150–151, 152
Public Works Loan Board (U.K.), 36, 240, 266
Public Works Loans Act of 1875 (U.K.), 36

Ratcliff, Richard U., 171*n*, 174*n*, 177*n*, 224
Rathbun, Daniel B., 171*n*, 174*n*, 177*n*, 188, 189
Reconstruction Finance Corporation (U.S.A.), 150, 184
Rehabilitation, 57–61, 197–200; early English legislation, 13–14; interwar Germany, 114–115, 117; war-damaged buildings, 121, 122–123; role of *Länder*, 122–123; United States, 169, 176, 197–200; investment problems, 200–202, 218
Rent Act of 1922 Germany), 115
Rent Act of 1946 (U.K.), 25
Rent Act of 1957 (U.K.), 34, 239
Rent control, 11–12, 18, 25–26, 31–34 *passim*, 66, 70–77, 115, 119, 123, 145, 146, 152, 155–157, 164, 232, 238–239; public dissatisfaction, 27; and slum development, 60, 197; as condition for subsidy, 18–19, 62–64, 132*n*, 147; and availability of housing, 92–93; influence on housing demand, 92–93, 102, 159–160; and maintenance, 107–108; and consumption goods expenditures, 108; and repression of private construction, 108–109; social welfare objectives, 241–242; and consumer price levels, 264–265
Rent Control Act of 1942 (Sweden), 71
Rent and Mortgage Interest Restriction Act (U.K.), 15, 16
Rents: in public housing, 16, 192, 217–225; relationship to income, 26, 75–76, 98, 108; subsidies for, 33–34, 191, 219–225 *passim;* relationship to costs, 52, 71–72, 114, 125–126; regional differences, 72–73; standards and, 73–74, 82; finance and, 82; and maintenance, 126; trends, 155–157; "black market extras," 156. *See also* Rent control
Resettlement Administration (U.S.A.), 150, 152
Riksbank (Sweden), 259
Romania, 10
Royal Board of Housing (Sweden), 110
Royal Commission on the Housing of the Industrial Population of Scotland Urban and Rural, 15
Royal Commission on Housing and Redevelopment (Sweden), 65
Royal Housing Board (Sweden), 68–69, 78–79, 95, 241–242, 265

Sabatino, Richard A., 28*n*, 29, 45, 48*n*
San Francisco Bay area, 188
Saulnier, R. J., 187*n*
Savings and loan association, 172–174
Schaaf, Albert Heeley, 177*n*, 189*n*
Schaeffer, 123*n*
Scotland, 15, 25–26, 60
Second Housing Act of 1956 (West Germany), 124, 137–138, 231
Senneby, Bengt, 84*n*
Servicemen's Readjustment Act of 1944 (U.S.A.), 163, 180
Shaftesbury Act of 1851 (U.K.), 13
Silk, Leonard, 62*n*, 63*n*, 65*n*, 66*n*, 68*n*, 100*n*, 103*n*
Size of dwelling. *See* Density; Standards
Slums: clearance and rehabilitation, 21, 23, 57–61, 151, 167–168, 197–200; subsidies, 21, 57, 60; U.S.A. 1892 survey, 145
Small Dwellings Acquisition Act of 1899 (U.K.), 38
Sohmen, Egon, 237*n*
Spain, 8–10
Standards, 11; Scotland, 15; certification of construction, 42–43; government role, 48, 108, 132, 138, 145, 197, 201, 222, 224; in public housing, 49, 55–56, 132, 199; trends, 68, 85, 97–98, 105, 109, 112, 118, 139–140, 157–163 *passim*, 224–225, 247–253;

rents and, 73–74, 82, 92, 126; finance and, 82, 124, 139–140, 209, 221, 222, 224, 242–243; multi-family dwellings, 92–95; working housewives and demand for amenities, 94; and costs, 73–74, 82, 92, 125; substandard units, 141, 161–163, 165, 169, 200, 252 (*see also* Rehabilitation; Slums); "model housing law," 145; occupant characteristics and, 163; income and, 217–218; and FHA appraisals, 219; "filtering down," 224–225. *See also* Maintenance

State Building Loan Office (Sweden), 68

State Housing Loan Bank (Sweden), 65

States (U.S.A.): rent control role, 145, 146, 155; loans and tax concessions by, 146; role in public housing, 190–196 *passim;* expenditures of, 204. *See also* Länder

Steel, Robert, 34*n*

Stern, Helwig, 118*n*

Stockholm: rent-income ratio, 75; construction costs, 81; coöperatives, 87; property ownership patterns, 90

Stolper, Gustav, 116*n*

Subsidies, 1, 11–12, 14, 31–34 *passim,* 66, 68, 79, 107, 240; to local government, 16, 18–19; 238; stimulation of private construction, 20, 137, 222–223, 231; class bias in, 24; rents and, 32–34, 62–64, 71–73, 123–127 *passim;* expenditures for, 38–42; 94–97, 235–237; costs and, 52–53, 71–73, 81, 115–116, 262–265 *passim;* encouragement of multi-dwelling construction, 56, 92–95 *passim;* for rehabilitation, 57, 60; rent allowances, 65–66, 85, 191, 192, 219–225 *passim,* 244; for pensioner housing, 85; and housing demand, 103; and standard of living, 108; for slum clearance and redevelopment, 198–200; by tax concession, 223–224. *See also* Finance; Public housing

Svenska Riksbyggen, 88

Sweden, 62–110; dwellings-population ratio, 6–7; value of construction, 7–8; national product and housing investment, 10–11; construction level, 10, 85–88, 233, 236, 253–256; housing policy, 11–12, 68–110 *passim,* 241–244; standards, 11, 247–253 *passim;* war impact, 66–68; rent control, 70–77; finance, 77–85; ownership patterns, 88–91; costs, 94–97, 253–256; needs, 100–103; rent subsidies, 220; government expenditures, 94–97, 237, 243–244; economic policies and conditions, 258–267 *passim. See also* Agencies, etc.; Legislation

Swedish Housing Loan Bank, 77

Swedish Mortgage Bank, 77

Switzerland, 4, 6–8 *passim*

Tax concessions: 123, 131, 133, 134–138, 146–147, 203, 231–232, 235–237

Tax Reform Law of 1948 (West Germany), 134

Tenant-Protection Bill of 1923 (Germany), 115

Tenants' Savings and Building Society (Sweden), 87–88

Tennessee Valley Authority, 154

Thornell, Stina, 74*n*, 80*n*

Torrens Act of 1868 (U.K.), 13

Town and Country Planning Act of 1953 (U.K.), 31

Truman, Harry, 165

Umrath, Heinz, 22*n*, 117*n*, 119*n*, 120*n*, 122*n*, 125*n*

United Kingdom, 13–61, 238–241; war damage, 4, 21–22, 25–26; dwellings-population ratio, 6–7; value of construction, 7–8; national product and construction, 10–11; standards, 11, 247–253 *passim;* government expenditures, 38–42, 237; impact of economic policies and conditions, 257–267 *passim. See also* Agencies, etc.; Legislation

United States, 12, 145–229, 244–247; value of construction, 7–8; national product and construction, 10–11; standards, 11, 247–253 *passim;* interwar programs, 146–152; government expenditures, 151, 202–204, 220–221, 235–237, 243–244; World War II programs, 152–157; postwar problem and objectives, 163–171, 204–229, 244–247; finance policies and programs, 171–190; public housing, 190–196; construction level, 233, 236; impact of economic policies and conditions, 260–267 *passim. See also* Agencies, etc.; Legislation; States

United States Housing Act of 1937, 151

United States Housing Authority, 151, 152, 154
United States Housing Corporation, 146
United States Shipping Board, 146
Urbanization, 13–14, 101, 120. *See also* Density; Population growth
Urban Mortgage Bank of Sweden, 77
Urban renewal, 197–202, 217–225 *passim. See also* Rehabilitation; Slums
Urban Renewal Administration (U.S.A.), 165
Urban Renewal Fund, 199
U.S.S.R., 10

Vacation homes, 94
Vällingby Center, 110
Veteran loans from state programs, 147, 219
Veterans Administration, 163, 165, 172, 180–184, 187, 189, 210, 215, 246, 265
Veterans Emergency Housing Program, 163–164
Virginia, 145

Wagner, Bernard, 133*n*
Wandersleb, Hermann, 121*n*
War damage and destruction, 4–12 *passim*, 21–22, 25–26, 120, 121
War housing, 154–155
Wendt, Paul F., 25*n*, 47*n*, 68*n*, 98*n*, 103*n*, 153*n*, 157*n*, 166*n*, 196*n*, 271*n*
Wertheimer, Robert G., 120*n*, 121*n*, 134, 135*n*, 136, 137*n*, 143*n*, 235*n*
West Germany, 111–144; war destruction, 4, 120; dwellings-population ratio, 6–7; value of construction, 7–8; construction rate, 8–10, 138–142, 233, 236, 253–256; national product and housing investment, 10–11; standards, 11, 247–253 *passim;* housing policy, 12, 123–127, 231–238; interwar conditions, 113–119; finance, 127–138; government expenditures, 141–143, 235–237; impact of general economic policies and conditions, 256–267 *passim. See also* Agencies, etc.; Länder; Legislation
Westminster, 13
Winnick, Louis, 159*n*, 161, 189*n*, 216, 227*n*, 249*n*, 261
Wisconsin, 147
Wolff, Reinhold P., 169*n*
Wood, Edith Elmer, 145*n*, 146*n*
Woodbury, Coleman, 198*n*
World War I impact on housing, 14–18, 62, 145–146
World War II impact on housing, 4–12 *passim*, 21–23, 66–68, 120, 121, 154–155
Wright, David McCord, 143*n*

Yugoslavia, 10

www.ingramcontent.com/pod-product-compliance
Lightning Source LLC
Chambersburg PA
CBHW031412270326
41929CB00010BA/1424

* 9 7 8 0 5 2 0 3 0 8 0 3 9 *